D1055667

▼

The Pre-Astronauts

THE PRE-ASTRONAUTS

Manned Ballooning on the Threshold of Space

Craig Ryan

Naval Institute Press   *Annapolis, Maryland*

© 1995 by Craig Ryan

All rights reserved. No part of this book may be reproduced without written permission from the publisher.

Library of Congress Cataloging-in-Publication Data

Ryan, Craig, 1953–

    The pre-astronauts : manned ballooning on the threshold of space / Craig Ryan.

        p.   cm.

    Includes bibliographical references and index.

    ISBN 1-55750-732-5

    1. Balloon ascensions—United States—History. 2. Atmosphere, Upper—Research—United States—History. 3. Outer space—Exploration—United States—History. I. Title.

TL618.R95 1995

629.13'0973—dc20   94-48540

Printed in the United States of America on acid-free paper ∞

02 01 00 99 98 97 96 95   9 8 7 6 5 4 3 2

First printing

Grateful acknowledgment is made to the following for permission to reprint previously copyrighted materials:

From *Man High,* by Lt. Col. David G. Simons, with Don A. Schanche. Copyright 1960 by Doubleday. Reprinted by permission of the publisher, a division of Bantam Doubleday Dell Publishing Group, Inc.

From *The Long Lonely Leap,* by Capt. Joseph W. Kittinger Jr., with Martin Caidin. Published by E.P. Dutton and Co., Inc. Copyright 1961 by Joseph W. Kittinger Jr. and Martin Caidin. Reprinted by permission of the authors.

TL
618
R95
1995

▼

for Kathy

▼

In a very real sense, these balloon flights have also set the stage for the coming drama of space flight. They have held all the adventure of man, with his courage, making the flights in his isolated cabin; and his fellow man on the ground launching him into his new frontier, following his flight, and worrying about him while he is making measurements and is himself being measured for his adaptability to a new role.

—Otto Winzen

We were *the space program.*

—Duke Gildenberg

Contents

▼

Preface

Back in the 1950s and early '60s, before liquid-fuel rockets had launched us full sail onto what John Kennedy would call the "new ocean," a small fraternity of daring, brilliant men made the first exploratory trips into the upper stratosphere to the edge of outer space in tiny capsules suspended beneath plastic balloons. Their backgrounds and motives were varied. They were doctors, physicists, meteorologists, engineers, astronomers, and test pilots. They saw things no one had ever seen and they experienced conditions no one was sure they could survive. Mostly Air Force and Navy officers, supported by a cadre of dedicated civilian contractors, they struggled with meager budgets, bureaucratic politics, and one another. Yet they were united in the belief that they labored on the cusp of a new age and each of them burned for his own chance to advance the coming era of space exploration. They made tremendous personal sacrifices and took great risks for the promise of spectacular adventure and the opportunity to uncover a few precious secrets of the universe.

This book examines the dramatic achievements of the postwar manned-balloon programs and the remarkable individuals who made them possible, and it argues for their rightful inclusion in the broad history of space exploration and astronautics. The stratospheric balloon programs supplied many of the systems and processes that would later be adopted by NASA. Some of these inheritances were acknowledged, others were not. And by the time Project Apollo was in full glory, the high-altitude explorers of the balloon programs had been largely forgotten—as had, unfortunately, some of the valuable lessons they brought back from the edge of space.

But in their day, before Gagarin and Glenn and American flags on the Sea of Tranquillity, these pre-astronauts *were* the space program.

▼

Acknowledgments

I am grateful to the many kind people who answered my questions, helped me locate research materials and identify potential sources, or put me in touch with others who could help. This is by no means a complete list of those Good Samaritans, but probably better than no list at all: James M. Bates, Eric Brothers, Chief M.Sgt. John R. Burton, Lloyd Cornett, Tom D. Crouch, David H. DeVorkin, Mike Gorn, Dr. Charles Gross, Richard P. Hallion, Michael Horan, George M. House, John Jensen, Bill Jolly, Gregory P. Kennedy, Jon Lee, Paul Maravelas, Wayne O. Mattson, Jeffrey Pearce, Robert Sleator, and Jane Vessels. A special thanks to J. Gordon Vaeth who went beyond the call of duty to help make sure I got it right. I am also grateful to the many generous and competent people who helped me at the Library of Congress, the National Air and Space Museum, the Space Center in Alamogordo, the University of Minnesota Wilson Library Special Collections and Rare Books department, and the Multnomah County Library in Portland, Oregon. My apologies to those I have neglected to mention.

I am indebted to the authors of all the books, articles, reports, and papers upon which my work came to rely so heavily. The titles of most of those works can be found in the bibliography, but a few deserve special mention. David DeVorkin's study of the scientific balloon flights of the 1930s and '40s, *Race to the Stratosphere,* with its superb analysis of the politics that attended those ventures, was particularly helpful. Tom Crouch's *The Eagle Aloft* provided a valuable historical overview of American ballooning. *Man High,* by Lt. Col. David Simons (with Don A. Schanche) and *The Long, Lonely Leap* by Capt. Joseph W. Kittinger Jr. (with Martin Caidin) were essential, as were George Meeter's accounts of the early days of space research at Holloman Air Force

Base (not only the polished pieces collected in *The Holloman Story,* but also the numerous press releases and bulletins written for the Air Force Missile Development Center). Also extremely helpful were three volumes of the NASA History Series, *This New Ocean: A History of Project Mercury* by Loyd Swenson Jr., James M. Grimwood, and Charles C. Alexander; *Chariots for Apollo: A History of Project Mercury,* by Courtney G. Brooks, James M. Grimwood, and Loyd Swenson Jr.; and *Where No Man Has Gone Before: A History of Manned Lunar Spacecraft* by William David Compton.

The following principals in the story allowed me to interview them: Dr. John Paul Stapp, Dr. David Simons, Joseph Kittinger, Clifton McClure, Bernard "Duke" Gildenberg, Francis Beaupre, Vera Simons, J. Gordon Vaeth, and George Hoover. Without exception, their graciousness and honesty amazed me. (Most also provided me with background materials. Dr. Simons entrusted me with precious slides made from photographs taken at altitude during his Manhigh ascent. Ms. Simons provided a number of her own photographs from the Manhigh and Strato-Lab days, and reviewed my accounts of many of the events discussed in the book.)

Thanks to Jim Stewart who listened patiently as I talked my way through this book, and who badgered me into finishing it. Thanks to Kayo Parsons-Korn for her illustration. Thanks to Julie Keefe for her help with the photographs. And thanks to Jessy Ryan for her help with the index. Special thanks to Scott Ellsworth who helped me through the early months of my research, who sent me documents I needed from Washington (often on short notice), and who read some of the early drafts and offered fresh insights every step of the way. I would also like to acknowledge a long-term debt to R. V. Cassill: a great writer and a loyal friend.

My thanks to the folks at the Naval Institute Press, especially Anne Collier and Mary Lou Kenney, to my editor Therese D. Boyd, and to my agent Al Zuckerman at Writers House whose unwavering confidence in a book on an obscure topic about people no one remembers by a writer no one has ever heard of has meant more than he knows.

Finally and most important, thanks to the three women I live with: my wife Kathy and my daughters Jessy and Caitlin.

▼

The Pre-Astronauts

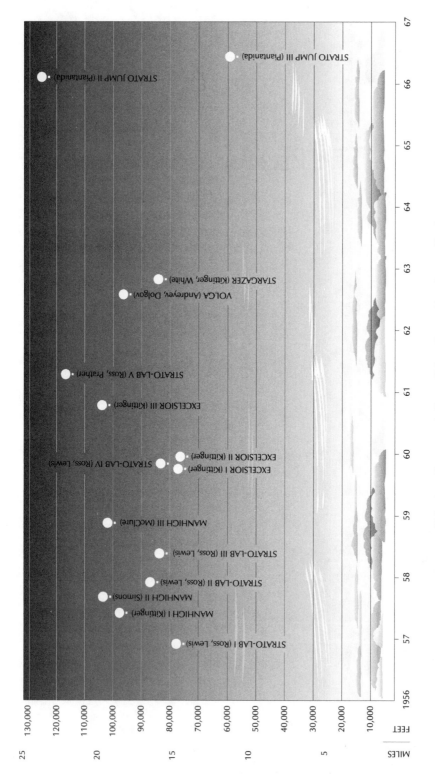

Altitudes of postwar balloon flights. (*Source: Kayo Parsons-Korn*)

Selected Postwar Manned Balloon Flights in the Stratosphere

Balloon	Date	Altitude (feet)	Pilots
Strato-Lab I	Nov. 8, 1956	76,000	Ross, Lewis
Strato-Lab II	Oct. 18, 1957	86,000	Ross, Lewis
Strato-Lab III	July 26, 1958	82,000	Ross, Lewis
Strato-Lab IV	Nov. 28, 1959	81,000	Ross, Moore
Strato-Lab V	May 4, 1961	113,740	Ross, Prather
Manhigh I	June 2, 1957	96,000	Kittinger
Manhigh II	Aug. 19, 1957	101,500	Simons
Manhigh III	Oct. 8, 1958	99,700	McClure
Excelsior I	Nov. 16, 1959	76,400	Kittinger
Excelsior II	Dec. 11, 1959	74,700	Kittinger
Excelsior III	Aug. 16, 1960	102,800	Kittinger
Stargazer	Dec. 13, 1962	81,500	Kittinger, White
Volga	November 1962	93,970	Andreyev, Dolgov
Strato Jump II	Feb. 2, 1966	123,500	Piantanida
Strato Jump III	May 1, 1966	57,600	Piantanida

"Just Another Day Wasted Away"

The balloon towered above the crowd, straining like an animal against the big ropes that bound it to the earth. Inflated with 80,000 cubic feet of volatile hydrogen gas, it had the power to pull a man, silently and surprisingly swiftly, into the upper reaches of the troposphere—even higher. The pilot, veteran Army Air Service captain Hawthorne Gray, stoically prepared himself for an assault on the human altitude record. A broad-faced, barrel-chested, bull of a man with big dreams and six years' experience with gas balloons, Gray, at age 38, was confident that he was equipped to face the conditions aloft. But in 1927 the upper atmosphere was still uncharted, fantastic territory. Airplane pilots had been as high as 40,000 feet, but no balloonist had ever gone beyond 36,000. Gray dressed in thick layers of wool and deerskin, with fleece-lined moccasins on his feet and an insulated helmet on his head, and he stowed several heavy blankets with his gear. He also made room in the cluttered wicker gondola of his balloon for three small cylinders of pressurized oxygen, a 50-cent thermometer, and a compact collection of instruments that would measure and record the qualities of the region he intended to visit. Finally, at a little after one o'clock on a March afternoon, he shouted, "Okay, let her go!" and lifted off the ground in Belleville, Illinois. As jazz played on a portable Atwater Kent radio, he laughed and waved bravely to cheering friends and crew. Then he was swept up, above the treetops and then higher. But no breeze whistled in his ear or fanned the pages of his flight log—he was riding on the wind, had become part of the invisible current. The radio continued to play as the ground melted away and colors faded into a vague geography.

Gray's ballasting system consisted of more than two tons of sand packed into dozens of 50-pound canvas bags that hung outside the gondola. In order to ascend, he pulled up a bag, slit it open with his knife, and then spilled the sand over the side. He expected to have to dump most of the sand in order to rise to altitude, but knew he would need to save some in order to slow his descent enough to ensure a safe landing.

Yet as he rose, the task of hauling the bags up, slitting, and emptying them proved too much even for the robust Captain Gray. All three of his knives became dulled by the canvas and sand and he resorted finally to clawing the bags open with his nearly frozen fingers. His efficiency deserted him, then his strength. With his oxygen supply growing steadily colder, cold enough to sting his lungs with each gasping breath, Gray passed out from hypoxia somewhere around 27,000 feet.

With ballasting interrupted, the big silver balloon leveled off, and then fell. It picked up speed until it was falling 1,200 feet a minute. The pilots of the Army pursuit planes following Gray watched helplessly, circling his descent path. And then, at the last possible instant, Gray regained consciousness in time to ballast frantically before crashing through a set of telephone wires and landing in a ditch near Ashley, Illinois—40 miles from where he started. Somehow, he crawled from the wreckage with nothing more than a sprained ankle.

Two months later, after fashioning an oxygen mask and rigging a heater for the tanks, he lifted off from Scott Field once again using the same aluminum- and rubber-coated silk balloon. This time he made it: to 42,240 feet—higher than any human being had ever been. But he could only remain there for a single spectacular moment. The environment above 40,000 feet is brutal and even if Gray had possessed the ballast necessary to maintain his height, he could not have survived it for long. Doctors had warned him to descend at the first sign of physical distress, and now a heavy pain began to well up in his chest. Gray opened a valve to release hydrogen and even though he closed it again after a few seconds, the balloon plummeted. He had almost no sand left with which to slow his descent, so he tossed over an empty oxygen cylinder. It had little effect. He had seriously overballasted. The price paid to reach this height had been too great.

At 8,000 feet, with an Army plane circling, Gray grabbed the rope that opened the valve on the balloon. He pulled it hard and tied it off to the gondola's railing. Then he scrambled awkwardly up onto the lip of the swaying, free-falling basket—and jumped off. The balloon sprang up as Gray pulled the D-ring on his Army parachute and spiraled slowly down into the warm, rich air to a safe landing near the town of Golden Gate, 110 miles from the launch site.

But the altitude record Gray coveted was withheld. The international sanctioning body, the Fédération Aéronautique Internationale, as well as America's own National Aeronautical Association, required that a pilot land with his craft. Disappointed, but determined as ever, Gray and his crew spent the rest of the summer and fall redesigning valves (adding heaters to keep them from freezing), and reconfiguring controls for ease of use. The ballast system was overhauled so that cutting sandbags would no longer be required, and all the oil—which had shown a tendency to freeze—was removed from the barographs and thermographs. Gray and fellow Army Air Corps medical researchers also carried out a series of experiments in which cats and birds were placed in a decompression chamber and subjected to high altitude–equivalent environments.

Then, in November, Gray tried once again. The conquest of some obscure, invisible peak in the suffocating vacuum of the stratosphere had, over the months, become a collective obsession for Gray and his crew. Publicly, the Army stressed that its balloon flights were conducted purely for scientific reasons, but something beyond research was clearly at stake. It was early afternoon when he lifted off from Scott Field for the third time that year. And even though it was late fall, temperatures on the ground were almost summer-like. As before, Gray tuned his radio to KMOX in St. Louis and was able to hear well-wishers on the broadcast toasting him as he rose.

Less than an hour later the balloon was at 20,000 feet, nearly four miles above sea level. In spite of the pleasant Midwestern weather below, at this altitude it was eight degrees above zero and snowing hard. Gray jotted a note in his log: "Symptoms of Ricketts." Ice began to form on the balloon and, in spite of the heating elements that had been added, on the faceplate of Gray's oxygen mask as well. Ole Oleson's orchestra played "Sunset," keeping the lonely pilot company. As Gray ballasted, the balloon continued to rise. The temperature plunged to 40 below. Swollen fingers tuned the radio to WLS in Chicago in time to catch a popular song called "Telling about Dying," and then to WLW in Cincinnati for the final strains of "Just Another Day Wasted Away." At 30,000 feet, his clock stopped. And as Gray threw over an empty oxygen cylinder for ballast, it snapped the radio antenna, isolating him instantly from the world below.

At 40,000 feet, Gray, by now severely hypoxic and shivering uncontrollably, scrawled the final entry in his log: "Sky deep blue, sun very bright, sand all gone." The Army planes had long since lost Gray in a thick cloud cover somewhere near the Illinois-Kentucky border and had returned to Scott Field. Later that afternoon, a farmer named Jack Fisher in the remote Cumberland Mountains village of Orlinda, Tennessee, saw a big balloon drift by and noticed something fall out of it: a pair of radio batteries and a note requesting their return to Capt. Hawthorne C. Gray.

The next morning, in Sparta, Tennessee, a strange object was discovered tangled in the branches of an oak tree. A young boy climbed the tree and found the burly Army pilot on the floor of the basket. The body was lifeless and slumped forward. An oxygen mask remained strapped to its face. Local physicians on the scene speculated that the cause of death was suffocation, or perhaps heart failure. Army investigators arrived to find that two barographs had survived and been recovered by the locals. The instruments disagreed as to the precise height at which Gray's flight peaked, but both showed maximum readings of somewhere between 43,000 and 44,000 feet. The barographs were immediately packed and shipped to Washington for calibration, accompanied not much later by the body of Hawthorne Gray, to be buried at Arlington National Cemetery at the request of his wife. The Distinguished Flying Cross would be awarded posthumously.

Early newspaper accounts speculated that Gray accidentally severed his oxygen hose. Later, the stories were revised to say that Gray had simply become so exhausted and cold that he could not physically open the oxygen valve on one of the tanks. Later still, Russell Owen, writing in the *New York Times,* guessed that decreasing atmospheric pressure ruptured one of Gray's internal organs, killing him instantly. And A. Leo Stevens, himself an experienced and widely respected aeronaut, announced that he thought Gray died either during the descent or upon impact. Stevens's assessment of Gray's flights was to the point:

> It is perfectly possible to send a balloon up to that height, but it is a different matter to get it down again safely. . . . It is lamentable that a brave man's life should be sacrificed because of a lack of forethought as to what must be faced after the balloon has gone as high as it can go.

Gray was resourceful and courageous but, like Icarus, he lacked discipline. Yet Stevens saw hope: "A larger balloon might reach that height with sufficient reserve ballast so that a safe landing might be made." The problems that kept Gray from realizing his dream were not insur-mountable. There were technical advances ahead: not only larger bal-loons, but improvements to the fabric of the balloon's envelope, elegant ballasting systems, superior lifting gases, better protective gear for the pilot, reliable and safe systems for delivering warm, pressurized oxygen to his lungs. New records would be set and then be broken again.

The flights of Hawthorne Gray were a dramatic success in one important sense: they inspired a generation of aeronauts and aeronau-tical engineers to focus their resolve and collective genius on the fron-tiers of our atmosphere. The record attempts of 1927 are a reference point. For almost another decade, balloonists on both sides of the Atlantic raced to set new altitude records. There were triumphs and there were failures, some of them tragic. By the time this flurry of high-altitude activity finally waned in 1935, the altitude mark for a manned balloon stood at more than 72,000 feet—deep into the stratosphere.

But the final—and most spectacular—chapter in the history of high-altitude manned ballooning, the era of the pre-astronauts, was yet ahead.

one

The Ghost of Muroc

During the long summer of the final year of the Second World War, the greatest collection of physicists ever assembled was camped on the Jornada del Muerto in the gypsum and saltbush wasteland of southern New Mexico. They hunted antelope and deer, relaxed with volleyball games and afternoon dips in the cattle-watering tanks, and worked feverishly on a government project so sensitive that not even their wives and families knew where they were or precisely what they were doing. The experiment they would conduct was a page from a pulp science-fiction novel: they would attempt to induce nuclear fusion in a rare man-made substance called plutonium. One of the men, a codiscoverer of this exotic new material, admitted that no one really knew what would happen if the experiment was successful and a critical mass of plutonium was achieved. "In spite of calculations," he confided in his wife before leaving for the secret site in the desert, "we are going into the unknown." Edward Teller, the great Hungarian physicist, calculated and recalculated the odds of the explosion igniting the atmosphere and transforming the planet into a star.

Then, on the morning of July 16, 1945, at 5:29, a technician flipped a series of switches and detonated the first atomic bomb. A searing light flashed across the earth, the bomb's heat cauterizing the desert and melting the sand into green glass. In a millionth of a second, the jackrabbits and rattlesnakes in the vicinity of Ground Zero were vaporized along with the 200-foot steel scaffold from which the bomb had been suspended. Witnesses reported the distinct smell of death about the Jornada for weeks afterward. When the thundering winds of the blast had subsided, the project's young chief scientist, Robert Oppenheimer, stepped from his bunker burdened with the sickening certainty that the world was, in that moment, changed forever. The collective genius of the Manhattan Project had unleashed a Promethean scourge. It had also, as would be clear a few weeks later, succeeded in ending the war, thereby setting the stage for the next inconceivable demonstration of mind over matter: leaving the planet.

This barren high-desert theater had been hand-picked for the atomic age's violent debut: a remote, mostly uninhabited, flat sweep of mesquite and yucca bordered on two sides by rugged mountain ranges and characterized by predictably dry weather, technically an extension of Mexico's Great Chihuahua Desert. And not long after the great blast at Trinity—Oppenheimer's mysterious name for the plutonium bomb site—over 100 German rocket scientists from Peenemunde, "Operation Paperclip" Germans who had surrendered to the Americans in the final weeks of the war, were shipped to El Paso, Texas, just to the south to create a U.S. guided missile program at Fort Bliss.

These celebrity prisoners of war had stupefied their Army interrogators with descriptions of detailed plans for sending instrumentation—and even human beings—to the edge of the earth's atmosphere and beyond. They discussed, in a remarkably matter-of-fact manner and in precise technical terms, multistage rockets and orbiting space stations.

Wernher von Braun and his colleagues launched the first V-2 rocket from American soil at the White Sands Proving Ground, a 40- by 100-mile corridor in the Tularosa Basin of New Mexico—which included Trinity Site—in the spring of 1946. A V-2 weighed about 14 tons; it was 46 feet long and capable of carrying its ton of explosives at supersonic speeds (which meant, to Londoners who had been on the receiving end of the V-2 attacks, that you never heard the thing until it was too late). During the last two years of the war, the Germans manufactured about 5,000 of them, many of which were captured by the Allies.

The atomic age was less than a year old, but as the screaming barrage of ballistic missiles pierced the wild blue yonder over the American desert Southwest, yet another brave new world—the space age—was born. Some 500 miles to the west, in the skies above the Mojave Desert of California, the Army was testing the first of its new X-series of rocket-powered airplanes: first glide trials, then propulsion tests, and then, in the fall of 1947, Capt. Chuck Yeager flew the liquid-oxygen and alcohol-fueled XS-1 faster than the speed of sound. Yeager reached an airspeed of 662 MPH. The X-1, with an airframe built by the Bell Aircraft Company and a liquid-propellant rocket engine built by Reaction

Motors, was capable of 6,000 pounds of thrust. But that was just the beginning. The Bell X-2's Curtiss-Wright engine would be capable of delivering 15,000 pounds of thrust. And as early as 1952, the NACA Committee on Aerodynamics would recommend the funding of research efforts to solve the problems of manned flight "at altitudes between 12 and 50 miles and at speeds of Mach 4 through 10." Aviation technology was exploding both literally and figuratively. The X-planes would rocket higher and higher, arcing farther and farther into the stratosphere, tracing their great rainbow trajectories across the skyscape of the last great frontier.

Human beings could now, with a new level of confidence and with resources and renewed energies freed from the shackles of global war, begin to contemplate space travel. Most of the fundamental problems of escaping gravity's prison had been solved. But in the rush to perfect the secrets of rocket travel, one element had been curiously neglected: mortal man. Somebody was going to have to *prove* that a human being was in fact fit for space before those who held the nation's purse strings would even consider underwriting such a brazen activity.

In 1919, while at Clark College in Massachusetts, Robert Goddard had seen the future and published a paper entitled "A Method of Reaching Extreme Altitudes" in which he had argued that a multistage rocket fired from earth would be capable of reaching the moon. This assertion was, almost predictably, ridiculed in the nation's press. The *New York Times,* in an editorial under the headline "A Severe Strain of Credulity," passed a typical judgment:

> That Professor Goddard with his 'chair' in Clark College and the coun-
> tenancing of the Smithsonian Institution does not know the relation of
> action to reaction, and of the need to have something better than a vac-
> uum against which to react—to say that would be absurd. Of course,
> he only seems to lack the knowledge ladled out daily in high schools.*

Indeed, in the late forties through the mid-fifties, "space" remained a dirty word in the Pentagon and in the halls of Congress. To mention the subject was to invite jeers. Those who wanted to be taken seriously did

---

*Goddard was still involved in valuable rocket research during World War II and would almost certainly have been a principal player in postwar rocket development had he not died in August of 1945.

not request money for space research, and especially not manned space research.

If progress was going to be made in the business of qualifying human beings for space travel, it would have to be driven by someone who, for starters, had little regard for his own professional reputation. It would require someone of considerable scientific sophistication, but also of practicality, someone who could come to hands-on terms with the real world of military politics. A man of vision who would be capable of deriving satisfaction from progress itself rather than personal glory. He would be an enigma, a lone ranger appearing unannounced and vanishing almost before you learned his name.

Not surprisingly, then, the Army Air Corps did not really understand who they had when they brought the man to Wright Field in Ohio in August 1946 to observe tests of the first American pilot-ejection seat. John Paul Stapp was an unassuming 36-year-old doctor who had been reared by strict Southern Baptist missionary parents in the jungles of Brazil. He had been schooled diligently by his fiercely idealistic and eccentric mother, forbidden to speak any language but Portuguese and the native Indian dialects until the age of 12. He was sent back to the States when he was 15 to live with relatives and to finish his education. He enrolled at Baylor University in Waco, Texas, and graduated with master's degrees in zoology and chemistry, living in near-total poverty and dining regularly on the school's lab animals—guinea pigs and pigeons, mostly. Stapp wasn't particular. "If it breathed it had protein," he said, "and if it had protein I ate it." A jungle childhood that included a five-year bout with malaria had left him with a distinctly unromantic view of creatures great and small. ("I was taught the value of human survival against our plant and animal antagonists.")

During his sophomore year, John Paul visited an uncle's family during Christmas break, and the trip changed his life. During his stay, an infant cousin crawled too near the fireplace, his bedclothes caught fire, and he was horribly burned. The suffering stunned Stapp, who personally nursed the boy for 63 hours before he died. Shortly thereafter, Stapp decided to become a doctor. He had found the trigger for the shotgun zeal he had inherited from his mother and father, the indomitable desire to save the world in spite of itself and in the face of all odds: the missionary spirit. "You might shake off the religion," he was fond of saying, "but you never shake off the missionary spirit."

Stapp earned his Ph.D. in biophysics at the University of Texas before enrolling in medical school at the University of Minnesota. After two six-month deferments, he joined the Army. He continued his studies as an intern, graduated, and was transferred to the Army Air Corps ("dumped" there, in Stapp's words, because of a frequently sprained ankle), and got his first taste of aviation medicine.

The war was over and von Braun's V-2s were already soaring from the New Mexico sands by the time Stapp witnessed the ejection-seat tests at Wright Field in 1946 and saw the opportunity to help close the widening gap between aviation technology and the pathetic vulnerability of the human pilot. The notion of explosively ejecting pilots from aircraft was novel: the Germans had done it first and handbooks obtained from captured Nazi pilots had taught the Americans what they knew. But there was still a lot to learn about the forces of acceleration and deceleration and their debilitating effects on the body—and a thousand other mysteries that pertained to pilot survival in the newborn space age. The Aeromedical Laboratory of the Air Materiel Command at Wright was a revelation to Stapp: the men there weren't academics ("pure scientists . . . the prima donnas in universities working in their nit-picking ways at academic doodlings to impress each other"), nor were they assembly-line armed-forces medicos (at an Army base in Arizona, Stapp had once examined the eyes, ears, noses, and throats of 600 men in a single day: "a nightmare relieved only by the thought that I might have been a proctologist"). The work going on at Wright was research on the sharpest cutting edge of medical science, research that held the gratifying promise of immediate practical application. It was a new, exciting field in which the rules were still largely unwritten, and in which innovation was desperately needed. But to Stapp it would become something more: a crusade to save lives.

With only a few months to go before his military obligation would be satisfied, Stapp reenlisted and volunteered to serve as a subject for tests of a liquid-oxygen breathing system with a converter that had been developed by the Bendix Corporation. In a modified B-17 with special ignition wiring that allowed it to reach stratospheric altitudes, Stapp made flight after flight to 47,000 feet in an unheated, unpressurized cabin in order to study the painful effects of the bends firsthand. In the process, he made the valuable discovery that it was possible to avoid the bends by breathing 100 percent oxygen for 30 minutes before takeoff.

Earlier that same year, the Aeromedical Lab at Wright had begun a program to study the effects of sudden deceleration based, again, on information obtained from the defeated Germans. German engineers had built a special track and a rocket-powered test vehicle. The entire apparatus had ended up in Soviet hands after the war, and Stapp was sent to Moscow to examine it. He pronounced the design "ingenious," and returned to Dayton to work on plans for developing a similar system for the Army.

Northrop Aircraft was awarded the contract to supply the track and test vehicle largely because it already owned a 2,000-foot B-1 launching track. Stapp traveled to Los Angeles to consult with Northrop engineers, and in April of 1947 he was transferred to Muroc Air Base (later to become Edwards Air Force Base) in the Mojave Desert to run the program. President Truman signed the Armed Forces Unification Act that summer, making Stapp an employee of the United States Air Force—but that didn't make it any easier for him to operate on anything that could even vaguely be construed as "space research," especially since he was an independent operator without suitable sponsorship and the proper connections among the service brass.

Few at Muroc even knew who Stapp was. He worked on his own with assistance only from a handful of civilian employees of Northrop who, in spite of their dedication, were neither sufficiently skilled in research nor trained in medical measurement or observation. He had a tiny budget and meager facilities. He acquired equipment and supplies mostly by barter, offering his medical services to Muroc personnel in return. When the Air Force wouldn't even construct a crash helmet for the project, Stapp convinced Dr. Charles Lombard at the University of Southern California to design and donate one. It was his first experience with a process of which he would become the undisputed master: bootleg research—unofficial projects that were authorized and funded at the lower levels of the bureaucracy. If you did it right, the "men at the mahogany desks"—in Stapp's words—weren't even aware of what you were doing. If your project was successful, and the brass found out about it, they'd congratulate you and take the credit themselves; if you failed and they discovered it, you might be discharged or court-martialed. The game required a cagey resourcefulness and swift efficiency. And John Paul Stapp was the hell-bent genius ghost of Muroc.

All that summer he ran tests on the B-1 track with a rocket sled built by Northrop called the "Gee-Whizz," an angular vehicle cobbled together from aluminum and rivets that resembled an industrial-strength soapbox racer. He would strap a 185-pound anthropomorphic dummy to the sled and send it hurtling down the 2,000-foot length of rail. Because of the tremendous power of the rocket engines and the experimental nature of the restraint systems, Stapp insisted that thirty-five test runs with the dummy be completed before a human subject would be allowed to attempt a rocket-sled run. On one of the tests, as the sled slammed to an abrupt stop at the end of the track, a harness ripped free and the dummy smashed through a one-inch thick wooden windscreen and catapulted some 700 feet out into the desert.

The first rocket-sled run with a human being aboard took place that winter, and the test subject was John Paul Stapp himself. Only one rocket was fired on that first ride, resulting in a top speed of just 90 MPH. The next day, Stapp ordered three rockets fired and achieved a speed of nearly 200 MPH. By May of 1948, Stapp had made the 2,000-foot run a total of sixteen times, subjecting himself to an increasing load of G forces as the sled accelerated down the track, and to an increasing load of negative Gs as the sled slammed to a stop at the end of the run. During the course of these rides, he sustained a string of injuries—bruises, abrasions, broken ribs, concussions, fillings lost from his teeth—but he became increasingly excited about the results of his research. The conventional wisdom among the brass at the Aeromedical Lab was that the human body could tolerate a maximum load of 18 Gs, or 18 times the force of gravity at sea level. The official textbooks had recorded this value as the absolute limit. Yet Stapp's rocket-sled runs had already proved that a man could withstand more than 18 Gs if properly trained and adequately restrained. In fact, Stapp himself had already survived 35 Gs. And not only had he painstakingly recorded every detail and measurement of every ride he had taken, but he had also recorded his subjective impressions with great care so that it would be possible to review not only what kind of physical punishment the test subject had taken but also how lucid he had been and how severely he had been affected by psychological stress.

Stapp took his results back to his superiors at Wright and asked for help. He needed a trained, motivated crew of researchers to help him compile and interpret the data and he needed qualified medical personnel on hand to monitor and evaluate the subjects. With adequate assistance, he argued, he would be able to shatter existing notions of what a pilot could endure in terms of gravitational forces. He felt he had earned the opportunity to move past the bootleg phase and into a full-scale research program. But soon after arriving back in Dayton, Stapp discovered that no help would be forthcoming. In fact, his superiors were horrified that Stapp had subjected himself and others to such tremendous G forces. They reminded him that 18 Gs was the human limit of tolerance, any bootleg data to the contrary notwithstanding. They ordered Stapp to desist from further human testing beyond the 18G limit. Period.

Bitterly disappointed, Stapp returned to his makeshift lab in the desert and drew up plans for a new series of tests—this time using chimpanzees as subjects. Several months later, officials from the National Advisory Committee for Aeronautics (NACA) came to observe the rocket-sled runs and to pick Stapp's brain. Here was an organization that *was* allowed to contemplate space travel and had a very pragmatic interest in the rocket-sled research. Rocket travel into outer space would be characterized by violent acceleration in the minutes following launch, and equally violent deceleration during reentry into the earth's atmosphere. The NACA asked to see a human rocket-sled run, and in spite of his orders, Stapp arranged for a relatively low-speed test using a human subject. The visitors were impressed, but Stapp's section chief promptly reported the violation to the brass at Wright, which resulted in a formal reprimand and another order to desist.

Stapp was eventually able to get the order rescinded, but in the meantime he defiantly resumed rocket-sled testing with human subjects. By December of 1951, he had carried out a total of 255 runs (including 73 with humans and 88 with chimps). By that time, he had reached the limits of both the propulsion system and the braking system of the Northrop sled. He had also published the first paper on the effects of massive deceleration on the human body, single-handedly rewriting the "book" on G forces and the limits of human tolerance.

Windblast experiments were also being conducted at Muroc during this period. Five days prior to his final sled run, Stapp went up in the back seat of a Northrop F-89 with the canopy cut away in order to subject himself to as much wind as he could find. After a Northrop copilot had died in the back seat of a similar jet during a high-speed emergency, researchers wanted to know how much wind a pilot could endure before he lost the ability to operate an aircraft's ejection controls. Stapp would root out the answer personally. The pilot took the F-89 up to 20,000 feet and tipped the nose down into a steep dive. Completely exposed to the elements while the jet reached a maximum speed of 570 MPH, Stapp proved that it was possible to handle all the ejection controls as long as he kept his elbows pinned tightly to his sides.

Designers of ejection-seat systems could now have confidence that pilots—even rocket pilots—were quite capable of surviving ejection at much higher speeds than anyone had thought possible, and those at NACA and elsewhere who were trying to work through scenarios for space flight could expand their notions of what was possible.

Stapp, meanwhile, returned to Dayton and the Aeromedical Laboratory already contemplating a new set of problems. He had gone as far as he could go with the current sled design and the forces of positive and negative acceleration. The next step would be to figure out a way to study the environment of space. If tremendous bursts of speed and sudden stops threatened to rip a human apart, the frozen vacuum beyond the earth's atmosphere promised an equally grim fate. One colleague described Stapp's attitude toward such problems as a zeal of hatred: he *hated* the fact that not enough was known to guarantee survival for the prospective space pilot, and he *hated* the natural forces that threatened to inflict pain and death on human beings. It was the raging, selfless hate of the missionary—and not the sort of mindset that is well received by a military bureaucracy.

By the time he returned to Wright, and in spite of his skill with bootleg research, Stapp began to acquire a reputation as a troublemaker. When a new unit of measure was needed to describe gravitational forces on the human body, Air Force researchers initially referred to a "jerk" as the force of one G acting on a body for one second. If you were exposed to 5 Gs for 10 seconds, you were said to have taken 50 jerks. Later, the unit of measure was officially changed to a "stapp"—the intent was to honor the man who had done so much to expand our knowledge of the effects of multiple G forces, but some of the men at the mahogany desks claimed it was because Stapp himself was such a jerk.

It was at Wright Field in the early fifties that Stapp first began thinking about balloons. Test subjects needed to get up above the atmosphere, out on the murky fringes of outer space, and to stay there long enough to take some measurements, conduct some experiments, get some subjective observations of the experience. Ballistic missiles were too unreliable, and their flights were no more than brief fiery arcs through the sky. The rocket planes in California also fell back to earth too quickly, and they carried a price tag that put them completely out of reach. More conventional aircraft were simply incapable of getting above the atmosphere. Balloons were the obvious answer—not only were they capable of rising into the stratosphere but, with a big enough balloon and enough ballast, they could stay there awhile.

And one other thing: balloons were cheap—relatively speaking.

Stapp envisioned a balloon-borne system that used a closed, pressurized capsule. It would be able to carry a human, if not into space itself, into a space-like environment where physiological and psychological reactions could be studied. The problems of designing a super-high-altitude survival system could be thoroughly worked through. Yet before he could get the approval for a high-altitude manned balloon program, he was transferred—fortuitously, as it turned out—to Holloman Air Force Base outside Alamogordo, New Mexico, and put in charge of the Aeromedical Field Lab where, under his tenure, valuable research in space biology and biodynamics would focus on hazards to human beings in the upper atmosphere. The German rocket men, under the Army's jurisdiction, were still at work on the bombing range just a few miles to the north, but the quonset huts and tents of the forties had been replaced by a sprawling complex of buildings and hangars and roads—miles and miles of paved and unpaved roads, eventually some 800 miles. Von Braun himself was gone, but the missiles were still screaming skyward from the White Sands.

And something else was rising into the blue desert sky by then—the undulating jellyfish of silvery plastic, rising and rising and expanding like the Trinity cloud as it rose, rounding into a bright, taut ball bouncing against the roof of the planet.

The Army had first conducted manned balloon operations in the Tularosa Basin in reaction to the Japanese balloon bombs that landed in Pacific coastal areas during the war.* In fact, balloons had been rising from central New Mexico even before the Peenemunde Germans had arrived with their V-2s. Scientists from New York University, among others, assisted with the early balloon research. One of the first postwar manned balloon flights sponsored by the military was launched

---

*More than 9,000 large rice-paper balloons, filled with hydrogen and carrying incendiary bombs, were launched by the Japanese from locations in Tokyo, Formosa, and the Kurile Islands in 1944 and 1945. Two or three years earlier, ahead of the Americans, the Japanese had discovered the jet stream and had reasoned that balloons launched into the swift-moving air current at about 30,000 feet might drift all the way to U.S. soil. (Americans discovered the 140-MPH jet-stream winds as B-29s plied them on bombing runs over Tokyo during the final months of the war.) Using a barometrically regulated sand-ballast system, about 1,000 of the Japanese balloon bombs reached the United States. Some of the balloons were retrieved from the beaches and forests of Washington, Oregon, and California. At least one made it as far as Montana. The Japanese spent approximately $200 million over two years on the balloon bombs.

from the Tularosa Basin in 1947 with the intent of crossing the Rockies and landing somewhere along the Eastern Seaboard. Unfortunately, the entire flight's supply of ballast was expended in the crossing of the Sacramento range to the east of Alamogordo and the balloon's journey ended just short of Roswell. A potential embarrassment, the aborted continental crossing was kept quiet and the pilot's name never released. "We were naive as hell," explained one of the NYU scientists.

But as the years wore on, balloon expertise in the Tularosa Basin matured. By the time Stapp arrived, the Balloon Research and Development Test Branch (affiliated with the Air Force Cambridge Research Laboratory), housed in a two-story sand-colored building out in the Holloman back country, represented the state of the art in scientific balloon operations groups.

By 1955, after years of sending fruit flies and mice and monkeys into the stratosphere, David Simons knew a great deal about the character of the upper atmosphere. In the late forties, Simons had been involved with Dr. James Henry in the first space-available animal research flights aboard the White Sands V-2s. The fins had fallen off the first New Mexico V-2, but most of the next sixty-three flights were successful to one degree or another.* For the scientists who participated, including Simons, it had been the research opportunity of a lifetime. James Van Allen, one of the prominent physicists who participated in the program, assessed the experience many years later:

> The drive for myself and my colleagues to go into space was not particularly inspired by science fiction, or the idea of manned space flight. . . . Our motivation was an improvement in technique for performing scientific experiments in a new way and to investigate matters which had previously been only areas of, let's say, educated conjecture.

---

*One that wasn't so successful created a near-international incident. On May 29, 1947, the gyroscope of a V-2 malfunctioned shortly after launch and sent the missile south. After a direct overflight of El Paso, it crashed into a hillside cemetery on the outskirts of Juarez, Mexico. No one was hurt, but Secretary of State George Marshall was reported to have placed a concerned call to the base at White Sands. Later, the suggestion was made that German rocket men who hated the heat and isolation of the desert had intentionally misfired the V-2 in hopes of getting the entire ballistic missile program transferred to a more desirable location. Whether there was any truth to this or not, launch facilities were eventually transferred to the Florida coast.

Charles Green, a General Electric physicist who worked on V-2 research projects, likened human knowledge of the upper atmosphere before the V-2 experiments to a fish's knowledge of the fisherman: we knew roughly what it looked like, but not what it was all about. Immediately after returning home from the Korean War, Major Simons was assigned to the Space Biology Laboratory at Holloman.

Upon his arrival in New Mexico, Simons was asked to lead a pioneering study on the effects of cosmic ray bombardment on living tissue. Cosmic radiation, composed of highly charged nuclear particles that are abundant beyond the thick band of gases that surrounds the surface of the Earth, was poorly understood and, like most things unknown, feared. What would happen to the rocket plane pilots and later space travelers when they strayed into that bleak zone at the top of the sky? Would radiation broil their skin, damage their brains, destroy their reproductive capacities? *Popular Science* magazine was willing to speculate:

> What these blockbusters [heavy-particle cosmic rays] may do to the body is conjecture—no one has ever been exposed to them. Space-medicine experts foresee that they may perforate the body with such wounds as sterilized needles would leave—and cause flashes of light as they strike the eye's retina, perhaps with permanent damage to vision.

And, in fact, early studies from the United States, Germany, and the Soviet Union all suggested that the potential damage might in fact be catastrophic.

This was virgin territory for Simons, not yet a space-medicine expert. Not only did he know relatively little about cosmic radiation, he had never had more than cursory exposure to statistical analysis of data. But he was intensely curious, and had deep interests in medical research and astronomy. Relishing the challenge, he began to educate himself, tracking down the published literature and the few experts in the field who were willing to share their knowledge and techniques.

Gone by this time were the volatile and wildly unpredictable V-2s—the nose cones had rarely come down in one piece anyway. The first recovery of live animal subjects had not occurred until September 1951, after an Aerobee rocket flight attended by Henry and Simons that had reached 236,000 feet. At Holloman, gossamer-thin polyethylene balloons were now being used to raise the research animals into the skies.

Interestingly, the early Air Force high-altitude balloon projects received "classified" designations not because of any particular technological or strategic sensitivity, but in order to keep the Society for the Prevention of Cruelty to Animals at bay. Work involving dogs—originally dachshunds because their sausage-like shapes had fit so snugly into the V-2 nose cones—and chimps was a special target for scrutiny. And in spite of the fact that all the research animals were extremely well cared for, handled humanely, and always anesthetized if an experiment had the potential to be traumatic, accidents did happen.

Not only were the balloons a fraction of the cost of missiles—they worked, most of the time. And they were much easier to track and recover than missiles. Simons was able to recover the mice and hamsters and dogs and cats and monkeys after their journeys and scrutinize them for signs of radiation damage. He began to suspect, after many months, that cosmic rays were actually relatively benign. They caused a few hairs on black mice to turn white, but there was no evidence of serious damage to the progeny of radiation-bombarded fruit flies or the brains of primates.

One of the main problems with sending living things so high in the sky was figuring out how to balance the temperature inside the capsules. Simons and the Holloman balloon crew used the mouse as a yardstick: one "mouse unit" equaled the amount of heat produced by a single laboratory mouse. They standardized on a 200-mouse-unit capsule in which they could accommodate various combinations of the small animals provided by the Air Force contractors. After gaining proficiency at launching and retrieving these payloads, they carried out most of the actual research flights in northern Minnesota and North Dakota because the most intense concentrations of cosmic radiation are encountered over the northern latitudes.

But it was back at Holloman on an August day when everything changed for Major Simons. He was in his office, busy with some paperwork, when his boss, Col. John Paul Stapp, walked in, sat on the edge of the desk, and asked him whether he thought it would be possible to put a *man* inside one of those capsules and send *him* up to the top of the atmosphere. Simons considered the question and, using the weight of an average man, quickly calculated that a 500-mouse-unit capsule would be required—two and a half times the size of the capsule they had been using. Sure, he said. There would be no great technical problem constructing such a capsule. Simons—tall, good-looking, with an analytical mind and a sometimes-arrogant manner—was suddenly curious.

Stapp quizzed him further, asking him whether in his opinion it would be safe to take a man above 100,000 feet—20 miles—and leave him there for, say, an entire day. Simons hesitated, puzzled, but answered that nothing he had learned to that point would seem to prohibit it.

"Dave," Stapp asked, "would *you* be interested in going?"

Simons was floored. He was a biomedical research man, a doctor. At Holloman he was surrounded by pilots from the Fighter Test Section. These were the elite jet jockeys, the shining stars, the razor-sharp Joe Hero types living on supersonic adrenaline, pressing toward the blurry edges of experience. They got the glory assignments. The scientists in their white lab coats with their clipboards and mechanical pencils did the grunt work. Simons recalled an earlier time, a year or so after he first arrived at the base and just after his first boss at Holloman had left. As he cleaned out the drawers of the man's desk, the very one he was sitting at now, he came across a curious drawing, a sketch of what appeared to be a manned space vehicle. He had laughed at the time: science fiction, Buck Rogers. Now he remembered the drawing as he formed an answer to Stapp's question.

The animals had allowed Simons to gather invaluable data on the upper atmosphere, but what he really needed now was an observer, someone who could monitor his own condition and report back the results. The doctor would be the patient and the researcher would serve as his own subject. There was no question. Of course he wanted to go, he said.

Stapp smiled and conferred upon David Simons the directorship of a new space biology program, one that would focus on humans. As Stapp put it, "The animals did nothing up there but breathe, eat, and defecate." They couldn't take measurements or make scientific observations. There was so much to learn that could only be learned with a human being on board. It was the next logical step. But it would be a difficult one. Simply keeping the pilot alive at the altitudes they were talking about would be a chore.

Stapp and Simons weren't the first to seriously consider such an undertaking. The Navy's Project Helios had intended to raise a human to a height of 100,000 feet beneath a cluster of 100 plastic balloons back in 1947. Unfortunately, the process of launching such a cluster had proved unmanageable. Yet it was with Helios that the concept of manned, scientific, high-altitude ballooning in the postwar period really began. And as Stapp and Simons began to contemplate their own blueprint for a near-space flight, the Navy's Project Strato-Lab had already announced its intention to raise a balloon-borne research platform into the upper atmosphere.

Stapp and Simons, however, had in mind more elaborate flights and more focused research objectives than anyone else had proposed. They wanted to study more than cosmic rays, pilot-escape problems, and high-altitude hardware. They were interested in the effects of a stratospheric journey on the body and mind of a human. And there was little desire to compete with other programs. There would be, as Stapp put it, no "track meets in the sky."

Most of the theoretical work behind the high-altitude programs of the Air Force had originated at Wright Field in Ohio. Following World War II, the Aeromedical Laboratory there had been staffed with its own brilliant coterie of German immigrants, including Hubertus Strughold, who would become known as the "father of space medicine." Strughold had developed the concept of the "aeropause": a region of the upper atmosphere in which "space-equivalent conditions" could be found. In spite of the fact that true space was thought to begin somewhere between 50 and 600 miles above the surface of the earth (an arbitrary designation no matter what number you settle on; an international agreement puts the figure at 100 kilometers—about 62 miles), Strughold argued that atmospheric space equivalence, in ever-increasing degrees, began at an altitude of approximately 10 miles up. He pointed out that instantaneous loss of consciousness due to oxygen deprivation occurs above 50,000 feet and that bodily fluids will boil at 63,000 feet. At 100,000 feet, more than 99 percent of the earth's atmosphere lies below. According to Strughold, "What we call upper atmosphere in the physical sense, must be considered—in terms of biology—as space in its total form." So, by Strughold's definition, the flight Stapp had envisioned would visit more than the stratosphere—it would enter space.

The Air Force's School of Aviation Medicine at Randolph Air Force Base outside San Antonio, under the direction of Col. Harry G. Armstrong, had also been instrumental in early high-altitude and high-speed human factors research. Armstrong had written the definitive text on aviation medicine and had himself established the height above the earth's surface above which an unprotected man's blood would boil in his veins. The Armstrong Line, drawn at 63,000 feet above sea level, was considered to be the precipice of space. It was at a conference organized by Armstrong in 1948 that Strughold coined the term "space medicine."

Stapp and Simons named their program Project Daedalus after the mythical Cretan architect and inventor who built wings for himself and his son, wings to deliver them from slavery. But after submitting the name to the Air Force for approval, they discovered that it was already being used by another project. It was probably just as well; Daedalus, after all, was a tragic figure who was ultimately punished by the gods for his pride and left cursing his own inventive skill.

So Simons and Stapp settled for their second choice, more mundane perhaps, but more straightforward and elemental. And while Project Manhigh would continue Simons's cosmic radiation studies, its charter was expanded: to determine the feasibility of manned space flight. Could a human survive for an extended period of time above the atmosphere? Could he perform work efficiently? Would radiation create havoc with the human body?

John Paul Stapp's own research at Holloman between the time of his arrival in 1953 and the beginnings of Manhigh had gained him the respect, if not the awe, of some of the most grizzled test pilots in the Air Force. Attitudes at Holloman differed significantly from those at Muroc. The Air Force had begun to get serious not only about high-altitude survival, but also about high-speed survival. If the limit of human tolerance to deceleration forces was not 18 Gs, like the textbooks said, then what was it? Stapp had gone as far as his equipment would take him at Muroc, but he had never claimed to have found the limit.

At Holloman, Stapp was given spacious, well-equipped facilities and a competent, well-trained staff of Air Force officers. He also received a 3,500-foot high-precision track, including rails a full seven feet apart, an ingenious water-braking system, and a state-of-the-art sled (designed and built, like its predecessor at Muroc, by Northrop) powered by nine rockets capable of delivering 40,000 pounds of thrust. Stapp intended to find the limit of human endurance, and he intended to do it himself. Stapp would later say that he used himself as the subject for his great rocket-sled experiments because he preferred to take the physical punishment personally rather than risk court-martial for killing some unlucky sergeant.

In the summer and fall of 1954, Stapp propelled down the 3,500-foot track at frightening speeds three times, only to slam to an abrupt stop at

Dr. John Paul Stapp is strapped in before his final Holloman rocket-sled run: "Subject had considerable apprehension and uneasiness with cold sweat of axillae and palms." *(Source: USAF)*

the end of the ride. Each time, in that final, horrible moment, Stapp was subjected to G-forces unheard of in the history of aviation. By December of that year, the rocket sled had taken its toll. Colonel Stapp had broken his ribs and wrists, and suffered several assorted concussions and hernias, hemorrhages in the retinas of both eyes, and searing headaches that lingered for days.

Wearing a blue wool flight suit, leather gloves, a special fiberglass helmet with a Plexiglas face shield, and with a rubber bite-block clenched between his teeth, he strapped himself into the rocket sled for the final time on December 10. A red flare was fired to signal two minutes until

The "world's fastest man" approaches the speed of sound. Joe Kittinger, in the T-33 overhead, is unable to keep up with Stapp on Sonic Wind. *(Source: USAF)*

ignition. "Subject had considerable apprehension," he would write later in his report, "and uneasiness with cold sweat of axillae and palms." Painted in bold black letters onto the side of the red and white sled was the name "SONIC WIND No. 1." Immediately behind him, the nine rocket engines were prepared to fire. Technicians in a concrete block-house 100 feet from the track kept an eye on the preparations through a periscope window and waited for the countdown—broadcast out to the track through loudspeakers—to reach zero, and then fired the engines. An explosion of smoke and fire leapt from the rockets and Stapp hurtled off, literally like a bullet—faster, in fact, than a .45-caliber shell shot from a pistol. He reached a speed in excess of 600 MPH and endured wind pressure of more than two tons. A Lockheed T-33 jet attempted to track and keep up with the sled but could not. Stapp, feeling the full weight of 20 Gs jamming his shoulders and head into the seat, pulled away in a deafening roar, a 35-foot tongue of fire and a cloud of white smoke boiling out of the rockets. At the end of the track, a precisely measured water barrier lay between the rails to catch a scoop on the front of the sled and—in conjunction with more conventional friction brakes—slam it to a stop. When the sled hit the water brake and the giant rooster-tail of water shot into the air, the Sonic Wind was traveling at very nearly the speed of sound.

At the precise moment that he slammed forward into his shoulder harness and his head snapped down, as the blood rushed into his brain like a wave pounding a cliff, Stapp, in massive deceleration, pulled an unheard-of 46.2 Gs—almost four tons. The weight of his body surging against the restraints at that moment was approximately 7,820 pounds.

The night before that final run, Stapp had made a point of drinking in the vermilion glory of the wide New Mexico sunset beyond the San Andres Mountains, aware that it was his eyes, his vision, more than anything else, that would be at risk in that moment of deceleration. He had already suffered multiple severe retinal hemorrhages. Afterward, as he was helped from the sled, Stapp casually remarked that he could not see. His entire vision was encompassed by a "shimmering salmon-colored field." He later described the pain in his eyes: "somewhat like the extraction of a molar without an anesthetic." It felt, he said, as if his eyes had been plucked out of their sockets.

One of the initial press reports claimed that Stapp had been critically injured during the run and lay in a coma in an Alamogordo hospital. Not so, according to Stapp: "I've never been unconscious from a sled run. . . . They took me to the base hospital, and I had two lunches because I hadn't had any breakfast."

Gradually, over a period of minutes, his vision returned and, later, his other injuries healed. The Holloman rocket-sled runs proved that windblast can be almost as dangerous as the deceleration forces themselves; Stapp had the blisters to prove what a single grain of sand can do to protective clothing and skin when it impacts at 600 MPH. Yet he had survived the worst of the dangers: no internal organs had ruptured and neither his heart nor his respiratory system had gone into arrest. On the morning after the big run, Stapp did begin to lose vision in his right eye. He sought out the opinion of the genial Holloman base surgeon, whose response was to offer Stapp a drink. Eventually, the fading vision resolved itself into a retinal image that would remain visible to Stapp, in his right eye, forever after: a perfect silhouette of the X-1 rocket plane.

The press called him "the world's fastest man." He made the cover of *Time* magazine and was the subject of the Ralph Edwards television tribute show "This Is Your Life!" If he had been exposed to the cold shoulder of the Air Force bureaucracy for too many years, he stepped now into the warm glow of celebrity. Yet his satisfaction was contained completely by his work and its results: He had proved that a pilot, if adequately clothed and properly restrained—and there was work to be done here—could survive an emergency bailout at 40,000 feet at speeds up to Mach 1.6.* Air Force jet pilots, understandably, were heartened with the findings. Stapp wanted to continue the experiments, wanted to build Sonic Wind No. 2 and experiment with speeds in excess of 1,000 MPH using a rotating gyro-seat that would simulate the random tumbling of a pilot ejection, but the men at the mahogany desks were resolute this time. Enough was enough. It was possible, they lectured him sternly, to push luck too far.

"Why," Stapp continued to ask, "are we always underestimating man?" While Stapp's work with human subjects on the test track came to a halt, the Holloman "railroad"—during his tenure as chief of the Aeromedical Field Lab—became an increasingly important research facility for the Air Force and, later, for NASA. By 1957, the track's length had increased tenfold from 3,500 feet to 35,000. Test vehicles were powered by rockets capable of delivering 350,000 pounds of controllable and variable thrust. By 1959, a ground speed of Mach 4—four times the speed of sound—was surpassed. The Holloman track, which Gemini astronauts were able to identify from space, celebrated its two-thousandth run in 1963 with a test that reached Mach 5.

The flight surgeon monitoring Stapp's condition during the rocket-sled experiments had been one Maj. David Simons. He had witnessed the devotion and quiet courage of his superior officer firsthand, and so he understood implicitly why Stapp was asking him now, months later, if he had the confidence to attempt the Manhigh flight himself. That was crucial. Simons knew more about the possibilities and risks than anyone. Unless he himself would be willing to ascend 20 miles into the sky

---

*Capt. Eli Beeding later survived a deceleration test that unexpectedly exposed him to 83 Gs for a fraction of a second. On that run, Beeding suffered a sprained back that landed him in traction at the base hospital. ("The first thing I felt was the spinal pain," he reported, "as if a baseball bat had been applied to the bottom of the back.") Rocket-sled experiments with anesthetized chimpanzees showed that they were capable of withstanding 135 Gs before significant injury resulted. The fatal limit was found to be somewhere in the vicinity of 247 Gs.

and remain for an entire day and night, it would be fundamentally improper to ask another airman to do the same. Stapp had established an ethic that other project leaders at Holloman would be challenged to follow.

"He was not addressing himself to the question of personal bravery or fear," Simons would write later, recalling Stapp's question about Simons's willingness to subject himself to the space equivalent environment at 100,000 feet. "He was asking about confidence, not fear."

David Simons first met a test pilot named Joseph Kittinger during the Holloman rocket-sled experiments. While Simons was on the ground monitoring Stapp's physical condition, Kittinger was above, flying the T-33 that attempted to track the speeding sled from the air. Captain Kittinger, "Little Joe," short of stature but tough and wiry with orange hair and a quick, engaging smile, was an experienced and passionate pilot. So when, in order to examine the effects of zero gravity, Simons needed an experienced pilot who could fly him on the big parabolic arcs known as "Keplerian trajectories" that produce a few seconds of weightlessness at their apex, Stapp assigned Joe Kittinger.

The trick was to power-dive steeply, build to maximum speed, and then pull back into a hard climb. The pilot must then maintain a steady speed and complete a huge, precisely rounded arc in the sky. At the very top of the arc, the pilot and his passenger experience the desired effect: a few precious moments of complete weightlessness and with it an almost dreamy, floating sensation. Air Force astronomer/physicist Heinz Haber had originally devised the technique, and pilots Scott Crossfield and Chuck Yeager had pioneered it. Yeager had described the disoriented feeling of zero gravity as "lost in space." (NASA astronauts preparing for the first Mercury flights would later come to Holloman for their zero-gravity training. Their Keplerian trajectories were accomplished in a big modified C-131 transport whose fuselage was emblazoned with the plane's name in giant letters: "How High The Moon.")

It was during that first zero-G flight together, completing the big parabolas in an F-89 Scorpion, that Simons got a glimpse of the real Joe Kittinger. Many test pilots avoided these medical research flights, but Kittinger loved the novel sensation of zero gravity and relished the challenge of flying the arcs perfectly so that the weightless moments at the top lasted as long as possible. In fact, both Kittinger and Simons became totally engrossed in the entire process. They had been up for two hours when Kittinger announced that they were already on reserve fuel and would have to return to the base immediately. Simons, nearly euphoric, was unconcerned. Even when Kittinger informed him that he was going to request an emergency landing because there wasn't enough fuel to complete the traffic pattern, Simons looked down and saw the Holloman runways and shrugged.

A few moments later, Kittinger reported a further interesting development: "We've lost number two engine. Fuel booster pump is out." By this time, Simons was becoming concerned. He knew Kittinger was an excellent pilot, but he also knew the tough-guy test-pilot mindset and the bravado that accompanied it.

With one engine gone and not much but fumes for fuel, Kittinger lined the F-89 up for landing. But the tower refused permission for a straight-on landing. "I'm coming straight in," Kittinger shot back. "I have lost one engine. Fuel is low. Repeat. Fuel is low."

The controller, agitated now, warned that Kittinger was on a collision course with an incoming jet on a perpendicular runway.

"Thanks for the information," Kittinger barked. "I'm coming in. Out."

Dropping down toward the runway, Kittinger discovered yet another intriguing problem. The landing gear would not release. Banking, he pulled around to line up with another runway, barely missing the Saberjet coming in across his path. The indicator still said no landing gear, but Kittinger lined up for final approach anyway. Maybe the gear was down and maybe it wasn't. Simons could see the firetrucks racing from the hangars below.

The gear was, as it turned out, down and locked and Kittinger executed a textbook landing. As they rolled down the runway, the engines finally sputtered and quit: the fuel tanks were dry. Simons recalls Kittinger turning, grinning broadly, and saying something or other about "luck."

Preparation for Manhigh was under way. The balloon and the gondola were painstakingly designed, redesigned, and constructed, piece by piece. Stapp delineated four conditions that a pilot would have to satisfy before he would be cleared for a stratospheric ascent: candidates would have to (1) pass a claustrophobia test to prove their capacity to endure a space smaller than a telephone booth for 24 consecutive hours, (2) survive a simulated altitude of 100,000 feet in a decompression chamber, (3) make a parachute jump to prepare them for an emergency, and (4) qualify for a free-balloon pilot's license.

Stapp also added two alternate pilots to the program. He wanted trained backups ready to go at all times in case something happened to Simons. The project's success would never be allowed to hinge on the availability of a single pilot. Joe Kittinger—who had heard about the program from Simons and had volunteered—was named an alternate along with a Holloman scientist. When Lt. Col. Oakley Baron, director of the Holloman Flight Test Division, received Stapp's request for Kittinger's services on Manhigh, he filled out the appropriate transfer papers, writing at the bottom of one, "Joe, here's your approval. More guts than brains. Good luck. Baron."

In spite of the fact that Manhigh would use a pressurized, closed-gondola system—a prototype of the plug-shaped space capsules that would become so familiar during the Mercury, Gemini, and Apollo days of the 1960s—it was decided that the pilot would wear the partial-pressure suit that was standard issue for high-altitude jet pilots. Should the Manhigh gondola lose pressure at altitude, an unprotected pilot would suffer explosive decompression: above 63,000 feet internal fluids vaporize instantly into expanding gas; the body inflates and literally explodes. The partial-pressure suit of the 1950s, a bulky and extremely uncomfortable piece of gear, made deliberately just a bit too short from crotch to collar, contained tubes that could be instantly inflated with oxygen. If pressure was lost, the oxygen inside the suit would surround and squeeze the body, creating a compensatory pressure similar to the cuff of a hand-inflated blood-pressure apparatus. It would not keep a pilot alive forever, but it might give him time to get down to a safe altitude.

The claustrophobia test required the subjects to squeeze into the suit and sit sealed inside a mock-up of the tiny 500-mouse-unit gondola for an entire day. In spite of uncomfortably high temperatures and some pain caused by the tight-fitting suit, not to mention the frustration of remaining in a cramped sitting position for so many hours, Simons had no trouble. Ever the efficient researcher—a man who would often shave with an electric razor in each hand to save time—Major Simons brought along some technical reports that required his attention and a book about Civil War balloon operations for background reading. Kittinger, likewise, completed his time in the mocked-up gondola without incident. The second alternate pilot candidate, however, proved the soundness of Stapp's decision to insist on such a test. This man completed his day-long lock-up, but during his subsequent physical was discovered to be on the brink of cardiovascular failure. And the scary part—the part that had a lasting effect on the thinking of both Simons and Stapp, as well as on the agenda of the Manhigh program itself—was that he had never been aware, never admitted even to himself, that he had experienced symptoms of acute claustrophobia. So determined had he been to complete the test and qualify for the Manhigh flight that he had managed to block out what would otherwise have been a truly harrowing experience. Even though a human pilot was going to be sent up in order to gain his personal observations, it would not always be possible to rely on a man's own evaluation of his physical condition. It was a dilemma Manhigh would struggle with to the end.

Simons and Kittinger (now the sole alternate Manhigh pilot) headed to Dayton, Ohio, and the Wright Air Development Center for their decompression tests. Again they had to wear the partial-pressure suit. But this time, instead of a stage-prop gondola, they entered the thick, steel tank of the Air Force's stratosphere chamber: a large cauldron accessed through an air-lock and surrounded by a bewildering tangle of pipes, valves, and wires. To Simons, this imposing monster resembled nothing so much as an execution chamber. After breathing pure oxygen for an hour to cleanse his blood of nitrogen bubbles that would otherwise expand and cause excruciating pain, the pilot sits alone in the chamber while the air is pumped out. At the equivalent of 100,000 feet above sea level, the chamber is an almost total vacuum. A leak in the suit in such an environment would bring death in moments, a risk requiring experienced technicians to monitor the subject closely. Both the suit and the men, however, emerged intact.

If the Manhigh gondola malfunctioned in some way during the flight and the internal pressure was lost, the pilot's only hope would be to descend as quickly as possible. There were two possibilities: If the pilot retained consciousness, he could strap on a parachute, open the hatch, and jump. Otherwise, the ground crew could remotely separate the gondola from the balloon and allow the entire vehicle to fall beneath a large cargo chute. It wasn't known what the chances of pilot survival might be in either case, but Stapp was insistent that his pilots have experience with the personal parachute they would carry with them into the stratosphere.

Kittinger had recently gotten his first taste of parachuting in El Centro, California, after being challenged by a group of Air Force jumpers in a bar one night. He had made his first jump the next day— "for the hell of it," he claimed. Now, under the auspices of Manhigh, he returned to El Centro with David Simons. Simons admitted that he wasn't exactly crazy about the idea. After taking a look at the C-47 that would take him up, he noted the position of the plane's tailpiece in relation to the door he would have to use and wondered how it would be possible to miss hitting the tail when he leapt out. But once in the air, in that queasy, unreal moment of no return familiar to anyone making his first parachute jump, Simons moved automatically to the open door as he had been instructed and pushed obligingly out into nothingness. Then, somehow, in disbelief, he felt his D-ring in his hand and the sharp tug of his harness. He sailed slowly, gratefully down.

As Simons returned to Holloman and the laborious regimen of preparing for Manhigh, Joe Kittinger remained in El Centro and enthusiastically completed the eight additional jumps that qualified him for a USAF paratrooper rating.

Several months later, Simons and Kittinger finally found time to work on the last of Stapp's conditions: a free-balloon pilot's license. In order to qualify for Civil Aeronautics Administration balloon licenses, each man would have to log 16 hours of flight time in an open-gondola balloon and execute sixteen takeoffs and sixteen landings. Most of the flying would be done over the farm country of Minnesota and, unlike his experience with jump training, Simons had no ambivalence at all about piloting balloons. He found it, as most do, one of the most pleasant ways to travel. It was peaceful, quiet, and magical. One hundred and fifty years earlier, a German prince had written of his first experience in a balloon: "The feeling of absolute solitude is rarely experienced upon earth, but in these regions, separated from all human associations, the soul might almost fancy it had passed the confines of the grave."

David Simons offered his own impressions:

Without wind whistling by your ears, you are in a strangely silent world, conscious only of the sounds of the countryside below. And you hear the noises of living on earth as you never have heard them before. They are remote, therefore not jarring; you are lifted above them, and therefore are not a part of them, so they come to you like sights and sounds in a dream.

There was a lovely irony here: humanity's first significant foray to the precipice of the only real frontier left—the vast, black sea of space—would be accomplished in the very oldest form of aircraft.

* * *

No one knows for certain when the first balloon was flown. The concept, after all, is rudimentary. All that is required is a fairly light, fairly strong sack and a heat source. An ancient pottery shard discovered in Peru reportedly contains a design that resembles a balloon. The evidence was at least convincing enough to inspire a group of balloon enthusiasts from the International Explorers Society, in 1975, to build and fly a balloon constructed entirely with materials and tools available to the pre-Incan Nazca civilization of the Andes. The envelope was constructed of a single strip of material sewn up in spiral fashion to form a large tetrahedron. Filling the balloon with the hot smoke of a tar fire, Englishman Julian Nott and a copilot ascended with the *Condor I* in a reed gondola to a height of 300 feet and returned to earth safely.

Nevertheless, the aristocratic Montgolfier brothers of France, Joseph and Etienne, are usually credited with launching the first manned lighter-than-air flight of modern times. It was Paris, 1783. On September 19, a colorful and intricately decorated linen balloon 40 feet wide and nearly 60 feet tall was carried 1,500 feet straight up and held there for eight minutes by the superheated air from a pile of smoldering straw and wool. A sheep, a duck, and a rooster were the passengers on this flight that brought cheers from a crowd of onlookers celebrating below in the Great Court at Versailles. It was not a manned flight, but it was close.

For nearly a century leading up to that flight, Europeans—primarily the Italians and the French—had been thinking about and designing various forms of aerostats that would float on the currents of the air as ships floated on the currents of the sea. But not even the Montgolfiers themselves, avid but amateur students of physics, understood precisely what physical principle caused their balloons to rise. The scientific consensus at the time was that a mysterious atmospheric agent in the smoke called *phlogiston* was responsible for the lift. To fill his *Globe,* first flown in August of 1783, Jacques Alexandre Cesar Charles used a substance he called "inflammable air." He poured sulfuric acid onto iron filings and produced hydrogen gas, which was sixteen times lighter than air, the lightest element known.

Nearly a year earlier, at the family home in southern France, the Montgolfiers' aviation career had begun with the recognition—Joseph's, initially—that a paper bag would rise when it was filled with smoke. After some experimentation with taffeta balloons in the late fall and winter, the brothers announced a demonstration for the Académie des

Sciences in the Annonay town square in June of 1783. They built a fire and suspended over it a paper and fabric bag that measured 35 feet in diameter and was held together with common buttons. Once the bag was filled with smoke, they released it and watched with the crowd as it sailed up some 500 feet and drifted off on the wind. Inspired by their success, and bankrolled by the family's successful paper factories, the Montgolfiers decided to head for Paris.

Almost immediately after the flight of the three animals thrilled Versailles in September, a race was on to raise the first human being over Paris: the Montgolfier hot air balloon versus the Charles gas balloon. A few weeks later, in spite of the fact that it was Charles's gas design that would dominate the next century and a half of ballooning, 30-year-old François Pilatre de Rozier, a physics and chemistry teacher, became the first man to fly. On October 15, 1783, de Rozier made a series of tethered ascents in a new Montgolfier hot-air balloon that featured a circular gallery attached to the base. With Joseph Montgolfier controlling the guide ropes, de Rozier rose as high as 80 feet: the world's first manned-balloon altitude record. A month after that, with a passenger, the marquis d'Arlandes (François Laurent), along to provide balance and the king and queen (the soon-to-be-deposed Louis XVI and Marie Antoinette) in attendance at the launch, de Rozier made the first free balloon flight, drifting with the breeze for nearly half an hour and reaching a height of 3,000 feet. The launch was well attended and the crowd was absolutely flabbergasted as it watched the handsome, pear-shaped balloon sail off on the northwest wind. The Montgolfier balloon was surely one of the most beautiful aircraft ever to fly—blue, gold, and red, decorated with garlands and zodiacal icons, draped with ornamental fabric bunting. The two aeronauts, dressed in blue-velvet suits and wearing plumed hats, fanned a small fire beneath the 56,000-cubic-foot envelope as they rose, and landed gently in a field a full five miles from the launch spot. Then, in December, J.A.C. Charles and a passenger ascended from the Tuileries Garden in a larger version of the gas-filled *Globe*. This was the year that manned flight was born. Forever after, human beings would have the luxury of looking down at their towns and countrysides from the perspective of the birds. It was a fundamental liberation.

The balloonist of the eighteenth century was part laboratory scientist and part raconteur. He knew enough chemistry and physics to select materials and construct a functioning aircraft, but he was also salesman enough to know how to raise the capital to fund his work and huckster enough to keep keen the public's interest in balloon activities. One of the most impressive feats of this period was the first air crossing of the English Channel in January of 1785. Jean Pierre Blanchard was a brilliant, arrogant Frenchman who was, by this time, already a name in aeronautical circles—as much for his insufferable personality as for his pioneering balloon flights (he had made his first ascent in Paris the year before). John Jeffries was a Boston physician, living in England, who had become enthralled with the idea of flight and approached Blanchard with an offer to fund a crossing of the Channel if he—Jeffries—could participate in the flight himself. The two reportedly quarreled like children over every conceivable aspect of the preparation. By the time they finally lifted off from the cliffs of Dover on that cold, clear winter morning, they were barely speaking to one another.

It was a dangerous stunt and the prospects for success were only marginal. They rose above the water in a small, black, boat-shaped gondola equipped with a rear rudder, four wing-like fins, and bright, silk-covered oars with which to "row" through the air, and drifted off toward the Continent. But before they reached even the halfway point, the balloon—round as a billiard ball and encased in a huge net—began to descend. They had chosen an eccentric—and weighty—collection of personal items with which to travel: scientific books, musical instruments, art objects, a telescope, a clock, among others. By the time they were three-fourths of the way across, they had ballasted nearly everything they had, including their life jackets, ropes, and even their pants. Blanchard grabbed the gondola's oars and frantically began to flail at the air—with absolutely no effect—while Jeffries attempted to steer with the useless rudder. Eventually, the oars and rudders were dismantled and thrown overboard for ballast. The balloon dropped down near the waves and began to skip off the surface of the water. Blanchard and Jeffries then took turns filling a flotation bladder with their own urine which they proceeded to toss overboard. Those few ounces made the difference. The balloon bobbed up and drifted far enough to land in a forest near Ardres. Blanchard and Jeffries, half-frozen and dressed only in their underwear, were terribly disappointed that crowds of admirers were not on hand to hail their arrival. (Blanchard continued his aeronautical adventures and, almost exactly eight years after his Channel crossing, he made the first free balloon flight in the infant nation across the Atlantic Ocean, ascending from a prison yard in Philadelphia with

Pres. George Washington in attendance—still attempting to pull himself through the air by means of oars.)

Balloonists began to compete seriously for altitude records around the turn of the century, beginning with the 1803 German ascent of Robertson and Lhoest, the 1804 French ascent of Gay-Lussac, and the Italian ascent of Andreoli and Brioschi in 1808, all of which topped 20,000 feet. In 1862, the Englishmen Henry Coxwell and James Glaisher only barely survived an ascent that probably reached 29,000 feet. Thirteen years later, Theodore Sivel and Joseph Croce-Spinelli died in an attempt to establish a new record. Their balloon, the *Zenith*, topped out at 28,000 feet; Gaston Tissandier, the third member of that flight, survived to become a well-known historian of ballooning. Then, in 1894, German meteorologist Arthur Berson rose to 30,000 feet. Seven years later, with his friend Reinhard Suring aboard, Berson reached a world-record altitude of 35,424 feet, a mark that would stand until the celebrated flights of the American Hawthorne Gray a quarter of a century later.

two

The Sport of the Scientist

Hawthorne Gray was the first balloonist to get above 40,000 feet, but the first successful stratospheric flight was the work of a clever Swiss physics professor named Auguste Piccard. And while Gray's three attempts at the human altitude record had been undertaken mostly in the spirit of adventure and conquest, Piccard's balloon flights four years later were accompanied by all the clutter and trappings of science. Piccard himself was perfectly cast for the role he would play: the prototype egg-headed, scatter-haired, white-aproned genius who held sacred the tenets of the scientific method. Many years after his great aeronautical achievements, he would write,

> The modern scientific seeker should not cast himself head foremost into these perils. The sport of the scientist consists in utilizing all that he knows, in foreseeing the dangers, in studying every detail with profound attention, in always using the admirable instrument of mathematical analysis wherever it can shed its magic light upon his work. If he is convinced in advance he has avoided all imaginable risks, and has neglected nothing in his plans, the scientist then has the serenity necessary to achieve success.

It comes as no surprise that Piccard did not listen to jazz orchestras on the radio during his trip into the uncertain serenity.

After a distinguished academic career at the Swiss Institute of Technology, Piccard developed an interest in atmospheric physics. In 1913, with his equally brilliant twin brother Jean, he flew a balloon from Zurich, across Germany, and into France taking air-density and temperature measurements. Both Piccards served in the Swiss army's Lighter-than-Air Service in 1915.

On May 27, 1931, Auguste and an assistant, Charles Kipfer, wearing inverted wicker chicken baskets and pillows on their heads as makeshift crash helmets, lifted off from Augsburg, Germany, beneath a 500,000-cubic-inch, hydrogen-filled balloon. Piccard's gondola was much better suited to a high-altitude flight than the open wicker basket of Hawthorne Gray. In fact, Gray's tragedy had been the inspiration behind Piccard's "capsule" design. (The U.S. Army had experimented with enclosed, pressurized gondolas, but had finally abandoned the idea as impractical.) The physicist's attention to detail and practical imagination are in ample evidence in his own description of the design problems he faced:

> We must have a hermetically sealed cabin, carrying breathable air at ordinary pressure, and able to resist this internal pressure even when the outside pressure will be no more than one-tenth of an atmosphere. Our lives depend upon the airtightness and the strength of this cabin. Let us, then, have a spherical cabin in sheet aluminum of one-seventh of an inch (3.5 mm.) thick. The diameter will be 7 ft. (210 cm.). Two observers, surrounded by their instruments, will be perfectly comfortable here, surveying the outside world through eight round portholes of a convenient diameter, that of 3.15 in. (8 cm.). To avoid the danger of breakage caused by the difference between the pressures prevailing on the two faces, these windows are constructed of two sheets of glass, each 0.3 in. thick, separated by a thin layer of air which contributes to thermal insulation. We thus prevent the formation of rime on the windows, even in the stratosphere, where the external temperature is in the neighborhood of −76 degrees F.

A Draeger apparatus, adapted from deep-sea applications, chemically removed carbon dioxide from the cabin atmosphere and rendered the interior breathable. It was the first closed-capsule system.

Shortly after the aluminum ball lifted off and floated over the factory chimneys of Augsburg, Piccard discovered a potentially disastrous air leak. An insulator for an electric sounder had broken and its installation hole was siphoning off the cabin's oxygen. Ever resourceful, Piccard went to work plugging the hole with a wad of cotton and some petroleum jelly that he had brought along for just that purpose. By the time the leak was stopped, pressure inside the gondola had dropped to below two-thirds of normal and the oxygen content of the air was badly depleted. Piccard, unfazed, dribbled a small quantity of liquid oxygen onto the metal floor of the gondola where it bubbled up at a temperature of –290 degrees Fahrenheit and evaporated, enriching the breathable oxygen mix inside the capsule.

A little later, another crisis presented itself as a barometer broke and spilled mercury on the capsule floor. Piccard and Kipfer frantically tried to get hold of the mercury blobs with their fingers before any of it found its way into the beginnings of a crack in the interior surface, but finally gave up in frustration. Piccard solved the problem nicely by attaching a rubber hose to a petcock on the cabin wall and, taking advantage of the pressure differential, vacuumed the mercury up with the hose. Kipfer watched through a porthole as the silver beads streamed into the air and drifted off.

In less than half an hour after takeoff, the *FNRS* (Piccard took the initials from the Belgian Fonds Nation de la Recherches Scientifiques, established by King Albert for the purpose of backing scientific endeavors, which had provided $14,000 to fund the project) had ascended more than nine miles and recorded an unprecedented altitude of 51,200 feet. Piccard and Kipfer had cracked the stratosphere.

And thanks to the closed gondola, the two men could peer out the portholes and enjoy a view never seen before. In his later writings, Piccard would attempt to describe what he saw. But somehow his scientific precision failed him. "Physicists cannot explain very well this colour of the stratosphere."

But now came that other part of the journey, the part that had tormented Captain Gray: safe return to earth. As Piccard and Kipfer looked out on the white peaks of the Bavarian Alps to the south, the direction they were heading, they made an awful discovery. The rope attached to the valve that should have allowed Piccard to release gas from the balloon had tangled with another rope and was completely useless. This meant that the *FNRS* would have little control over its own descent. As the evening came on and temperatures cooled, the gas in the balloon would contract—and the capsule would drop. Piccard had no idea where they would land, but he did know two things: it would be night and they would be lost. He decided to conserve all remaining ballast for the crucial final moments of the flight.

"There we were," Piccard wrote, with typical dramatic flair. "Prisoners of the stratosphere." Nevertheless, he continued to collect cosmic ray data and other atmospheric measurements that were the acknowledged justification for the flight, while keeping one eye on the hole in the gondola and adding gobs of petroleum jelly as necessary. As the great balloon drifted, he became concerned that it might eventually come down in the Adriatic Sea. By late afternoon the descent was only beginning, and it was eight o'clock that night, well after sundown, before the two men were finally back into the troposphere. The temperature was falling and the gondola, itself falling rapidly now, became enveloped in a thick fog. At 15,000 feet, they opened the portholes and allowed the stale interior of the aluminum ball to fill with fresh mountain air. The fog vanished. They could clearly see the jagged moonlit ridges of the Tyrolian Alps looming ahead. Moments later, after bouncing off a steep snowfield and sailing over a glacier cut with dark crevasses, Paul Kipfer pulled the rip-panel strap and instantly emptied the envelope of gas. The gondola struck the ice, skidded a few feet, then came to rest.

Both men were unhurt, although the gondola's 400 pounds of scientific equipment were badly damaged. They spent a very cold night in the *FNRS,* roping up early the following morning for a long walk down the slopes. Fortunately, both men were experienced mountaineers and were able to descend the glacier in relative safety, if not ease. After a few hours they were spotted by a patrol of skiers and escorted to the village of Ober Gurgl, Austria. It took thirty men to carry the balloon envelope and the assortment of instruments off the glacier. The gondola itself was abandoned to the mountains where it was recovered a year later by a team from the University of Innsbruck.

Both pilots were knighted and their achievement was heralded around the world. Piccard told the press, "I made this flight because I had agreed to do so, but I cannot expose my wife and children to another such period of mental distress." Yet the following year he made another flight, this time launching from Zurich and attaining an altitude of 53,152 feet. On this second flight, which lasted 12 hours and touched down in a field south of Lake Garda in Italy, Piccard made the first stratospheric radio broadcast: "All is going well. Observation good." When he visited America in 1933 to lecture on his cosmic radiation experiments and research into what he called his "rocket plane," the Swiss celebrity was accorded a treatment befitting visiting royalty. Among other brash pronouncements, Piccard predicted that a closed-capsule system based on his design would one day carry a human being all the way to the moon.

Twenty years later, Piccard recalled the first of the many celebrations that honored that premier visit to the stratosphere, given by the Swiss Aero-Club a few days after the flight. The president of the club had delivered a speech in which he expressed the hope that the new world altitude record would stand for many years to come. Piccard recalled his own response: "'It will be a fine day for me,' I said, 'when other stratospheric balloons follow me and reach altitudes greater than mine. My aim is not to beat and above all not to maintain records, but to open a new domain to scientific research and to aerial navigations.'"

In 1937, Piccard turned his attention to the design of deep-sea bathyscaphes where he applied much of the knowledge he had gained working with pressurized balloon gondolas.

During Auguste Piccard's American visit in 1933, officials of the upcoming Chicago World's Fair tried to recruit him for a stratospheric flight they hoped to launch that summer. Piccard was flattered and considered the offer, but eventually decided to return to Europe. Before leaving, however, he nominated an alternate pilot: his twin brother, Jean. Jean Piccard had studied chemistry in Zurich, Munich, and Lausanne, and taught at the University of Chicago, before settling in America for good in 1926. He taught at the Massachusetts Institute of Technology for three years and then took a job developing and testing explosives for the Hercules Powder Company in Wilmington, Delaware. He was as passionate, eccentric, and intensely curious as his famous sibling—and anxious for a chance to visit the stratosphere himself. Jean began designing a gondola and an envelope immediately. But the project's sponsors faced other problems: Jean Piccard was not a licensed balloon pilot. Someone who could manage a large balloon in flight and land it safely once the journey was over would have to accompany him into the upper atmosphere.

Ward T. Van Orman seemed like a natural choice. He had been working with a variety of lighter-than-air vehicles at Goodyear-Zeppelin (which had built the Navy dirigibles *Akron* and *Macon* and would manufacture the balloon) since 1917, but he was also regarded as the most successful civilian balloonist in the nation's history, having surpassed— among others—Hawthorne Gray to capture first place in the 1926 Gordon Bennett balloon race, neither Van Orman's first nor last victory in that most prestigious of aeronautical competitions.* But Van Orman did

---

*James Gordon Bennett, a New York newspaper publisher, established an international aeronautical competition in 1906. Balloons of all sizes and shapes would lift off from a prearranged spot and a cash prize, along with the Gordon Bennett cup, would be awarded to the pilot who landed the farthest from the starting point. Six different nations hosted the Gordon Bennett competition from the years 1906 through 1938;

not like the idea of attempting such a challenging flight with Jean Piccard. He had first met Piccard at the Goodyear plant and had been uncomfortable around him from the beginning. Piccard's eccentric nature and lack of aeronautical experience were bad signs, Van Orman was sure. He said no to the Chicago people, but recommended a friend, Navy lieutenant commander Thomas G. W. "Tex" Settle—another great balloon racer who had enjoyed success in the recent European Gordon Bennetts—as the man to take his place.[*]

Tex Settle was a supremely capable aviator (he would become the only human being in the history of flight qualified to pilot a glider, an airplane, a free balloon, a blimp, and a rigid airship) who badly wanted a chance at the stratosphere. He had listened avidly to Auguste Piccard's lecture to the National Geographic Society in Washington, D.C., earlier in the year and had afterward engaged Piccard in conversation about techniques and equipment. The World's Fair sponsors fired off an invitation by telegram to a flabbergasted Settle and he accepted once he was able to obtain permission from his Navy superiors. By special arrangement, Settle—whose duty assignment at that time was inspector of naval aircraft—was allowed to participate in the Chicago project as a civilian. But he too became worried that Jean Piccard would be a disruptive presence in the gondola and asked permission to make a solo ascent. After some consideration, and in spite of Piccard's threat of a lawsuit, the sponsors agreed.

Lieutenant Commander Settle gained an intimate knowledge of the principles and peculiar difficulties of lighter-than-air flight while serving on Navy dirigibles in the mid-1920s. Like Auguste Piccard, Settle had studied Hawthorne Gray's experiences and understood that a

---

during that time, a total of 351 balloonists participated. Aeronauts from the United States won ten of those contests and Belgium was close behind with seven victories.

[*]Later that year, competing in his final Gordon Bennett, Ward Van Orman nearly died when his balloon was caught up in a thunderstorm and swept deep into the dense forests of Quebec. He was eventually rescued, but he spoke of the ordeal as a horrible nightmare and announced that he was through with flying. However, he did continue his lifelong work with flight technology. In 1927, in preparation for a race, he had developed an altimeter so sensitive it could measure a balloon's fall or rise in increments as small as four feet and an altimeter alarm that would alert him when his balloon had reached a predetermined altitude. Later he would contribute to the development of some early pressure suits and pioneer a self-sealing fuel tank for aircraft.

sealed-cabin gondola was the best solution for manned stratospheric flight. In fact, a Settle-designed closed gondola, a seven- by three-foot capsule called the "flying coffin" (evidence of a sense of humor if not good public relations instincts) had actually preceded the *FNRS* and even been authorized for construction by Rear Adm. William Moffett, chief of the Navy's Bureau of Aeronautics—but a budget-conscious Congress had killed the idea before it could get into production.

There is no question that Settle and his sponsors wanted above all else to claim the human altitude record, but the Chicago flight did have its scientific justifications: the gondola would carry (1) ultraviolet ray experiments that would attempt to determine whether or not the hypothesized layer of ozone existed and, if it did, to determine precisely where it was, and (2) a number of cosmic ray experiments designed by Nobel-winning physicists Arthur Compton and Robert Millikan.[*] Cosmic radiation had been discovered around 1900 and, by the thirties, it was known to consist of high-energy, fast-moving particles that originate somewhere outside of our atmosphere. But the ultimate source of these rays remained a mystery.

The proposed flight began to be referred to as the Piccard-Compton flight, and the balloon was called *A Century of Progress* after the theme of the World's Fair. Both the Goodyear-Zeppelin balloon and the gondola (manufactured by the Dow Chemical Company) were patterned after Auguste Piccard's successful system, but a number of improvements had been made. The spherical gondola, for example, was the same diameter as Piccard's, but was constructed of a strong, nearly pure magnesium alloy ⅛th of an inch thick that was a full third lighter than its aluminum counterpart. This alloy, chemically extracted by Dow metallurgists from a briny liquid pumped from deep wells near Midland, Michigan, and called Dowmetal, would be used for a number of subsequent flights.

---

[*]Arthur Compton was a cowinner (along with C.T.R. Wilson) of the 1927 Nobel Prize for physics. They proved the existence of photons, as well as the dual nature of light as both particle and wave. In the early forties, Compton was the director of the Metallurgical Laboratory at the University of Chicago when the first self-sustaining atomic chain reaction was achieved.

Robert Millikan was awarded the 1923 Nobel for physics for his work on the elementary electronic charge and the photoelectric effect. He served as director of the Norman Bridge Laboratory of Physics, and later as president, of the California Institute of Technology, where he began his cosmic ray studies.

The balloon's rubberized-fabric envelope was bigger than Piccard's, with a capacity of 600,000 cubic feet. It looked massive even as it lay in folds on the white dropcloths that had been spread for its protection on the turf of Chicago's Soldier Field. The balloon was surrounded by some 700 steel cylinders of hydrogen and miles of tubing. When it was fully inflated in the predawn hours of August 5, 1933, it rose to the height of a fifteen-story building. With a crowd of 20,000 spectators cheering from the grandstands, *A Century of Progress* lifted off from the stadium at 4:05 A.M. Onlookers could take pride: America was going to the stratosphere.

The great balloon ascended quickly to 5,000 feet where Settle had planned to level off and wait for the sun to heat the hydrogen molecules trapped in a giant bubble at the top of the envelope. He valved some gas to check his ascent, a normal procedure. But the gas valve stuck open and began spilling the entire contents of the gas—which had been donated by the Union Carbide and Carbon Company—into the sky. Settle had had trouble with the valve even before launch. When he pulled and released the graphite-coated valve cord to test the system, he failed to hear the telltale whack of the valve doors slamming shut and worried that the cord's movement had been restricted in the folds of the heavy balloon. He hoped that as he ascended and the balloon filled out, the cord would be freed. He also understood that even if hydrogen were indeed escaping in the moments before the launch, the launch had to proceed for safety's sake. It was important to get the volatile balloon out of the stadium either way.

Fifteen minutes after takeoff, barely enough time for the crowd to file out of the Soldier Field bleachers, *A Century of Progress* dropped ingloriously onto the Burlington Railroad tracks less than two miles away. A contingent of Marines was hastily called in to protect the balloon from greedy souvenir hunters who were busy hacking pieces from the envelope with pocket knives. The Marines eventually dispatched the mob, leaving bloodstains and cigarette burns on the rubbery fabric in the process.

A disappointed and chagrined Tex Settle announced to the world, "I am sorry that I put on a poor show." After some prompting, he admitted that he wanted to attempt a second flight, and the sponsors—the World's Fair itself, the National Broadcasting Company (NBC), and the Chicago Daily News—agreed to consider it.

Seven weeks later, on the last day of September, another high-altitude balloon took to the sky—but not over Chicago. This one, *Stratostat,* was built and flown by the Soviet Red Army. Comdr. Georgi Prokofiev and two other men (Ernest Birnbaum and Konstantin Gudunov) rose to a reported height of 62,304 feet, surpassing Auguste Piccard's mark by almost 9,000 feet. The Soviets claimed to have conducted a number of scientific experiments, including one that dealt with cosmic radiation. And even though the altitude mark was never verified or sanctioned by the FAI, which did not officially recognize the USSR in those days, U.S. Rear Adm. Ernest J. King (who succeeded William Moffett at the Navy's Bureau of Aeronautics) publicly praised the Soviets for their "very marvelous performance."

And that, certainly, is how the flight of the *Stratostat* was viewed in the USSR. Even though the standard-issue official proclamation insisted that the stratospheric flight had been conducted purely for scientific reasons, Prokofiev's ascent was a significant event in terms of Soviet morale. A massive, exuberant rally in Moscow celebrated the feat. Walter Duranty, cabling his report to the *New York Times* directly from Moscow, wrote, "Yesterday's events did more to strengthen the Kremlin's prestige and stimulate the masses than anything the writer has known before. The psychological effect in Russia is comparable to the effect in the United States of Lindbergh's flight to Paris." The *Century of Progress* crew was likewise affected by the flight of *Stratostat*. Settle, Goodyear, and Dow were all acutely aware of their competition on the other side of the world. And, in fact, it was *Stratostat* that guaranteed the necessary support for a second *Century of Progress* attempt.

In many respects 1933 may not have been a great year for the Americans or the Soviets, but it was a banner year for high-altitude balloon ascents. Every few weeks, like clockwork, another of the huge gas bags lifted off. Less than two months after the Soviet flight, Tex Settle tried again. The balloon had received some 1,800 patches to repair the damage done by the souvenir seekers, and the troublesome valve cord had been repositioned and encased in flexible tubing to assure its efficient operation. This time Settle took along a copilot, Marine Corps reservist Maj. Chester Fordney. It was an odd choice: Fordney had never been in a balloon in his life and had certainly never harbored ambitions to make a record-breaking flight. However, he had not only led the contingent of Marines who had been called in to save the balloon following Settle's first attempt, but he also had a keen interest in science and was in charge of a mathematics exhibit at the World's Fair. Fordney's father, who was at that time commandant of the Marine Corps, thought Major Fordney was crazy for tying up with an adventurer like Settle. But Settle liked the young man and had him assigned to operate the scientific instruments and monitor the experiments that, as always, would be the flight's announced justification.*

With Settle hanging in the ropes on top of the gondola, they took off on the morning of November 20, this time from Akron, Ohio (where they were able to inflate the balloon inside a giant Goodyear-Zeppelin hangar). The balloon, now bearing the insignia of both the Navy and the Marines, drifted east, rising to maximum altitude somewhere over Pennsylvania. It was the first successful stratospheric balloon flight launched from American soil, and Settle and Fordney became the first Americans to take a pressurized cabin beyond the atmosphere. The barograph showed 59,000 feet, but the FAI later announced the official mark as 61,237 feet—higher than Piccard's record, but still short of the height reported by the Russians.

Only a few hundred spectators gathered to watch the liftoff this time. But many, many more followed Settle and Fordney on their radios. For the first time, conversation between the balloon and its ground crew was broadcast live. Listeners nationwide were able to hear crackling voices from the stratosphere. And when radio contact was lost during the balloon's rapid descent, the audience—like the audience for any high drama—suffered for its heroes.

The round gondola landed gently in the soft muck of a New Jersey marsh a few miles from Delaware Bay and—interestingly—only a few miles from the residence of Jean Piccard. The two men decided, wisely, to spend the night in the gondola and find their way out of the marsh the following morning. But since they had jettisoned the radio batteries as ballast during the descent, they had no way to contact their crew or alert an anxious nation. Search parties by the score poked about in the swamps where the balloon was presumed to have come down. South New Jersey merchants reported a run on hip waders. A few hours after

---

*One such experiment carried plant-disease spores aloft. Another would expose fruit flies to cosmic radiation for the purpose of monitoring subsequent changes in their sexual reproduction. The fruit flies had become an in-joke among the crew who presented Settle and Fordney with a box of sanitary napkins for their trip into the stratosphere just in case the radiation up there should turn out to cause a "sex change" in the pilots. Ironically, the napkins proved invaluable for soaking up condensation that formed on the interior walls of the gondola.

dawn, Fordney plunged into the cold water and waded five miles across the marshland until he found a boy who took him to a phone.

Among the myriad messages of congratulations the new stratospheric explorers and their crew received, one from the Soviet Commissar for Foreign Affairs, Maxim Litvinoff, was particularly noteworthy: "Hearty congratulations on your great achievement. I am sure your colleagues in the Soviet Union have watched with greatest interest your flight. May both our countries continue to contest the height in every sphere of science and technique."

The FAI sanctioned the flight as an altitude record and America celebrated Settle and Fordney as the new world-record holders. But Settle, in a piece for the *New York Times* immediately after the ascent, did not claim a record. Instead, he marveled at the intense public fascination with these trips into the "greatest of all unexplored regions—the region of night beyond the earth's atmosphere." Settle went on to point out that the entire endeavor was regarded somewhat less romantically by its participants. He wrote,

> There probably is plenty of poetry about the dead quiet, the bitter cold and the queer coloring of the stratosphere, but we had little or no chance to consider such things. We were seldom permitted the time to look out the windows of our gondola or to contemplate the scientific advance that made it possible to live in security and comfort up there, where until only a few years ago no human being could breathe. Ballooning, whether to the stratosphere or to heights where man is no stranger, is chiefly work.

Not long after the flight, Tex Settle—anxious for a change of scenery and new challenges—asked for sea duty and was given command of a Navy gunboat in China. From 1934 to 1937 he commanded the *Palos*, known as the "Flat-Bottomed Queen of the Yangtzee." He joined the Cleveland Rocket Society in the days before the war, marking himself as one of the visionaries who saw the inevitability of the space age many years before it came to pass. He would go on to win the Navy Cross for heroism during World War II, later be named head of the Naval Assistance Program to Turkey and Norway, and eventually become a vice-admiral of U.S. Amphibious Forces, Pacific Fleet. He never realized a long-held ambition to serve as U.S. ambassador to the Soviet Union, but his tremendous energy never waned. At age 80 he continued a lifelong habit of ascending stairs three at a time.

The landmark *Century of Progress* flight was Chester Fordney's one and only claim to national fame. He made no more balloon ascents. He pursued a career in law enforcement following his stint with the Marines and was later elected sheriff of Loudoun County, Virginia. He died in 1960.

Early in January of 1934, the National Geographic Society and the Army Air Corps announced their intention to raise a manned balloon an unprecedented 15 miles above the earth's surface. The new joint venture planned to construct a balloon five times the size of the one flown by Settle and Fordney, one capable of lifting an elaborate flying laboratory and three men. And it would be done quickly. Spokesmen promised that the largest balloon ever seen would fly that summer.

Strato-watchers would not have to wait that long. On the last day of January, the massive Soviet balloon *Osoaviakhim I* was launched. Rumor had it that Josef Stalin was irritated by the success of the Settle-Fordney flight and had ordered a Soviet attempt to coincide with the 17th All-Union Communist Party Congress in Moscow, despite a forecast of severe winter weather. The Russian balloon was constructed and flown by three civilian aeronauts: Fedosienko, Wasienko, and Vsyskin. By mid-morning they reported a peak altitude of 67,585 feet, but apparently the balloonists had duplicated Hawthorne Gray's blunder—they expended too much ballast in order to reach their maximum height, and failed to properly monitor their descent. The *Osoaviakhim* fell too fast and the ropes securing the gondola to the envelope began to strain. On the famous Red Army balloon *Stratostat,* the foot ropes had been attached to a net that surrounded the entire envelope; on the *Osoaviakhim,* the ropes were merely attached to a large belt that ran horizontally around the envelope's base—a fatal flaw. One by one the ropes popped. At 1,500 feet, the last one gave way and the gondola shot earthward like a cannonball. It came down near the village of Potish-Ostrog, 150 miles east of Moscow. All three men were killed on impact. A panel chaired by Commander Prokofiev, who had piloted the successful Red Army balloon in 1933, concluded that the civilian pilots likely never even knew they were in danger until the final moments. Another version of the story maintains that the *Osoaviakhim*'s portholes iced over during the rapid descent, making it impossible for the three men inside to jettison ballast or escape from the freefalling gondola.

A million Muscovites marched solemnly past Red Square in tribute. It may have been the biggest outpouring of Russian public grief since the death of Lenin. Indeed, the ashes of the three aeronauts were ceremoniously entombed in the Kremlin Wall.

Among the few instruments to survive the crash were the barographs. They proved, claimed the Soviets, that the tragic flight had in fact reached a height of 72,178 feet—by far the highest that humans had ever been.

By July, *Explorer*—as the National Geographic/Army balloon had been named—was ready to go. The rubberized-cotton envelope, constructed of 3,520 separate pieces of fabric held together by 300 gallons of rubber cement, had a capacity of 3 million cubic feet, dwarfing all balloons that had come before. And every bit of that capacity would be required. The laboratory/gondola, a two-tone Dowmetal sphere painted white on the top and black on the bottom, nearly $8^{1}/_{2}$ spacious feet in diameter, was outfitted with a diverse and compact assemblage of delicate measurement devices, cameras, radios, and other gear, all designed to be as lightweight and as small as possible. Nevertheless, the entire rig weighed more than a ton. The total cost of the balloon, gondola, and instrumentation came to about $60,000, underwritten primarily by National Geographic and fully insured by Lloyd's of London.

While the original impetus for what the twin sponsors hoped would be a series of ascents was a new human altitude record, that would not be the justification for the expense and risk. The National Geographic Society's magazine assured its readers that travel into the stratosphere was more than a stunt: "Mere attainment of altitude . . . is not a primary object. It is desired to reach the loftiest attainable height above the earth to explore conditions there." In fact, a convincing fivefold scientific agenda was developed. The stated goals were: (1) to measure the intensity and direction of cosmic rays; (2) to locate and measure the thickness of the ozone layer; (3) to collect air samples from the stratosphere; (4) to ascertain whether spores or bacteria (i.e., life of any kind) exist in the upper atmosphere; and (5) to determine whether the traditional barographs and thermographs measure altitude more accurately than the more recent photographic techniques.

A talented and experienced trio of Army officers was chosen to make the flight: Capt. Albert Stevens, Capt. Orvil Anderson, and Maj. William Kepner. There wasn't a more disciplined or dedicated flight crew. Stevens, who had been the driving force behind the flight from the beginning (he was responsible for convincing National Geographic to get involved), even contributed several thousand dollars of his own money to the project.

Once the construction of the balloon and gondola had begun, the next task was to locate a suitable launch site. Kepner and Anderson, both veteran balloonists who knew exactly what they were looking for, toured the western half of the United States searching for the ideal spot. While in Denver, Kepner was asked by the chamber of commerce to describe his fantasy site. He replied that it would be a hole or canyon about 400 feet deep surrounded by vertical walls. This would allow the crew to inflate and launch a large balloon while protected against a sudden gust of wind. The bottom of the hole, Kepner went on, should be a grassy meadow served by a 20,000-volt power line. Also, a roadway capable of handling large trucks and a railroad should run along the edge of the meadow. As an afterthought, he added that it would also be nice if the site could contain a good trout stream.

After much scouting, Kepner and Anderson found their dream spot in the Black Hills gold-mining country near Rapid City, South Dakota. It was a vertical-walled canyon with a grassy meadow at the bottom— almost exactly as Kepner had described. Rapid City even agreed to build the roads and string the power lines. And, as luck would have it, a lovely trout stream did in fact snake its way through the canyon. It would become known as the Stratocamp, and later as the Stratobowl.

As flight preparations began, a small village for more than 100 support personnel sprang up near the canyon, its construction supervised by Anderson. South Dakota National Guardsmen and troopers of the 4th U.S. Cavalry assisted with the seemingly endless support tasks. Nearly a quarter of a million cubic feet of hydrogen arrived in hundreds of cylinders that were carefully stacked and immediately buttressed with sandbags and covered with fresh-cut pine boughs to protect them from the sun's heat. A giant liquid-oxygen generator truck from the Army Air Corps was maneuvered into place. As launch day approached, a two-inch layer of sawdust was laid down in a giant circle 200 feet in diameter in order to provide a suitable carpet on which to spread out the envelope. Once inflation began, the area immediately around the launch site was sealed off in order to protect the balloon.

William Kepner's "cast off" order came at 6:45 on the morning of July 28. Kepner remained outside the capsule, on the slippery top of the sphere, clutching the big ropes and directing the launch crew. As a huge ring of searchlights lit up the canyon, the balloon rose majestically and steadily into the sky, the flags of the National Geographic Society and the United States of America suspended in the rigging. The Chamber of Commerce of Rapid City had installed safety railings on the cliffs overlooking the Stratobowl. More than 30,000 spectators were present at the launch and could watch Anderson crawl through a porthole and join Kepner on top of the capsule. By the time the balloon reached 15,000 feet, both men were back inside and the capsule had been sealed. At 40,000 feet, *Explorer* leveled off to allow cosmic ray measurements to be taken. A 14-foot arm with a propeller allowed the balloonists to control rotation of the gondola as the measurements were made. Then, at 60,000 feet, well into the stratosphere, a rip appeared in the lower part of the rubberized envelope. Kepner, speaking to a nationwide radio audience on a special lightweight transmitter supplied by NBC, assessed the damage:

> The bottom of this balloon is pretty well torn out and it is just a big hole in the bottom here. I don't know how long she is going to hold together.

And then, moments later:

> And this fabric—there is so much of it and it is partly torn and coming down—you see, it acts as a parachute and then it lets go and occasionally tears an extra chunk out and the thing is getting to look pretty much like a huge sieve on the underneath side.

Explorer began to fall, and then fall faster. The tattered fabric twirled and whipped about in the wind, bits of it tearing off and flying away. The men fought the temptation to pop one of the hatches. In Stevens's words:

> No one made a move toward the lever. To have opened it [at that altitude] would have meant almost instant unconsciousness from change of pressure. Our tissues would have expanded suddenly, somewhat as would those of certain fish drawn hurriedly to the surface from ocean depths, and the results would have been both distressing and disastrous.

They bided their time, watching the altimeter and waiting for the capsule to reach a tolerable altitude. Finally, at 20,000 feet, the ports were punched open and the three men, dressed in thick airman's leathers and wearing helmets and goggles, quickly strapped themselves into parachutes. Anderson crawled out, hanging precariously from the foot ropes.

Stevens and Kepner remained inside. The radio transmitters continued to operate and hundreds of thousands listened to the ordeal as the three prepared to jump. By this point there was little left of the balloon's fabric, the entire structure having all but collapsed. Then, a static spark caused by the friction of ripping fabric ignited what was left of the hydrogen inside the envelope and *Explorer* exploded. At 5,000 feet, the gondola was in terminal freefall.

Anderson was the first to leap free at 3,000 feet. His D-ring had caught on something and prematurely released his chute. He gathered the fabric and jumped, throwing the canopy to the wind. Stevens, fighting against the wind pressure surrounding the falling sphere, followed at 2,000 feet and was momentarily bombarded by pieces of falling balloon fabric. Kepner barely got out in time for his parachute to open, jumping at a height of only 500 feet above the ground. Seconds later, the gondola smashed onto a Nebraska farmer's drought-parched cornfield, black dust billowing up to mark the spot. The aeronauts all landed uninjured beneath their chutes only minutes ahead of souvenir hunters who, ignoring a blistering mid-day heat, descended on the scene, eagerly collecting fragments of the ill-fated balloon. Some would later mail the bits of cloth to the pilots requesting autographs. The Dowmetal sphere was, according to Stevens, "crushed like an eggshell." (National Geographic's decision to insure the gondola and its contents proved prescient.) An axe, supplied by a local farmer, was required to free what was left of the scientific instruments from the twisted hunk of metal. Most of them were total losses, though some film records were salvaged. So were the barograph recordings: *Explorer* had missed the world altitude record by 624 feet.

The Army wasted little time assuring a stunned public that future ascents would in no way be curtailed. And the following January, Dr. Gilbert Grosvenor of the National Geographic Society (which had footed most of the $60,000 cost of *Explorer*) proclaimed that the next *Explorer* flight would occur in June 1935. Grosvenor went on to assert that the new balloon would boast an astonishing capacity of 3.7 million cubic feet. Also, significantly, a new lifting gas would be used for the first time: helium. Grosvenor called it a "wonder gas." It could lift almost as much as hydrogen but it was much less volatile, effectively eliminating the danger of explosion and fire.

Before *Explorer* would have an opportunity to make a second flight, however, Jean Piccard would finally get his chance. As agreed, the

Century of Progress sponsors had turned both balloon and gondola over to Piccard following the successful Settle-Fordney flight. But it was apparent from the beginning that sponsorship for a Piccard flight would be a problem. National Geographic, Goodyear-Zeppelin, and Dow Chemical all declined to offer support. Piccard had announced that his wife, Jeanette, would serve as pilot for the proposed flight while he would handle scientific chores, and Jeanette (an ardent feminist) suspected that the prospect of a woman pilot was what drove the big sponsors away. This explanation is plausible, but simplistic: Jeanette Piccard not only lacked aeronautical experience, she also lacked a balloon pilot's license. In the end, a coalition of sponsors, mostly smaller private companies, agreed to foot the bill for the flight.

While Jean negotiated with the scientific community, eventually convincing cosmic ray specialists William F. G. Swann and a reluctant Robert Millikan to provide instrumentation for the flight, Jeanette learned to fly balloons. Her teacher, the 1927 Gordon Bennett winner Ed Hill, guided her through the requirements for a lighter-than-air pilot's license. Apparently Hill had faith in the Piccards, because he also agreed to serve as flight director for the stratospheric attempt.

The patchwork balloon was inflated with hydrogen and launched, along with the refurbished capsule, from an airfield outside Dearborn, Michigan, in the early morning of October 22, 1934. During a prelaunch ceremony, Jean and Jeanette had received a bouquet from their sons and listened to a small band play "The Star-Spangled Banner," then quickly ducked into the round capsule—along with their pet turtle (the Piccard reputation for eccentricity intact)—and readied themselves for the journey they had dreamed of for nearly two years. Albert Stevens was on hand to provide advice and later to track the Piccards' flight by airplane.

The balloon rose quickly to a peak altitude of 57,579 feet. And although it must have been satisfying for Jean to surpass his celebrated brother's mark, it was still well short of the height reached by Settle and Fordney with the same balloon. The Piccards landed near Cadiz, Ohio, at 2:45 in the afternoon where the press converged on the site. No record had been set, and negligible scientific results had been achieved, yet the Piccards were treated like celebrities, with a special emphasis on Jeanette, the first woman to experience the stratosphere. When asked if she, a mother, would be willing to risk such a flight again, she replied, "Oh! Just give me a chance."

In 1937, Jean and Jeanette Piccard reached 11,000 feet beneath a double cluster of ninety-two 350-gram latex balloons they called *Pleiades*. The Piccards' interest in ballooning, and their continuing thirst for the international fame that had befallen Auguste Piccard, never waned. After the war, the Piccards became central—though predictably controversial—figures in the Navy's Project Helios. In his sixties, Jean explained, in straightforward terms, the lure of the heights: "Going with open eyes into new territory is always an interesting and useful thing to do." In 1965, Robert Gilruth, director of NASA's Marshall Space Flight Center and former associate of Piccard, appointed an aging Jeanette Piccard to serve as an honorary special consultant to Project Apollo. It was an attempt to publicly link the American space program with the heroic age of high-altitude ballooning. A radiant Mrs. Piccard, cloaked in mink stole and elbow-length gloves, was photographed at North American Aviation in California, standing in a mock-up of the Apollo Command Module, waving to the assembled crowd.

Orvil Anderson was born in Springville, Utah, in 1895. He grew up on the family ranch and attended Brigham Young University. When America entered World War I, Anderson enlisted in the Army and found himself assigned to an aviation group. A year later, as a second lieutenant, he was appointed an instructor at the Army's balloon school in Omaha. And by the summer of 1935, Captain Anderson was an accomplished flier in many types of aircraft—but most especially the gas balloon.

Albert Stevens had grown up across the continent in Maine. Nine years older than Anderson, he spent several years working as a mining and electrical engineer in the gold fields of the western United States before the Great War broke out. He was sent to Europe as an Army observer, where his photographic expertise earned him the rank of captain. He was later made chief photo officer of the First Army. While on leave in 1924, Stevens completed a massive photographic map of the upper Amazon River basin using his own aerial techniques. In 1932, he took the first photos of the moon's shadow on the Earth during a total eclipse of the sun. It was a great team: Anderson in charge of maneuvering the *Explorer* balloon, the largest lighter-than-air craft the world had ever known, and Stevens serving as the photographer and instrument caretaker aboard the floating lab.

The number of aeronauts had been reduced to two because of complaints of cramped conditions during the previous journey, but another factor may have at least influenced the decision. A superstition had begun to take hold in ballooning circles that crews of three were simply bad luck. The 1875 flight of Sivel, Croce-Spinelli, and Tissandier had left two dead, the *Osoaviakhim* and *Explorer I* flights were disastrous as well. The great successes of the 1930s had been accomplished by pairs, and so the *Explorer II* team would attempt to add to that tradition. Now, if only the balloon would hold together. Publicly, both Stevens and Anderson were upbeat about their prospects. But the malfunction of the first *Explorer* balloon and the recent deaths of the Russian balloonists cast a shadow over *Explorer II* preparations and created a stressful atmosphere for the pilots. In the weeks before the launch, Stevens became known for his long, solitary walks in the Black Hills.

Soon June had come and gone. Mechanical delays and numerous repairs to the balloon itself held up progress and, as summer slipped into fall, wind and rain became the enemy. Finally, after a six-week hold due to weather, everything came together on a crisp November morning. The balloon, again constructed by Goodyear-Zeppelin (only this time inflated with helium), unfurled and rose to the height of a thirty-one-story building. And the crowds were back. An estimated 20,000 gathered in and around the snow- and ice-encrusted Stratobowl, braving the near-zero temperatures. The residents of Rapid City and environs were as dedicated to the project as the sponsors and crew: local residents raised and donated $13,000 toward the ascent of *Explorer II*.

The pressurized helium that would be used for the first time as a lifting gas was stored in 1,685 steel cylinders on the periphery of the launch site and pumped into the balloon through 400-foot hoses that fed the gas into the envelope from forty cylinders at once. Over 100 soldiers at thirty-six snubbing posts kept their grips on the restraining ropes and held the gondola to the earth as the giant balloon took life and towered above them like some amorphous deep-sea creature struggling to free itself. The circle of floodlights illuminated the bottom hundred feet or so of the undulating fabric, the rest stretched up into the darkness.

In spite of a wind shear seconds after liftoff that nearly blew the balloon into one of the jagged canyon walls—the quick release of 75 pounds of fine lead-shot ballast onto the heads of spectators solved the problem—everything went smoothly. The big *Explorer II* gondola left the grassy meadow at precisely 8:00 A.M. and ascended at a leisurely pace to a new world-record altitude of 74,000 feet at 12:30 P.M.

Anderson and Stevens were the first human beings ever to report seeing the curvature of the Earth with their own eyes. Their observations might have been more detailed, but the glare of the sun at altitude made viewing from one entire side of the gondola useless. The fan that was suspended from an arm on the exterior wall of the gondola was supposed to allow them to rotate the aircraft to avoid sun glare, but its blades proved ineffective in the thin air of the stratosphere. Later, in a memoir published by National Geographic, Stevens recalled his own observations:

> The earth could be seen plainly underneath through the lower porthole and hundreds of miles in every direction through the side portholes. It was a vast expanse of brown, apparently flat, stretching on and on. Wagon roads and automobile highways were invisible, houses were invisible, and railroads could be recognized only by an occasional cut or fill. The larger farms were discernible as tiny rectangular areas. Occasional streaks of green vegetation showed the presence of streams. Here and there water could be seen in the form of rivers or lakes, especially if the sun was reflected from the water's surface.
>
> No sign of actual life on the earth could be detected. To us it was a foreign and lifeless world. The sun was the one object that commanded our attention; we were temporarily almost divorced from Mother Earth.

They remained at that altitude for an hour and twenty minutes—Anderson would later claim that they could safely have gone 5,000 feet higher—and then began their descent. Journalists on the ground who had followed the balloon's drift eastward were able to watch the entire ascent; the sight of *Explorer II* at altitude was likened to a pearl on a stickpin held at arm's length.

The arsenal of state-of-the-art scientific gadgetry was vastly expanded for this flight: instruments captured all sorts of meteorological data and measured the electrical conductivity of the stratosphere. There were temperature and barometric readings, air samples, cosmic ray studies, sunlight and skylight experiments, wind direction and velocity measurements, samples of bread and strawberry mold that would be examined later to determine the effects they had suffered due to altitude and cosmic rays. And there was the photographic equipment. Stevens took pictures during spare moments, including the first motion pictures shot in the stratosphere.

There was also, of course, communications equipment. *Explorer II* had maintained radio contact throughout the flight and it had been broadcast not only nationwide, but also in Europe. Stevens had been able to chat with the pilot of an airplane over the Pacific Ocean and with a reporter in a newspaper office in London. Listeners reported that the reception was so clear they could hear Geiger counters aboard the gondola ticking away, counting cosmic rays while the aeronauts conversed with their ground crew.

At about 1,000 feet above the ground, the two men began tossing overboard some of the important scientific instruments and air-conditioning chemical containers to fall beneath their own individual parachutes. This would protect certain crucial recorded measurements and key pieces of equipment from a rough landing inside the gondola, and protect Stevens and Anderson from chemical burns in the event of a crash landing. In another protective measure, the two men slipped on padded football helmets borrowed from Calvin Coolidge High School in Rapid City. As it turned out though, there was no need to worry. The landing at 4:13 P.M. in an open prairie near White Lake, South Dakota, was described as "soft as a feather."

The National Geographic Society was thrilled with the flight, and relieved that the photographic equipment and scientific instruments had returned undamaged. The balloon envelope was cut into one million commemorative bookmarks for Society members. And Orvil Anderson had the perfect answer when a reporter asked for his impressions of the flight. "Boy," he answered, "I sure got a kick out of being at the top of the world."

Needless to say, the two men were lionized—but not, certainly, as pioneering researchers. They were celebrated, instead, as intrepid explorers. They were sanctified heroes at a time when America needed heroes. A *New York Times* editorial captured the public mood:

> Thus it happens that STEVENS and ANDERSON must now be regarded as the legitimate descendants of the navigators who demonstrated that the earth is a sphere and who began to map land and water. The air is just as much a part of our earth as Europe or the Pacific Ocean. Until recently explorers have only crawled over the globe. It is time that we discovered something about the sea of gas in which we are immersed. We live only in the dregs. So we hail the crew of Explorer II not merely as record breakers but as Vikings of the atmosphere. They bid us look beyond the tenuous layers where meteors and auroras glow, and wonder if we shall rise to heights where the stars and the sun blaze day and night in a perpetually inky sky.

Yet the ascent and safe return of *Explorer II* was more an ending than a beginning. In a few short years the world would find itself once again drawn inexorably into the maelstrom of global war.

The 1939 Gordon Bennett race was to have been held in Poland, the trophy having been won the previous year by Polish Army captain Anton Janusz. But when German panzers rolled across the border late that summer, Polish aeronautical aspirations suffered a double blow: not only was the Gordon Bennett classic canceled, but a high-altitude balloon flight that had been in preparation for nearly two years was also scrapped. Janusz himself would have been the pilot for the attempt on *Explorer II*'s altitude record. The United States, under a special export license granted by the secretary of state, shipped 220,000 cubic feet of helium from Texas to Poland in July to support the stratospheric attempt. Captain Janusz visited the United States that same month to discuss his attempt with Albert Stevens and to arrange for the helium shipment. When war broke out in Europe before the balloon attempt was ready, the Poles released the helium into the atmosphere to guard against its being captured by the Germans and Janusz himself headed for the Polish front.

Two decades more would pass before the next manned stratospheric balloon would break the bonds of those "tenuous layers." The second great paroxysm of high-altitude lighter-than-air flight had reached a glorious end. But with all the lip service paid to scientific discovery, what, in the end, did these high-altitude balloon flights of the 1930s really discover? Both the *Century of Progress* and *Explorer* gondolas were crammed full of scientific equipment and carefully prepared experiments, but in the end neither program made any earth-shattering contributions to scientific understanding. The truth of the matter is that none of the experiments carried aloft by stratospheric flights in the 1930s required the presence of a human being. If science had really been the *raison d'être* of these flights, unmanned balloons would have made more sense. An unmanned balloon could go much higher much less expensively and much less dangerously. Interestingly, Robert Millikan, who had supplied cosmic radiation experiments for the *Century of Progress* flights, was asked to do the same for *Explorer*. He declined. Millikan eventually became a vocal opponent of scientific research funds being used on manned balloon flights, charging that the scientific agenda for *Explorer* was a "sham," and that manned balloon activities in general were a passing "fad."

But these flights were more than publicity stunts. They did serve a purpose beyond setting altitude records, even if it was never explicitly acknowledged by their sponsors. All of the American—and Russian—stratospheric flights of the 1930s were designed, as much as anything else, to restore public morale during dismal times and to rebuild a shaken public's faith in their societies. According to historian David DeVorkin, these flights were "compelling symbols of romantic journeys of the human spirit with which each and every citizen could identify and vicariously experience, as indelible as the opening of the American West in the popular imagination." The Viking metaphor in the *Times* editorial was not far from the mark.

Without science, however, the flights would never have occurred. The political and practical realities of the day required the participation of both scientific and military institutions in order to legitimize the programs and to empower them to acquire the necessary funds. It would be hard to justify spending huge sums of money during a global depression simply to set an altitude record, but it seemed to make some sense if the goal was to learn more about cosmic rays and the ozone layer. At least it *sounded* better. Later, in the 1960s and '70s, much would be made of rocks and dust that were brought back from the moon. Moon rocks provided tangible scientific booty for a public spectacle that in reality served a very different—some would argue, more important—purpose.

In the postwar days of the mid-1940s, the notion of sending humans into near-space by means of balloon found yet another justification when an extraordinarily imaginative Navy officer, George W. Hoover of the Special Devices Center at the Office of Naval Research (ONR), got wind of some work going on at the General Mills Corporation in Minneapolis. Inspired by its progressive founder, James Ford Bell, General Mills formed an entire department to pursue high-altitude balloon work and staffed it with the top men in the business—among them immigrant balloon builder Otto Winzen and the irrepressible Jean Piccard (who, at the age of 60, still dreamed of a high-altitude research flight he called Project Helios and who had correctly anticipated a renewed availability of research funds following the armistice).

As then–Lieutenant Commander Hoover remembers it, "The whole thing started when a man named Winzen walked into my office and asked, 'How would you like to go to 100,000 feet?'" Immediately impressed, Hoover listened intently as Winzen expounded on the new designs and plastics he was working with at General Mills. After awhile, Hoover cut Winzen off and told him, "Okay, you've got a job."

Piccard, still in possession of the old *Century of Progress* gondola, had already submitted formal proposals to both the Army and the Navy. Hoover, who was as impressed with Piccard as he had been with Winzen, was a pilot who had come up through the ranks and was interested primarily in the immediate and practical applications of a high-altitude flight. Already running some 60 projects for the ONR, Hoover was intrigued with the military research potential of high-altitude balloons and saw Helios as a vehicle that would facilitate the study of the aerodynamic properties of missiles. Hoover, an accomplished practitioner of bootleg research, convinced the Navy to enter into an odd alliance with General Mills, Piccard, and Winzen. Hoover was fascinated with the notion of dropping things from 100,000 feet in order to study the behavior of various payloads at supersonic speeds, but he saw other uses for such a program, among them the opportunity to study aircraft cockpit designs at very high speeds with an eye toward the protection of military pilots. Helios also had its purely scientific side, represented in part by Urner Liddell, head of both the physics and nuclear physics sections of the Scientific Branch of the ONR's Planning Division, and by W.F.G. Swann of the Bartol Research Foundation of the Franklin Institute who had contributed to the Piccards' *Pleiades* flight.

But Helios never flew. The plastic balloons, arrayed in a spherical cluster, proved impossible to inflate and launch as a balanced system. And the technical difficulties encountered in getting the large collection of balloons to behave were appropriate metaphors for the human and organizational problems that burdened Project Helios almost from the outset. When Jean and Jeanette Piccard had first offered their gondola and their project to the ONR, it had been on the condition that the Piccards themselves make the flight. The Navy quickly vetoed that notion and phased the Piccards out of the picture, selecting—as a substitute pilot—balloonist and airshipman Lt. Harris F. Smith, USNR. According to George Hoover: "Jean Piccard knew what he was talking about. But his wife . . . that's another story." A bitter Jean Piccard blamed, among others, Otto Winzen at General Mills.

But even without the Piccards, the organizational tangle that attempted to administer Project Helios imploded, in spite of the fact that the highly respected Tex Settle, the man who had unseated Jean Piccard in the original *Century of Progress* flight, was brought in as coordinator of technical operations. Factional disputes within the Office of Naval Research, and between the ONR and the Office of the Chief of Naval Operations, burdened a program already struggling to justify its very existence. Finally, and sensibly, Helios was split into an unmanned scientific/military balloon program (to be known as Project Skyhook) and a manned high-altitude balloon program that would not become operational for several more years (to be known as Project Strato-Lab).

George Hoover became the driving force behind Project Skyhook, which immediately inherited his original vision for Helios. By 1949, the ONR, working with General Mills and other contractors, was dropping scientific payloads called FFTVs (free-fall test vehicles) from high in the stratosphere above the White Sands Proving Ground in New Mexico where they could reach supersonic speeds. Hoover consulted with Wernher von Braun, who took a keen interest in the Skyhook flights. Over the years, Project Skyhook would become a hugely successful and constantly evolving scientific and military program using unmanned balloons for a wide variety of research applications.

George Hoover, a visionary in the realm of super-high-altitude research, would later become a prime mover behind Project Orbiter, the United States' original satellite program, and would receive a prestigious medal from the British Interplanetary Society for his work on high-speed and high-altitude aircraft. Hoover, who was aware that an influential naval commander had declared in 1947 that the Navy would never have any interest in research above 60,000 feet, became—like John Paul Stapp—supremely accomplished in the art of coercing a complex and change-averse military bureaucracy into doing valuable things even when it had gone on record as not wanting to do those things.

Project Strato-Lab, the manned-balloon component of Helios's legacy, would go on to launch five manned flights into the stratosphere beginning with the flight that broke *Explorer II*'s altitude record in 1956.

By the spring of 1957, the Air Force's Project Manhigh was almost ready to fly. A balloon envelope was near completion and the gondola needed only finishing touches. But funding, which had been a battle from the start, continued to worry David Simons and John Paul Stapp. In spite of the fact that high-altitude balloon work was cheap compared with the costs of other Air Force projects, such as intercontinental missile research, the costs of the balloon programs themselves had risen dramatically since the days of the animal flights a few years earlier. The hamster and mouse flights from Holloman had cost between $5,000 and $10,000 a shot in 1954. But with the addition of safety features and provisions for an expanding collection of onboard research equipment that was mandated for human flights, the total cost for a closed-capsule flight now exceeded a quarter of a million dollars.

More than once, the project had gone broke. Both Simons and Stapp flew regularly to Baltimore to argue their case at the Air Research and Development Command (ARDC) headquarters. Space research was not a popular notion with the public or the Air Force in those days, and perhaps only the support of Brig. Gen. Don Flickinger (chief of human factors research for the ARDC and one of the few admitted space enthusiasts in the Air Force) had kept the Holloman balloon crews afloat at all. Stapp had even diverted precious funds from his own rocket-sled work to buy equipment and pay contractors for Manhigh. The economics were a day-to-day, week-to-week distraction. "I think they eventually funded the rocket sleds," Stapp would remark, "because they hoped somehow I'd kill myself." But whatever money he had been able to obtain for Project Manhigh had come with the warning that he would be court-martialed if he ever killed anyone else.

Simons, then, was shocked when Stapp announced that he wanted to add a test flight to the agenda. The justification made sense, though: if they gambled everything on a full-scale medical research flight and something went wrong, especially something disastrous that jeopardized the pilot (like a malfunction with the pressure suit), the entire project would almost certainly be canceled. However, if they launched a scaled-back test flight first, they would have a chance to troubleshoot the entire system and correct any design or process flaws that cropped up—without cost to the program's reputation. An additional flight, however, would cost money, and money was the one variable they could never completely control. Simons hated the idea of sinking their remaining resources into a test flight. Yet, seeing the logic of Stapp's strategy, he agreed; testing the system would be the prudent thing to do. Not only would they gain some valuable insights into the business of launching a manned balloon, but Simons personally would gain experience as a pilot, experience that would pay dividends on the real flight.

Then Stapp dropped his second bomb.

"I want Kittinger to make the test flight," he said.

Again, Simons was stung. He had never considered that someone else might fly the Manhigh balloon before he did. He wondered why it was necessary to bring in an alternate when he, the principal pilot, was ready and willing. Stapp explained that the main goal of the project was the lengthier research flight that Simons would make. It made no sense to risk him on the test flight, which would be essentially nothing more than a checkout of the hardware. In addition, since Stapp would operate as ground flight surgeon monitoring Simons's condition on the research flight, he wanted Simons to have a chance to train him. Again, the arguments made sense, but Simons still had nagging doubts that somehow he was being grounded because he was a doctor, a scientist, rather than a test pilot. Stapp would later say that what he had wanted for the test flight was someone with lightning reflexes and a proven ability to respond to emergencies. "I didn't want much. Just the sharpest pilot I'd ever met."

Simons knew Stapp and Kittinger both were impatient with his constant poring over research reports and cosmic ray data. He felt outnumbered, and he began to fear that he might never get the chance to complete his work and to observe firsthand the illusive wonders of the stratosphere. He feared that Manhigh might be somehow compromised by Kittinger's ambition and become another in a series of dubious high-altitude manned balloon programs that cloaked themselves in the stage-prop garb of science, and that the medical research agenda would be quietly squeezed out. Kittinger, on the other hand, became increasingly suspicious of Simons's motives: "He didn't want anybody to steal the thunder; he wanted to be the first one up there. He pouted about that the whole time."

But there was nothing to be done. Simons might have been the project director for Manhigh, but John Paul Stapp was a full colonel. Simons agreed to the test flight with Kittinger in the gondola, and turned his attention back to the planning. He told Stapp that everything would be ready to go by June 1, weather permitting.

Two companies submitted bids to the Air Force for the contract to build the balloon and gondola for Manhigh: General Mills and Winzen Research, Inc. Both had been making balloons and conducting launches for several years, and both had been involved in high-altitude experiments. David Simons personally inspected both facilities, interviewed their engineers, and ratified the decision to select Winzen, based in Minneapolis and known to the public principally as the manufacturer of plastic bags. General Mills' management was extremely disappointed to lose the Manhigh contract. But in spite of the big company's past successes, particularly with the Navy's Project Skyhook, Simons was convinced that Winzen's techniques and capabilities were significantly superior. "They had better quality control. And that," he added dryly, "was of some interest to me." In addition, Simons had been working with Winzen balloons at Holloman since the early animal flights and had complete faith in the company and its staff.

Otto Winzen, the charismatic president and co-owner of Winzen Research, called his innovative polyethylene-lined cardboard box (a durable, disposable container) the Fluid-pak, and it was a commercial hit. In the mid-fifties, a tin milk can cost about $10, versus 35 cents for a Fluid-pak. Winzen pointed out to buyers that they could reduce their factory head-count by 35 percent since the cans would no longer require cleaning, sterilization, or retinning. But while plastic consumer items paid the bills, Otto Winzen was really interested in only one thing. The Fluid-pak (along with plastic tarpaulins, barge covers, and highway curing blankets) merely bankrolled the real focus of Winzen Research: the balloon. Ninety percent of the company's research expenditures went directly into plastic balloons.

In the days of Hawthorne Gray, balloons were made of rubber-impregnated silk or cotton. Those balloons were then filled with gas until the lift equaled the weight of the balloon, rigging, and payload. An extra amount of gas, called *free lift,* was added, which created an imbalance that caused the balloon to rise. As it rose and the air pressure outside the balloon decreased, the gas expanded until a maximum altitude was reached—at which point, if no gas were released—the rubber fabric would burst.

But Winzen was an innovator, and his plastic envelopes were different. The first plastic balloons in the mid-1930s, created by Jean Piccard, had been made of cellophane and had an unfortunate tendency to crack at low temperatures. Winzen turned eventually to a new synthetic called "polyethylene resin," which was first used to insulate electrical cabling on submarines. This new material, produced from ethylene (a petroleum derivative), was light, relatively cheap, and unaffected by ultraviolet radiation. Winzen convinced his manufacturing sources to find ways to extrude thinner and thinner plastics. His balloons were thinner than a human hair, a tenth the thickness of a bread sack. They were also nonextensible (in other words, they did not expand like rubberized materials). And, while stronger than cellophane, and generally impervious to extremes of heat and cold, they were still terribly fragile. Great care was taken with these envelopes, and when even the tiniest pinholes were discovered, they were immediately patched with adhesive tape. Balloon launch crews wore gloves, worked in socks, and were required to submit to fingernail and jewelry checks before being allowed to handle the wispy acres of polyethylene.

The first Manhigh balloon was constructed of seventy long gores of polyethylene DE 2500 resin "A" film that were heat-sealed together and then bound by strips of fiber-acetate tape, running vertically, to create a harness around the plastic panels. Each tape encircled the balloon and was connected to an aluminum collar at the base. It was the tape, then, that bore the weight of the gondola, not the delicate balloon itself.

One more important difference between these new plastic balloons and traditional rubber ones: the base, or lip, of the new balloon was no longer closed tight. It remained wide open to allow excess gas to spill out, a design necessity since the plastic itself would not stretch as its contents expanded. With this system, a balloon would rise to its maximum altitude and float. The helium supply regulated itself. If it expanded too much, the excess was simply forced out into the atmosphere.

Otto Winzen, who had emigrated from Germany in 1937 and studied aeronautical engineering at the University of Detroit, spent World War II in a series of internment camps. The armistice brought his release and he immediately became an important figure in the rebirth of high-altitude ballooning that occurred shortly after the war. As chief engineer at the Minnesota Mining and Manufacturing Company—and later with General Mills—he sold plastic balloons to the Navy. Teaming up first with Jean Piccard and the Navy on Project Helios, Winzen launched his first nonextensible (unmanned) balloon in 1947; it rose to about 100,000 feet. Soon he was working not only with Navy physicists on Project Skyhook (cosmic-ray research flights launched from ships off the coast of Greenland and near the Galapagos Islands in the Pacific), but with the Air Force on a program called Moby Dick (cover name: White Cloud). Moby Dick, while ostensibly a project to study wind currents and other atmospheric conditions in the stratosphere, employed Winzen's balloons for photographic reconnaissance missions (i.e., aerial spying) over the Soviet Union. With a central plotting facility at Lowry Field in Colorado, more than 500 Moby Dick balloons were released from sites all over the United States, with roughly half of the instrument packs eventually being recovered. The Soviets became aware of the balloons and a diplomatic spat ensued. John Foster Dulles originally claimed that the Winzen aerostats were weather balloons, but finally reneged and had the entire program killed—but only after 8 percent of the Soviet Union and China had been recorded photographically by balloon-borne cameras. (Moby Dick presaged another soon-to-follow "aerial reconnaissance" fiasco: the U-2 spy-plane incidents.)

But credit for the early success of Winzen Research does not belong solely to Otto Winzen. Not long before going to work at General Mills, Winzen met and married the teenage daughter of a Detroit society photographer named Habrecht—a contact he made through Jean Piccard. And when Winzen left General Mills,* his young wife Vera arranged to borrow money from her parents to fund the founding of one of the world's first plastic balloon companies. Winzen was a visionary, a restless man with a vivid imagination and boundless energy—but he was not much for details. The day-to-day discipline of running a factory and attending to the thousands of little tasks that make a business go were never his strong suit. Fortunately, Vera, who dropped out of art school somewhat reluctantly to take over duties at Winzen Research, was very good at it. Not only did she supervise personnel and train them to handle polyethylene and build giant balloons, she constantly improved the construction techniques and redesigned the envelopes themselves. During her decade with Winzen Research, she obtained four patents and established herself as the finest plastic balloon builder in the world. And in spite of the fact that Otto named himself president and his wife vice-president of the new venture, she retained—as a condition of her parents' financial participation—two-thirds ownership of the company.

As a young girl, Vera Habrecht had followed her father outside to look at the sky and listen to him describe the wonders to be found there. She would gaze at cloud formations as her father described the meteo-

---

*By 1948, things had soured among the original balloon contingent at General Mills. During a period of months in the late forties, the principal players in the high-altitude balloon business, not only Winzen but also the founders of the company that would later become Winzen's chief competition, Raven Industries, left General Mills to build their own balloons and gondolas.

rological conditions that produced them. He would take her to local air-fields to watch the planes take off and land, and to blimp hangars where the giant aerostats were tethered. So when her dreams of finishing art school and devoting her life to painting and sculpture were interrupted by Otto Winzen's dreams of stratospheric exploration, she entered a world that held its own array of attractions. She was enchanted with the ethereal sensations of balloon flight and earned her gas-balloon pilot's license in 1957. And the magic of those days in the air would stay with her and affect her aesthetic vision for the rest of her life. "What I liked about flying," she recalls, "was the freedom, being in the open. I still have a very vivid memory of rising up through a cloud. It was a nice, fluffy, fair-weather cloud. The experience of being in that cloud and then coming out . . . just incredible!"

But it was difficult in the beginning. Her first memories of Winzen Research are of scrubbing the floors and walls of the company's first building alongside Fleming Field outside of Minneapolis. The company was so busy that she sometimes worked three shifts. At first, she hired two "balloon girls" to help her with construction of the plastic envelopes. The number of assistants later grew to 120. After many months of building extensions to the original building to keep up with the company's growth, Winzen Research moved to a huge new facility in Bloomington that housed an electronics lab, a model and machine shop, an environmental physics lab, and facilities for the flight operations staff. And as time went on, the new building too had to be enlarged to make room for the ever-larger balloon tables required to handle the demands for bigger and bigger balloons.

The tables were custom-made for the construction of a particular size and design of balloon. First, the Winzen engineers would work out the dimensions of a single gore of material. Then carpenters built a special table to fit the gore, which might be 500 feet long. The balloon girls bellied up to the huge table and worked at attaching the load tapes to the polyethylene—by hand at first, then later using special tape machines that ran around the outside edge of the table. Vera Winzen was proud of her staff. Very few mistakes were made during balloon construction and not a single balloon girl was ever fired for negligence on the job. Part of the success can be credited to good training methods, frequent task rotation, and liberal rest periods, but also important was the entire company's sense of connection with the fruits of their labor.

Whenever an important scientist or military officer visited the plant, he was always taken to meet the manufacturing staff. And whenever a Winzen balloon was launched, Vera Winzen made sure the team of balloon girls that had built the balloon was on hand at liftoff.

"To see what you've made come alive," Vera would say, "that's pretty damned exciting."

While some of the early stratospheric research flights were conducted in the service of Cold War–related intelligence contracts for various government agencies, others were made to allow contractors and manufacturers of rocket instrumentation to test their gear. As demand for the plastic balloons grew, so did the challenges facing the Winzen engineers. Bigger balloons were required to lift bigger payloads, but bigger meant harder to construct and handle. It was always a dicey business because there was never the luxury of testing an individual balloon before using it. Once a polyethylene balloon was inflated, it could never be used again. (Balloon crews sometimes gave the plastic envelopes to farmers when a balloon would be recovered in their fields. The polyethylene was prized as a covering for hay and as wrapping for freezer-bound produce and meat.) And, as Winzen himself was fond of pointing out, "Balloons are the most complicated of all aircraft. The thermodynamics and physics involved are still not thoroughly understood."

Wind is the great enemy of plastic balloon launches, which explains why most launches are conducted at dawn when the air is calmest. But the balloon people at Holloman came up with an inflation device called a "covered wagon" that increased their odds of avoiding the random gust that could slice apart the thin polyethylene in a few seconds. This device consisted of a 40-foot flatbed trailer onto which a headboard and sideboards of pipe and iron had been attached. The metal frame was then sheathed in plywood and covered by nylon, with a nylon top to enclose the "wagon." The inflation occurred inside this cavity, where the balloon was cradled and protected from the elements. Once inflated, it could be released with relative confidence.

The big teardrop-shaped monsters continued to get bigger. The first polyethylene balloon, built for Project Skyhook in the mid-forties, had only been about seven feet in diameter. By the time Simons, Stapp, and Kittinger were preparing for the Manhigh test flight, Winzen Research was rolling out balloons 300 feet high and 200 feet in diameter. These silvery leviathans were capable of lifting a 3,000-pound payload. And they kept getting bigger. In Otto Winzen's estimation, "It almost appears that there is no limit to the size of plastic balloons which can be built or flown." Before the project was over, these delicate bags would have volumes of 10 million cubic feet, greater than that of the giant *Hindenburg* dirigible that exploded and burned in Lakehurst, New Jersey, in 1937.

three

"Come and Get Me"

In the weeks leading up to the test flight, which would become known as *Manhigh I,* most of the activity occurred at the Winzen Research plant in Minneapolis. The framework of the gondola, fully laden now with instrumentation and communications equipment, sat uncovered on a bare warehouse floor where technicians could access the crowded interior. On launch day, the frame would be hoisted by crane and lowered into the alloy shell that formed the gondola's exterior.

When Joe Kittinger arrived from Holloman, he began immediately to familiarize himself with the vehicle. He bombarded the technicians, and especially Winzen's chief engineer, Don Foster, with endless questions. He climbed into the gondola and tested the feel of the nylon-web seat; he studied the scores of controls and backup controls; he memorized the locations of all the major functional components. There was a lot to learn.

Winzen's gondola was a remarkable piece of economy and ingenuity. Imagine an upright, tubular capsule about the size of a telephone booth: eight feet tall with a diameter, at the widest point, of three feet. Its three separate sections were welded together. The large center section, an aluminum alloy casting, served as the load-bearing member. This section and the rounded top piece would hold Kittinger in a pressurized, artificial atmosphere of 60% oxygen, 20% helium, and 20% nitrogen. The top piece was attached to an aluminum ring from which the entire assembly would be suspended from the balloon itself. The bottom section contained the main 24-volt battery to power the gondola's electrical and communications systems, as well as a 12-volt back-up battery. It also housed the oxygen regeneration system, which consisted of chemical scrubbers (lithium hydroxide, sodium hydroxide, potassium hydroxide, lithium chloride, and magnesium perchlorate were all used during the course of Project Manhigh) that would extract both moisture and toxic carbon dioxide from the capsule atmosphere, and a five-liter bottle of liquid oxygen (sufficient for a 48-hour flight).

As Kittinger sat inside the gondola, he could marvel—with a test pilot's critical eye—at the design. Everything inside, all the major systems, were color-coded. The prime color was a light shade of green; electrical components—as well as the release lever for the pilot's parachute, Kittinger noted—were red; the hardware for the six portholes was blue; the capsule shell release buttons were yellow; and the main instrument panel was black and white. Everything had been positioned strategically and arranged ergonomically so as to make the vehicle as comfortable, efficient, and safe as possible. Every major system on board the gondola, from the oxygen supply to the radios, was supported by a redundant system that could be activated in case the first one failed.

The functional beauty of the entire Manhigh system would have pleased Auguste Piccard, but his favorite component might well have been the air-conditioning system. The direct solar heating of the gondola during the day, as well as the heat generated by the electrical components and the pilot's own body, dictated the necessity of some sort of cooling mechanism. But it had to be light and small. Credit for the solution goes to the Standards Laboratory at Holloman: a simple can of tap water became a stratospheric air conditioner (or, as the engineers would refer to it, a "water-core heat exchanger"). Because the boiling point of water decreases as atmospheric pressure decreases, at 112,000 feet water will boil at about 32° Fahrenheit, the temperature of ice at sea level. The can of water, when vented to the outside near-vacuum environment, begins to evaporate. The heated air from the capsule is blown by a fan through the lower chamber that contains the can of water; the warmer air is picked up by the water vapor and vented outside. Only cool air is recirculated to the capsule above. At night, when the sun is no longer heating the capsule, the pilot simply turns the fan off and allows his body heat to build up. It is hard to imagine a more elegant or suitable piece of bootleg engineering.

As the crew prepared for the early summer launch, David Simons watched with interest, and increasing concern, Kittinger's own exhaustive personal preparations. The young test pilot spent hours each day

Otto Winzen, Joe Kittinger, and Dr. David Simons pose with the *Manhigh* gondola at Winzen Research. *(Source: USAF)*

The *Manhigh* instrument panel. *(Source: USAF)*

sitting in the gondola, taking its measure, getting the feel, practicing with the hardware and reviewing procedures that would be used during the flight. The idea was to eliminate guesswork and surprises; he wanted to know everything that anyone else knew about the vehicle and the journey he was about to make. This, Simons understood, was a healthy impulse for anyone who flew experimental aircraft. The test pilot must have absolute confidence in his vehicle, must know it inside and out, must believe in it. But Simons, still smarting at the selection of a test pilot for the maiden flight, found himself wishing that Kittinger was as curious about the scientific aspects of the flight as he was about the Winzen gondola.

> Although Kittinger was far more alert and perceptive that any pilot I had known, and grasped the sometimes difficult concepts of science more quickly than most other untrained observers, there was not time to give him the detailed instruction in meteorology, astronomy, and physiology that I knew would be invaluable to the Manhigh balloonist. I doubt if he wanted to get that technical anyway.

One of the things that Kittinger did want to know was what he should do if the capsule began to depressurize. Don Foster replied that he should first check for leaks around the portholes and the main seal. Next, switch the oxygen regulator to "manual" and fill the cabin with pressurized oxygen.

And if that doesn't work? Clamp the faceplate down on the helmet. If pressure continues to drop rapidly, inflate the suit and separate the gondola from the balloon. A cargo chute would drop the gondola slowly enough for a survivable landing—about 20 MPH.

Kittinger wanted to know why it wouldn't make more sense to use his personal parachute and bail out of the gondola. He was told that he would be safer inside the aluminum shell. But Simons was not convinced that Kittinger really believed it.

Simons was nursing a concern, partially shared by Stapp, that perhaps Joe Kittinger was overly fascinated with the possibility of bailing out at a high altitude. Ever since jump training at El Centro, Kittinger's fascination with the notion of higher and higher jumps had been obvious. Later, Simons would write:

> He relished the delightful experience of parachute jumping so much that Stapp and I feared his preoccupation with jumping would leave him eager to find an excuse to bail out of the capsule. Neither of us knew for sure whether Kittinger would live through such an experience. But we were dead certain that the Manhigh program would not survive it. If he bailed out, it would probably cost us the capsule. In order to jump, the lower half of the capsule containing power supply and air-regeneration equipment would have to be jettisoned. Even if we could find it, the jettisoned section would be nothing but a crumpled mass of aluminum.

Stapp and Simons met privately with Kittinger in Otto Winzen's office and told him explicitly that the only justification for abandoning the gondola during the flight was a fire in the cabin. And even then, the first course of action would be to try to control the fire with the extinguisher on board. Kittinger agreed. Yet as Simons left the office, he was unconvinced. For some reason, he did not completely trust Kittinger. But why? He wondered if he was jealous of Kittinger's assignment to make the maiden flight, or if he was merely reacting to Kittinger's own ambitious nature.

> Difficult as it is to be completely objective with oneself, I tried, and slowly I perceived the source of my disenchantment and my growing fear of Kittinger. His motives for wanting to fly the Manhigh balloon

into this exotic and hostile realm where no man had been before were pure, but they differed from my own. Joe quite frankly acknowledged that to him the flight was a mixture of a sporting and professional challenge as an aviator. He wanted to be the first man to do it for no other reason than to prove that it could be done. He wanted to be the first to see what it was like to float along the rim of the atmosphere.

I had some of the same motivation—the desire to be first just for the sake of being first—but I was trying to swallow it for the sake of an orderly research program. A much more powerful motive for my desire to fly the capsule was the purely scientific urge to go into unexplored territory to study it. I was far more interested in the frontier than the covered wagon that would take me there.

The Manhigh system as I saw it was primarily a laboratory, one in which I could conduct experiments that would be impossible in any other laboratory. I looked upon myself as little more than an integral part of this complicated scientific machine.

The wariness I was beginning to feel for Joe clearly was due to a growing realization that his test flight could destroy the scientific apparatus I had spent a year and a half helping to devise and planning to fly.

I was afraid that he might accidentally or impetuously squeeze me out of my own research program. When boiled down to that single source, the fear seemed groundless. Still I could not get it out of my mind. Nor could I convince myself that Kittinger had abandoned his urge to use the Manhigh capsule for a parachute test.

Vera Winzen watched the rift between David Simons and Joe Kittinger gather and build: two men, each brilliant in his own way, anxious to be the first human being to experience space-equivalent conditions. To some degree, their competition would catalyze the Manhigh effort. But if the private battles became too pitched, the entire project was in danger of annihilation. "They were both emotional guys in different ways," Vera observed. "They had different motives and they were different kinds of people. However, both wanted fame and glory. That was the core of the competition."

The chief meteorologist for Manhigh was a remarkable man from the Holloman balloon unit named Bernard "Duke" Gildenberg. Gildenberg, a self-described "balloonatic," had been involved with scientific ballooning at Holloman from its earliest days. He had been part of the

New York University program that had worked on the early animal flights with the Army and had created balloons to facilitate detection of Soviet atomic tests. He had even helped capture cats from Alamogordo neighborhoods to be used as research subjects. But his specialty was assessing wind patterns. If a small load was dropped with a parachute from 100,000 feet, it was said, Duke could pinpoint the landing spot within 100 yards. As Simons put it, "If Duke Gildenberg looked up at a clear summertime sky above the Sahara desert and said it would snow within five minutes, I would start looking for a pair of snowshoes."

Gildenberg's interest in high-altitude operations, however, was not limited to weather forecasts. He loved to fly balloons; earlier in the project he had volunteered as an alternate pilot and had briefly been considered as a subject for the test flight. He passed the claustrophobia test, the pressure chamber test, and the parachute test. But a landing mishap in New Mexico during a free-balloon training flight with both Kittinger and Simons aboard eliminated him. During a hard landing in a 15-MPH wind, Simons was thrown into Gildenberg, fracturing some of the meteorologist's vertebrae, snapping two of his ribs, and forcing Duke back into his original role—less glory, but perhaps an even greater responsibility. Gildenberg would set the launch date and give the final approval to launch. He would have the authority to cancel the flight up until the last instant, but the project would pay a high price for an eleventh-hour shutdown. By that point, the pilot would have been sealed into the gondola for several hours while the interior atmosphere was stabilized and the ideal pressure achieved. And after inflation of the envelope had begun, a cancellation would mean a waste of huge quantities of expensive helium gas.

Gildenberg predicted that stratospheric winds above Minnesota would be calmest around the beginning of June, a time that would also probably produce low ground winds. He set the launch date for June 2, 1957. The original plans specified that the launch would take place in a wind-guarded iron pit near Crosby, Minnesota—the North Woods equivalent of the Stratobowl. Yet as the day approached and the weather remained still, the launch site was moved to nearby Fleming Field, an airport in South St. Paul. It was a measure of the project's faith in Duke Gildenberg's weather forecasts.

Launch day was dead calm at dawn. Many hours earlier, Kittinger began the unpleasant job of fitting himself into the torturously tight USAF MC-3 partial-pressure suit. (As Kittinger described the sensation, it felt "like being loved by an octopus.") A miniature microphone was taped to his chest to allow the ground crew to monitor his heartbeat and respiratory rate.

After Kittinger was sealed inside the familiar capsule, and the entire structure was hoisted and then lowered into its aluminum container, the process of flushing the interior air and replacing it with the artificial atmosphere began. The air we breathe consists of about 20 percent oxygen and a little under 80 percent nitrogen. The air Kittinger would breathe during the flight would have three times as much oxygen and about a quarter as much nitrogen. Twenty percent of the mixture would contain the inert gas helium; this would cut down on the chances of a fire, a real concern in any oxygen-rich environment. But, as Kittinger spoke through an intercom with Ed Archibald, the man handling the gas mixture, a side effect of the helium was evident: Kittinger sounded like Mickey Mouse. The Manhigh pilots eventually became adept, through practice, at using muscle control to lower their voices into a less comical range.

It had been obvious from quite early in the project that substantial quantities of helium would be essential for the safe operation of a project such as Manhigh. Helium, one of the "noble gases," is colorless, tasteless, odorless, and—most important—nonflammable. And while, with the exception of hydrogen, helium is the most plentiful element in the universe, it is relatively rare on Earth. Most of the world's commercially produced helium comes from natural gas wells in the southwestern United States. The gas is cooled until it condenses into a liquid, leaving a mixture of uncondensed helium and nitrogen. This mixture (known as "crude helium") is further cooled until the nitrogen also condenses into liquid. The remaining helium gas is then purified by filtering it through charcoal at extremely cold temperatures.

Huge quantities of helium were required to launch a balloon the size of *Manhigh I.* Otto Winzen, who had learned over the years how to manipulate military bureaucracies, managed to get massive Navy-owned tanker trucks suitable for transporting helium loaned to the Air Force and—with special approval from the National Bureau of Mines—to get them filled with the precious gas and delivered to the launch site.

At 4:00 A.M., the gondola was loaded onto a pickup truck and driven to Fleming Field. Since the can-of-water air conditioner in the bottom chamber of the gondola would not work until it reached the stratosphere and the pressure dropped radically, the crown of the capsule was packed with dry ice to keep Kittinger from overheating while waiting for launch. As the truck moved slowly south out of town, a roiling carbon-dioxide cloud unfurled like a jet's vapor trail from the dome of the cylinder standing upright in the pickup's bed.

For Kittinger, the time had finally come. Last-minute weather reports had been checked, wind directions at a variety of altitudes noted. The entire flight trajectory had been plotted and replotted. He had trained off and on for 17 months, had endured the isolation tests and decompression tests, and learned to live with the gripping misery of the partial-pressure suit. Now he was ready for the payoff. The truck arrived at Fleming Field around 4:30. As Kittinger sat anxiously in the tiny capsule, his blood denitrogenizing, a crew of Winzen technicians ran through dozens of checklists. They could hear the staccato squawking of radios coming from the communications vans and the shouts of the launch crew. And then they could hear nothing but the eerie rocketlike whine as the valves were opened and helium flowed through the inflation sleeve and into the long polyethylene bag. The cargo parachute was attached to the gondola's nylon suspension lines. Shortly before 6:30, the sky slowly spreading color across the pancake flats and the air dead still, Duke Gildenberg gave the final okay and the balloon was released. Kittinger later said that he never felt a thing. Simons had asked him over the radio moments before liftoff if he was all right. Kittinger had responded with his typical "No sweat."

It was physically impossible for him to see straight down, but by using a mirror attached for just that purpose, Kittinger could watch the earth shoot away from him. He relaxed. This was it.

Manhigh I rose at a steady 400 feet per minute, the imprisoned gas slowly expanding and filling out the envelope. Stapp and Simons watched anxiously from the ground, their necks aching as they strained to keep sight of the balloon. The ascent rate climbed to 500 feet per minute as Kittinger approached the tropopause. This would be the riskiest part of the ascent. Temperatures would plummet, jet-stream winds would shift. At 100° below zero, the balloon's thin plastic would become a brittle shell. If the winds shifted too severely, the shell might shatter like a glass Christmas-tree ornament. But there was nothing anyone could do now except wait and watch and hope for the best.

Kittinger turned his attention quickly from the sights in the mirror back to his chores. The first was to test the VHF radio that would be his voice communications link with the ground. But a mechanical failure of the transceiver's selector knob made it impossible for Kittinger to determine the frequency to which the transceiver was tuned. No matter what he tried, he was unable to transmit voice messages to the ground. He could still receive the voices of Simons and Stapp, but he could not respond. This was a real blow to the flight plan, for while the gondola was equipped with a telegraph-style key that allowed the pilot to transmit in Morse code, composing messages in laborious streams of code would consume valuable time that might divert attention from other important chores—especially since Kittinger had not used Morse code since his aviation cadet days. Nevertheless, he began tapping out his first message: "N-O S-W-E-A-T." And it was not just bravado. Stapp, monitoring Kittinger's heartbeat and respiratory rate at that precise moment, noticed nothing more than an incidental rise in either. Stapp and Simons were now tracking the balloon from Sikorsky H-21 helicopters, buzzing across the farm country below.

At 45,000 feet, *Manhigh I* hit the tropopause, where one-half of all high-altitude balloon failures occur. Kittinger felt a violent jolt as a 100-MPH blast slammed into the gondola. The huge balloon was flung nearly horizontal in powerful gusts that came in a hammering series of blows. The teardrop profile of the polyethylene envelope was smeared into grotesquely distorted shapes as the wind snatched, fingered, and released the balloon. These were terrifying moments for Joe Kittinger, who had no choice but to believe in the Winzen design and the painstaking construction of the entire system, trusting it all to hang together. This moment, the hard-bitten test pilot would write later, "absolutely frightened the hell out of me."

And then, suddenly, it was over. The jet stream was now below the balloon and *Manhigh I* resumed its steady ascent. Kittinger returned to his checklist of chores, transmitting data patiently through the telegraph key: "R-E-P-O-R-T F-O-L-L-O-W-S . . . T-E-M-P-E-R-A-T-U-R-E I-S 4-5 . . . I F-E-E-L G-O-O-D." As the balloon rose through the stratosphere, and through all of the altitude records posted during the previous decades, the huge swollen gas bag rounded out—the volume of helium doubling every 18,000 feet—until its shape was that of a perfect ball. The ascent slowed. Kittinger stayed busy reading meters and transmitting numbers back to earth.

But if *Manhigh I* was a test of human resolve and will to reach the top of the sky, a final examination that had begun decades earlier with the flights of Hawthorne Gray and even before, it was not over yet. As

Kittinger reported the contents of the gondola's oxygen supply, he realized immediately that something was wrong. The gauge showed that the oxygen supply was already half gone. At this point in the flight, the tank ought to have been almost completely full. He read the gauge and repeated the reading to the ground crew. After some anxious moments and simple deduction, Foster sent word up to Kittinger: somehow, he reported, the Winzen technicians must have installed the oxygen system's aneroid backwards. The oxygen supply was being released into the stratosphere and only the incidental bleed-off was actually flowing into the cabin.

Kittinger understood the implications at once. He would need to begin descending soon if he wanted to survive. Perhaps it was already too late. And yet his compulsion to reach terminal altitude was powerful. He felt the collective will of the entire project pushing him up. He shut down the cabin oxygen system to stop the loss of oxygen and used the oxygen supply to his pressure suit to service the interior of the gondola.

Then, finally, the balloon stopped. The altimeter registered 96,000 feet. Kittinger, hanging motionless in the void, peered out one of the gondola's small portholes. Only Ivan Kincheloe, an Air Force captain who had reached 126,000 feet in the X-2 rocket plane the year before, had ever been this high. And Kincheloe was only there for a phantom moment as his swept-wing rocket reached the top of its ballistic arc and quickly fell back to more familiar regions. But here aboard *Manhigh I* there was no screaming jet roar, no sickening thrust, no blurred vision. Kittinger marveled in silence at the deep, deep blue-black of the sky above the atmosphere's horizon, and seethed because he had nothing with which to send his descriptions back but a clumsy telegraph key.

"How does it feel to be the highest human?" Stapp asked.

Kittinger tapped back, "G-R-E-A-T."

The oxygen gauge now showed two-tenths of one liter of oxygen left, very likely not even enough to allow a return to earth. Kittinger, realizing that he would have to descend, began to release helium from the balloon in preparation for the return trip. Moments later, Colonel Stapp's voice came across the radio ordering Kittinger to begin his descent immediately. In awkward, halted Morse code, Kittinger sent his reply: "C-O-M-E A-N-D G-E-T M-E."

David Simons almost choked. It was his worst nightmare come true. He knew of the obscure syndrome pilots referred to as the breakaway— or break-off—phenomenon. High-altitude jet test pilots had reported it as a dreamy, hallucinatory state that beckons one higher and higher. A 1957 study by pioneering Navy researchers Dr. Ashton Graybiel and Carl Clark showed that feelings of extreme isolation and physical separation from the earth were experienced by about 35 percent of high-altitude, solo pilots.* Ross and Lewis had reported a similar sensation on their record-setting balloon flight in the Navy's *Strato-Lab I,* and some had likened it to divers' "rapture of the deep" that accompanies the bends. It was a dangerous false sensation of freedom and detachment. Some had speculated that Hawthorne Gray had been seduced by the "breakaway" on his final flight. And Simons now feared that Kittinger had succumbed. He also wondered whether Kittinger had found his excuse to bail out and skydive back to earth.

Stapp grimly repeated his order to descend. The ground crew waited for a reply. Then it came: "V-A-L-V-I-N-G G-A-S." Kittinger was on his way down.

Later, Kittinger would grin and shrug off the entire incident. "Well, God, they said: 'The guy's got euphoria! There's something wrong with him!' I was just trying to be funny, and they got a little excited, I guess."

The descent went according to plan. The idea was to slowly valve just enough gas to achieve a rate of 800 feet per minute. Duke Gildenberg monitored Kittinger's altitude and issued valving instructions. Then, as the balloon neared earth, the pilot would have to drop ballast in order to slow the rate of descent for a landing. The mechanics were tricky— gas balloons were incredibly sensitive—but Kittinger was an ace. Below, members of the crew circled in a C-47, waiting for the balloon to punch through the band of clouds that had slipped in during the flight. Radio transmitters tracked the location.

Kittinger's luck—and oxygen—held out. Simons spotted the balloon as it drifted out of the clouds. The helicopter carrying Simons and Stapp raced to the site. The gondola dropped toward a gently rolling meadow

---

*Graybiel and Clark were only two of the most prominent Navy researchers to make important contributions to aerospace medicine. Graybiel is known primarily for his pilot disorientation studies, and Clark for his role in the Navy's acceleration/deceleration research. The world's largest and most sophisticated human centrifuge was located at the Naval Air Development Center in Johnsville, Pennsylvania. At the end of the device's 40-foot arm was a vehicle called the Iron Maiden: a capsule filled with water, contained in which was a compartment for a human being. Clark, the John Paul Stapp of the Navy, took many research rides in the Iron Maiden in the 1950s, suffering tremendous G and anti-G forces.

Indian Creek: Joe Kittinger emerges from the *Manhigh* gondola following the test flight. *(Source: USAF)*

A jubilant Kittinger is attended to by Dr. David Simons. Stapp would later tell the press: "Not a red hair of his head had turned grey." *(Source: USAF)*

and landed in the current of a small, muddy tributary of the Mississippi called Indian Creek, 80 miles from the launch site. At the instant of impact, the balloon was electronically released from the gondola. The plastic envelope tumbled and sailed lazily across the rolling meadows of Minnesota. An old man and his grandson scrambled off into the brush with their fishing poles and tackle boxes when the capsule plopped into the water.

Not only was the pilot okay—Kittinger flashed his trademark grin as he stepped from the gondola and pulled off his helmet ("Not a red hair of his head had turned grey," Stapp later bragged to the press)—but the capsule itself was remarkably undamaged. The flight had been both disaster and triumph. The VHF radio had failed and the oxygen system foul-up had come within minutes—if not seconds—of killing the pilot. The duration of the flight had been drastically curtailed. And yet Kittinger had shattered the world altitude record. Demolished it. A man had gone nearly 19 miles into the sky and sat, for a few incredible moments, on the very edge of outer space. Above him, the sky had been ink black in the middle of the day; below, the earth had been merely a filmy, indistinct, slightly distorted map of the upper Midwest.

The gondola was trucked back to the Winzen plant for inspection and Kittinger was taken to a nearby hospital for examination. The aftermath of *Manhigh I* involved analysis of the data and the attempt to understand why the radio had failed. And while the engineers wrote their technical reports, David Simons ran the flight over and over in his mind.

He continued to wonder if there was anything to the notion of the breakaway phenomenon. How much could the pilot of a super-high-altitude vehicle be trusted to perform and report on his own condition? Had there been anything more to Kittinger's "come and get me" comment than a cocky test pilot's attempt at a joke? Most accounts of *Manhigh I*—newspaper stories, magazine articles, full-length books—mention the "come and get me" line. Its drama, like the peppery character of Joe Kittinger itself, is irresistible. And yet Joseph Kittinger's own book about his exploits ignores this part of the story. Why did Kittinger neglect his own best line?

"I suspect that he probably wasn't very proud of it," David Simons speculated many years later. "He had a test pilot mentality, and he had a streak of kid in him." To Simons, the breakaway phenomenon had been a real concern. It was something, in his mind, that had threatened to destroy his research project. "It was kind of a stupid thing to do. But it was his idea of a joke. He had that streak in him."

Kittinger himself never understood the reaction. "I was just trying to be funny—and they got panicky." Kittinger was convinced that the problems with *Manhigh I* had nothing to do with any kind of breakaway rapture, but with a lack of adequate testing. "You don't neglect testing of the equipment before you go. It would not have been a very difficult task to put that capsule in an altitude chamber and test it before the flight, but they didn't do it." The reasons for not testing the entire system in a stratosphere chamber had to do, mostly, with a lack of funds. But one thing was for sure: Stapp's decision to include a test flight had been sound.

As he thought back to those years in the late fifties when he and his team had first sent a human into the upper stratosphere, David Simons reflected on the motivations of his pilot. "One of the reasons that Kittinger didn't like me was because I was a scientist," he said. "He wasn't interested in medical research. He just wanted to do something nobody'd ever done before."

While David Simons and the rest of the team settled into their laborious preparations for the research flight, *Manhigh II,* Capt. Joseph Kittinger was awarded the Distinguished Flying Cross and became a certified American hero. He would have no more to do with Simons's Manhigh project ("[Simons] was looking for an excuse to get rid of me anyway"), but neither would he rest on his laurels. Kittinger, only 28 years old, would see the stratosphere again—and in singularly spectacular fashion.

four

Floating at the Ceiling

Until just a few years before the turn of the last century, all science really knew about the upper atmosphere was that it was cold and that the air was thin. The concept of regions, or layers, of atmosphere was still unfamiliar; it was assumed that as one ascended, the air simply turned progressively colder and thinner. Prior centuries of observation and speculation had failed adequately to describe and define our canopy of gases that a former scientist for the Office of Naval Research calls "a text of the physical sciences, containing within its seemingly limitless area the answers to many of those riddles of physics and chemistry which man has long unsuccessfully attempted to solve by earth-bound investigation."

In 1896, the French meteorologist Leon P. Tisserenc de Bort launched a series of unmanned sounding balloons. Attached to the balloons were various measurement devices that recorded conditions aloft. When he recovered these instruments, de Bort was astonished at what he found. At an altitude of somewhere between six and eight miles, he learned, there is a sharp transition in the character of the atmosphere. Above the transition point, weather all but ceases to exist: there are no clouds, no rain, no wind. De Bort called it the "stratosphere." He coined another term, "troposphere," to describe the band of dense air that we think of as our atmosphere.

As man learned to fly, and discovered ways to propel himself farther and farther from the earth's surface, he came up against some powerful obstacles. The first thing was the cold. De Bort's balloons showed that temperatures in the upper regions could reach at least −70° Fahrenheit. But there were ways to protect people and equipment from a freezing environment, or at least to minimize the damage. A far more serious problem was oxygen-poor air. Without a proper supply of oxygen to feed the blood, the brain literally self-destructs.

The early balloonists pushed themselves and their balloons higher and higher into the sky; as they did so, they found themselves beginning to choke, and finally—if they went high enough—to suffocate. As early as 1803, only 20 years after the first balloon flight, Etienne Robertson, in an ascent that he claimed reached 23,526 feet, experienced these symptoms. And in 1804, in one of the early scientific flights, Joseph Gay-Lussac ran into similar trouble at 23,000 feet as he attempted to gather air samples. That same year, Count Francesco Zambeccari and two passengers in a hot-air balloon were swept up into rising air currents over the Adriatic Sea. The count's postflight report mentioned some of the other difficulties awaiting visitors to extreme heights:

> We had difficulty hearing each other—even when shouting at the tops of our voices. I was ill and vomited; Grassetti was bleeding at the nose. We were both breathing short and hard, and felt oppression of the chest. Because the balloon rose so suddenly out of the water and bore us with such swiftness to those high regions, the cold seized us suddenly, and we found ourselves covered with a layer of ice.

Louis Lauriat, who made a large number of free balloon ascents all over North America in the 1830s and '40s, encountered some unexpected dizziness and shortness of breath on one flight that reached 24,500 feet. Lauriat reported that he had been forced to breathe three times to get the equivalent of one breath of air at sea level. His lips turned blue and swollen, his eyes bulged in their sockets, and he experienced severe pain in both ears. His pulse rose and his blood vessels began to swell, resulting in a throbbing headache. Finally, blood began to flow from his nose so freely that Lauriat had trouble stanching it. Clearly, one did not want to go much higher than that without some preparation and some protection, not to mention a great deal more knowledge about the upper atmosphere than Lauriat or his contemporaries could lay claim to.

The British Association for the Advancement of Science sponsored James Glaisher and Henry Coxwell in a flight that may have reached 30,000 feet (or higher) in 1862. Glaisher, a meteorologist, and Coxwell, the best-known balloonist in England, had no idea what was waiting for them in the upper atmosphere. They assumed that balloonists who had run into trouble with altitude had simply ascended too rapidly. Dressed in street clothes, without gloves or caps, they launched in a rainstorm at Wolverhampton and rose in a balloon built by Coxwell himself. They carried a number of scientific experiments, containers for air samples, instruments with which to make various measurements, and several pigeons in small crates. At 15,000 feet, it was 18° and ice was beginning to form on the instruments and the neck of the balloon. At 25,000 feet, it was 5° below zero and both men were seriously hypoxic. Their hands and lips had turned a distinct blue and their eyes were bulging grotesquely. In spite of his condition, Glaisher continued to take measurements and to throw the occasional pigeon overboard to observe its behavior. (The birds dropped sluggishly until they were out of sight.)

At 28,000 feet, Coxwell realized that he could no longer reach the cord that would allow him to control the gas valve on the envelope. In other words, the two men had no way to descend. The celebrated balloonist grabbed the iron ring around the base of the balloon in an attempt to pull himself up and grab the rope, but his bare hands froze fast to the metal. Somewhere near 30,000 feet, Glaisher began to convulse and then passed out. (Later, he would recall the moments before he lost consciousness: "I dimly saw Mr. Coxwell, and endeavored to speak, but could not. In an instant intense darkness overcame me, so that the optic nerve lost power suddenly.") Coxwell was still fighting, lunging for the rope and trying to grab it with his teeth. Finally, he succeeded and—in spite of the bloody loss of a tooth and bouts of vomiting—managed eventually to bite through the rope and spill the contents of the balloon. After a crash landing in which both men survived, Coxwell claimed that his final reading of their barometer had shown 35,000 feet.

Later, as the world began to learn of the character of the atmosphere and the role played by oxygen and air pressure in respiration, there were those who doubted the tale, claiming that no one could survive at that height without oxygen. It certainly strains the limits of credibility. At the very least, we can safely say that no one has since managed to survive a similar ordeal.*

Scientists nearly 100 years before Coxwell and Glaisher had been able

---

*Mountaineers have scaled all 29,028 feet of Mount Everest without supplemental oxygen, but their ascents require many days during which their bodies have a chance to partially acclimatize to the altitude. Balloonists rise quickly and face the full, immediate effects of oxygen debt.

to observe what happens to the flame when a candle is covered by an air-tight belljar, and had watched the death throes of mice trapped in an air-tight vessel, but they did not comprehend the physical principle at work. In fact, the mystery remained unsolved until a British theologian who dabbled in chemistry, Joseph Priestley, proved that he could keep a flame in a belljar burning, or a mouse alive, by introducing what he called *dephlogisticated air*. What Priestley had actually done was to heat mercuric oxide and capture the vapor—it was this essence that allowed the flame to burn and the mouse to breathe. A few years later, Lavoisier identified this substance as the gas *oxygen* and showed, as had Priestley, that it was crucial to respiration. And as people began to climb the higher mountain peaks and, later, lift themselves into the sky, they discovered that the oxygen content of the air decreased as one ascended.

But lack of oxygen was not the only impediment to respiration at high altitudes: the stratosphere is a vacuum—there is no air pressure. In 1648, a Frenchman named Florin Perier first proved Pascal's theory that the weight—or pressure—of air decreased as one ascended above the level of the sea. Perier constructed a crude but effective barometer and found that the mercury inside the instrument's glass tube rose to a level of about 26 inches when read at the base of a 3,500-foot mountain while it showed only 23 inches at the summit. It was a landmark experiment, proving that the barometric pressure of air does indeed decrease as altitude increases. There would be obvious implications for airmen of all sorts because without sufficient air pressure, the crucial oxygen transfer cannot occur in the lungs. And without that transfer, brain damage and death come rapidly.

In the later years of the nineteenth century, science turned its attention to the composition of the sky, where new oddities were revealed. The dangers of overexposure to ultraviolet radiation from the sun were already common knowledge, and in 1912 Victor Hess discovered cosmic radiation by sending balloon-borne electroscopes up to 16,000 feet. A few years later, Robert Millikan would show that these mysterious rays (more precisely: minute, ultra-high-speed radioactive particles), unlike oxygen and air pressure, increase steadily as one ascends. And unlike ultraviolet rays, there was no way to effectively shield humans from cosmic radiation. And there was no way to know what risk, if any, these cosmic bullets might pose for high-altitude explorers.

So aeronauts not only had to protect themselves from the bitter cold and devise a way to breathe in the thin air, they also had to fight the deadly effects of decreasing air pressure and somehow shield themselves from the poorly understood dangers of radiation. It was not an inviting scenario.

Balloonists, of course, were better situated to study these questions and make the necessary observations than were airplane pilots who, at extreme altitudes, had to fight their machines as well as the elements. Free balloon pilots could truly explore the upper atmosphere because, beyond managing the ballasting and valving operations, they were indeed free to observe, record, experiment, and reflect.

As early as 1874, European aeronauts were groping for solutions to the challenges of high-altitude survival. The threesome of Sivel, Croce-Spinelli, and Tissandier, reaching 28,000 feet that year, carried bladders of oxygen from which they could breathe when the air got thin. Before leaving the ground on their record attempt, Sivel and Croce-Spinelli had approached Paul Bert and volunteered themselves as subjects in the great French physiologist's decompression experiments. Bert had constructed a steel chamber from which he could remove the air and simulate the environment of any desired altitude. He sealed the aeronauts inside and began pumping out the air, reducing the pressure to the equivalent of 24,000 feet. Bert also had bags of oxygen and nitrogen under pressure in a second chamber; a hose connecting the two allowed the balloonists to inhale the gas whenever the effects of the simulated altitude became severe. They survived the decompression chamber in fine shape, but were less fortunate on the actual flight.

At an altitude of 25,000 feet, the aeronauts were overcome by hypoxia—the oxygen bags could not deliver sufficient quantities of the gas to their blood. All three became weak, then numb, and finally passed out. Only Gaston Tissandier ever woke up. Later, considering himself a very lucky man, he described the dreamy delirium of severe oxygen debt: "The body and mind weaken little by little, gradually, unconsciously and without one's knowledge. . . . One becomes indifferent; one no longer thinks of the perilous situation or the danger; one rises and is happy to rise."

As the century turned, people were no longer content to regard the heavens as merely a blue tableau. They demanded to know what was up there and many were willing to pay the price to find out. Balloons were pushing higher and higher. The German physics professors Arthur Berson and Reinhard Suring reached 35,424 feet in 1901. The word "stratosphere" came into vogue, and the challenge of the barren layer of atmosphere above our own took powerful hold on the mind of the armchair adventurer. American historian Tom Crouch writes that, in the years surrounding the Great Depression,

> the stratosphere was far more than a layer of sky that began roughly ten miles above the surface of the earth at the equator. The word stratosphere conjured up images similar to those that *darkest Africa* had evoked in the nineteenth century or the names Arctic and Antarctic in the early twentieth. Like an unexplored continent, it was a region to be visited by only the most intrepid explorers, members of well-financed and well-equipped expeditions.

By 1957, the stratosphere had become much more than a dream for David Simons. In fact, preparations for the full-scale stratospheric research flight, *Manhigh II,* now completely consumed his life. And if the project was reasonably well equipped and well staffed, well financed it was not. The mechanical malfunctions of *Manhigh I* had been corrected, but Colonel Stapp now insisted on a full-dress rehearsal in a decompression chamber before he would approve the launch. A complete run-out of the system had never been done before the test flight, and it had come back to haunt them. Meanwhile, accountants estimated that the project would require an additional $14,000 to meet expenses.

The timing could not have been worse. A soaring national debt, rising unemployment, and an economy in recession had caused drastic cuts in research funds across the country. The Air Force was hit especially hard. Project Manhigh had no way to make up the deficit. Simons and Stapp sat dejectedly in an office at Winzen Labs and discussed canceling plans for the research flight, crating up the equipment and supplies, and trying again at a more advantageous time. Privately, however, both men were certain that if momentum were lost, there would be no second chance.

As a last resort, David Simons, who always had Otto Winzen's ear, tried to convince Winzen to free up some of the company's funds. But the company was struggling, too. In order to keep its experienced workforce, Winzen Research had been forced to keep wages competitive with General Mills. Organizers, starting with the Teamsters, had attempted to unionize the plant. A labor contract was finally signed by Winzen and the Oil, Chemical, and Atomic Workers Union after many long hours of arbitration that had distracted the company's management.

Vera Winzen had initially opposed the suggestion that Winzen Research help fund Project Manhigh. (More than once she had found herself at odds with both the Air Force men and her husband over operational details. When she heard David Simons and Otto Winzen discussing the possibility of putting a chimpanzee into the capsule with the pilot for *Manhigh II,* she remarked, "One monkey on this flight is enough.") But in the end, with all the money and energy already invested in the project, she agreed that it was the only way to assure a second flight and, finally, to protect her parents' investment.

Otto Winzen called Simons and Stapp into his office and announced, with both pride and relief in his voice, that the directors of Winzen Research would agree to supply the remaining capital. The truth was that Winzen wanted another shot at the stratosphere as much as Simons did. Not only because he wanted to vindicate his technicians and materials after the screw-ups on *Manhigh I,* or because he wanted more publicity, but because he was himself caught up in the obsession. He was on the line with Manhigh as surely as if he were aboard the gondola.

If Kittinger's test flight had failed to generate funds for Manhigh, it had at least drawn plenty of attention to the Minneapolis team now readying the system for the research flight. Not only was private industry eager to participate, but other branches of the service became interested as well. A radio communications vehicle was offered by the Office of Naval Research. Two helicopters, complete with full flight crews, came courtesy of the Army.

Scientists and scientific instruments also began to arrive in Minneapolis. Film emulsions and tubes filled with mold were donated for the purpose of cosmic ray studies. Dr. Herman Yagoda from the Air Force's Cambridge Research Center prepared photographic plates that would be taped to David Simons's arms and chest. These plates would record "hits" of cosmic ray particles. Tiny hash-mark tattoos were inserted under Simons's skin to allow the plates to be positioned so that examiners could pinpoint the exact spots at which particles of cosmic radiation had impacted. For many years after the flight, Simons would be examined to monitor possible effects of the radiation.

From the National Bureau of Standards came a sealed barograph to record the altitude. No such device had ridden on *Manhigh I* since the USAF generally discourages attempts at records of any kind. Approval was obtained for *Manhigh II,* however, after (thanks to Otto Winzen) *Life* magazine agreed to pay the $3,500 it would cost to retain an FAI exam-

Otto Winzen, Vera Winzen, David Simons, and John Paul Stapp with *Manhigh II* gondola. *(Source: Winzen International)*

iner and an officially calibrated barograph. David Simons had little personal interest in the quest to certify an altitude record, but he was not opposed to it, either: "I didn't care. I saw no reason why we shouldn't get credit for a record if we set one, but that wasn't why we were going."

Unlike NASA programs of the sixties, which would employ a new vehicle for each flight, the Manhigh project was able to use the same sturdy aluminum gondola throughout. The capsule that would carry David Simons on the research flight was the same one that had been

Don Foster, David Simons, and Otto Winzen before the research flight. *(Source: Vera Simons)*

retrieved from the creek bottom following Kittinger's flight. Some significant alterations were made to the gondola in preparation for *Manhigh II,* however. General Electric had been given the contract to overhaul the oxygen and communications systems. (Lockheed also worked on the gondola.) A more sophisticated telemetering system would monitor Simons's heartbeat, respiration, and body temperature. A spot-photometer was included to allow Simons to measure—with great precision—the brightness of the sky at extreme altitudes. In addition, a small telescope was now on board and—if time allowed—would afford Simons the opportunity to engage in some stratospheric astronomy and gaze at stars and planets without the intervening haze and blur of Earth's atmosphere.

Three days prior to the launch date, Simons was placed on a special restrictive diet in preparation for his trip to the stratosphere. Since the objective of the research flight was to raise a man above 100,000 feet and keep him there for 24 hours, the pilot would be denied the use of full toilet facilities for not just the day and night he would spend at altitude, but also the additional hours it would take to establish the capsule's artificial atmosphere, launch, ascend to a height no balloonist had ever reached, and then return to Earth. It was important, therefore, to restrict preflight food intake to "low residue" foods that would be absorbed almost totally by the body: lean beef steak, fish, gelatin.

The launch date, however, was delayed several times due to weather, requiring Simons to remain on the low-residue diet. Using a Minneapolis motel room as his personal preflight quarters, Simons would receive the latest weather briefing, and then swallow Seconal tablets each night before climbing into bed. The sedatives were a precaution against restless sleep. It was crucial that a pilot on such a mission be completely rested at the outset. Simons would also be awakened in the middle of the night so that a nurse could take a blood sample from his finger. As weather continued to forestall the launch date, Simons began referring to the nurse as Vampira.

Duke Gildenberg issued a favorable weather report on August 18 and so, once again, the ritual began. Simons went to sleep that afternoon still somewhat discouraged at the string of delayed launch dates, yet hopeful that Gildenberg's latest report would still be valid when he awoke. It was. The weather over the northern plain states was completely cloudless and the winds were mild. As Simons was awakened, as the photo plates were taped to his forearms and the microphone that would relay his pulse and respiration to the ground was taped to his chest, as he began the difficult process of squeezing into the custom-tailored partial-pressure suit, Duke Gildenberg continued to study his weather charts and to monitor conditions across the entire western United States. In spite of the long-hoped-for break in the weather, Gildenberg knew that to launch now would be a gamble. A violent storm over the southwestern states could move up into the Great Plains and continue northward, sliding under *Manhigh II*

Prior to the flight, David Simons autographed Vera Winzen's portrait of him inside the gondola. The inscription was added after his return: "Vera, Thanks for saving a perfect balloon. It gave me a perfect flight." *(Source: Vera Simons)*

while it sat at altitude, and block a return to Earth. The scenario was not likely, but it was well within the realm of possibility. The current high-pressure zone over Minnesota looked relatively stable. But if they waited long enough to verify that, it would be too late to begin launch preparations. And the chance that another ridge of high pressure would move in before autumn was slim indeed.

Later, Simons characterized the dilemma facing Manhigh's chief meteorologist: "He knew as well as I did that financially, if for no other reason, it was now or never. We literally could not afford delay."

Gildenberg did not share his knowledge of the southwestern storm with Simons until later. He knew that the forecast required by the project—calm winds and clear weather for 36 hours—simply would not happen. And he knew that Simons would have been furious about another cancellation. He decided, with the support of his top meteorological advisors, to bend the rules. Besides, he was absolutely confident that *Manhigh* could overfly the threatening weather system. He announced that the launch was on. *Manhigh II* would wait no longer.

At 10:00 on the evening of August 18, Simons climbed into the familiar gondola and settled into the web seat. Otto Winzen handed him a box of food for the journey: Air Force ration cans, fruit juice, sandwiches, candy bars. Simons could look up and see a cardboard disk with good luck messages he had gotten from his family. They had pasted a map of the moon onto the cardboard and written this message below it: "When you reach this, come home." (David Simons's wife and four children would wait out the flight at home in Alamogordo, camping out in the backyard "so we could be under the stars with Daddy.") As Simons surveyed the cramped quarters, he found another message taped to the wall. This one said, "Have all the fun you want, but don't jump up and down"; it was signed "Otto Winzen" and referred to Simons's tendency to bounce when he was excited. And then, at 10:40 P.M., as Vera Winzen—who served as her company's official photographer—snapped photographs and Colonel Stapp, in typical fashion, saluted the brave young doctor with a pun ("Major, you are about to reach the high point of your career"), David Simons was sealed into the gondola to begin the establishing of capsule atmosphere and the denitrogenizing of his blood.

Later, Simons would describe his emotions.

My body tingled with the mixture of apprehension and excitement that is born of the finality of commitment to an unknown. It was a pleasant sensation, the same sort of feeling I suppose that forces other men to demand the chance to make of themselves fools or heroes; to willingly, even eagerly embrace an event whose hazards may range from the discovery of unforeseen cowardice to death. Already I was beginning to savor the anticipation of overcoming the hazards, commanding the event; the thrill of winning infinitely enhanced for a scientist by the thrill of discovery.

At 11 P.M., the gondola was hoisted onto a truck to be transported 140 miles west to the open-pit iron mine near Crosby, Minnesota. In spite of an uncomfortable, jostling ride, Simons was able to get a little sleep on the trip. As in *Manhigh I,* a 50-pound chunk of dry ice on top of the gondola was used to cool off the interior until the water-can air conditioner could operate. Nevertheless, conditions inside were alternately too hot or too cool. Simons complained several times that he was sweating profusely inside the pressure suit. He tried to remain calm. He ate two cheeseburgers and managed, in a delicate half-standing operation, to urinate twice during the wait.

The winds at Crosby were four knots, higher than the Manhigh crew would have liked, but not high enough to scrub the launch. As a soupy ground fog swirled eerily around the floor of the mine, the balloon was inflated by hoses from the helium tanker trucks and the envelope was attached to the gondola. Everything was going remarkably smoothly. And then, during inflation, the first real problem developed. A plastic band called a "reefing sleeve," reinforced with adhesive filament tape, caught around the base of the envelope and pinched the balloon's opening. Unless it could somehow be removed, the flight would have to be canceled. The offending band was 70 feet off the ground, causing the crew to scramble for a very tall ladder. After some delay, a ladder was located and rushed to the inflation site by firetruck.

Removing the tape and the plastic sleeve without damaging the delicate, billowing polyethylene fabric would require expert hands. And the most expert hands available belonged to the person who had worked with the polyethylene from the very beginning: Vera Winzen. And so, with six crew members balancing the ladder on top of one of the helium trucks and steadying it with ropes, she climbed to the top and, using a pair of shears, carefully snipped the plastic band away. Her efforts cleared the way for the historic launch of *Manhigh II.*

At 9:22 A.M. on the morning of August 19, 1957, David Simons had already been sealed inside the capsule for nearly 11 hours. But now the waiting was over. Duke Gildenberg gave the okay and the tethering cables were released, freeing the balloon. A mild surface wind pitched the gondola toward the looming 400-foot-high cliffs of the mine, but it just missed striking the rock as it cleared the lip. Spectators stationed on the cliffs applauded, along with the crew down in the mine itself, as *Manhigh II* ascended into the transparent morning sky.

The balloon climbed steadily—about 1,100 feet per minute—and without incident. Inside the gondola, David Simons was luckier than Joe Kittinger had been. This time, the VHF radio worked perfectly and the

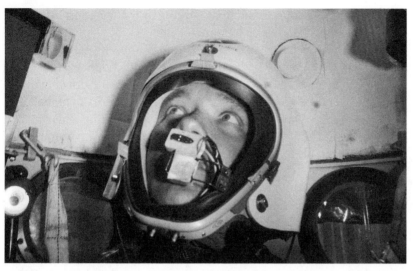

David Simons snaps a self-portrait at 101,500 feet, floating at the ceiling. *(Source: David Simons)*

pilot's voice could be heard clearly on the ground as he described the cloud formations and the wonderful coloration of the sky. As the balloon continued its ascent, Simons began to take photos out the portholes.

Manhigh II was tracking over the ground, heading westward, at about 20 MPH. Otto Winzen's brigade of vehicles followed. This caravan included several trucks and vans, three airplanes, and three helicopters. Winzen himself directed all vehicles from a central command post inside the Navy's communications van. Colonel Stapp, also in the van as flight surgeon, monitored the pilot's physical condition.

Due to light jet-stream winds, the balloon breached the tropopause without incident and continued its ascent into the stratosphere. At 74,000 feet, Simons stepped on the foot pedal that activated his radio transmitter and described the appearance of the balloon to his ground crew. It looked, he said, "like a lady holding onto her skirt . . . it drapes down so gracefully. The fimbriated edges wave very, very gently in the breeze." At this point in the flight, Simons also remarked that the sky was becoming much darker.

The experience was totally enthralling, and not just for the sights. There was also the eerie hush, a strange sonic void that Simons found hard to relate. "It's like no earthly quiet," he would say. "On earth there are always traffic sounds and dogs barking or the wind just whistling. But in space there's nothing but quiet."

And then, not much later, Simons found himself at 101,500 feet: "floating at the ceiling. . . . The balloon was gently bouncing like a basketball being dribbled in slow motion in an upside-down world." Almost 20 miles above the surface of earth. Higher than any balloonist had ever been. David Simons looked down below from where he had come only two hours and eighteen minutes before. It was the rarest of views. Later, in his technical report on the flight, Simons would record his impressions.

Looking down, I thought I could see Lake Michigan to the east. . . . Above me, I saw something I did not believe at first. Well above the haze layer of the earth's atmosphere were additional faint thin bands of blue, sharply but faintly etched against the dark sky. They hovered over the earth like a succession of halos. They are apparently thin shells of dust on whose presence scientists had previously only theorized. My field of vision from that altitude covered a radius of at least 400 miles, or more than half-a-million square miles of the United States.

As Simons returned his sights to the planet below, he let his eyes run across the hazy brown and green geography that stretched to the horizon. As he tracked the endless grid of section lines of the farm country and noted the way they converged in the distance, it dawned on him that he was seeing something else that others could only imagine. He was seeing the curvature of the earth. Stevens and Anderson had reported a slightly bowed horizon, but Simons believes that he was the first human being to ever really appreciate with his naked eyes that we live on the surface of a ball. "You wouldn't see it in a cursory glance," he reported. Even at nearly 102,000 feet, the effect was subtle. But it was there. And the sight was stunning.

Another sight out the portholes of *Manhigh II* proved to be almost literally indescribable: the colors of the sky as seen from the stratosphere. Simons was not the first stratospheric explorer to notice the colors; in fact, every balloonist who had gotten above the tropopause had remarked on the strange, deep hues that matched no colors known. And in anticipation of this phenomenon, the Air Force's Cambridge Research Center had supplied Manhigh with a set of color samples that included every subtle shade of color that could be perceived and reproduced with pigment. Simons attempted to match the deep bluish-purple color that occurred between the horizon and the utter blackness of space above. None of the color samples matched the color he was seeing.

Simons attempted to describe the sight to his crew on the ground.

I tried to compare the color charts to the sky color, the green . . . one was too green, the other too purplish violet, because this sky has the blue of an ocean blue, pure clean lapis lazuli blue, at the interface between the dark purple sky above, and the white typical of looking through the atmosphere horizontally toward the horizon. The color above this band is deep indigo, intense, almost black . . . in fact, the point is, what little color is there is very deep and very intense . . . although there isn't very much. It is nearly black.

Simons groped for words but, like others before him, never seemed to find the right ones. Later, he would try again as he reflected on the experience. By then, the description had been reduced to metaphor. In the upper regions of the stratosphere, physics and poetry are accustomed bedfellows.

Where the atmosphere merged with the colorless blackness of space, the sky was so heavily saturated with this blue-purple color that it was inescapable, yet its intensity was so low that it was hard to comprehend, like a musical note which is beautifully vibrant but so high that it lies almost beyond the ear's ability to hear, leaving you certain of its brilliance but unsure whether you actually heard it or dreamed of its beauty.

In the classical conception of the world, the sky was an exalted region. Author Clive Hart summarizes the pre-Renaissance understanding of the atmosphere: "As one ascends toward heaven, the purity of experience increases both in a spiritual and physical sense." But David Simons, even as he drank in the wonders of the planet and found himself enthralled with the fantastic, spectacular vastness of the all-encompassing vacuum of space, was never unaware of the shackles that tied him to mortal pursuits. The grip of the pressure suit and the tight aluminum confines were both torment and savior. And his self-imposed regimen of scientific tasks continually pulled him away from prolonged meditation. Simons hoped to complete some twenty-five experiments during the course of the flight: astronomical observations of the moon and Venus, meteorological observations of cloud formations, astro-physical observations of the *aurora borealis,* biomedical observations of his own physical and mental reactions to the stress and discomfort—not to mention monitoring the effects of cosmic ray bombardment on his own body.

He had scheduled free time to allow himself to observe and contem-plate, but a review of *Manhigh II's* technical reports and radio transcrip-tions reveals that even during these "free" periods, Simons relaxed by pho-tographing, filming, and making observations with the five-inch telescope. In fact, with the continual regimen of chores and the nearly predictable emergencies, it is amazing that the Manhigh pilots were able to even notice the view out their windows, much less enjoy what they saw.

Not long after reaching peak altitude, as the *Manhigh II* gondola hung suspended over Detroit Lakes, Minnesota—as if on cue—things started to go wrong. Simons was interrupted in the middle of his astronomi-cal observations by the radio crackle of Otto Winzen's voice. "We've got a problem, Dave." Winzen informed Simons that all high-frequency radio transmissions had been lost. This meant that not only was the telemetry information (pulse, respiration, body temperature) no longer available to the ground crew, but that the tracking vehicles no longer had a high-frequency beacon with which to track the balloon. In addition, the VHF voice radio frequency had begun to shift, raising the possibil-ity that Simons might at any moment lose all radio contact with the ground. Winzen and Stapp agonized over the decision before them.

With the sun due to slip beyond the horizon within a few hours, the question was obvious: Should *Manhigh II* attempt to remain aloft through the night, or should descent begin immediately? Simons asked for Colonel Stapp's judgment. Stapp told Simons, in essence, "It's up to you, but understand that if VHF radio contact is lost, you'll spend the night up there alone."

Simons took a few moments to think. For all practical purposes, he was alone anyway. The potential loss of voice contact was not really a problem, except that he would then be required to make tape-recorded and handwritten notes on his observations. An annoyance, to be sure, but no reason to scrap the rest of the flight. The bigger worry was the loss of the high-frequency contact. The lack of tracking data was not a show-stopper; with the armada of both land and air vehicles, surely they would be able to find him when he landed the next day. It was the lack of telemetry data that presented the most serious danger in David

Simons's mind. The capsule temperature had been building up, higher than had been expected, and Simons was not sure why. He expected the problem to disappear as the cooling temperatures of night came on, but it would have been reassuring to know that Stapp was watching his body temperature closely. Simons was also exhausted. His last real sleep had been nearly 24 hours earlier. His knees ached and his back hurt due to the sitting position he was trapped in. It would have been comforting to know that his crew could keep tabs on his respiration and pulse, and would be able to know when stress began to take too great a toll.

But the overriding concern for Simons at this point was the list of things left to do, a list he had spent two years preparing. He needed to observe the sky at night, look for stars. But more than anything he needed to remain at altitude in order to be able to observe the effects of a day in the upper stratosphere on the principal research subject: himself.

Resolved, he spoke to Winzen and Stapp. "With your permission, I'm staying up here. There's nothing, repeat, nothing wrong with the system. If you can stand the doubt, we'll make it through the night."

Stapp immediately sent word that permission to continue the flight was granted. Simons thought he heard relief in the older man's voice.

The issue settled, Simons returned to his celestial observations. But very quickly he became aware that his level of performance was dropping. He noticed that his movements were more sluggish than before and that his speech had become slightly slurred. The cabin temperature was still uncomfortably warm: 77°. He snapped a series of photographs of the horizon before realizing that he had neglected to put film in the camera.

Colonel Stapp, in the radio van now parked at Fargo, North Dakota, interrupted Simons to ask when he had last eaten. Somewhat chagrined, Simons admitted that his last food intake had been the cheeseburgers he had eaten on the ground. He had been too busy and had simply neglected it. He immediately ate a chocolate bar and hoped that the subsequent rise in his blood-sugar level would boost his concentration.

As he finished his snack and glanced out through the portholes again, Simons noticed a change in the colors of the sky. The sun was closing the gap with the horizon and as it did, a stunning pallet of colors, some familiar, others not, began to move and blend in an unexpected, brilliant wash. Simons would say later that the sunset from his vantage at the top of the stratosphere was the single most startling sight his eyes had ever seen. For an entire hour he sat rapt, tearing his attention away only briefly to record his impressions on a tape recorder and for a grateful ground crew that was already in darkness, the sun having set for them long before *Manhigh II* saw the last dying rays of daylight.*

Paradoxically, I was still suspended in the full light of the sun, and to my back, somewhere over Colorado and the Dakotas, it still bathed the earth. But in front of me, over Lake Michigan, Wisconsin, and Minnesota, it was setting. And a curious reversal of night and day met my eyes. High in the atmosphere, where the sun still shot its rays, the ever deepening blue sky was acquiring a greenish, sunset tinge. But below it, closer to the earth, was a giant demarcation line which looked like a faded rainbow arching from south to north across the eastern horizon. And beneath the line was the darkness of night covering the earth below. The daylit sky was above, the darkened sky below. And as the sunset progressed, the rainbow arch rose ever higher, drawing with it a curtain of blackness. Where the darkness had not yet fallen, the changing sunlight majestically shifted its colors through the atmosphere, deepening here to a fiery red, fading there to a salmon pink, then to a pale yellow. Above the slowly changing colors was a layer of blue so clear that it was as if someone had lifted a veil from an ordinary blue sky to leave it polished and bright and clean with no scattered light to diffuse it.

When the last of the sun had disappeared and the red afterglow had begun to melt into the horizon, Simons looked up and noticed a black sky alight with stars—thousands of bright, pinpoint lights that shone with a steady glow. ("The stars glow like an animal's eyes. . . . I have a ringside view of the heavens—it is indescribable.") The moon, he told his ground crew, looked like a thin, gauzy cloud. "Interestingly enough, that gauzy layer I was just referring to has the damndest things going around to the north, turns out to be an *aurora borealis* arch." Simons's written account includes more discoveries.

---

*This phenomenon, a balloon in the stratosphere remaining in the light—and continuing to reflect bright sunlight—while the earth below is in darkness, was thought by the Air Force to explain the vast majority of UFO sightings. During the 1950s, these sightings increased in frequency along with the Navy's and Air Force's balloon operations, and Air Force studies showed a direct connection between balloons in the stratosphere at dusk and dawn and reports of UFOs.

Looking at Earth's horizon from maximum altitude on *Manhigh II:* "I have a ringside view of the heavens—it is indescribable." *(Source: David Simons)*

Close behind the setting sun trailed Venus. . . . I picked her up just a few degrees above the horizon and watched for sixteen minutes as she set in the wake of the sun. Her plunge below the horizon was almost as spectacular. From my vantage point far above the earth, I was watching the setting planet through a double thickness of atmosphere, just as you look through two thicknesses when you peer through the curving side of a drinking glass. This led to a rainbow effect as the bright planet's light passed through the bands of air. It twinkled slowly in brilliant colors, each holding for about a second, then shifting suddenly to another: first green, then red, then yellow, as if a giant stage-light color filter turned slowly between Venus and my eyes.

Moments later, when an observation of a setting Jupiter failed to yield a similar light and color show, Simons checked his altimeter to determine whether his position in the sky might not be changing. It was. *Manhigh II* was losing altitude. Altitude loss at twilight was, to a certain extent, expected. As the helium cooled and contracted, the balloon would not be able to maintain a constant height above the ground. How much drop to expect was not completely clear, but Simons believed he was falling faster than he should have been. He decided to jettison one of the spent batteries, which amounted to 100 pounds of ballast. This, he was confident, would allow him to maintain an overnight altitude of well above 80,000 feet.

But *Manhigh II* continued to drop. Why? As Simons sat forward and looked toward the earth below him, he suddenly understood. He had seen the heavy blanket of clouds scooting beneath him long before twilight and had watched their undulating tops take on the colors of the setting sun. This was the developing cold front that had concerned Duke Gildenberg. Simons realized that the clouds had cut him off not only from the ground but from much of the reflected heat and infrared radiation of the earth's surface. The helium contraction was accelerated and *Manhigh II* was falling. The balloon *would* level off, that was a certainty, but when? Simons thought of the storm front and wondered how high the tops of the thunderheads had been. He recalled that storm clouds sometimes boiled up to 50,000 feet, maybe a little higher. There was plenty of buffer, clearly, between *Manhigh II* and the storm, but it was unsettling nevertheless. Simons would write in the *Manhigh II* technical report,

> The clouds were becoming sirens, beautiful but hazardous. Although fascinatingly lovely to watch, especially impressive for their fine detail and fantastic forms like giant cauliflowers or brains lighted from within . . . like flashing neon displays, the clouds shot through with sporadic pulses of light that showed up in a gorgeous pattern of puff and shadow.

After reporting to his ground crew at a little after midnight, Simons slumped forward and let his head fall against his chest-pack parachute to try to sleep. Moments later he jumped awake as a bright flash of white light illuminated the gondola. He thought of the 300-foot radio antenna that was dangling beneath *Manhigh II:* a lightning rod reaching down into a powerful storm. Simons quickly checked for fires or evidence of a lightning hit. He found nothing. He checked his altitude and noted that he was still dropping. He'd be at 70,000 feet soon.

For the first time during the flight, David Simons was afraid. What would it be like to sink into the thunderheads and be incinerated in the instant crack of a billion volts? What would it be like if the balloon burst and he punched through the storm like a falling rocket?

And then another intense flash of light struck the gondola. Simons was near panic now. Even the slightest spark in the oxygen-rich environment of the capsule and the whole thing might explode like a bomb. He knew he could not afford to drop much more ballast or he would not have enough to make a safe descent once the storm was past. Again the cabin was bathed in a flash of white light.

David Simons slumped into his seat. He wanted to laugh, but he was too tired. He understood now. It was not lightning at all but a photoflash strobe light on an automatic camera that was programmed to go off every five minutes and record the instrument panel. Condensation from the roof of the gondola had dripped in and short-circuited the electrical connection earlier in the day; now the wires had dried out and the camera had come to life—and nearly scared the pilot to death.

As *Manhigh II* drifted northward and darkness settled in, an exhausted Simons radioed the ground crew that he wanted to try once again to sleep. Over the next few hours, he slept fitfully: dozing, waking to make a few observations, maybe eating a candy bar, then sleeping again. After a half-hour nap at 1:00 A.M., Simons woke to find his altimeter reading 71,800 feet; minutes later he was down to 70,000. After another short period of sleep, he read 69,800. He dropped some more ballast.

At 4:15, still in darkness, Simons was jolted awake by a sudden drop of 500 feet. The altimeter showed 68,000 feet, and *Manhigh II* was still falling. The gondola was also beginning to spin wildly beneath the balloon. Simons reasoned that the envelope must have split. He wiped condensation off one of the portholes and looked out—and saw at first glance what had caused him to drop so rapidly. It was a dark, distinct thunderhead—perhaps a mile or two away, and it stretched up as high, if not higher, than David Simons in his alloy capsule. A downdraft from the storm had sucked him down like a leaf. It did not seem possible. The textbooks said clouds did not rise this far into the stratosphere. Simons, an amateur meteorologist, wanted to find comfort in this "fact," but instead he felt the fear returning and felt it encircle and grip him. He thought of the antenna scraping the top of the storm and he steadied himself as best he could. The view from a second porthole confirmed the seriousness of Simons's dilemma: he could no longer see the stars, meaning that he now had clouds *above* him. He had literally dropped into the storm. He radioed the crew.

Otto Winzen replied, "Are you certain about the altitude? If you're at 70,000 feet I don't see how you could be so close to the thunderheads."

"I'm right on top of them," Simons said, with some irritation. Then he reported his intention to drop 100 pounds of ballast in the form of a pair of reserve batteries mounted on the landing ring below the gondola. Winzen replied that this would send a fairly severe shock up the cables to the balloon itself and expressed doubt about the ability of the envelope to absorb it. In the night-time cold, the gossamer-thin polyethylene would be a fragile, brittle shell that could shatter and pitch the gondola into the middle of the storm.

Simons made the decision, with Winzen's reluctant approval, to risk dropping ballast. The storm had completely halted all airborne tracking of the balloon, which would lengthen the time it would take his crew to find him if he were forced down. But the idea of hanging around and risking being sucked into the storm was too much to bear. He fingered the switches that would release the batteries, and then pressed them. The shock wave would shoot up the cables to the balloon, encircle the surface, and then return to rock the gondola. He knew from previous ballast operations that it would take exactly four seconds for the shock to reach the balloon and exactly four seconds more for it to return. He counted to four, then to eight: the gondola jumped hard.

Simons sat back into the web seat and sighed. The balloon began to rise rapidly as it pulled away from the thunderheads and ascended once again into the weatherless, upper reaches of the stratosphere. As the tension drained from his body, he began to feel cold. The temperature had dropped steadily since sundown. He read the thermometer: 34°. In spite of the cramped surroundings and his nearly overpowering fatigue, he decided to try and wiggle into the thermal oversuit that had been stowed in the gondola. The suit had been designed to be easy to put on, but it still took Simons 25 difficult minutes to complete the job.

Shortly after six o'clock in the morning, Simons reported a momentary flash of bright green light: evidence of the sun about to crest the horizon. As the sun rose, Simons struggled again to describe the curling braids of color he watched forming and blending and melting in the sky: "reddish blue-purple," "weak, watery pink, white light," "a very dark, foreboding, formless blue that grades off into a slate gray amorphous color."

At 7:30, after taking a urine sample, Simons ate a breakfast of cold ham and eggs, sliced peaches, and a nut roll. The warmth of the ascending sun pulled the balloon up: the altimeter read 93,000 feet. Above the balloon was the inky blackness that Simons recalled—fondly now—

from the previous day. He found himself impatient with the rate of ascent.

I felt as if I no longer belonged to the earth on this morning. My identity was with the darkness above. As I ate, the sky around me and above me grew darker. I knew that I was returning to the altitudes I had visited the day before. It was right. That was where I belonged. I was separated now, emotionally as well as physically, from the earth.

At 100,000 feet, Simons could see the trailing edge of the thick cloud bank that had been beneath him through the night. He described the formation that he said resembled a steep, limestone cliff:

This cloud layer which terminates as an overhanging shelf is so solid it gives one a feeling of being in heaven, above the rest of the world where you can look down over the edge and see the poor, faltering mortals. It's a strange sensation: a quiet world, peaceful, bright and dark at the same time.

Not until later would Simons be able to identify these emotions as a classic manifestation of the breakaway phenomenon, the false sense of superiority and security that seems to lure humans, siren-like, farther and farther from the earth. The causes in this case were most likely fatigue (physical and psychological), stress, and the cramped isolation inside the gondola. An additional explanation for the lapse in Simons's concentration would not be discovered for another few hours.

At a few minutes before 10:00, Simons dropped another 60 pounds of ballast (which, he noted, left him with a total of 300 pounds), and by 10:30 the altimeter aboard *Manhigh II* read 121,000 feet. This would shatter the existing balloon altitude record if the barographs could validate it, but an altitude record was not of much concern to anyone on the Manhigh crew at this point—and especially not to David Simons. It was time now to begin the descent.

Or almost time. In spite of Simons's stated desire to attempt to descend through a hole he could see in the cloud cover, Otto Winzen vetoed the plan as too dangerous. The jet-stream winds might grab the balloon and pull it right into the storm. Instead, Winzen suggested that Simons wait at altitude and give the storm a chance to drift farther east. Meanwhile, Colonel Stapp paced nervously in the Fargo field beside which the van was parked.

Simons agreed—reluctantly. Feeling exhaustion beginning to take control of his muscles and his thoughts, he was suddenly anxious to start down. It would be a journey of many hours and one that would require a great deal of concentration. He was ready to go. The capsule, he noticed, was again becoming uncomfortably warm. Minutes later he caught himself recording some simple omnirange bearings backwards. His efficiency was clearly tapering off.

Moments later, Colonel Stapp—back in the van—requested a respiration reading. Simons quickly timed his breathing and reported that he was taking 44 breaths a minute. This respiration rate was of immediate concern to Stapp—normal respiration for a body at rest is between 12 and 16 breaths a minute—but Simons's complete lack of concern in reporting such a reading was perhaps more alarming. Simons was a doctor and knew full well that 44 breaths a minute was outrageously high.

Simons was asked to report the carbon dioxide level in the capsule. After a few moments spent with a CO_2 analysis kit, he reported a level of 4 percent carbon dioxide. "Recheck that reading" came the voice from the ground. After a second reading, Simons reported the same level: 4 percent. This was a huge problem, and even Simons, weary and distracted though he was, knew it. The CO_2 level should have been much lower. In fact, in preflight preparations, the maximum allowable CO_2 level in the capsule had been set at 3 percent. The atmosphere Simons was breathing—at well over 20 miles above the surface of the earth—was bordering on poisonous. It was potentially the most threatening situation the Manhigh program had faced.

Stapp acted immediately. "Gentlemen," he announced to Winzen and the others in the van, "I don't mean to sound derogatory, but down with Simons, I say." David Simons was informed that, in view of the emergency, he was no longer in control of the flight and that from that point on all decisions would be made on the ground. Stapp would issue the commands and Simons would execute them. The first command came almost immediately. Simons was instructed to begin valving gas for the descent.

The next instruction was for Simons to close the face shield on his pressure suit and activate the oxygen system that fed the suit. Simons did so and found that the pure oxygen cleared his head almost immediately. He remained tired and scared, but now he felt that at least he could function rationally. He thought through the problem with the chemical scrubbers that were supposed to be cleansing the capsule atmosphere of the CO_2 he exhaled, and reasoned that the anhydrous lithium hydroxide had cooled so much during the night that its absorbent qualities had gone partially dormant. If this were true, the CO_2 level should drop as the capsule remained in the warming glow of the daytime sun. And, in fact, as the day wore on, the level began to creep slowly down into the safe range.

But the sun's heat created another problem. At about 11:30 in the morning, Simons took note of the capsule temperature. It was 82°, warmer than at any time during the previous day. Perhaps it was fatigue, but Simons found the heat nearly unbearable—especially trapped as he was inside the bulky pressure suit. He could activate an air cooler to counter the heat, but he did not dare expend any more of his emergency power supply. If he exhausted all of his batteries before he was on the ground, everything aboard *Manhigh II*—including the communication system—would go dead. He feared the possibility of landing some-where on the deserted prairie and not having even enough juice to blow the explosive bolts that would open the capsule and allow him to crawl out. Somehow, he would have to endure the heat. He forced himself to concentrate on the valving operation, to think his way through the suf-focating heat.

Gildenberg provided instruction on when to valve and for how long. There was an art to it. Because the rate of descent doubles as one drops through the tropopause and into earth atmosphere, it was imperative that the rate be held down early in the descent. But Simons began to wonder if the valving regimen he was following was too conservative. *Manhigh II* was fast running out of power, of oxygen, of pilot efficiency. The flight schedule called for Simons to be back on the ground by 3:50, the time at which it was estimated the reserve power would be depleted. Yet at 3:30 the altimeter still read 70,000 feet with a descent rate below 400 feet per minute.

Simons asked for, and received, permission to turn the two-way radio off for a while to conserve power. He continued to valve helium, mon-itoring his rate of descent. The ideal rate of descent in the stratosphere was 400 feet per minute. If Simons could achieve this before entering the jet stream, his rate would climb to about 800 feet per minute as he fell through the troposphere. At that speed, the *Manhigh II* balloon would set the capsule down hard but safely. Simons intended to valve until he reached 400 feet per minute, and then leave the valve open an additional two minutes. He expected that this procedure would keep him right around 400 feet until he hit the tropopause. But due to a mis-calculation, Simons's final two minutes of valving occurred precisely at the time he was passing through the tropopause.

He watched the needle on the gauge as it tracked his speed and real-ized, too late, that he had overvalved. Moments later *Manhigh II* was falling at 1,300 feet per minute and on course with a sure-fatal crash land-ing. Simons quickly turned the radio back on to consult with the crew. He had 200 pounds of ballast left: not much given his extreme speed. Winzen told Simons to drop half the ballast at 4,000 feet, and save the rest until he was only 300 feet above the ground. The hope was that 100 pounds of ballast dropped at the very end of the descent would provide a puff of lift sufficient to keep the impact from crushing the capsule.

At 5:00, *Manhigh II* was at 25,000 feet. There was not much for Simons to do but wait until it was time to drop the first batteries. He opened one of the portholes. The cold, fresh air rushed into the capsule like a blessing; at 12,000 feet Simons lifted his face shield and breathed deeply. He was immediately energized. Out the open porthole he could clearly see the farms and roads of Aberdeen, South Dakota.

At 4,000 feet, just as the balloon fell through a thin patch of clouds, Simons pressed a switch and released an emergency battery pack. He could feel the gondola slowing down. At 300 feet he dropped the last battery pack and again felt the braking. The only power left was a small battery that would allow him to cut away the balloon once he was on the ground, and then blow the bolts that would release him from the capsule.

He came down in the middle of a newly plowed flax field near the town of Elm Lake, South Dakota, landing hard enough to jerk his fin-ger off the balloon release switch. The balloon immediately pulled the gondola onto its side and began to drag it across the soft furrows. After an anxious moment, his finger found the switch and the giant polyeth-ylene bag that had been so meticulously taped and glued was cut free. It billowed up like a startled jellyfish and sailed off on the western wind.

For a moment Simons remained still within the capsule. He was back on earth now—405 miles from where he had launched the morning before, but safe and well. The research flight that had been the objective of Project Manhigh was complete. He had prevailed over long odds, meager funds, a deadly storm, and near-toxic carbon dioxide levels. He was the first man to spend an entire day and night in the stratosphere, the first man ever to float down into a thunderstorm, the first man to ascend above 100,000 feet in a balloon. Stapp may have selected Joe Kittinger to make the test flight because of the test pilot's proven ability to maintain efficiency in the face of punishing circumstances, but David Simons had just completed one of the greatest feats of endurance and perseverance in aviation history. And now he was back. But curiously, the thought that held him as he lay tight in his restraints, sideways on a South Dakota farmer's field, was that he wanted to go back. In spite of the fact that he had already been forced to endure the confines of the capsule and the glove-like constriction of the pressure suit for more than 44 hours, he wished, briefly, that he could return to that rarefied place where the sun rising and falling painted fantastic pictures on the sky.

He blew the bolts on the hatch and wriggled out. The sun was bright and the dense air heavy with fresh flax. Across the field, a few hundred feet away, Simons could see an old draft horse slowly approaching with two riders, a man and a young boy. He pulled off his helmet and called to the farmer and his son.

"Hello. How are you today?"

"Howdy," the farmer replied matter-of-factly. Simons tried to imagine what this man and his boy would make of the strange, plug-shaped capsule that had just returned from a journey to the edge of space. He tried to imagine what they would make of him, the stranger in the thick, bulky pressure suit. Had they seen the balloon drift away? How could he explain to them how he came to be here, what he had seen and experienced? Might they mistake him for some alien creature, a Martian? But the man and the boy were silent. They slipped slowly off the big farm horse and the man handed his son the reins, as if they were completing some chore they had performed a thousand times.

Just then, a helicopter carrying Stapp and Winzen and other members of the Manhigh crew came into earshot. As the chopper came thumping across the sky, the farmer's son suddenly grew visibly excited.

"Look! There's a helicopter," he cried, his eyes round and unblinking, genuine awe breaking across his face. "I always wanted to see one of them."

five

"This Is God"

On August 24, 1957, Lt. Gen. Samuel E. Anderson, commander of the Air Research and Development Command (ARDC), pinned the Distinguished Flying Cross on David Simons in a ceremony in Baltimore. The citation referred to a "valor above and beyond the call of duty . . . under conditions never before experienced." For a brief period following the flight, the Manhigh crew were the darlings of the press. Simons was the "daring young Air Force officer" and "the gallant major." An op-ed piece in the *New York Times* titled "The First Space Man" suggested that *Manhigh II*'s pilot had risen to the rarefied heights as a representative not of his branch of the service or his country, but of all mankind: he "made the trip for all of us. Organized society took this step toward space as it has taken others in the past and will take many more." A jovial Colonel Stapp assured reporters that Project Manhigh had plans to send a bigger gondola up, big enough to hold five men and capable of remaining in the stratosphere for a week. (Winzen Research had already submitted an unsolicited proposal to the Air Force for just such a balloon-borne floating laboratory to be called Satelorb. After a lukewarm reception, Otto Winzen later took the idea to NASA—with similar results.) Manhigh had proved, Stapp announced, that human beings could live outside of Earth's atmosphere. And David Simons had proved his mettle as an aeronaut: "He was sort of a one-man band," Stapp explained, "keeping alive with one hand, watching dials, conducting experiments, and snapping cameras with the other. Dave could sit in a gondola, handle 20 emergencies, and not die once."

But the sensation of glory and the satisfaction in a job well done were short-lived. Simons found himself increasingly annoyed with the fickle attentions of the press. They did not understand the real significance of what he had done, nor why he had done it. And because of their professional cynicism, they were incapable of really appreciating it. One of the reporters at the postflight press conference went sniffing for an angle: "Was it a spiritual experience?"

Simons measured his words and spoke as a scientist:
I have a deep regard for the steady, progressive march of mankind. I consider myself extremely fortunate to be able to move a step forward in the gradual pushing back of the frontier of progress. My spiritual experience here was tantamount to that of a biologist looking into a microscope and discovering a new virus.

The reporter challenged the response, accusing Simons of "humanism."
"To me," Simons said, "this is God: to contribute to the progress of mankind."

Then, from the back of the pack of reporters, one said to another, "They've bottled everything else this guy has done this week. Might as well bottle his religion and have a look at that, too."

Whereas Tex Settle in the thirties had complained that the press made too much of his stratospheric flight with their talk of "poetry," Simons was frustrated because the press, in a sense, made too *little* of the flight of *Manhigh II*. Plainly, he was more awestruck than they.

Simons was especially angered by the implication that the unstated goal of Project Manhigh, from the beginning, had been to set an altitude record. He bristled at the suggestion that he was in it for personal glory. "I had a profound resentment toward people who thought the scientific part of it was an excuse," he would say. "I felt maligned."

Simons had always been conscious of an undercurrent of opposition even from within Manhigh, and he knew it had to do with motives. He was a medical man. He did not want to test aircraft or ride rocket sleds. He wanted data. "After I saw Kittinger and Stapp in operation," Simons explained, "I understood it [the desire to set records]. But I always felt that the record has to be secondary." He could appreciate the fact that there was room in the Manhigh program for more than one set of motivations—and that many people had made vital contributions to the program's success. Still, it galled him to be lumped in with the record-setters.

For Simons, the most important work of *Manhigh II* was still to come: the laborious sifting and analyzing of the data. And there was bad news on that front right away. Shortly after the flight, Duke Gildenberg tried to listen to one of the voice tape-recordings. The recorder used on the flight was one of the earliest portable tape recorders and had never inspired high confidence. Sure enough, the tape Gildenberg selected was blank. As it turned out, not all of the tapes were blank, but several were either blank or badly garbled. It was a serious blow. Since a big part of the flight's purpose had been to gather information on the effects of space travel on the pilot, the pilot's spoken observations, it could be argued, were some of the most important data of all.

But there was worse news. An accountant from Winzen Research informed Simons and Stapp that all of the funds the company had put up on behalf of *Manhigh II* had been exhausted. There was not even enough left to maintain a skeleton staff to organize and document the raw data. In fact, the project had racked up a $60,000 cost overrun. They were dead broke.

In early October, a dejected David Simons traveled to Barcelona to attend the annual conference of the International Astronautical Federation, where he presented a paper describing his experiences in the stratosphere. While the conference was in session, on October 4, an international news story broke that would, in short order, breathe new life not only into Project Manhigh, but into the entire field of space research and exploration—just as surely as it would rock the faith of the American public in the superiority of its own scientific and military know-how. The Russians, ahead of the United States in rocket technology, had succeeded in launching a 200-pound satellite called *Sputnik* into orbit around the earth. This aluminum-plated sphere with collapsible antennae circled the globe once every 90 minutes and would remain in orbit for 92 days.

Less than a month later, *Sputnik II* was fired into orbit. This satellite was larger, over 1,100 pounds, and, in addition to a number of scientific measurement devices, it included a pressurized compartment and a passenger: a dog named Laika. *Sputnik II* was much heavier and went twice as high as the first satellite. This one remained in an elliptical orbit for 163 days. The world was in awe; the Soviet public was jubilant. Sergei Korolev, the genius behind the intercontinental rockets propelling the celebrated payloads into space, looked to the future: "The time will come when a spacecraft carrying human beings will leave the earth and set out on a voyage to distant planets—to remote worlds. . . . The way to the stars is open."

In preparation for the International Geophysical Year, an 18-month period from the summer of 1957 through December of 1958, President Eisenhower announced in 1955 that the United States planned to establish artificial Earth satellites as part of its contribution. The IGY was intended to carry on the tradition of organized international scientific cooperation that had begun with the International Polar Year in the late nineteenth century. The period of 1957–58 had been selected because of the unusually high sunspot activity expected during that time. But while the Soviets had pursued the goal of earth orbit relentlessly, the United States had squandered its own scientific and engineering talent in a fruitless series of debates, false starts, and bureaucratic bickering. The biggest roadblock to American success had been the political incorrectness of the entire field of space research. Until *Sputnik,* "space" had continued to be the dirtiest of dirty words, and U.S. scientists who knew what it would take to put objects into orbit could not get funding or even serious attention from their government. When Dr. Hugh Dryden was appointed deputy administrator of NASA in 1958, he recalled the pre-Sputnik days: "If you mentioned the word *space,* your appropriations would be cut for wasting the people's money on foolish things."

George Trimble, who was vice-president of engineering for the Martin Company at the time, shocked the panel at a congressional hearing in 1959 when he explained why the national space program found itself in second place:

> Almost 12 years ago a group of people with whom I was associated designed a large vehicle capable of orbiting the Earth. . . . With the clarity of hindsight, it can now be said that the machine would have worked well, that the Space Age would have been ushered in five to six years earlier. . . . None of us went ahead with the job because the American people decided not to. We did not know how to sell it to them.

It was a catch-22. The Department of Defense had a "show me" policy that required anyone submitting funding requests to prove the practicality and usefulness of the idea, but no idea was judged practical unless it was already part of DOD's agenda. Ironically, the turgid bureaucracy that the West associated with the Soviet system had crippled American efforts to put a satellite into orbit. "In a sense," aviation and astronautics authority Martin Caidin would write, "we might say that the United States presented a huge scientific-political boycott of the future."

Sputnik had surprised nearly everyone but the U.S. scientific community and top officials in the government. Aware of Soviet progress, they had systematically kept that information to themselves. Even after October 4, 1957, the government continued to con the American people by publicly denigrating the Russians' achievement. A spokesman for the Office of Naval Research claimed that *Sputnik* was just "a hunk of iron"; the United States could have sent its own satellite up at any time, he insisted, but simply saw no reason to do so. Eisenhower himself said that the Russians had only succeeded because they "captured all the German scientists in Peenemunde" after the war—an ironically embarrassing charge since all the key Peenemunde men, including Wernher von Braun, had already surrendered to the Americans before the Russians arrived. In fact, down in Huntsville, von Braun and the Army had for some time been begging government officials for permission to carry out their own satellite program. But a combination of xenophobia (von Braun had become a U.S. citizen in 1955 but was still considered an ex-Nazi), a reluctance to entrust space exploration to the military, and lobbying efforts by General Electric, who was the contractor for the Navy's competing Vanguard program, kept "our" Germans on the sidelines.

Even if *Sputnik* had not come as a complete surprise, it succeeded in making everyone in the West—including government officials—very nervous. Within days after the launch of *Sputnik I,* Eisenhower assured the American public that these achievements by the Soviets in no way implied any shift in the military balance of power. But he also sounded a warning: "We could fall behind, unless we now face up to certain pressing requirements and set out to meet them at once." The Cold War, which had become the unchallenged central theme of national politics since at least 1949 when the Soviets exploded their first atomic bomb, was still running full tilt, and the *Sputniks* invested Nikita Khrushchev's icy prediction of the year before with a new chill. "We will bury you," he had promised the West.

On January 31, 1958, a year that would be fraught with ominous international conflict, a fraying around the edges of the balance of powers (the U.S. invasion of Lebanon, the bombing of Quemoy and Matsu by the new Communist power in China, Fidel Castro's seizure of Cuba), the United States put its first satellite, *Explorer I,* built by the Jet Propulsion Lab at the California Institute of Technology, into orbit. A few months later the Russians countered with *Sputnik III.* This one contained a small laboratory's worth of scientific instrumentation and would remain in orbit for nearly two years. Outer space had become an arena of the Cold War, and technological achievement had become a full-scale political battle.

Shortly after the *Sputnik* story broke, Simons received an urgent cable from Brig. Gen. Don Flickinger, assistant for bioastronautics at the ARDC headquarters in Baltimore, ordering him back to the States. Flickinger, Simons would say, "spoke our language" (although not every-one connected with Manhigh shared this opinion; some saw Flickinger as a prescient careerist who gambled that his support of space research would eventually pay dividends). With Russian hardware circling the planet and transmitting its celebrated "beeps" back to Earth, Pentagon opposition to space research was fading fast.

A conference was quickly convened to consider the question of putting a man in space. Or, more to the point, of putting an *American* in space. In spite of the Russian lead in rocketry, and in spite of the DOD's neglect of the Air Force's biomedical research efforts, the United States felt that it retained a significant advantage in the field of space biology and space medicine. If this was true, the advantage had been maintained thanks largely to the high-altitude balloon programs. The practice of using rock-ets to send research animals into the stratosphere had been discontinued in the United States in May of 1952, while the Soviets had continued apace with hundreds of their own animal rocket flights. But now that the *Sputnik* gauntlet had been thrown, the animal rocket shots were soaring from the New Mexico sands again by 1958. Research balloon launches would also be stepped up. A heavy increase in UFO sightings in the months following *Sputnik* can be attributed only partly to paranoid hyste-ria, for the atmosphere was fairly flooded with the otherworldly-looking plastic balloons.

After the conference in Baltimore, General Flickinger called Simons aside and ordered him to return to Holloman and complete analysis of the *Manhigh II* data. The funds, he promised, would be made available. Where only a few weeks before, "space" had been a fool's epithet in the struggle to garner money from the Air Force, it suddenly looked like the passkey that could unlock the golden coffers. Flickinger would go on to champion the Air Force's "Man in Space Soonest" program (which would evolve into Project Mercury). And in the wake of *Sputnik,* both the Army and the Navy also rushed to release funds for programs that might lead, eventu-ally, to putting a man in space. In addition, Flickinger told Simons, Project

Manhigh should begin preparations for a third manned stratospheric balloon flight to be scheduled sometime during the following year.

"The people who had opposed me earlier," Simons observed, "were suddenly telling me how to do it." There were new stakes, higher stakes. There were political, perhaps moral, implications.

"The real challenge we face," Sen. William Fulbright announced, "involves the very roots of our society. It involves our educational system, the source of our knowledge and cultural values." Manhigh would, at least for a while, be on the very forefront of America's drive to put one of its own into space.

For David Simons, this looked like resurrection.

Manhigh II had proved a number of important points. Yes, a human, when properly trained and equipped, can survive in a space environment. You can keep him warm, give him an atmosphere to breathe, protect him from the extremes of temperature, isolate him from the effects of a vacuum. The flight had reached a ceiling altitude of 102,000 feet; the altimeter on the gondola that had indicated a much higher mark had been in error. And while Simons had not literally entered outer space, he had experienced the *de facto* equivalent. For the most part, the communications and telemetering systems had functioned properly. There had been some problems with overheating of the cabin and condensation on the portholes of the gondola, and some problems with the partial-pressure suit, but these were imminently solvable. Still, as Simons culled the data and listened to what survived of the voice tapes, he understood that a very large question remained unanswered, one that would require a very detailed answer before any serious effort to launch a human into outer space could proceed: How do you pick the pilot and, once you have picked him, how much decision-making power do you give him? Under what conditions do you rescind that power? Maj. Charles Berry, an Air Force physician who would later go on to work with NASA's Mercury astronauts, had studied human response to prolonged isolation and concluded, in a paper published in the spring of 1958, that "the psychological problems presented by the exposure of man to an isolated, uncomfortable void seem to be more formidable than the physiological problems."

Simons recalled Kittinger's "come and get me" response on *Manhigh I,* and he recalled his own experience with the breakaway phenomenon. What might happen to a man, psychologically, aboard an orbiting space vehicle? Could he be trusted to make rational decisions? What about fatigue and wild fluctuations in temperature? How big a role would stress play in the effectiveness of a space pilot? What effect did the artificial breathing atmosphere have on the brain over a period of time?

These were the questions that a third *Manhigh* flight might be able to answer. The chief focus would no longer be on the hardware or cosmic rays or the ozone layer, but squarely on the human element (both physiological and psychological), on human processes and human dynamics. The entire Manhigh program from this point on would have to test not balloons or capsules, but *humans* and the way they interacted with each other. This was, at least to Simons's way of thinking, a tougher question. But it was one that was right up his alley.

Unfortunately for Simons, just as the planning for *Manhigh III* kicked into high gear, John Paul Stapp was abruptly reassigned to Wright-Patterson Air Force Base and Col. Rufus Hessberg replaced him as chief of the Aeromedical Field Laboratory at Holloman. It is unclear why this action was taken at this particular time. Some suspected General Flickinger of a personal vendetta against Stapp (the Revenge of the Mahogany Desks); others believed that unnamed powerbrokers in the Air Force had become nervous about all the bootleg research out in the desert and wanted to put a damper on the "frontier mentality" of programs like Manhigh.

Simons, who had hoped to succeed Stapp as chief of the Aeromed Lab, was retained as project officer for Manhigh, but he no longer controlled the program. And he no longer had a boss willing to run interference for the zealots possessed by the missionary spirit, willing to hide the true believers in his own shadow while they pulled crazy stunts that tended to scare the hell out of the bureaucrats. The bootleg days at Holloman were over, he realized—probably for good. One Air Force man who had worked in the Aeromed Lab both before and after the reign of Stapp and Simons describes what Hessberg's arrival meant to space research (not Hessberg personally, but the forces that eliminated Stapp and installed their own in his place), and takes issue with the notion that the Air Force embraced the idea of space travel following the flight of *Sputnik:*

At this time no decent, intelligent, sane Air Force officer would find his hat over there in that damn place. Those guys over there were proud to be doing what they were doing—they knew they were different—and there were thousands of people on that base who'd go a long way to go around that damn place. They wouldn't volunteer for any of the flights. . . . They were scared to death to be associated with it. There's no way to convey this now. Buck Rogers! They used to make fun of you. . . . And it was a long time, not until after *Mercury,* that it changed. . . . So Hessberg was sent down here to get 'em to QUIT ALL THIS SHIT! And the project that he didn't want to have was *Manhigh.*

While Stapp and Simons had never really seen eye to eye, with Stapp gone Simons was left exposed. In spite of his brilliance, David Simons had never been a very popular figure as the project leader for Manhigh. And the celebrity that attended his monumental flight in *Manhigh II* did not help endear him to his colleagues. A thick cloud of professional jealousy hung in the air following the Manhigh flights. It wasn't only Joe Kittinger and John Paul Stapp who had had disagreements with Simons. Duke Gildenberg explains, "There was a personality conflict between Simons and everybody else. Dave was great at his stuff, but he was so involved with it, he didn't know how to handle the people involved."

So while Simons (now a lieutenant colonel) would continue to play a key role in the Manhigh program—the Air Force could not afford to waste Simons's expertise and depth of knowledge—he would no longer pull the strings and make the whole thing dance.

At Holloman, planning for the next Manhigh flight began in earnest. One of the goals would be to formalize the process for selecting the pilot. Manhigh would essentially develop a procedure for the eventual selection of pilots—or *astronauts,* as they would come to be called—for orbital flight.

But before the pilot for this third Manhigh flight could be selected, another question loomed: Who would select him? And what criteria should be used? of it. A few years earlier, Flickinger participated in a symposium sponsored by *Collier's* magazine that considered the selection criteria for space travelers. There was some speculation that perhaps drugs and hypnosis might be employed to probe for characteristics like ingenuity, intelligence, judgment, and courage. In fact, batteries of astronaut qualification tests had already been envisioned in great detail by the Army (von Braun) and the Air Force (Strughold, Haber, Henry, and Stapp). But until Manhigh, it was all mere theory. "What we're looking for," the *Collier's* symposium concluded, "are people with specific attributes and unusually stable personalities."

The notion of a scientific "panel of experts" that would assume ultimate responsibility for making decisions during the flight grew out of conversations between David Simons and Capt. George Ruff, an Air Force psychiatrist. If it was impossible to give irrevocable decision-making control to the pilot—and the lessons of the earlier flights pointed to this conclusion—then those in whom this power would be vested must be selected as carefully as the pilot himself.

But what expertise would this scientific panel of experts need? After some debate, a panel was assembled by Colonel Hessberg. David Simons would be retained in the role of flight surgeon, monitoring and evaluating the medical condition of the pilot. He would also act as director of the panel of experts. George Ruff would act as consulting psychiatrist should any human stress–related emergencies arise. Capt. Eli Beeding, who had worked with Stapp on the rocket-sled deceleration experiments and who had been considered as a Manhigh pilot himself, was selected as the panel's physiologist. Duke Gildenberg would continue in his role as Manhigh's meteorologist. Vera Winzen directed the group of civilian contractors working with the Air Force; this group included Lee Lewis, the former Navy Strato-Lab pilot, who would be in charge of the balloon itself and the launch process. Dr. Herman Yagoda would bring his expertise in cosmic radiation to the panel. Donald Foster was named project engineer and was assisted by Vern Baumgartner. Others were added who could offer intimate knowledge of upper-altitude sky brightness, astrophysics, and astronomy. The idea was to provide a composite brain for the flight; the pilot would essentially be the eyes and ears and hands. Observations would be relayed to the panel of experts by the pilot, and the panel would in turn act on that information and send orders to the pilot.

This strategy would not only invest the *Manhigh III* flight with a level of scientific knowledge and decision-making expertise that would be impossible to obtain in a single pilot, it would also relieve the pilot of the enormous responsibility for a continuous series of critical decisions. The pilot, in fact, would not be required to have any particular scientific or technical knowledge at all.

One notable absence from the panel of experts was Otto Winzen. Two months earlier, Winzen and a Holloman scientist, Air Force captain

Grover Schock,* were badly injured in a balloon crash near Ashland, Wisconsin. Winzen and Schock were both considered serious candidates to make the third Manhigh flight—in fact, Simons had originally recommended them to General Flickinger as the most promising candidates—and were working to complete their gas-balloon pilot training in a Winzen-built training gondola called the Sky-Car. In an attempt to land before winds swept the balloon out over Lake Superior, the envelope was manually cut loose prematurely and the gondola fell about 100 feet to the ground. "Somebody panicked," Vera Winzen said. "I don't know whether it was Otto or Schock." An Air Force observer in a C-47 reported that the balloonists had overvalved and gotten themselves into a dangerous pattern of up-down oscillations and lost control of the aircraft. Schock was an inexperienced lighter-than-air pilot and Winzen's expertise was mostly with ground launch crews. Winzen also reportedly had a great fear of landing in water. As the balloon approached the lake, he removed the cover from the cut-down switch, and then separated the gondola. The two men, strapped into their seats, free-fell and the impact snapped the bones in Schock's legs and in one of Winzen's wrists. It also literally turned Schock's heart around, nearly closing the aorta. Winzen was in serious condition when he was admitted to a local hospital a few hours later, but Schock got the worst of it: in addition to the heart and leg damage, his throat was slashed open and he suffered a variety of head, back, and stomach injuries. He was listed in critical condition. Both men survived, but both would be confined to hospital beds as the final preparations were made for *Manhigh III*.

The same requirements that had been placed on both Kittinger and Simons were retained for pilot candidates for this third flight: 24-hour

---

*Working in the Holloman zero-gravity program in the early fifties, Schock pioneered simulating subgravity conditions underwater in the indoor swimming pool at Alamogordo's School for the Visually Handicapped. He lowered into the deep end of the pool a 600-pound iron contraption featuring a chair that could be rotated horizontally around a pole that itself could be positioned at any desired angle along a huge arc above the chair. By blindfolding subjects in this subgravity environment and slowly manipulating their position with respect to the "horizon," Schock was able to show that human beings quickly lose their spatial orientation as the body's mechano-receptors lose their coordination. Schock published his findings in a landmark paper titled "Some Observations of Orientation and Illusions When Exposed to Sub and Zero Gravity," which earned him the nation's first doctorate in space physiology.

confinement (or claustrophobia) test, high-altitude pressure chamber test in a partial-pressure suit, Civil Aeronautics Administration free balloon pilot's license, and a parachute jump. But new requirements were added. In addition to a detailed preselection interview and a complete physical evaluation, candidates for *Manhigh III* were required to undergo a rigorous psychological/psychiatric evaluation, a physiological stress-response test, and a grueling centrifuge multigravity-response test.

The preselection interview, while concerned with the candidate's basic scientific knowledge and his medical and family history, was conducted primarily to determine motivation. The interview probed at the subject's values and tried to determine why he wanted to go up in the Manhigh capsule. Did he want to explore new frontiers and contribute to the advancement of science, or did he want to prove to the world how tough he was? Was he a team player or a cowboy?

Once six good candidates had emerged from the preselection interview, they were given routine flight physicals and then sent to the Lovelace Clinic in Albuquerque to be subjected to a four-day evaluation. On the basis of this detailed battery of tests, one of the candidates was disqualified for a combination of excess body weight, potential heart trouble, and less-than-perfect eyesight. Another was disqualified for moderate high-frequency deafness, moderate difficulty distinguishing red from green, high blood cholesterol, and being physically too large to fit comfortably into the capsule. The examination process was thorough and unforgiving.

The remaining candidates proceeded to the claustrophobia and pressure chamber tests, followed by the psychological and psychiatric observations. Next came the physiological stress-response testing, supervised by Capt. Charles Wilson. Candidates were required to do curious things like submerge their bare feet in a bucket of ice water and keep them there for seven minutes while pulse and blood pressure were monitored. They had to log time in a "heat box" while fatigue response was measured. Candidates were denitrogenized on 100 percent oxygen and told to exhale into a pressure-resistant tube at a 40,000-foot equivalent air pressure. This tested resistance to hypoxia and cardiovascular response in a low-pressure environment.

Another potential Manhigh pilot was eliminated from consideration following this series of procedures. The three remaining candidates proceeded to the human centrifuge, a high-tech version of the world's most gut-wrenching carnival ride. The centrifuge's big arm could whip the subject around at tremendous speeds, testing reaction to increasingly heavy G-forces and gauging any tendency toward motion sickness.

Taken together, the candidate qualification process was an exhausting and exhaustive regimen. The remaining candidates had all performed remarkably well over the many days and weeks of probing, testing, and confinement. But by the time it was over, a clear favorite had emerged. Candidate D had distinguished himself in a number of ways. He had demonstrated an exceptionally high maximum breathing capacity and had consistently outperformed the other candidates during the stress and response testing. He proved himself alert and effective even under extreme conditions and he demonstrated a remarkable ability to evaluate his own performance under tremendous strain. He also exhibited a carefully dispassionate maturity that would bode well in emergencies. Following the 24-hour confinement test, this candidate was asked his impressions.

> It . . . wasn't a matter of whether you had to grit your teeth and bear it, hold yourself or anything, it was just a difficult job and you just had to sit there and do it. I never forced myself to do it; if I had had to, I would have come out of there because I don't think you should go on the Manhigh flight when you are under that much strain.

And in the centrifuge test, whereas the other candidates had approached the process and apparatus with obvious dread and had shown real discomfort, candidate D, according to the *Manhigh III* technical report, "thoroughly enjoyed the experience, appearing disdainful, rather than awed by the acceleration, considering it a form of amusement."

Candidate D was 26-year-old 1st Lt. Clifton McClure, a ceramics engineer and pilot extraordinaire. He impressed everyone who examined him, not only with his physical health and alert composure, but with his psychological stability and his ability to withstand extreme discomfort and stress. His most evident trait, however, was an intense curiosity about all the processes, equipment, planning, and training that went into Manhigh. He wanted to touch, evaluate, and understand it all. And even though his role in the upcoming flight would be—as previously stated—the eyes, ears, and hands, this didn't imply that he was not mentally acute. In fact, more than 30 years later, David Simons would remain in awe of the qualities of McClure's mind: "I've never to this day met anybody any smarter." Duke Gildenberg was similarly impressed: "He was an absolute monster; he was great."

One member of Project Manhigh was reluctant to jump on the McClure bandwagon. Vera Winzen overheard the young lieutenant bragging about flying planes under bridges and sized him up as a daredevil. "McClure was a nice man," she admits. "There's no question that he was cooperative, willing, etcetera. He went through all the tests and you never heard a squeak or a peep out of him." Still, McClure's confidence came across to her as recklessness. And in spite of her subsequent role on the third flight's panel of experts, she had no say at all in the selection process. That was an Air Force matter. But she did have definite opinions about the result: "I think Joe Kittinger would have been the wisest choice. Joe had already been up. He knew what to expect."

By the time the lengthy selection process had delivered Clifton McClure to Project Manhigh, it was mid-September (1958) and the weather window was in danger of slamming shut on *Manhigh III*. The flight was scheduled to originate from Minnesota, in the tradition of *Manhigh I* and *II*. But according to Duke Gildenberg, the launch was going to have to occur before the end of the month due to uncertain high-altitude winds in the northern latitudes. He would guarantee nothing after the first of October. McClure's training was put on the fast track and completed on September 28. The following day, the entire crew went north to prepare for a launch from the iron mine outside of Crosby on October 1.

In a preflight press conference, McClure was offered up to the same cynical journalists who had proved so annoying to David Simons. McClure, however, managed to charm his inquisitors with his contagious optimism, his crackling energy, and his South Carolina drawl. He had been nicknamed "Demi" at birth, he said, by the doctor who delivered him, to commemorate "the first Democrat born" on the night of Franklin Roosevelt's first presidential election. He told the press how much he loved to fly (he had gotten his first pilot's license at age 11, had been a jet instructor, had flown the tricky Keplerian trajectories in an F-94C in the Holloman zero-gravity program, and was an avid sailplane pilot to boot). He told them about the time he used a small trainer to tail a flock of ducks all the way down to tree-top level for the purpose of studying natural flight formation.

McClure told reporters how much he enjoyed his Manhigh training. He had only recently graduated from Air Force pilot training and, with his heavy engineering background, McClure had feared that the Air Force would bury him in some deadly desk job somewhere. His chance meeting with John Paul Stapp—McClure's astronomy professor at Texas A&M had furnished the introduction—and subsequent invitation to try out for Manhigh had been a stroke of luck.

The invitation hadn't simply come out of the blue. McClure had worked a number of ground-pounding jobs at Holloman before Simons or Hessberg even knew his name. "It was supposed to be a detriment to your career to get assigned out there. But I didn't care what I had to do. I would've carried garbage out in the morning just to be there." He worked on a big solar furnace that was being designed to test re-entry heat loads, but he kept his sights trained upward on the space-equivalence research flights. Along with Stapp, McClure had been certain for years that humans were going into space. He had watched the progress of the first two Manhigh flights closely and had begun to burn with the desire to make his own stratospheric flight. He volunteered for baseline testing that had been done in preparation for the pilot selection process and had resolved to outperform his competition and get himself noticed.

> I started getting myself evaluated along with the rest of these people. And I beat 'em every time. That was my objective. I'd say, "Well, there's ten people who've done this." I'd look at what they'd done and I'd say, "Now, I'm going to do this at least twice as good as the best guy there." I just kept at it, and when it ended up, I was there.

And now that he had emerged from the selection process and the training, he was clearly there: in heaven. The reporters believed it when he told them that it had all been great fun. Except for the practice flight in Davenport, Iowa, when a sniper had hopped out of a Cadillac and taken seven rifle shots at the balloon. "I'm a better shot myself," he bragged. "In fact, if I'd had a rifle with me, he might have found that out." (It's not difficult to imagine Vera Winzen on the periphery of the small crowd of reporters, in the shadows, eyes narrowed slightly, lips pursed.)

McClure later claimed that the press conference scared him much worse than anything that happened on the flight itself. And given the way the flight of *Manhigh III* went, that is a most remarkable statement.

On the morning of the twenty-ninth, McClure downed his low-residue meal, swallowed his Seconal, and went to sleep. He was awakened that

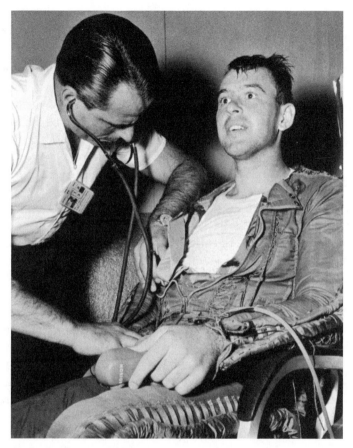

Candidate D, Clifton McClure, is examined following a claustrophobia test. "I started getting myself evaluated along with rest of these people. And I beat 'em every time. That was my objective." *(Source: USAF)*

evening and helped into the olive-green partial-pressure suit. But before the prelaunch procedure could go any further, Gildenberg announced that weather conditions had deteriorated. The launch was off.

Gildenberg and Colonel Hessberg met immediately to weigh the possibilities. The launch could be moved to New Mexico where the weather would be less of a problem, but the cosmic radiation experiments aboard the gondola would be useless, the radiation concentrations over the southwestern United States being unacceptably low. After an analysis of weather patterns, however, the decision was made to launch from

Holloman. The cosmic ray experiments were expendable. Besides, they couldn't risk infinite weather delays in Minnesota. If *Manhigh III* did not fly in October, Gildenberg warned, it likely would not fly at all that year. And if it did not fly that year, they both understood, it might not fly—period. The race to solve the puzzle of how to put a human in space was moving too quickly. If Manhigh wanted to contribute, the time was now. A few months earlier, Congress had passed the National Aeronautics and Space Act of 1958. And three days after the aborted Crosby launch, back in Washington, D.C., a new organization, a civilian space agency, the National Aeronautics and Space Administration or NASA, was formally established. NASA was the successor to the National Advisory Committee for Aeronautics (NACA), which had been founded during World War I. The NACA's charter had been "to supervise and direct the scientific study of the problems of flight, with a view to their practical solutions." Orville Wright had served on NACA's first advisory board. The initial budget for NACA had been $5,000. The new charter called for NASA to use whatever aeronautical space capabilities it could develop "for the benefit of all mankind." In contrast, the first annual budget for NASA was in the vicinity of $100 million. And NASA was not simply starting from scratch with lots of money and congressional blessing; it also inherited facilities and personnel from NACA, as well as several ongoing projects from the military including the Army's Explorer program, the Navy's Vanguard program, and the Air Force's F-1 engine program. The intention was clear: to put the nation's space-related eggs into a single bureaucratic basket.

The entire crew, along with the Manhigh gondola and the balloon and all the associated hardware, including trucks and tracking vehicles, were rushed south to Holloman. The new target date was October 6. Gildenberg declared that, in spite of a cool breeze on the evening of the fifth, the weather on launch day stood a good chance of being calm enough to launch.

Once again, McClure was fitted into the partial-pressure suit and the white helmet with the Air Force insignia above the eyes. He was lowered into the capsule, the capsule was sealed, and the interior atmosphere was flushed and refilled with the familiar mixture of oxygen, nitrogen, and helium. Dry ice was placed on top of the capsule to keep the heat down inside. The hoses were fitted to the balloon envelope and the helium pumps were started. As technicians scurried around in the eerie predawn light, prospects for a successful launch looked quite good. Lee Lewis, who had ridden the Navy's record-setting *Strato-Lab* balloon to 76,000 feet in 1956, and who now served as Winzen's operations chief, cautioned the balloon handlers and others in the vicinity to treat the envelope with special care. Only two Manhigh balloons existed, and it would take several days—not to mention a great deal of additional money—to get more balloons from Winzen Research.

By 9:00 that morning, the balloon was filling nicely. The breeze that was supposed to have died down by now, however, began to flare up and tug at the huge plastic bag. There were some nervous moments as the balloon rippled and lurched. Then, suddenly, a gust snatched the billowing polyethylene and slapped it down onto the hard pavement of the Holloman runway. There was a pause. Then the giant balloon burst. The crew stood silent, horrified, eyes raised to the morning sky watching the confetti of clear plastic flutter and dart and fall to the ground. It was a terribly disappointing moment for the entire crew that had labored so hard to make the launch of *Manhigh III* happen on schedule, but the most disappointed man on the base that day was Clifton McClure, sealed inside the gondola. McClure wanted to go up with *Manhigh III* more than he had ever wanted anything in his life. And now only a single polyethylene envelope remained.

That night, a little before midnight, McClure was once again sealed into the capsule that had been wrapped with a reflective metallic blanket that resembled tinfoil. The hangar buzzed with the familiar suite of prelaunch preparations and the Balloon Branch's information office was crowded with wire service reporters, radio and TV crews, beat writers from nearby papers, and freelance journalists working on feature stories. There was a certain heightened sense of purpose to the activities this time since everyone involved knew that the project was down to its last balloon. Once the capsule was wheeled out onto the runway and attached to the balloon, and once the helium came whistling through the tubes and inflation began, there was no turning back. Even if the balloon envelope itself was in fine shape, it could not be reused once it had been unrolled and inflated to any degree at all. It was a one-shot deal.

Before being hoisted into the gondola, McClure pleaded with Colonel Hessberg: please, for God's sake, make sure that nothing goes wrong this time. Please.

Once he was sealed inside, the capsule atmosphere flushed and reestablished, all McClure could do was wait. He settled himself into the web seat and tried to stay calm despite the tremendous anxiety he felt. His eyes ran over the instrumentation and survival equipment that surrounded him: tape recorders, cameras, light meters; spectral spot-photometers, oscillometers, cosmic ray scintillometers; measurement and recording devices to capture climatic conditions, precise altitudes, air-pressure variations; the tubes of the primary and secondary air-regeneration systems; the blower for the air-cooling system and the communications hardware. Occasionally a voice over the radio would ask for a temperature or pressure reading. At one such request, McClure turned his upper body quickly left to glance at the air pressure gauge. In so doing, his hand bumped against the emergency personal parachute, which hung on the capsule wall.

At first he could not believe it. But as he looked down onto the floor of the gondola, across his knees and around his legs, he saw hundreds of square feet of white nylon lying in folds. He had accidentally hit the tightly packed chute and the restraining pins had popped out. The parachute was now a useless pile of fabric. Ironically, McClure and others had opposed the presence of the personal chute in the *Manhigh III* capsule in the first place. They argued that the large cargo chute between the gondola and the envelope was a sufficient safeguard against a balloon failure. But after Hessberg had been given control of the project, he insisted on the parachute's inclusion. "Hessberg was a parachutist," McClure explained.

> He felt that a personal parachute offered additional safety, but what it did was compromise everything about the project. The way they'd designed this cabin, it was the smallest cabin a man could occupy and still do anything. If they could have made it smaller, they would have. It was a design requirement. They knew they were going to have trouble in space flight with weight and volume. There wasn't anything about it at all in the way of size. And that parachute was hanging right there in the only space I had. God, I hated it when he handed me that damn thing.

McClure did not report the parachute incident right away. He was too appalled to speak. Due to the position of the capsule and the placement of the portholes, no one outside could see the lower section of the interior. Technicians continued to scurry around the capsule and out onto the runway. McClure weighed the options. Then he stepped on the microphone switch and asked for Hessberg. The voice of Capt. Eli

McClure before being sealed into the gondola: "It was the smallest cabin a man could occupy and still do anything. If they could have made it smaller, they would have." *(Source: USAF)*

Beeding crackled through the radio and asked what he wanted. McClure hesitated.

If he answered and reported what had happened, Hessberg would have no choice but to cancel the flight. The decision would be automatic. The capsule would be opened and the entire procedure would have to begin again, probably the next day or the next. He was not sure whether the balloon envelope had been rolled out. If they were forced to start over, they could be grounded by weather again. Duke Gildenberg was forecasting deteriorating conditions over the upcoming days. Who knew how many more chances were in the cards?

I was the only person that was physically in a position to evaluate the possibilities of repack; anyone else would be required to make a deliberate safety-of-flight compromise with another man's life, and this is no decision. I brushed off Captain Beeding's answer and withdrew into the loneliest corner that I could find during the entire flight. I felt immediate repugnation [*sic*] toward my decision not to tell Captain Beeding because dishonesty seemed to lurk in such a decision, yet I knew at the same time that, again, I was the only person alive that had a decision in the matter.

He closed his eyes and recalled one particular day of his Manhigh training. He had been practicing with the capsule when he had noticed someone unpacking and repacking the personal parachute. There was no need for the pilot to bother himself with the procedure for packing it, but McClure's curiosity had gotten the best of him. He had never packed a parachute himself and he watched carefully as the chute was packed. He asked questions. He saw how it was done, how the folds were handled, how the lines were gathered and tucked.

Now, leaning over, McClure began to try to impose some semblance of order on the mass of material. Captain Beeding noticed the pilot's strange position. He picked up the radio microphone.

"You okay in there?" he asked.

McClure straightened. "Fine, sir."

Beeding resumed his duties and McClure returned to his own. He decided he was going to repack the chute. There was not enough room, and he did not have enough mobility in the tiny confines, trapped in the bulky pressure suit. But he did have time. Plenty of time. If he went slowly and methodically, he was certain it could be done. But he would have to do it right, and he would have to do it without alerting anyone outside the gondola.

Two hours later, documenting every step of the process on the portable tape recorder and stopping occasionally to read gauges and answer questions over the radio, McClure had the chute folded into what he was confident was the proper configuration to be loaded into the pack. With the parachute pack up on the wall, it required a great deal of strength to push the burgeoning nylon into the pack far enough to allow the restraining pins to be inserted. McClure strained awkwardly, pushing as hard as he could. Finally, he succeeded in slipping both pins into place. The chute was packed. He sighed and slumped back into the seat.

It was now 3:30. There was still some time before dawn. He turned

The inflation of *Manhigh III.* Clifton McClure, sealed in the gondola at left, awaits his shot at the stratosphere. *(Source: USAF)*

his eyes back to the chute and noticed something. The restraining pins were in backwards. Backwards! He had struggled so hard to work them into place that he had neglected to orient them first. He touched each pin lightly. He was not sure if it would make a difference. He debated.

Then, wearily, McClure pulled the pins and began again. By 5:00, he was finally done. The chute hung squarely on its hook on the gondola wall, perfectly packed and properly secured.

At 6:51, *Manhigh III* lifted off into the sparkling clear of a bright blue sky just as the first rays of the rising sun crept over rugged Sacramento Peak. Inflation had gone without a hitch and cool, calm weather had prevailed over the Tularosa Basin. The launch procedure complete, the panel of experts boarded the Air Force bus that would serve as a command center during the flight. The bus was equipped with a speaker system that allowed the experts to listen to McClure's voice communications. If anyone needed to talk to McClure, he could step out of the bus and into the communications van where a microphone was available. A C-47 outfitted with a conference table, microphones, and headsets sat on the tarmac nearby. The plane would serve as an airborne command center in the event that the balloon drifted off course and out of radio range of Holloman.

At 24,000 feet, McClure reported a capsule temperature of 89°. This raised some eyebrows in the command bus. After some discussion, it was agreed that the high reading could probably be explained by the fact that the temperature gauge had been positioned directly above the air generation system and was measuring the incidental heat of that system rather than the true temperature of the gondola. In fact, more serious trouble was brewing. For reasons that are not entirely clear, the CO_2 cap on the gondola had not been replenished before launch, and the gondola had left the ground with a mostly evaporated quantity of dry ice. In spite of the fact that the dry ice had worked well for both Kittinger and Simons and had kept them relatively cool until the water-can stratospheric air conditioner had kicked in at higher altitudes, this detail was neglected for McClure's flight. And coupled with the excess heat generated inside the capsule—and the partial-pressure suit—by McClure's parachute-packing activities, temperature control threatened to become a major issue.

Manhigh III passed through the tropopause with its 50-MPH winds and −73° temperature without incident. At 90,000 feet, McClure spoke to David Simons:

> I see a blanket like a halo or a glow from a fluorescent tube where the horizon should be—but I can't find the horizon. The halo is shaded into a band of blue like the normal sky. But a few degrees higher it fades into still deeper blue, and then ten or fifteen degrees higher into black, almost complete black—the black gets darker and darker.

McClure, his excitement rising as he surveyed the scene, continued his description, striving for objectivity but occasionally lapsing into the same awestruck gush of words that had characterized Simons's reports:

> I see the most fantastic thing, the sky that you described. It's blacker than black, but it's saturated with blue like you said. I honestly can't describe it to you. I'm looking at it, but it seems more like I'm *feeling* it. It's literally indescribable! Then as I look upward there's this huge brightly white balloon and completely surrounding it this blackness so much darker than what I used to think was black. I have the feeling that I should be able to see stars in this darkness but I can't find them either—I have the feeling that this black is *so* black it has put the stars out!

He had anticipated it and tried to imagine what it would be like, but it was more spectacular, more mysterious than he had been able to envision. It was a supreme privilege to be where he was, seeing the things that he was seeing, and he was determined to drink in every detail, every subtlety.

By 10:00, McClure was floating at 99,600 feet. Because the balloon was drifting toward the northwest much faster than had been anticipated, the panel of experts boarded the C-47 shortly after noon. Onboard *Manhigh III,* McClure ate lunch. But he did not have any of the bootleg diet of cheeseburgers or standard-issue rations that had sustained Simons on *Manhigh II.* This time, the Air Force nutritional lab at Wright Field had prepared meals that could be eaten in a weightless environment. The foods had all been creamed and packed into neat toothpaste-size tubes. Not too appetizing, but efficient. After lunch, McClure made a series of observations with the heavy spot-photometer aboard the gondola. He reported feeling fatigue at about this point, but no one on the ground was concerned.

A little later, as McClure began to give his regular pilot report, his voice was noticeably sluggish. He reported the reading of the suspect capsule temperature gauge. It now read several degrees above 90.

Simons immediately asked for a body temperature reading. McClure reported: "101.4."

There was near panic in the C-47 that was now airborne, tracking the balloon. The tension level among the panel of experts was almost off the chart. Duke Gildenberg's assessment of the drama of the situation: "It was like a Hollywood movie."

Eli Beeding swore and asked for a recheck. McClure read his temperature again: "It's 101.4." A gauge on his suit provided a constant reading from a rectal thermometer.

Simons informed the rest of the panel of experts that they might be in serious trouble. If the capsule temperature readings were even close to correct, the close-fitting partial-pressure suit might induce fever. He told McClure to check the mercury thermometer stored in the dry-bulb temperature-humidity kit. They needed to know with certainty how hot it was in the gondola. Simons also ordered McClure to drink some water immediately.

Unfortunately for McClure, he could not get any water to come from the drinking-water container through the tube. He sucked hard on the tube, but it was no use. He got out the dry-bulb kit and reported the reading on the thermometer. Simons cringed when he heard it: "97 degrees." The capsule was becoming an oven.

The panel of experts huddled. George Ruff explained that his rule of thumb when conducting stress tests had always been to stop when the subject's temperature began to climb. It was a clear danger signal that could not be ignored. McClure was already severely overheated. There was no question. *Manhigh III* should descend right away.

Hessberg asked whether or not McClure might be able to tolerate the temperature until sunset when the lack of radiant heat would help bring it down. Could he last until dark? Simons said no. It was still six hours until sundown. No human being could tolerate the kind of heat McClure was experiencing for that amount of time and retain any efficiency at all. Even remaining conscious would be a struggle. Simons agreed with Ruff: McClure would have to come down. Now.

Lee Lewis suggested that McClure might unhook the hose from the fan to the air regeneration system and try to blow cool air into the pressure suit. It was a trick Lewis had used with some success on an overheated Strato-Lab flight two years earlier. But when this was suggested to McClure, the panel learned that McClure had already thought of it himself and tried it. Unfortunately, he reported, the air blowing through the hose was hot. However, he had managed to get the drinking water system working again and had gulped down several mouthfuls of cool water. It seemed to help.

McClure called down to the panel of experts. He told them that he was aware they had some real problems. But he also told them that in spite of the heat, he was feeling okay. A little tired, maybe, but aware and in control. And although the capsule temperature was continuing to rise, he said he was sure he could hold out until sundown.

"I don't want to come down," he said. "Repeat. I don't want to come down."

Simons, speaking as flight surgeon, firmly repeated his advice to the panel. *Manhigh III* must begin to descend immediately. To wait any longer was to take a terrible risk. After a brief moment, Hessberg nodded. It was agreed. But before the order to descend was given, George Ruff questioned how McClure would react. Was he under so much stress that he might act unpredictably to disappointing news? They were all very aware of how badly McClure wanted to stay in the stratosphere.

In the meantime, McClure was peppering the panel of experts with his own barrage of probing questions aimed at assessing *their* state of mind. McClure could plainly hear the stress in the voices that spoke to him and he initiated a volley of psychological give-and-take designed to reveal whether *they* were panicking or not, and whether *they* were acting rationally. Were they overreacting? Could he trust them to make a sound decision? What clues were they looking for in him and how were they interpreting them?

The panel had an additional dilemma on its hands. The preflight briefing had made it clear that the panel would allow McClure to call the shots only until an emergency intervened. The problem was that the briefing had also stressed that the panel would be completely honest with the pilot on all matters. The experts would not keep important information from McClure. They would not attempt to shield him from the facts, no matter how sobering. And they would never, under any circumstances, mislead him.

These promises were now put to the test as both sides—McClure on the one hand and the panel on the other—struggled to evaluate the other. Hessberg radioed McClure and told him to descend into the tropopause. The air moving past the gondola might help cool things off, he said. But he did not tell McClure the whole truth, that the panel had already made the decision to terminate the flight. It was a clear violation of the briefing agreement.

McClure objected immediately, as if he sensed the message behind the message. He would not be able to descend far enough fast enough to do any good, he said. The best thing would be to remain at altitude and wait for nightfall. He again requested permission to remain in the stratosphere.

Hessberg said no. McClure tried again to argue his case. After a moment, Simons grabbed the microphone. He told McClure that it was medically necessary for him to come down. There was no choice. It was a direct order.

There was a silence from *Manhigh III,* sitting now at a peak altitude of 99,700 feet.

The premature descent created a number of special problems for McClure, and for those on the ground. The two most alarming were the fact that *Manhigh III* was now going to touch down at night, very possibly in remote, mountainous terrain, and that Clifton McClure might very well be unconscious when he landed. As he valved gas to begin the descent, his body temperature had climbed to 104.1° and metal surfaces inside the capsule were already hot enough to blister skin. His vision swam, fading in and out.

Somehow, McClure maintained consciousness. Meanwhile, the C-47 had landed at a small airstrip on the western edge of the White Sands Missile Range in order to direct the balloon's descent.

At 4:00, *Manhigh III* was still at 85,000 feet. The capsule temperature was registering 118°, as high as the gauge could go; McClure's body temperature had reached 105.2. The panel of experts—and David Simons in particular, who understood that devastating brain damage was also a possibility—feared for their pilot's life. It was a brutal combination of heat and stress. How much could a man tolerate? McClure's radio transmissions were punctuated now by weak grunts and groans.

Back in the information office at Holloman, the press had begun to buzz. They had gotten word that the cooling system aboard the gondola was not working properly and that McClure might be in some kind of danger, but no details were available. Nearby, another interested party was following the fate of Clifton McClure and *Manhigh III*. In a small Alamogordo back yard, young Laurie McClure stayed glued to the eyepiece of the telescope with which she and Clifton had so often watched stars and satellites. Laurie had tracked the entire flight of *Manhigh III,* and still had the balloon in sight as it began the long, torturous descent. Luckily, she was not aware of the extreme heat situation onboard the gondola or the grim council of the project's experts as they debated how best to try to save her husband's life.

The panel of experts considered the possibility of remotely blowing away the balloon and dropping the gondola under the big drogue chute. This would mean a 20-MPH crash landing, however. And since the balloon was currently directly above the jagged peaks of the San Andres Mountains, the plan entailed additional risks. For one, the thin alloy shell might crumple and crush the pilot against a wall of rock. For another, the harsh chemicals used in the air regeneration system (potassium hydroxide and lithium hydroxide) might leak out and burn McClure. Lee Lewis could attest to the possibility: both he and copilot Malcolm Ross had been burned by similar chemicals following a crash landing on one of their Navy balloon flights.

Hessberg decided not to cut the balloon away unless they were sure that McClure had lost consciousness. If that occurred, McClure would not be able to trip the switch to cut away the balloon once he was back on the ground. The gondola might be dragged over a cliff or across the rocky desert floor. But as long as he was awake and aware, it would be better to wait and hope that he could ride it out.

Shortly after 5:00, voice radio transmission sputtered and cut off completely. The communications system had malfunctioned, apparently somewhere on the ground. Even the Morse code that had come in handy for Kittinger was not an option. There was now no way to know whether McClure was conscious or not.

Simons checked the telemetered readings. Body temperature was an almost unbelievable 107° Fahrenheit. But looking at the relatively normal and fairly steady heart-rate and respiration numbers convinced him that McClure might indeed still be conscious.

Aboard *Manhigh III*, the feverish Clifton McClure was not only still conscious but was monitoring his rate of descent and managing the touchy ballasting operation as he had been trained. Unfortunately, most of the ballast switches were not operating by the time he passed through the tropopause. He was able to slow his rate of descent to 900 feet per second, but that was all. It would be a very hard landing. He considered bailing out with his personal parachute, the one he had struggled to repack, but he doubted whether he had the strength to get the chute on, blow the top off the capsule, and get out safely. He decided to stay onboard and take his chances.

Things got worse. Not only was he burning up, but he had a terrible need to urinate. He had gone through the exhausting gyrations necessary to manage the operation once that morning while the capsule was still on the ground, and the prospect of repeating them now was almost too much to consider. But McClure remembered having heard that a full bladder could burst and kill a person in an impact accident. He was not sure if it was true, but it sounded possible. So he spent several long excruciating minutes extricating himself from the partial-pressure suit in the cramped space, careful not to jostle the personal parachute, and managed, finally, to pee in a bottle. When he was through, the effort left him almost completely sapped of energy.

It was dark now, too dark to make out many details of the landscape below. But he could see shadowy outlines that he guessed were mountains. He flipped on the beacon light.

He knew that the highest mountains in the vicinity stood at about 12,000 feet. His altimeter now read 20,000. It would not be long. First, forcing himself to concentrate, he carefully shut the valves of the air regeneration system so that the chemicals would remain sealed inside. He switched on the emergency power system and switched off the fan and the radio. Then he had a thought and took a moment to speak into the portable tape recorder. He suggested that the prelanding procedure should include the jettisoning of any remaining liquid-oxygen tanks in order to avoid the potential fire hazard. Incredibly, with a body temperature above 107°, McClure was envisioning improvements to the system and making notes for the benefit of future flights.

The gondola dropped through 15,000 feet, then 10,000. McClure tightened his restraining straps and steeled himself for impact. He watched the altimeter.

Then came the bone-jarring thud. The gondola tipped, then righted itself. McClure quickly reached for the balloon cutaway switch and pushed it.

A helicopter carrying Lee Lewis, George Ruff, and Don Foster arrived at the landing site first. It was a good 4,000 feet up into the San Andres range. Lewis had seen the balloon drift away, so he reasoned that McClure was conscious. But he also knew that he was past the threshold of heat exhaustion and would require immediate attention.

The helicopter landed as near the gondola as possible. As Lewis, Ruff, and Foster scrambled up toward the landing site, the top of the gondola popped open and fell away. As they approached, they saw an amazing sight: Clifton McClure standing up, pulling his helmet off and . . . nobody could believe it . . . grinning!

Lewis yelled at McClure to sit down and wait for a stretcher and for George Ruff. McClure climbed out of the gondola as Ruff arrived. A stretcher? He vetoed the idea. After all, he pointed out, he had already come nearly 20 goddamn miles from the top of the stratosphere. He would walk the final few feet on his own power, thank you very much.

A quick physical back at the helicopter revealed that the remarkable candidate D had a body temperature of 108.5°. At the base hospital, McClure found David Simons and Rufus Hessberg waiting anxiously.

"I don't know what all the fuss is about," he told them. "I just started to simmer, heat up, and boil all over." He flashed a grin. "I don't have to be treated like an invalid, you know."

Joe Kittinger, who had continued to follow the progress of the Manhigh project, expressed his admiration for what McClure had accomplished: "He's the only one who could've survived. He was just a tough, tough guy and he did a great job getting down alive." Kittinger also expressed his opinion on the handling of the launch and the oversight that allowed *Manhigh III* to lift off without a sufficient dry-ice cap on top of the gondola: "It was ridiculous to send him off without that cap."

Who or what was responsible for the overheating? The Air Force admitted to unspecified problems, but declined to say what they were. An official spokesman obfuscated: "Something went wrong with our calculating about insulation and temperatures." A headline in the *Washington Star* tried to capture the drama—"Nearly Baked in AF Balloon Error"—but its reporter got no closer to the truth.

The Manhigh III technical report does not do much better. It is an odd document, in some ways a metaphor for the star-crossed flight. Rather than the focused work of a single author, as the technical reports for the first two flights had been, this one—published a full two and a half years after the flight—became a compendium of observations and speculation.

> The various chapters of this report were prepared by the individuals who were in charge of the numerous and complex tasks of this project. The reader has, therefore, the opportunity to follow the phases of the flight from different points of view. The repetitions involved in this procedure show the many difficulties encountered during the MANHIGH project, and especially during the MANHIGH III flight.

In other words, the report offers no consensus, but rather a collection of sometimes contradictory "truths."

Simons would later suggest that the exertion of the parachute-packing episode may have contributed to abnormal temperatures inside the partial-pressure suit and the gondola. In his section of the report, however, Simons states that Winzen engineers made a launch-time decision not to repack the CO_2 cap.

> Apparently because Lt. McClure was reporting a cooler, more comfortable temperature this morning than he had the day before, the contractor engineers responsible for the capsule decided not to repack the dry ice cap but to send it aloft without additional cooling. On both the previous MANHIGH FLIGHTS, this cap had been repacked with dry ice within an hour before launch.

Vera Winzen's judgment is harsh. She believes that McClure's repacking of the parachute *was* responsible for the overheating: "Essentially, he blew the experiment and he didn't tell anybody. It altered everything inside that capsule, because he expended so much energy in putting it together. I would much rather have seen him abort the flight at that point. . . . It scared us all to death."

It does not appear in his section of the report, but Clifton McClure would later claim that David Simons simply forgot to make sure that the dry ice was in place that morning. But was loading the dry ice really the job of the project officer? "Here's what happened," McClure says.

> Colonel Simons *volunteered* to pick up the CO_2. And when he did that, I heard a sergeant kind of groan under his breath. I said, "What's the matter?" And the sergeant said, "A colonel shouldn't be picking up dry ice." I said, "Why?" And he said, "Cause he'll probably forget it. Nobody can chastise him and he's got too much to do. He ought to give it to somebody else." And he was right. And so I said, "Colonel, why don't you leave that CO_2 to somebody else?" And he gave me a dirty look, you know. And that was it. *He forgot it!*

Yet McClure is uncomfortable laying the overheating of *Manhigh III* at the feet of David Simons.

> I really don't think he deserves to be criticized. . . . I think he's one of the terrific people whom I've been fortunate to know. He *was* different. If he wasn't different, he wouldn't have been there. I hate to blame Colonel Simons because there are a lot of guys getting a lot more credit that haven't done a damn thing. And that dude was out there. You can't make an error if you ain't doing anything. These type of errors? I'll take 'em any day. Because at least they're out there doing something.

One hour after *Manhigh III* touched down in the mountains, Clifton McClure's temperature was down to a manageable 100°. And by the next day, during the postflight conference, he was alert and full of the energetic curiosity that had been so apparent during the selection process. McClure sat with the panel of experts around a conference table at Holloman and discussed what had gone wrong—and what had gone right—with the flight. He told them everything he could recall about his ordeal. He tried to explain, in a stream of consciousness, how he had been able to survive the heat during the long descent. That feat was based partly on a trick he had learned while taking heat-stress tests for the Air Force baseline studies: playing dead.

I leaned over with my head against the spot photometer, and when I went to tune the transmitter or anything, I was real careful to be extremely slow, and I didn't try to do anything I knew I wouldn't have to do, and I would try to relax and go to sleep that afternoon. To think that my feet would be relaxed, to relax my hands, tried to make my back feel the same way, and my neck, just try to drop everything except what I needed. And still, I could feel my heart pounding all in the top of my head, but it was awful hot. If you know what I mean, your heart no longer beats without you knowing it and your pulse is transmitted to the brain and it kind of hammers in the top of your head, and I was real hot.

Air Force interrogators were interested in some visual images, hallucinations most likely, that McClure had reported at 95,000 feet. They asked for him to repeat what he had seen.

About two hours after 95,000, after doing a little work for you people—very little, you were so considerate—I closed my eyes again and all I could see was little blue and green flickers of light—it was generally more like an aurora or something. It was an area of light that came and went.

One of the interrogators tried to interpret. "Under stress, in fact, under extreme stress," he suggested, "some people see virtual images, but they appear so real that you can almost reach your hand out and touch them."

The response is classic McClure. "Oh, no, it was nothing like that," he assured them. "No, it wasn't any image at all—no, these were just splotches of light that came because I was so blamed hot."

In other words, the stress was a piece of cake. He could handle all the *stress* they could throw at him. It was the blamed *heat* that had been the problem.

There was general admiration for the job McClure had managed to do under heat-stress conditions that exceeded anything either Simons or Ruff had thought humanly possible. In spite of a body temperature that might have crippled or destroyed the average pilot's ability to function, McClure had not only functioned but continued to act rationally and even entertain creative thoughts. Heat-stress tests during the selection process had established individual heat/humidity tolerances based on height, weight, and a number of other factors. Each candidate had been subjected to an environment that represented 90 percent of the conditions that should result in heat prostration for that individual and then given a series of stressful tasks to perform. McClure had performed well during the tests, but what he had done on the actual flight was something else again: McClure had absorbed 137 percent of the heat his baseline said he could tolerate. Nobody could explain how he was able to do it. McClure himself suggested only that he had learned, during the preflight tests, how to exert some control over his own temperature by restricting all movements to the absolute minimum.

Ruff suggested that perhaps the project had inadvertently uncovered some very important truths about pilot selection. The Air Force's space biology experts were already generally agreed that physiological problems were nothing compared to the psychological problems faced by a man isolated in a space capsule. Maj. Charles Berry of the Aeromedical Laboratory, who would later play a key role in training the Mercury astronauts, took this knowledge with him to NASA. But the Manhigh braintrust had already identified a valuable attribute of the perfect astronaut: psychic stamina.

David Simons reflected on the lessons learned on *Manhigh III*:

An essential quality necessary to an astronaut would be stamina; not in a purely physical sense but in a psychophysiological sense: a combination of deep physical reserves plus the all-important emotional determination to use those reserves. In our selection program we tried to delve into motivation of the candidates, and we tested them almost mercilessly for pure physical potential, but we did not stress stamina, particularly psychic stamina, as a quality in itself.

The project had been lucky. In the relentlessly tough-minded Clifton McClure, the Air Force had stumbled onto the profile of the ideal space traveler. In spite of the fact that *Manhigh III* had been unable to remain at altitude for the planned duration, great value had come from the attempt.

The Manhigh program dissolved not long after the third flight. The entire Space Biology Branch of the ARDC was abolished in 1959 as the big research dollars for space exploration began to funnel toward NASA, which had little interest in plastic gas bags. Balloons had carried man to the edge of outer space; rockets would now be required to take him all the way there and place him into orbit.

Initially, following Manhigh, David Simons resumed his activities at the Air Force's School of Aerospace Medicine, continuing his work on cosmic radiation. He was forced to contend with inadequate funds, poor facilities, and meager staffs—and Simons was no master of bootleg research like John Paul Stapp. Simons believes that his divorce and subsequent marriage—to the former Vera Winzen—caused political problems that hindered his abilities to operate effectively.

While his reputation was still untarnished in the days following the celebrated flight of *Manhigh II,* Simons had been contacted by Wernher von Braun. Von Braun, who was still working for the U.S. Army, wanted Simons to help design a closed capsule for the Redstone rocket project. Simons visited the Redstone facilities and found that he and von Braun were quite compatible. They saw eye to eye on most of the technical issues surrounding the development of a manned space capsule and Simons was sure that they would make a great team. Unfortunately, the realities of interservice politics intervened. Neither the bureaucracies of the Army nor the Air Force would issue the necessary clearances that would have allowed Simons and von Braun to run the joint project they envisioned. According to Simons, "Neither branch could decide who'd get the credit."

In the months following the demise of Manhigh, Simons approached NASA with proposals for several biomedical research projects to no avail. "What I was offering was so far ahead of anything they understood, it wasn't comprehensible to them," he would say. He needed an organizational benefactor, but was unable to find anyone in charge of the medical research groups at NASA who he felt would be sympathetic.

Much of the work of Project Manhigh—the most meticulously planned and thoroughly researched series of high-altitude balloon flights in history—set the stage for NASA's exploration of space in the 1960s. Most of the key players on Manhigh were debriefed by NASA. Duke Gildenberg remembers a shift in the attitude of the press after the third flight, as if the reporters were beginning to grasp the tangible connection between these balloon ascents and honest-to-God space travel: "There were even articles in the newspapers calling us astronauts." In spite of the minor scientific contributions, and there were several, the most immediately useful results of the program were its capsule design and testing, and an entire decision-making process that would be largely inherited by Project Mercury. In fact, Mercury was in reality only a modified and expanded version of the "Man in Space Soonest" scenario.

To the Air Force personnel who worked on Manhigh, it seemed as if NASA simply took the ideas and the technologies and then claimed to have invented them. John Paul Stapp spoke for many when he charged that Manhigh originated "every system for survival that went into Mercury. They just copycatted it."

In fact, NASA got more than its survival technology from the balloon programs. In October of 1957, two months after the second Manhigh flight, the Air Force convened a secret meeting at the NACA Ames Research Center outside San Francisco to discuss the design of a proposed suborbital glide bomber called DynaSoar. At that meeting, engineer Max Faget expounded on a breakthrough concept: a man-sized, plug-shaped capsule with a flat bottom and a big cargo parachute, a vehicle capable of atmospheric re-entry, he said. That moment is considered by some to be the real genesis of the American space program, despite the fact that Manhigh had already built such a capsule and taken it into the stratosphere not once, but three times. A few months later, Otto Winzen remarked optimistically, "It is now generally recognized in scientific circles that the manned balloon capsule is the prototype of the manned space cabin." If so, the scientists kept it to themselves.

David Simons and others would continue to harbor some bitterness over the lessons learned during Manhigh that were ignored or deferred in the partisan rush to place an American on the surface of the moon. Robert Gilruth, who ran Project Mercury for NASA, claimed that high-altitude balloons were less than ideal research platforms for space applications because they simply did not simulate enough aspects of space flight—massive acceleration, zero gravity, atmospheric re-entry.

In spite of the fact that Manhigh had worked out an effective and safe artificial capsule atmosphere in which oxygen was mixed with nitrogen and helium, NASA would continue to pressurize its space capsules with 100 percent oxygen for many years after. When three Apollo astronauts were killed on the launchpad during a test of the rocket engines in 1967, an outraged David Simons asked why. Gus Grissom, Ed White, and Roger Chaffee were asphyxiated when a fire broke out in spacecraft 012. Chaffee died in his seat, while Grissom and White struggled frantically to open the command module's hatch before being overcome by fumes. The explosive-opening hatch of earlier days had been replaced by an inward-opening mechanical hatch after Grissom's Mercury flight when an unexplained premature opening after touchdown had swamped and sunk the capsule. The new hatch required capsule overpressurization on the ground and at low altitudes to maintain its seal. It took more than five minutes for workers in the launch tower to open the hatch. The pressure suits the men wore had melted and partially fused with the molten nylon inside the smoldering capsule. The charred bodies of Grissom and White were almost impossible to separate from the interior of the cabin and from each other.

NASA's internal investigation listed two main conditions that led to the disaster: (1) the sealed cabin, pressurized with pure oxygen, and (2) the "extensive distribution of combustible materials."[*] By innuendo, the investigation pinned the blame for the disaster on its principal contractor. According to NASA reports, the agency and its contractors had been "unaware of the intensity and speed of fires fed by pure oxygen. . . . No one, it seemed, realized the extent of fire hazards in an over-pressurized oxygen-filled cabin." Frank Borman, an astronaut who served on the Apollo Review Board investigating the fire, claimed that nobody connected with NASA had ever seriously considered the possibility that highly flammable materials in an overpressurized environment of pure oxygen created a fire hazard. Yet it was well known, both inside and outside of aviation circles, that pure oxygen is one of the most flammable substances on earth. In fact, a closed vessel filled with pure oxygen and pressurized to 16 pounds per square inch, as was spacecraft 012, constitutes an oxygen bomb. Years earlier, the Russians had prohibited the use of pure oxygen in their space research projects because of the extreme danger. Even the United States' Department of Defense had declared that pure pressurized oxygen was far too volatile for closed capsule experiments.[†]

The contractor's engineers had pleaded with NASA *not* to use pure oxygen. North American's Charlie Feltz emphatically told NASA officials, "It's the wrong thing to do." But NASA pushed back, pointing out that a multigas environment would require separate regulators and a sensor. Besides, they pointed out, sixteen successful manned missions had already used a pure oxygen system without a hint of trouble. The

---

[*]At the astronauts' insistence, numerous strips of Velcro had been introduced into the cabin. The newly invented material was wonderfully convenient—especially in a weightless environment. Unfortunately, it is also flammable. The fumes that killed the three men were from burning Velcro and nylon netting.

[†]The widows of the three astronauts brought a negligence suit against North American Aviation, the principal capsule contractor, and eventually received out-of-court settlements.

disagreement ended with North American insisting on a written order from NASA requiring them to build a pure oxygen capsule. NASA obliged. North American also fought NASA on the inward-opening hatch that necessitated the dangerous overpressurization and made emergency escape all but impossible, another battle it lost.

Could NASA really have been unaware of the dangers? In March of 1965, NASA crew systems experts in Houston had debated the desirability of a one-gas versus a two-gas system and had come to the conclusion that a one-gas system was preferable due to its reduced complexity. (The environmental control system aboard Apollo, supplied by the Garett Corporation of Los Angeles, already consisted of eleven separate subsystems.) The experts also noted that a one-gas system would be much lighter. The danger of fire in a pure oxygen system, they believed, could be reduced to an acceptable degree by keeping flammable materials out of the cabin.

In spite of the successful use of a multigas system on Project Manhigh, the chief medical officer at NASA's Manned Spacecraft Center in Houston would claim that "at the time of initial Apollo development, no multi-gas system suitable for space flight had ever been demonstrated." This was self-serving nonsense. NASA had continued using pure oxygen for two reasons: weight and simplicity. Multiple-gas atmospheres required additional hardware, and additional hardware added weight to a program that was frantically reducing weight everywhere it could.

NASA's dilemma was profound. Each pound of weight added to the command module required an additional 80 total pounds of thrust from the three engine stages below. Apollo engineers were obsessed with weight by necessity, even when it compromised the reliability rate of the spacecraft in terms of pilot survival; official NASA policy stated that the rate was 99.9 percent, meaning that the acceptable astronaut loss rate was one in a thousand. And multiple-gas systems required another level of complexity: the gases would have to be mixed properly, which would entail more hosing, more regulators, and more monitoring equipment.*

---

*After the launch-pad disaster and subsequent investigations that cited "many deficiencies in design and engineering, manufacture and quality control," NASA made a number of changes. Most combustible materials were replaced or removed from the capsule, and a multigas cabin atmosphere was introduced. Some at NASA argued that a nitrogen-heavy atmosphere ought to be used and that sea-level pressure should be maintained inside the capsule, but this was incompatible with the end-of-the-decade deadline, since it would require rebuilding and strengthening the

Clifton McClure was an expert in high-pressure gas systems. How did he assess the Apollo fire? "Things are set in motion by things that happen way back," he would say. "The fire was decided ten years before it happened." Around the time of *Manhigh III,* McClure had occasion to discuss cabin atmospheres with some early NASA contract workers from McDonnell-Douglas, who told him they were planning to pressurize Mercury capsules with 100 percent oxygen. McClure was shocked. He recalls saying, "You can't do that. It's too dangerous," and their answer: "We'll change it later, but we've got to go with this right now because of weight." Over the years, McClure paid attention to NASA cabin atmospheres, watching for signs of a change.

But when they got to *Gemini,* they didn't change it. And then when they got to *Apollo,* they didn't change it. Now what did they do? The Russians had a hatch blow off and kill three astronauts, so that influenced the design. They said, "We'll fix it so it can't blow off. We'll make an inward-opening hatch with a type of lock that seals by pressure and we'll put 2 psi overpressure and we'll keep it sealed on the ground." When they went to 2 psi overpressure with that inward-opening hatch, they guaranteed the loss of life of those people. Something in there's gonna light.

As the sixties wore on, McClure wrote, called, and begged NASA to change the atmosphere. "It was like being in an insane asylum. If you can imagine in the olden days being up on the hill and seeing all these Indians down there with all this war paint on, and running down the hill and saying, 'Indians! Indians!' And they said, 'What are you talking about?' Like there wasn't no Indians."

Put simply, NASA used pure oxygen because to have done otherwise would have slowed them down—even though the tragedy eventually delayed the Apollo manned flight test by some 18 months and cost about 410-million additional taxpayer dollars. Speed was on at least an even footing with safety in the race to beat the Russians to the moon. The space program had finally become a track meet, pure and simple.

And the lessons of Manhigh had already been buried under the rotten bulk of bureaucracy.

---

spacecraft so that it could withstand that kind of internal pressure. NASA eventually settled on a 60% oxygen/40% nitrogen mixture during launch, with the nitrogen gradually cut back during ascent so that the astronauts would be breathing 80% oxygen once they were in space.

six

Truth or Consequences

A brief press release written at Holloman on November 16, 1959, announced that aviation history had just been made. The Air Force had set a new altitude record for a manned open-gondola balloon. This was not a pressurized capsule like the one used on Project Manhigh, but a more traditional "open" system in which the pilot's only protection from the vacuum and the cold was his partial-pressure suit. And, the statement continued, after reaching a peak altitude of 76,400 feet, the pilot had jumped out. It was the longest parachute jump ever attempted. According to the Air Force, the entire endeavor had gone according to plan. A story in the *New York Times* the following day reported that the pilot felt no ill effects from either the flight or jump.

From all indications, the operation—part of the Air Force's little-known Project Excelsior—had been a rousing, unqualified success. But the press release did not tell the whole story. In truth, the flight had been a disaster. And the long freefall back to earth had nearly killed the pilot, Capt. Joseph Kittinger Jr.

In April of 1958, after fulfilling his duties to Project Manhigh and enjoying the satisfaction of turning over proven hardware to David Simons for the Manhigh research flight, Joe Kittinger returned to Ohio as project engineer in the Escape Section of the Aeromedical Laboratory of the USAF Wright Air Development Division, reporting to Colonel Stapp. For the following two years, he worked on a number of projects pertaining to emergency escape from disabled aircraft at extreme altitudes. It was clear, by this point, that humans were going to travel into space and that they would for various reasons want and need to get outside of their vehicles, both for purposes of scientific exploration and for emergency escape. And Stapp's missionary hatred for the forces that threatened a human's well-being in these enterprises had fueled a number of research projects intended to solve at least some of the problems. Kittinger served as project officer for one of the most productive of these efforts, Project Excelsior.

Stapp chose the Latin word *excelsior* for the project. It means, literally, "ever upward." But the focus of Project Excelsior was not on what happened on the way up so much as what happened on the way down. The goal was to solve the peculiar problems of high-altitude bailout. An amazing 1943 jump by Col. Randy Lovelace had demonstrated one way *not* to do it. Lovelace, a doctor who had never jumped before, leapt from a B-17 at 40,200 feet in an attempt to simulate a high-altitude emergency; a static line opened his parachute immediately. The violent tumbling that often followed ejection from a high-speed, high-altitude aircraft had been documented, and one theory held that an immediate chute opening—if practical—might arrest the tumbling. But parachutes do not function very well at extreme altitudes, and it was a long, cold, brutal ride down. Lovelace lost consciousness, but not his life. It remains one of the highest openings ever survived.

By the end of World War II, the word was finally out: when ejecting from a craft at extreme altitude, the immediate objective should be to lose as much altitude as quickly as possible. Although supplied with a perfectly good parachute, a pilot should not—must not—open it. Not yet. In the stratosphere, or the upper regions of the troposphere, to pop the chute is, for all intents and purposes, to commit suicide. The dangers are fourfold: it is unbearably cold, the air pressure is practically nonexistent, the emergency oxygen supply is by definition quite limited, and the jumper is traveling much faster than at a lower altitude, so fast that the shock of a parachute opening threatens to rip apart both the fabric of the chute and the fabric of the pilot. A pilot must fall into warm, thick, breathable air before the parachute can be used with confidence. No matter how terrified, a pilot must resist the temptation to pull the D-ring and must find the discipline to freefall.

Ever since human beings first began to fall through the air from great heights, we have been aware of the body's tendency to tumble, roll, and—in a particularly unfortunate scenario—spin around an axis that runs through the pelvis, perpendicular to the ground. If the motion is not counteracted, the pilot will spin faster and faster, hundreds of times a minute, and die long before reaching the earth. The flier was therefore faced with a cruel dilemma: open the chute immediately and risk the tortures of the upper atmosphere, or attempt a long freefall and risk the centrifugal punishment of the flat spin.

In 1954, the Air Force founded Project High Dive to confront the problem of flat spin and to solve the riddle of high-altitude freefall. Jets were soaring to tremendous heights, catapulted through the skies at blinding speeds, and occasionally they broke apart, caught fire, or simply exceeded the pilots' abilities to control them. It was necessary for a pilot to be able to leave the craft and get back to the ground safely, which meant being prepared to freefall for many thousands of feet.

For three years, High Dive, led by Capt. Henry Neilsen, looked for the answer. This team dropped carefully constructed and anthropo-morphically accurate dummies from a wide range of altitudes. They studied the movements of the falling, tumbling bodies, looking for clues that would suggest a way to achieve some sort of stability. Later, they conducted endless experiments with experienced Air Force test jumpers. Four possible methods by which the pilot might achieve stability after a high-altitude bailout were investigated: (1) employing the body-control techniques of skydiving, (2) stabilizing an ejection seat that would accompany the pilot throughout the descent by attaching a small para-chute to the seat itself, (3) stabilizing an ejection seat with small fins that would give it characteristics of aerodynamic flight, and (4) stabilizing the falling pilot with a small drogue parachute that would provide con-trolled freefall.

By 1957, however, in spite of many promising discoveries (especially in the area of survival gear and parachute systems) and countless pages of technical reports describing valuable research, the High Dive team was formally dissolved. The secret eluded them to the end.

It was Kittinger's conclusion that they had done good work but had simply gone down the wrong track. He decided to retain most of the High Dive crew for Project Excelsior. "They were a bunch of real sharp guys there at Wright Field, but the trouble was they were parachute jumpers, not pilots. They just took the wrong approach." Some of the earlier high-altitude bailout experiments at Wright had been handled less than professionally. Two Air Force doctors who had worked on bal-loon bailouts back in the early fifties had been written up in *Collier's*, where they explained to reporters that they never slept before a big jump, but instead paced the floor endlessly and threw up all night as they contemplated the fearful task ahead. Once Stapp began to manage these programs, the entire mentality of the high-altitude bailout business changed overnight. Melodrama and histrionics were replaced by the matter-of-fact, steely confidence of the modern-day test pilot. And as Stapp would point out, the Air Force no longer recruited their test pilots from the backfields of the football squads, but rather from the honor rolls of the graduate schools.

When Excelsior was founded several months later, Kittinger and Stapp realized that they had a huge head start. The work done by the High Dive crew afforded them many examples of what to do and what not to do in pursuit of the answer to the question of how to stabilize a human in high-altitude freefall. First, they examined the four proposed methods explored by High Dive.

After a number of test jumps and a careful review of the experiences of USAF test jumpers before him, Kittinger—like his predecessors on High Dive—rejected method 1: the use of skydiving techniques to stabilize the jumper. Sport jumpers had known for years how to manipulate their bodies in order to achieve a stable, comfortable freefall position, one that gave them the ability to glide through the air and maneuver themselves into any position they desired: to turn, to somersault, to dive. But what had been discovered by many pioneering test jumpers like Col. A. M. Henderson, Capt. Edward Sperry, Capt. Henry Neilsen, and the most experienced of them all—M.Sgt. George Post—during numerous ejection tests and again during the freefall work on High Dive, was that while a jumper's attitude could be maintained fairly easily in a sport jump in ideal conditions at relatively low altitudes, it was an entirely different matter in emergency conditions at high altitudes. Sport jumpers had every advantage not available to frantic pilots forced to fire their ejection seats in the savage world above 30,000 feet. Pilots, clothed in bulky suits, leave their jets and are immediately subjected to deceleration forces akin to jumping out of a car at Autobahn speed and smashing into a wall. They tumble, out of control, disoriented, perhaps in shock. Even if they had received the weeks of training necessary to develop good freefall technique, they would be hard-pressed to demonstrate it here as they rush through the air at speeds two and three times what they had ever experienced before. Skydiving techniques were simply not an option for the typical pilot in an emergency.

The second method, attempting to stabilize an ejection seat with a small parachute that would provide just enough—but not too much—drag, proved equally unsatisfying. High Dive had shown that while such a parachute could eliminate the danger of end-over-end tumble, it could not counteract the real enemy: flat spin.

The third method—which was essentially another approach to stabilizing an ejection seat that pilots could "ride" all the way down into breathable air—showed more promise. This method required installing stabilizing fins to give the seat the aerodynamic profile it needed to soar through the air. In fact, the British adopted such a design in some of their ejection-seat technology in the late days of World War II, and with some success. But after rigorous testing, Project High Dive had also eliminated this method. No fin- or wing-mounted ejection seat tested proved capable of maintaining sufficient stability in emergency conditions.

That left method 4, which proposed that pilots should fall free of their ejection seats, but upon separation from the seat should deploy a small stabilization chute that would allow them to maintain a consistent posture with respect to the ground, yet which would not slow them down appreciably or detract from the ultimate goal of losing altitude at a rapid rate. High Dive had eventually settled on this method as the most promising, and had searched hard for a parachute system that would provide a controlled freefall. Unfortunately, the success rate of test jumps with such a stabilization system never exceeded 50 percent.

Yet as Project Excelsior kicked into gear and Joe Kittinger began making his own test jumps, he was quickly convinced that a stabilization chute for the jumper was the answer. And the highly experienced, dedicated crew Colonel Stapp had placed at his disposal would help him prove it. But among the many deeds performed by the brilliant pilots, medical officers, and flight technicians who were part of Excelsior, the contributions of one in particular stand out as critical: Francis F. Beaupre, inventor of the breakthrough multistage parachute system. It was an unconventional design, and one that did not immediately win favor with everyone. Beaupre remembers a meeting at Wright in which he was told categorically by experienced Air Force parachutists that his design would never work. He also remembers Stapp overruling the objections of prevailing opinion and forcing the "experts" to listen to Beaupre's ideas. In Kittinger's measured estimation, Beaupre was "one brilliant son of a bitch, but he would have been fired a dozen times if he hadn't had Stapp protecting him."

Beaupre served for two and a half years as a parachute rigger in the U.S. Navy during World War II where he experimented with a number of chute designs. During this period, he built and then test-jumped his own variations on the standard parachute system. In 1947, after assignments in Texas and Florida, Beaupre left the Navy and went to Wright Field as a civilian to work with the Air Force on a series of emergency escape systems that depended on new types of parachutes. By the time of Project High Dive, Beaupre had begun to work on the concept of a multistage chute that would release a small canopy that would serve to stabilize a human during a long freefall from extreme heights.

Early tests of Beaupre's multistage system went very well. As dummies were tossed out of airplanes with this new type of chute strapped to their backs, a static line deployed the first stage of the chute, which allowed a small stabilization canopy to fill with air. The dummies then freefell in a controlled, feet-down position until they reached a predetermined altitude where an aneroid device cut away the smaller chute and deployed the main canopy. But there was an unreality to these early tests, which were all conducted at tropospheric altitudes in which the falling bodies were traveling at speeds well under 200 MPH. What was needed next was a parallel series of tests at stratospheric altitudes. Unfortunately, Project High Dive did not command the resources to obtain planes capable of those heights.

So they turned to the only available alternative: the balloon. High Dive released dummies from a number of balloons at altitudes ranging from 68,000 feet all the way up to Manhigh-equivalent heights of 102,000 feet. But balloon drops presented certain problems. Unlike a jump from a speeding airplane in which the craft's airspeed creates a predictable airstream that will inflate a small chute cleanly and fill it with air, a balloon has a constant airspeed of exactly zero. It was one thing to release a dummy feet down and allow a static line to open a stabilization chute, and quite another to hurtle a dummy from a balloon and—in simulation of actual emergency exit conditions—cause it to tumble and twist as the static line is pulled and the chute is deployed. In these conditions, the small chutes invariably fouled around the limbs of the falling dummy.

When Project Excelsior began in the spring of 1958, Kittinger and Beaupre talked about the need for true high-altitude tests of the multistage design. They were convinced that the concept was sound and that the stabilization chute would work in conditions that provided a sufficient airstream. But if they were going to ask pilots of the new generation of jets and rocket planes to trust such a mechanism, they needed more. They needed successful test jumps—human jumps—from the upper stratosphere.

Excelsior inherited not only High Dive's unanswered questions, but its resource restrictions as well. There would be no rocket plane from which to toss dummies or eject test jumpers. If Beaupre's chute was going to be tested, they would have to use balloons. This suggested, of course, that Kittinger might yet get his chance to jump from the edge of space.

First, however, the riddle of how to safely deploy the stabilization chute would have to be solved. And as Kittinger and Beaupre combed through the piles of data that had been accumulated from the scores of dummy and live drops carried out by Project High Dive, they finally stumbled across the clue they needed. The problem of flat spin in freefall, which the stabilization chute was attempting to counteract, did not seem to manifest itself until just before the falling body reached terminal velocity. A man in freefall could remain fairly stable without much effort at all in the first seconds after he left the aircraft; it was as his rush through the air reached its maximum velocity that the killer flat spin became a threat. The dummy drops from the High Dive balloons verified this.

Since it would take someone jumping from a balloon at 100,000 feet nearly 24 seconds to reach terminal velocity—a speed which, in the extremely thin air, was estimated at something close to 700 MPH—a body might be able to freefall for some distance before being in danger of succumbing to a really high rate of spin. Kittinger and Beaupre thought they could afford to let the jumper fall for somewhere between 16 and 18 seconds—and reach approximately three-quarters of his terminal velocity—before needing to deploy a stabilization chute. And traveling at 400 or 500 MPH by that point in the fall should produce more than enough air resistance to pull the small chute cleanly from the pack.

Francis Beaupre went to work on a variation of his earlier multistage chute. Since a pilot bailing out under emergency conditions could not be counted on to pull a ripcord after a delay of 16 to 18 seconds, the system would have to include a timing device to release the stabilization chute. As Kittinger would write three years later: "Our entire program soon began to evolve about his design and modifications, and the BMSP—the Beaupre Multi-Stage Parachute—carried in its design philosophy the chances of survival for airmen and astronauts who would storm the heights into space."

While Beaupre attended to parachute design, Kittinger and the rest of the team turned their attentions to the myriad other problems inherent in a super-high-altitude freefall. There was more data from High Dive to digest, as well as some fresh theoretical work to do, but Joe Kittinger was not a scientist like David Simons. Kittinger was strongly biased toward "real world" tasks and was impatient with formulas and charts. He scorned what he called the "hordes of engineers and scientists who are sometimes stunned to discover that their weighty classroom endeavors avail them little in the field, where common sense, practical experience, and a grim determination to solve a problem—to say nothing of that rare and indefinable thing we call feel—are essential." After all, he would write after Excelsior was over, "mathematical tables were of little use in producing the first batch of penicillin, and the Wright brothers at Kitty Hawk never held a degree in aeronautical engineering." So Project Officer Kittinger avoided the office and took his grim determination up into the skies over Holloman Air Force Base. Kittinger was a veteran of only eleven parachute jumps when Project Excelsior began in April of 1958. By July he had twenty-one jumps from a range of altitudes as he worked to gain confidence and proficiency.

But while Kittinger plied the desert skies, some hard technical work was being accomplished on the ground by T.Sgt. Robert Daniels, who was in charge of testing and certifying the life-support systems that would be used: the partial-pressure suit, the helmet assembly, and the oxygen system—all of which were interrelated. The problems Daniels faced were perhaps more critical even than those faced by Otto Winzen's staff on Project Manhigh. On Manhigh, after all, the pilot's personal life-support system was essentially a back-up in case the capsule oxygen system failed. On Excelsior, there would be no capsule system; the gondola would be open to the elements throughout the entire ascent, and would be left behind completely once it reached peak altitude. The pilot's personal life-support system would have to work perfectly.

The reasons for using an open-gondola system were primarily economic. In spite of the successes of Manhigh—and, perhaps in some part, because of them—John Paul Stapp was back in bootleg mode for Excelsior. When he inherited the high-altitude bailout project at Wright Field, the program was down to its last $30,000 and suffering from a noticeable lack of prestige. Joe Kittinger's description of the climate at Wright following Project High Dive is reminiscent of the environment at Muroc during the early rocket-sled tests: "The average person at Wright Field in the parachute business wanted nothing to do with Excelsior. First of all, it had to do with space and space was a dirty word. Second of all, it was something that they had never thought of themselves—so there was internal resistance at Wright." There was also resistance in higher circles. Stapp and Kittinger traveled to Washington seeking permission to make the unprecedented jumps that were the objectives of Excelsior. There was considerable concern among the mahogany-desk set that Kittinger, a walking breathing prime cut of USAF grade A choice hero following his flight in *Manhigh I,* would be killed. Leaders of the Aeromedical Lab had already made it clear that it would be Stapp's hide if anything happened to Little Joe.

"The gun was loaded against Stapp," according to Kittinger. He claims that Air Force brass, including General Flickinger, were looking for an excuse to run Stapp out of the Air Force. "Lesser mortals are usually jealous of a person who's a greater mortal. And that's what Stapp was. And they knew it. But Stapp, unfortunately, was not a politician. He was a scientist, he was a visionary."

So while the Air Force allowed Project Excelsior to continue, it withheld full approval for the actual flights. It also refused requests for budget increases. If the project was going to accomplish anything, it would have to do it without even the limited funding that Manhigh had received. Project Excelsior would have to be done, in Duke Gildenberg's words, "for peanuts."

Stapp ordered the change from closed-capsule to open-gondola system in order to cut costs and reduce complexity, much as NASA had done and would continue to do in its race for the moon. It would be more dangerous without the protection of a capsule atmosphere during ascent, but Kittinger insisted that he was willing to take on the risks, and Stapp was confident that Kittinger would reduce those risks as far as was humanly possible. It was a carefully and shrewdly calculated gamble. And because of the reduced level of protection for the pilot of an open-gondola system, and because both Stapp and Kittinger were involved, Excelsior would become one of the most relentlessly safety-conscious research projects ever undertaken. In Duke Gildenberg's opinion, the project was run more like a NASA manned rocket program than a balloon research flight. Exacting hardware testing, especially in altitude chambers, went far beyond anything attempted on Manhigh. Numerous "point-of-no-return" check systems were implemented with precisely specified contingencies and redundancies, and several NASA doctors assisted in Excelsior testing and training. Later, these same doctors took the lessons learned on the high-altitude escape work with

Kittinger and Robert Daniels and applied them directly to the testing and training of systems and astronauts for the Apollo program.

Daniels was a perfect choice for Excelsior. He had been working with pressure chambers and altitude survival gear for 16 years, and he maintained a healthy distrust of all mechanical devices—especially those thought to be fail-proof. Every piece of equipment that Kittinger would wear into the stratosphere was personally and methodically tested by Robert Daniels. As the weeks and months of 1958 rolled on, Daniels spent long nights inside decompression chambers—at great peril to his own health—checking and rechecking every possible piece of the puzzle. On one simulated flight, a safety cable on his helmet snapped. The helmet was explosively torn from Daniels's head at the equivalent of 86,000 feet. It took exactly four seconds for the effects of the powerful vacuum to render Daniels unconscious. It came very close to killing him on the spot. Luckily, a technician was monitoring the "flight" closely and was able to pressurize the chamber and rush to Daniels's aid, saving him. Daniels was precisely the type of dedicated team member that characterized Excelsior and that Kittinger valued so highly. During this period, Daniels was drawing his down-to-earth Air Force pay of $5,100 per year, and that included an extra $55 per month worth of hazardous-duty pay.

A full-pressure, rather than partial-pressure, suit was considered for Excelsior. Scott Crossfield had done an excellent job designing a full-pressure, astronaut-style system for pilots of the X-15 rocket plane and Kittinger had been involved in testing it. The first full-pressure suit for pilots, designed by aviator extraordinaire Wiley Post and developed by the B. F. Goodrich Company back in the mid-thirties, had been modeled on similar suits used by deep-sea divers. Such a suit would indeed have been safer for a pilot above the atmosphere, since it completely surrounded a body with an absolute pressure. But, much to Crossfield's displeasure, Kittinger elected to use the standard-issue partial-pressure suit worn by Air Force jet pilots (and by Kittinger himself on *Manhigh I*). There were two reasons for the choice. First, Kittinger wanted to demonstrate to Air Force pilots that the suit provided for them on their routine high-altitude flights was in fact safe and dependable. He wanted to show everyone that he believed in the partial-pressure suit enough to trust his own life to it under extraordinary conditions. If part of the rationale for Excelsior was to prove the validity of high-altitude bailout for the Air Force pilot, then standard-issue gear was the only choice for a realistic test program. Second, the full-pressure suit was quite a bit heavier and bulkier than the partial-pressure suit. The test subject would enjoy much greater mobility by sticking with the more familiar suit.

The survival equipment selected and laboriously tested and retested by Sergeant Daniels through the winter, spring, and following summer consisted of much more than a suit, because the survival gear would have to work in tandem with various pieces of monitoring and communications equipment that would accompany Kittinger as he plunged through the stratosphere. The layer closest to the jumper's body consisted of a nylon girdle (into which electrodes had been sewn) encircling the jumper's chest; wires from the electrodes fed into a small transmitter that would send telemetry data on heartbeat and respiration to medical officers on the ground. The data would be simultaneously captured by recorders contained in an instrument kit strapped to the jumper's rear end as he fell. Over this nylon girdle, the jumper would wear long, waffle-weave underwear for insulation, and on top of that a set of heavy cotton longjohns. The next layer would be the partial-pressure suit itself. But before the jumper could be lifted into the suit, he would have to pull a rubber collar down over his head and ensure that the rubber formed a gasket-like seal around his neck. Only then would the jumper be hoisted up and literally dropped down into the suit itself.

And that was only half the job. Once inside the MC-3 partial-pressure suit, the jumper would don another set of heavy, quilted long underwear, and over that, a heavy winter flight suit. By this time he would resemble a well-fed honey bear. For the jumper's feet, four pairs of socks: cotton socks, special pressure socks, electrically heated socks, and finally heavy wool socks—all stuffed inside a pair of rubber boots designed by the Army for arctic use. For the hands: nylon gloves, then inflatable pressure gloves, topped off with a pair of World War II–vintage electric flight gloves familiar to B-17 pilots. An experienced arctic explorer who had been consulted for ideas on keeping the extremities warm had prescribed wool gloves and mukluks, but in the end only electric elements provided enough heat under stratospheric conditions.

And the jumper still had to strap on his parachute system and instrument pack, and pull his helmet down over his oxygen mask. It was quite an assemblage of gear—all of which had to perform as intended. There was very little margin for error. And Robert Daniels (known to the crew simply as "Dan") tinkered with it all until he was satisfied.

* * *

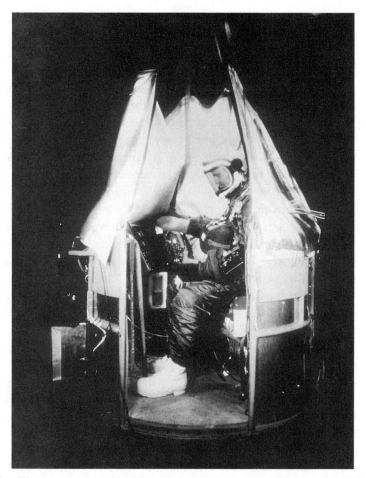

Joe Kittinger gets comfortable with *Excelsior*'s open gondola. *(Source: USAF)*

The Excelsior gondola itself was in many ways a simpler vehicle than the one the Manhigh team had created. This time there was no need to seal, pressurize, or heat the interior. No artificial atmosphere had to be mixed and maintained inside a capsule. The vexing problem of condensation on portholes would not be an issue. But it would be a mistake to assume that the Excelsior team simply hooked a sophisticated basket onto a balloon.

The Excelsior gondola was constructed on a tapering cylindrical frame of tubular steel, covered by an aluminum skin. The entire gondola weighed about 800 pounds. The shape was reminiscent of a tepee, four and a half feet in diameter at its widest point. The top section of the tepee was wrapped in a reflective aluminum curtain intended to lessen glare and reduce the effects of solar radiation. The tepee's open "door" section extended for the full height of the gondola (less than six feet). A wet-cell battery was attached to the gondola's exterior, along with some other instrumentation and communications packages. A liquid oxygen converter capable of supplying several hours worth of breathable oxygen was also attached. An instrument panel inside the gondola contained a pair of altimeters, a rate-of-climb indicator, a thermometer, an oxygen-quantity gauge, a helmet-pressure gauge, and switches for activating the items of electrically heated clothing. Radio transceivers, HF and UHF, were also mounted inside. Eleven separate cameras (both still and motion)—insulated by plastic water bottles and aluminum foil—were arranged strategically to capture every important aspect of the flight and the jumper's exit.

So, in spite of the fact that *Excelsior* would employ an open gondola, it had a great deal more in common with the capsule design of Manhigh than with the open baskets of the Montgolfiers and Hawthorne Gray.

Engineers at the Air Force Cambridge Research Center designed the balloon envelope and rigging, yet the balloon was constructed not by Winzen Research, but by the company that had lost the Manhigh bid, General Mills, Inc. The balloon was made of the familiar polyethylene, but was reinforced with much heavier seams. At full inflation, the envelope would measure 300 feet top to bottom, and 200 feet across at its widest point. It had a total capacity of nearly 3 million cubic feet.

By fall, the Beaupre Multi-Stage Parachute was ready. It was supposed to function as follows: At a predetermined interval after the jumper has left the craft, ideally allowing a freefall to three-fourths of terminal velocity, a timer automatically opens one compartment of the parachute backpack and releases a very small (18-inch diameter) pilot chute, which is propelled out into the airstream by a spring device. As the pilot chute catches air and pulls tight, it in turn pulls the actual stabilization chute, attached to the pilot chute by a three-foot length of nylon cord, from the backpack. As the stabilization chute fills, it pulls about three-quarters of the main parachute canopy from the pack. But the main canopy is kept from opening at altitude by restraining bands of nylon webbing attached to the backpack's shoulder straps. When the jumper reaches a predetermined altitude, sufficiently low to allow him to breathe and open the main chute safely, an aneroid trigger releases the nylon webbing from the shoulder straps and allows the main 28-foot parachute canopy to deploy and fill with air.

As parachute designs go, this was a complicated rig that depended on all stages and mechanical devices operating properly. It would be a disaster, for example, if the nylon webbing pulled loose in the stratosphere and allowed the main canopy to open early. It would be equally disastrous if the timer or the aneroid failed for some reason. To guard against this latter problem, Beaupre provided manual overrides for both opening devices, giving the jumper the ability to reset the intervals or fire the timers at any point during the jump.

It was an ingenious solution to the problem of flat spin—in fact, it represented one of the very few innovations in parachute design since 1919—but one that still lacked its trial by fire. Beaupre and his assistants had already conducted 140 dummy drops of the BMSP. The dummies had been tossed out of airplanes at extremely low altitudes (500 feet above the ground) and dropped from gas balloons at altitudes in excess of 100,000. But live jump tests were now required to troubleshoot the system and give the Excelsior crew confidence that it could be trusted to perform in the most harrowing conditions.

The live tests were conducted in the familiar airspace above Holloman in New Mexico. Kittinger assigned four men to make the test jumps: Capt. Harry Collins, Lt. Ray Madsen (a veteran of Project High Dive and now an operations officer for Excelsior), George Post (jumpmaster for Project Excelsior and probably the most experienced parachutist in the entire Air Force), and Kittinger himself. On October 27, all four climbed into a C-130 Hercules turboprop transport plane and roared off into the desert skies. The big four-engine airplane circled its way slowly up to 30,000 feet. The flight crew lowered the ramp in the rear of the plane. The jumpers, ensconced in their suits and breathing pure oxygen, could see the ground rolling past nearly six miles below.

Kittinger was the first to jump. He fell for seven seconds, rolling and tumbling but not spinning, before the first timer fired. The pilot chute popped out and dragged the stabilization chute with it—and immediately the wild body movements stopped. Kittinger reported perfect stabilization almost instantly. He continued to drop in a controlled, feet-down attitude until the aneroid fired the second timer at 18,000 feet, automatically releasing the webbing and the main canopy. It was as perfect a demonstration of Beaupre's design as could have been hoped for.

George Post jumped next in a repeat of Kittinger's experience. Then came Collins. The BMSP performed flawlessly. There was nothing to troubleshoot. Everything worked. Unfortunately for Ray Madsen, before he could get out of the C-130, the pilot found himself above a ragged layer of clouds and ordered the final jump canceled. Madsen was bitterly disappointed; he had worked tirelessly on the preparations for the jump and badly wanted to contribute to the test, but given the complete success of the first three jumps, there was no need to push luck and risk a fourth jump in marginal conditions.

On November 7, 1959, the Excelsior jump team received what they had been working toward for more than a year and a half: authorization for a full-scale stratospheric flight and jump. It came in a letter from Colonel Stapp who had proved himself a sufficiently able politician with the Air Force brass after all. "Gentlemen," it read, "enclosed is your passport to the upper atmosphere."

The flight of Excelsior was cleared for takeoff.

Launch day was set for November 16. While the project's ultimate goal was to prove the survivability of freefall from a height in excess of 100,000 feet, this maiden flight was only targeted to reach 60,000. In spite of the resounding success of the BMSP in the live jump tests, the system was still untested in actual stratospheric conditions. A test flight to—and jump from—60,000 feet seemed like a prudent first step.

The launch site would be prepared on the outskirts of a small town in New Mexico's Rio Grande Valley, across the San Andres from Holloman, called Truth or Consequences—an apt and sobering name, under the circumstances. This spot was quite a bit further west than the launch site for the third Project Manhigh flight had been, a full 60 miles from Holloman. It was extraordinarily desolate terrain dominated by the bleak geology of an ancient lava flow.

The launch crew, led by Sgt. Melvin Johnson, left Truth or Consequences at 11:00 on the night of November 15 to prepare the site. At 1:00 the following morning, Francis Beaupre entered Joe Kittinger's room in the Buena Vista Hotel and woke him. It was a 20-mile ride to the launch site. The night was cold, temperatures in the twenties, and the clear desert sky was lit with a crowded panorama of stars. Kittinger and Beaupre arrived at 2:00. The scene at the flood-lit launch site was busy and professional, but also palpably tense. The Excelsior crew worshiped Joe Kittinger and each man felt the responsibility bearing down on his own shoulders. Kittinger joked with the men, singing songs and slapping backs and doing his best to relieve the pressure on his team. It was a classic Kittinger performance. He was the one about to risk his life, and yet he was the one reassuring the crew. It was simply a matter of good, thorough preparation. It was a business like any other. No special theatrics were called for. If the engineering is done properly, everything will work out just fine.

Kittinger, in spite of his jolly behavior, was full of private anxieties. He received a quick weather briefing—conditions were ideal—and then entered a big trailer parked on the periphery and strapped on an oxygen mask to begin the process of denitrogenization. While the pure oxygen cleansed Kittinger's blood, Robert Daniels, his assistant Clarence Klinger, and jumpmaster George Post set about dressing him in the array of insulating garments, survival gear, and communications equipment he would wear into the stratosphere. Once that process was complete, the bulky form that contained Joe Kittinger somewhere inside its layers and layers of fabric and wires was led carefully down the trailer steps and allowed to recline on a bed of rolled-up tarps on the ground. The gondola would require another 30 minutes of preparation. Kittinger felt fortunate that there was no need to sit sealed inside the gondola for hours before launch, as had been the case with Manhigh. Instead, he relaxed and allowed himself a bit of contemplative stargazing.

When it was time, Kittinger was helped up and Beaupre attached the parachute harness. The BMSP was attached to the harness and squared up on Kittinger's back. A reserve chute was strapped to his chest; it would open automatically if the main canopy for some reason did not. The crew then had him sit down on top of the boxlike instrument kit that was attached; it would function as a seat on the ascent, but would also accompany him during the quick return to earth. This kit contained the oxygen that Kittinger would breathe during the jump, a tape recorder, a movie camera, and batteries to operate them. The entire package weighed 60 pounds. Other pieces of Kittinger's personal gear were double-checked. In one knee pocket of the flight suit was a radio set; in the other, batteries to operate it. To the left wrist Daniels strapped a small box that contained an altimeter, a stopwatch, and a small mirror with which to view the operation of the deployed parachutes. To the right wrist was attached a small knife.

About 45 minutes before the scheduled launch, Kittinger was lifted into the gondola. This was no small task: while Kittinger was not a massive man—he weighed about 160 pounds—his total weight with all of his clothing and survival equipment came to 320 pounds. Carefully, he was assisted into a sitting position on the styrofoam seat. Holes cut in the styrofoam contained plastic water bottles that would provide a heated surface, another ingenious bit of high-altitude thermal engineering. The water would freeze as the gondola rose, but in the process of freezing would produce heat. Eighteen bottles of water would produce 1,080 watts of heat. (The theoretical types with their slide rules, the engineering "hordes" that Kittinger disparaged, had provided some welcome warmth for the project officer's backside.)

As the tanker truck rolled in to begin pumping helium into the polyethylene envelope, Daniels fitted the helmet over Kittinger's head and secured it to the collar of the pressure suit. Once satisfied that the seal was firm, Daniels opened the valve that allowed oxygen to flow from the instrument kit into the helmet.

As members of the crew tapped him on the shoulder for luck and moved away from the gondola one by one, Kittinger could see the clear, silvery plastic rising above him in a ghostly dance as it filled with the invisible gas. All around the site, men were running soberly through checklists and making last-minute double-checks of the processes for which they were responsible. Kittinger watched the activity from his seat on the platform that held the gondola and marveled at the teamwork and dedication of his crew. He thought back to the launch of *Manhigh I;* he had been frightened then, wondering what awaited him in the stratosphere's deadly vacuum. It was different this morning. Everything was right. It *felt* right. The fear was still there, but now it had form. Stapp had counseled Kittinger not to think of the stratosphere as the *absence* of qualities necessary for life: air pressure and oxygen. Don't think of the vacuum as "nothing," he said, because then you'll underestimate it, no matter how careful you are. Instead, think of the vacuum as a deadly enemy: real and palpable and seeking to destroy you. Think of space as a million poison fingers clawing at your suit and helmet, looking for a way in, feeling for the human being inside, wanting nothing so much as to inject their executioner's venom into your guts and brains. Never forget that those poison fingers are out there, scratching at your pressure suit and your helmet. Fight the poison fingers. Hate them with the full-blown bull-rage fervor of the missionary.

The last crew member to leave the gondola platform was Daniels. Convinced, finally, that he had done everything that could possibly be done—and done most of them numberless times—Daniels stepped away to watch the launch with the rest of the team. The sun was coming up now; the stars had faded and the bare ridges of the Fra Cristobal range loomed on the western horizon, the San Andres range in silhouette to the east casting mammoth shadows that reached all the way to the launch site.

Kittinger could hear the muffled cracks of the restraining cables being blown free and could feel the insistent tugging of the helium.

"I felt the first quiver of motion, and the world fell away beneath my feet."

A small menagerie of aircraft was already airborne, poised to observe and track the flight of the great balloon. A B-57 bomber circled the launch site and a C-123 transport flew a zigzag pattern back and forth across the balloon's planned ascent path. A recovery helicopter hovered nearby, waiting to pick up Kittinger at the end of his long fall back to earth, or—if something were to go wrong—to respond to an emergency.

The balloon rose at a steady rate of 1,200 feet per minute. Kittinger would later report that there had been almost no sensation of movement in the ascent, and no sound at all beyond the intermittent crackle of ground communications in his ear. Capt. William Blanchard, the project medical officer, was Kittinger's sole voice contact. In addition, Blanchard was able to monitor the telemetered information from the electrodes on Kittinger's chest. By prearrangement (based on lessons learned on Project Manhigh), Blanchard had absolute command of *Excelsior I*. He had unequivocal power to abort the flight at any time for any reason. There would be no debate, no discussion. Blanchard was God for the next hour or so.

Kittinger spoke into his helmet microphone, reeling off oxygen supply and pressure readings, altitude, ascent rate, temperature. He also, according to plan, took a moment every so often to record his impressions and describe his feelings. This would give Blanchard a chance to evaluate the subject's emotional response to events and would provide a glimpse of his psychological state.

The balloon passed cleanly through the tropopause, drifting slowly to the east and over the sharp crags of the San Andres. As it rose, the gondola and balloon revolved slowly—a phenomenon familiar to Kittinger from his previous stratospheric flight. In themselves, these slow revolutions presented no particular problem; however, as the balloon rose and the air thinned, Kittinger found the intense glare of the rising sun more and more annoying. As he rotated and turned into the sun, the bright flash blinded him and temporarily interrupted his view of the gondola's instrument panel. The higher he went, the worse the glare became. He became especially concerned about his inability to keep a visual lock on the helmet pressure gauge—probably the single most important measurement in terms of survivability.

Irritation quickly turned to alarm when the helmet faceplate began to fog up. The faceplate was constructed of two layers of clear plastic separated by an almost transparent layer of gold film that carried an electrical charge to prevent fogging. But condensation began creeping into Kittinger's vision. The combination of the condensation and the regular (and worsening) moments of sun blindness totally obscured his view of his instruments. He was flying blind.

Then, as *Excelsior I* neared 58,000 feet, real problems began. As Kittinger squirmed in his seat, straining to see the crucial instrument panel, he realized with horror that his helmet was inching up and gradually rising from his shoulders. A crushing panic exploded in his head. He froze in his seat, afraid to move. If the helmet continued to rise and pulled the nylon bladder loose, breaking the seal around his neck, he would die within seconds. He sat paralyzed, unwilling even to speak into his microphone. He recalled Daniels's accident in the chamber; his helmet had literally blown straight up and off his head. Only the lightning reactions of the monitoring personnel had saved his life.

Another incident raced through the pilot's mind. Back in Ohio, Kittinger had himself been at 100,000 feet in the decompression chamber when the same thing had happened. The helmet had begun to creep up off his shoulders and pull at the restraining cable. It had risen nearly 12 inches from its original position, then stopped. The same fear had gripped him then. Explosive decompression was every bit as cruel in a chamber as in the stratosphere. Only the pressure of the nylon bladder kept the helmet from popping free. The helmet slipped upward, then slipped again. Because this incident had occurred while Kittinger was making a simulated exit from the gondola, the position of his body at the time the helmet slipped was such that the monitoring crew was not aware of what was happening. Finally, as the helmet continued to slip, Kittinger fought his instincts and forced himself to speak, in spite of the vibration it might cause in his throat and neck. Luckily, the helmet microphone picked up just enough of his voice to alert the crew. They pressurized the chamber instantly.

But at almost 60,000 feet in an open gondola, it would not be possible to pressurize the environment. And the nearest monitoring crew was 12 miles below. Because of the problems with the helmet during the chamber tests, however, Daniels had added an additional safety feature: he had attached several lengths of nylon parachute cord to clasps on the helmet, and then tied the cord to the parachute harness. In spite of his fear and the pounding of his heart, Kittinger forced himself to trust those bits of cord. In reality, he had no choice. Blanchard's calming voice on the radio attempted to reduce tension as far as possible.

At about this point, the condensation on the helmet faceplate began mysteriously to recede, allowing Kittinger once again a view of his instrument panel—in between the blinding flashes of the sun. It was comforting to be able to verify helmet pressure and to read his gauges again, but Kittinger read one particular gauge with alarm: his altimeter said 65,000 feet. In the previous frantic minutes, he had missed his planned jump altitude, which was now nearly a mile below him. Immediately he opened the valve on the balloon to check his ascent. But with the sun shining on the huge expanse of polyethylene, the helium was heating up now and *Excelsior I* continued to rise even as gas spilled from the envelope.

Kittinger announced to Blanchard that he was going to prepare to jump. First, he cut free the 200-foot radio antenna that hung down below the gondola. Then he began to disconnect himself electrically from the gondola, finally activating his own oxygen supply in the instrument pack he had with him and severing the umbilical to the onboard supply.

Carefully, very carefully so as not to jostle his helmet more than necessary or rock the tiny gondola, he leaned forward in his seat and looked out over the lip of the gondola floor at a gray-brown earth impossibly distant and surreal. He glanced at the altimeter one last time: 76,000 feet, more than three miles above his intended jump altitude. He grabbed the instrument panel with both gloved hands and tried to pull himself into a standing position, but he couldn't do it. It was as if a seat belt were holding him in place. He glanced around him for evidence of some obstruction, but found nothing. He knew that the original styrofoam seat form, which had suffered from the months of testing, had been replaced prior to the flight. He concluded that the new seat must have been cut slightly smaller and had expanded in flight just enough to grip the instrument pack. He tried again to release himself, but still he was held fast in a sitting position. Finally, in a panic, he lunged forward with all his strength. The instrument kit ripped free and he found himself standing in the open door of the gently swaying, slowly twisting aluminum can.

The only sound was the hiss of his own labored breathing. Only a few tasks remained. Kittinger grabbed awkwardly for the lanyard that would activate the first timer on the BMSP. The idea was to pull it free, start the cameras that would record his exit from the gondola, and then fall forward into space. But it was difficult to get a decent grip with the bulky pressurized glove. He pulled several times, but the lanyard would not come loose. He pulled again, with all the strength he could summon. The timer knob came free this time. Kittinger dropped the lanyard, punched the start button to activate the cameras, paused for a brief moment, and then—almost with relief—he let go of everything and tumbled out.

seven

Aerial Maniacs and Birdmen

As Kittinger left the familiar world of the gondola, he took a deep breath of oxygen—and held it. He was out in the stratosphere now, out into the vacuum. But something was wrong. He was out, he could feel his heart hammering inside his chest, but . . . nothing was happening. He wasn't falling. Why? How was that possible? He wasn't moving. He was hanging in space, suspended. It was as if time had stopped, as if he had stepped into some frozen, static dimension. He wanted to fall, to speed away from the gondola toward the earth, but he wasn't moving.

His mind could not accept the fact that he was *not* falling. That he was hanging in the middle of nothing. He should have been plunging through the air, picking up speed at a tremendous rate. His mind groped for some explanation, some clue. In a terrible moment of wonderment and horror he thought that he was too high, that he was somehow (how?) beyond the pull of gravity. He considered that he might never fall, but simply float until his oxygen ran out.

He glanced down at his arms, but there was no rippling of the fabric of his flight suit—no evidence of wind or motion. There was no sound—not even the rasping suck of his own breathing.

Then he became aware of a subtle vibration centered in his back. He remembered the stabilization chute and he tensed expectantly for the opening shock. But nothing came. He assumed the worst, that somehow the little chute had failed to open. Or that it had already opened and fouled. The image of dummies spinning at hundreds of revolutions per minute whirled through his mind. He struggled to shake off the panic. He groped for the chute, tried to find where it was wrapped around a shoulder or leg and pull it loose. But his hands found nothing.

Then, somehow, he began to roll and in seconds found himself on his back looking up at the black sky. He realized that he was now aware of motion of some sort, that he *was* moving. And after another moment, he felt himself beginning to twirl and knew that he was entering a flat spin. By adjusting the position of his arms, Kittinger found he could reverse his direction of spin. He'd done 60-second unstabilized freefalls in training. He knew the techniques. He would just have to skydive down. But no matter how hard he tried, he could not stop the spinning altogether.

Kittinger was still disoriented and unable to comprehend that—in spite of the absence of a sense of motion and the irrational fear that he was not falling at all—that he was in reality traveling at a speed well over 400 MPH, and accelerating, through air that was 104° below zero. There was no atmosphere to scream past his helmet, yet he was at that point moving faster than any living creature had ever moved without an engine.

Suddenly, Kittinger was jolted hard from his position in the sky and sent into a high-velocity flat spin that was beyond any effort to halt. Moving his arms or his legs had no effect now. He was helpless. The spin continued to accelerate. Kittinger tried to read the altimeter on his left wrist but found it impossible to pull his arm in close enough to his faceplate to read the dial. He began to pray and think about dying.

First, his vision grayed around the edges and he realized that he had lost all peripheral vision. Moments later, the universe receded, darkened, then went black.

When Joe Kittinger regained consciousness, he was lying on his back on the soft gypsum sand of the desert, his main parachute canopy wrapped tightly around his neck and the fuzzy gurgle of a helicopter beating a muffled thump somewhere in his brain.

As Kittinger came to in the desert heat, groggy and grateful to be alive, muttering thanks to his God and to the dedicated men of the Excelsior crew, he represented a very long line of airmen, numbering in the tens of thousands, whose lives have been saved by a simple invention that was at least 200 years old: the parachute.

Legend has it that the Emperor Shih Huang Ti jumped safely from the top of the Great Wall of China under a large umbrella-like chute in the fourteenth century. Leonardo da Vinci made drawings of a large pyramid-shaped parachute in the late fifteenth century and wrote convincingly in the *Codex Atlanticus* about how such an apparatus might provide sufficient air resistance to safely lower a person from the sky.

Other early parachute-like designs were reportedly developed in Siam in the late seventeenth century.

But it was eighteenth-century France that produced the modern parachute. Many of the lessons learned in the experiments with balloons were relevant to the concept of the parachute, and the development of both devices occurred nearly simultaneously. The Montgolfier brothers themselves dropped sheep and other animals from towers beneath small fabric canopies in the mid-1770s. The outcome of these drops cannot be confirmed—it would of course be a fairly simple trick to *drop* a sheep beneath a parachute, but a more impressive one to demonstrate that the creature was good for much besides mutton after its impact with the ground.

A professor at the Paris Conservatory of Art and Handicrafts, Louis-Sebastien Lenormand, advocated the parachute as a safety device that would facilitate escape from burning buildings. Lenormand designed and built his own 14-foot chute with which he apparently jumped safely from the top of the Montpelier Observatory in 1783. But the first confirmed manned parachute drop from an aircraft is credited to Andre-Jacques Garnerin on October 22, 1797. Garnerin, a former physics student who had learned ballooning in the French army and spent three years as a prisoner of war in Austria, rode a smoke-filled balloon to an altitude of 3,200 feet above Paris. A canopy of linen was attached to the basket by a separate set of cords, and when Garnerin cut the cords attaching the basket to the balloon, he plummeted and the canopy popped open. (Meanwhile, the balloon darted up and—for some reason—the volatile hydrogen exploded.) The large crowd that had assembled in the Parc at Monceau to witness the spectacle heard the snap of the parachute canopy open and watched as Garnerin's small gondola twirled and swayed wildly on the descent, swinging Garnerin so violently that he was lifted above the level of the chute itself at one point. He landed safely, but airsick and badly shaken by his historic ride. Well over a century later, the taciturn Wilbur Wright would characterize Garnerin's feat as one of the most courageous acts in the history of aviation.

Garnerin made scores of exhibition jumps throughout Europe—many of them with his wife and his niece, who became the first women parachutists. His most spectacular leap came in 1802 when he dropped with a white canvas, umbrella-shaped chute from a hydrogen balloon 8,000 feet over London with the royal family in attendance. But the problem of oscillations during the descent continued to plague him. A

French astronomer named Lalande suggested that Garnerin's problem was a flaw in the basic design of the canopy. Air trapped inside tended to spill out at some point on the canopy's periphery, he observed, creating an imbalance that swung the chute to one side—as the canopy swung back, air then spilled out the other side and in turn rocked the canopy back again. Lalande argued that a small aperture in the apex of the canopy would allow a controlled amount of air to escape, solving the swaying problem, but not appreciably affecting the overall air resistance of the parachute.

Chutes designed to test this theory proved that Lalande was exactly right. A hole in the top of the canopy provided stability and eliminated oscillation—and made the drop a more tolerable, even exhilarating, experience.

In the very early years of the twentieth century, another important innovation in parachute design appeared courtesy of an American, Charles Broadwick. Broadwick invented and personally test-jumped the first "packed chute" system. Before Broadwick, jumpers ascended with their parachutes somehow suspended or—in some cases—already fully opened beneath a balloon. Broadwick folded his chute and stuffed it inside a backpack that could be worn like a vest. As he fell, a cord attached to the opening flap of the pack pulled the pack open and released the parachute. This gave the parachutist the freedom to ascend comfortably inside a balloon-borne gondola and then, for the first time, to literally jump out. Not only did Charles Broadwick have sufficient faith in the Broadwick Safety Pack to test it himself, he trusted his packed chute enough to let his 15-year-old daughter use it herself in 1908. The baby-faced, 85-pound Georgia "Tiny" Broadwick became the first American female parachutist and eventually racked up more than 1,000 jumps using her father's invention.

Another milestone in the history of parachuting occurred in 1912 when U.S. Army captain Albert Berry made the first parachute drop from an airplane. Berry did not use the Broadwick chute, but one packed into a cone suspended beneath the Benoist plane. He climbed out of his seat, slid down the axle to a trapeze bar, harnessed himself to the 36-foot muslin parachute, and released at an altitude of 2,500 feet over an area on the outskirts of St. Louis. To the amazement of most, he landed safely.

When war broke out in Europe a few years later, the practical value of parachutes was demonstrated. In 1914, balloonists were regularly sent aloft to serve as spotters for artillery units, and they were invariably equipped with parachutes. A tethered balloon makes a splendid target for enemy fire, and many balloonists lived to fly again only after an emergency descent under a cotton canopy.

One of the great tragedies of modern aviation, however, is that an appalling number of World War I airplane pilots were either not equipped with parachutes or lacked the necessary trust in the devices to use them under emergency conditions. The Germans embraced parachutes first and were saving pilots' lives with them by 1917. The British followed suit; some Royal Air Force pilots used a chute known as the "Guardian Angel." But in spite of the sickening spectacle of pilots jumping senselessly to their deaths from the falling wreckage of burning aircraft, the Allies in general continued to stubbornly scorn the use of the parachute—arguing that the device would surely not work in emergency conditions, or that if the canopy did open, the hapless pilot would be a target for enemy fire and would be sliced apart in mid-air long before reaching the ground. The presence of a parachute onboard a plane was even thought by some wartime fliers to be evidence of lack of confidence in one's craft, or even of cowardice.

The American World War I ace Maj. Raoul Lufberry was one of the most vocal opponents of the parachute. Lufberry declared: "Me for staying with the old bus every time!" Lufberry took his own advice when his plane was shot down in May of 1918 and rode the old bus straight to his death. A parachute could have saved his life.

Immediately after the war, the Army asked the parachute unit at new McCook Field, across the Great Miami River from downtown Dayton, Ohio, to develop a reliable parachute that could be mass-produced and made available to American military pilots. The first of many innovations introduced by this group was to construct parachutes out of silk rather than cotton. Habutai silk from Japan, they discovered, was not only flame-resistant, lighter, and easier to pack, but it was also much stronger. In addition, it held up better under constant use and extended the useful life of a parachute to about seven years.

The McCook Field group also focused its attention on one of the design deficiencies that some felt had kept the parachute from gaining acceptance with the Allied forces. Because parachute opening devices were invariably attached somehow to the aircraft (as in the classic Broadwick chute, which relied on a static line to pull the chute from the backpack as the pilot fell away), the risk of some motion or obstruction interfering with the opening was always present. If a burning plane was spiraling down or tumbling end over end, it was difficult for a jumper to exit cleanly and be assured that his chute would open. It was hard to engender trust in such a system. What was needed was a chute that could be opened manually by the pilot once clear of the aircraft. The group of expert jumpers and parachute designers at McCook, under the direction of Maj. E. L. Hoffman, took up this task with gusto in the final months of 1918.

Leslie Irvin and Floyd Smith, civilian employees of the Engineering Division Equipment Section, conducted almost constant experiments through the early months of the postwar period, tossing dummies out of planes and observing their behavior with various types of canopies and opening devices. Together, they settled on a design for a manual-opening parachute and, by April of 1919, were ready to test it.

The canopy of the prototype chute measured 28 feet in diameter. The chute's wearer, after leaping clear of the aircraft, would pull a metal ring on his chute pack, which would pull a short steel cable that removed the pins from the compartment holding the silk canopy. As the pins were extracted, elastic bands snapped outward, pushing the silk out into the wind. Smith and Irvin had incorporated a small pilot chute into the design; the wind would catch the pilot chute immediately, and it would pull open the main canopy.

There were doubters at McCook. It was generally believed at the time, even in aviation circles, that it would not be possible to fall through the air even for a few seconds and still maintain the ability to pull the ring on a parachute pack. As a man's body plummeted, the received wisdom went, he would acquire speed so rapidly that the breath would be sucked from his lungs and he would lose consciousness almost at once. And even if he didn't pass out, he would be so stricken by panic that he would be unable to reason or to remember even a simple pro-cedure. Even if he were to maintain coherency through some force of superhuman will, the air rushing by at such velocity would render him unable to move his limbs—he would be paralyzed and unable, physi-cally, to raise his arm and pull the opening ring.

Irvin and Smith scoffed at these arguments. In spite of an absence of hard evidence, they insisted that their chute would work and announced that they were willing to put themselves on the line to prove it. Smith climbed into the pilot's seat of a de Havilland DH-9 biplane and Irvin strapped on the experimental parachute. They took off from McCook and leveled off at 1,500 feet above the field, traveling at an airspeed of about 100 MPH. A small, grim crowd of Army personnel had gathered outside the hangars to watch what many of them felt would be a suicide.

As they watched, an outwardly confident but privately anxious Leslie Irvin dove headfirst over the side of the plane and fell for nearly 600 feet. Then he reached up and pulled the ring free. The pilot chute unfurled, and an instant later the big white canopy snapped open. Irvin drifted down toward the field to great applause, smiling and laughing to himself all the way down. In his excitement, Irvin neglected to concentrate on his landing and broke his ankle, ending up in the local hospital. A few days later, Floyd Smith duplicated the feat with a perfect opening and trouble-free landing. Almost immediately, before Irvin was even released from the hospital, the Army ordered 300 of the new parachutes. Without further ado, Leslie Irvin went into business and opened the world's first parachute factory. Clearly, this was an idea whose time had come. Unfortunately, it came just a few years too late for the hard-luck fighter pilots of the Great War.

In spite of the success of the new manual-opening chute, pilots continued to resist the notion of freefall. Irvin and Smith, along with another McCook test jumper named Ralph Bottriell, had shown that the new design worked at relatively low altitudes. But what if a pilot was forced to bail out three or four miles up? In the thin air found at higher altitudes, the argument went, a man would fall too fast. His chute would not deploy under such conditions—there was simply not enough air—and the pilot would speed to a sure death. Against the exhortations of his friends and colleagues, Bottriell asked Major Hoffman to approve a jump from an airplane at 20,000 feet—and after some consideration, the request was granted. It was suggested, however, that both pilot and jumper carry oxygen bottles with them on their climb to altitude. Bottriell disregarded the idea. There was enough air to fill a parachute, he claimed, and there would likewise be plenty of air to breathe.

While Bottriell was correct about a jumper's ability to fall through the air at any altitude, he was wrong about a human being's ability to function at 20,000 feet without a supply of pressurized oxygen. Neither Bottriell nor his pilot took any special precautions as they made the climb to 20,000 feet in an open-cockpit LePere biplane during the summer of 1921. At altitude, both men struggled to fight off the extreme cold. They quickly found themselves drowsy and their vision blurred. Bottriell pulled himself up and tried to steady himself enough to climb onto his seat in preparation for his jump. As he grabbed hold of the edge of the cockpit and leaned forward, the manual-opening D-ring snagged on something and the elastic bands popped the silk chute from its pack. In less than a second the rushing wind grabbed the canopy and jerked Bottriell from the plane in a single motion, as if he were a puppet, and pulled him completely through the three-inch-thick ash-wood tail section of the biplane, obliterating the rudder and sending the aircraft into a lurching skid. The LePere flipped and shot earthward.*

Amazingly, Bottriell was still alive. But more amazing, perhaps, was that his parachute had survived the sudden impact and was lowering its cargo gently toward the ground. Bottriell was in shock and still hypoxic. He was also suffering intense pain. He examined his left arm, where the worst of the pain seemed to be located. The fabric sleeve of his flight suit had disappeared and his bare arm looked like it had been hacked up with a meat cleaver. Even in his traumatic state, he understood that he would have to stanch the flow of blood from the arm or he would bleed to death before he reached the ground. Bottriell grabbed a handful of the shroud lines and somehow found the strength to haul himself high enough up with his right arm so that he was able to wrap another set of lines around the injured left arm, just below the shoulder, and fashion a makeshift tourniquet. He fell the rest of the way in this arrangement, barely managing to fight off unconsciousness. Luckily, he landed in the field of an alert farmer who immediately provided the necessary first aid. Two months later, with a badly scarred arm, Bottriell was jumping again.

The following year, Capt. Albert Stevens—who would make the record-shattering balloon ascent to 74,000 in *Explorer II* thirteen years later—was assigned to the Photographic Section at McCook. In a desire to take some high-altitude photos from a Martin bomber, Stevens wanted to be flown at least two miles higher than Bottriell had gone and proposed to parachute back to earth after completing his photographic chores. (Stevens had harbored an interest in parachuting and chute design for nearly two decades. In fact, he had proposed a manual-opening chute as early as 1908.) Wisely, he and his pilot took along containers of pressurized oxygen. At 26,500 feet, Stevens jumped out and opened his chute

---

*The pilot, a Sergeant Madan, regained control of the LePere and managed to land safely. A month later, Madan's luck ran out and he died after losing control of a Sopwith *Camel* over rural Ohio.

immediately. In spite of some turbulence that made for a choppy ride down and nearly incapacitated Stevens with motion sickness, everything went relatively smoothly—proving that a manual-opening parachute was in fact a workable system for returning a pilot to earth without an airplane, even from extreme altitudes.

Another significant event occurred at McCook a few months later. Test pilot Lt. Harold Harris went up in a Loening monoplane fighter equipped with experimental ailerons and lost control of the plane. As the Loening spun crazily through the air, Harris—who had never attempted a parachute jump before—jumped free and pulled the ring on his manual-opening chute, becoming the first airplane pilot to save his life with the new style of parachute. Harris also became a walking vindication of the McCook designers' insistence that the system would work in actual emergency conditions.

Not all of the parachute milestones of the 1920s occurred at McCook Field. In 1924, Sgt. Randall Bose of the Aviation Section at Mitchell Field in Long Island, New York, made his own history. Bose was a believer in a human's ability to fall through the air from almost any height and maintain not only consciousness, but also the ability to perform maneuvers and operate a parachute. But in spite of the proven success of the manual-opening chutes, most pilots still were not convinced. They admitted that you could hold yourself together for a few seconds while you fell free of a disabled plane, but it simply was not physically possible to survive an extended fall without some sort of braking mechanism.

Bose proclaimed that he could fall for a thousand feet, open his parachute, and land safely. Most of his friends at Mitchell tried to discourage him, but one put Bose on the spot and bet him that he couldn't—or wouldn't—do it. So, a few days later, Randall Bose jumped out of an airplane at an altitude of 4,500 feet—and refrained from pulling his D-ring. He fell, rolling slowly into a head-down position, for 1,500 feet. The onlookers below watched first with horror, then in stunned amazement, as they saw the flash of white silk bloom from the falling shape. They could hear the report of the canopy as it cracked open and dropped Bose gently to the ground.

After collecting on his wager, Bose tried again almost immediately. This time he fell 1,800 feet before opening, but the second experience proved a bit more difficult. On his repeat jump, instead of a gentle roll, Bose found himself in a flat spin. The spin accelerated rapidly, so fast that Bose was a propeller-like blur to the spectators watching. Only seconds before losing consciousness, Bose managed to pull his D-ring. The parachute leapt from the backpack and twirled with the jumper's body. Eventually, the wind resistance of the chute slowed the rate of spin and brought a stunned Bose safely to earth.

In two successive jumps, Randall Bose had proven two things: (1) a human could survive an extended freefall as long as he could maintain control of his body position, and (2) a human in freefall was at the mercy of mysterious forces that threatened—almost randomly—to wrest that body control away from him. Obviously, there were still secrets in the sky.

A year later, Sgt. Steven Budreau jumped out of a bomber over Selfridge Field in Michigan and completed a textbook freefall of 3,500 feet, twice the length of Bose's. And in 1928, an enlisted man from the Navy's parachute training school freefell for 4,400 feet.

In spite of the resources at their disposal, the various branches of the armed forces had no monopoly on leading-edge parachute activities. While the parachute groups of the Army and Navy celebrated their successful freefalls in the 3,000- to 5,000-foot range, a barnstorming self-described "aerial maniac" by the name of Arthur Starnes was already way ahead of them. By the end of the 1920s, Starnes could already claim several 7,500-foot freefalls—and as far as Starnes was concerned, he was just warming up.

Art Starnes made his first parachute jump at the age of 18 with a barnstorming troupe at an airfield outside of Charleston, West Virginia. The technology at hand was crude, and the only "dummies" available to test the chute designs were unflappable young men with hearts for adventure. Starnes describes one of the early parachutes:

> The chute that I was using was of a balloon type, packed in a large bag. In turn, the top of the bag was lashed securely to the inner base strut, or the upright supporting the two wings nearest the body of the plane or fuselage. Instead of having a harness there was a large rope loop with a piece of garden hose covering it. Inside this peculiarly constructed loop I placed one leg for support before making my descent, so that I would stay with the parachute until it reached the ground. The rope was tied to a large wheel fourteen inches in diameter which was on the level with my chin when I was seated in this makeshift harness. There was no safety material at all.

Starnes had a colorful career as a professional stuntman, pilot, wing-walker, and parachutist throughout the Midwest and South in the 1920s and 1930s. And in spite of his moniker, "Aerial Maniac," Starnes was a stickler for careful planning, solid preparation, practice, and common sense. His work on the problems of freefall was usually one step ahead of the military's. By the early thirties, Starnes was jumping from altitudes approaching 20,000 feet and falling for 3½ miles before opening his chute. And by the end of the decade, Starnes reached the conclusion that extended freefall was much more than a novelty—it was a survival skill. Because of decreased air pressure, lack of oxygen, and frigid temperatures, pilots who were forced to leave their planes in the upper altitudes—essentially anything above 15,000 feet—were well advised to freefall into more hospitable regions before using their parachutes.

As the war in the Pacific began to unfold in the final days of 1941 and the winter months of 1942, another compelling argument for the efficacy of freefall revealed itself. When Allied airmen took fire or lost control of their planes in combat, they typically bailed out and—regardless of altitude—opened their chutes. As they floated down, their white silk canopies became fat targets for Japanese fighter pilots who zeroed in on the jumpers, gunning them down by the scores.

Art Starnes took notice. Without a formal education or military affiliation of any kind, and commissioned by no one but himself, Starnes had—two years earlier—undertaken a research project to prove that it was possible and indeed desirable to freefall even from extreme altitudes above 30,000 feet. In April of 1942, Starnes published his findings in a book titled *Delayed Opening Parachute Jumps and Their Life-Saving Value.* The dedication was short and passionate: "This little volume is dedicated to those courageous American airmen who were ruthlessly attacked and destroyed by their Japanese opponents while helplessly floating to the ground with their parachutes."

Starnes's study, carried out between the spring of 1940 and the fall of 1941, called for a series of six jumps that would allow him to test both equipment and procedures. The exit altitude of the initial jump would be 12,500 feet, the second jump would be from 18,500 feet, and so forth through the final jump, which would be from somewhere above 30,000 feet—a height at which no one had ever attempted to leave an aircraft.

Starnes designed a number of items of special high-altitude gear and spent many hours testing them in simulated high-altitude environments inside a decompression chamber at Northwestern University in

Chicago. The weight of the clothing and apparatus that Starnes planned to jump with came to just over 100 pounds. Fully decked out, he resembled an alien creature from a bad science-fiction movie, laden with mysterious wires and encrustations of pumps and gauges.

As he took off in the Gruman amphibious plane that would take him up for the first test jump, Starnes was in full regalia. His head was encased in a combination leather helmet/oxygen mask that included a windscreen, heated goggles, and a microphone with which to communicate to the pilot and ground crew. On his right hip hung an electrically driven movie camera with a 200-foot film magazine; his left hip held the transmitter that would broadcast his voice and heartbeat. He wore an altimeter on his right forearm. His body was covered by an electrically heated suit; his gloves and boots were likewise heated. On his chest, on top of an aluminum breast plate, was strapped a combination pneumograph/barograph to provide reliable measurements; on his back was a calibrated stopwatch that would be activated by static line. In addition, and most important, Starnes wore a 28-foot, manual-opening parachute in a backpack, and a 24-foot reserve chute in a chestpack. His total weight, fully laden, was 286 pounds.

As he proceeded through the series of jumps, Starnes tinkered with his equipment and experimented with body position in freefall, enduring rolls, tumbles, and even moderate flat spins. He also tried different airplanes and, on the final two jumps, tried using a small stabilization (or, as he called it, "anti-spin") chute during freefall.

Finally, on October 24, 1941, Starnes was ready for the big one. He ascended to an altitude of 31,400 feet over Chicago in a modified Lockheed Lodestar and prepared himself. At an airspeed of 165 MPH, Starnes jumped into air that measured –48° Fahrenheit. Deploying the three-foot antispin chute, he fell for nearly two minutes, achieving a terminal velocity of 230 MPH. He dropped to 2,100 feet above sea level (an unheard-of freefall of 29,300 feet), where he opened his chute and drifted safely to earth, landing in a cow pasture on the edge of town.

Afterward, Starnes described the experience to the crowd that had gathered to witness the event.

I had only two moments of fear. The first was as I stood in the open door of the plane, trying to get enough oxygen inside my helmet and wondering if my equipment would clear the door frame. But the second, more frantic sensation, was when my goggles frosted up in a cloud bank at 23,000 feet and my body went into a series of violent spins.

Starnes went on to describe his efforts to arrest the spins. Nothing had really worked, and he had continued spinning up until the moment he pulled his D-ring. The flat spin would remain a nemesis to high-altitude parachutists, but Starnes had proved to the world that it was at least possible to survive such a jump.

In his published report, Starnes offered pilots advice on how to clear their eustachian tubes during a long freefall ("by swallowing . . . by a lower jaw action . . . by opening the mouth wide and shouting at intervals"); how to bail out of an airplane safely ("Don't stick your foot out to see how cold it is," he warned. "Never jump standing up . . . dive out"); and how to counteract unpleasant body rotations on the way down ("I find rapid somersaulting with the legs drawn up uncomfortable"). In spite of his own use of the antispin chute, Starnes concluded that such a device was neither "practical or necessary" and advised jumpers against its use. He also claimed that extended freefalls, even very long ones, needn't be practiced. He did recommend a few static-line jumps for all pilots, however—chiefly to remove the apprehension of having to make an emergency jump. The mind is completely clear and facile during freefall, he advised. The important thing is to remain calm and to be alert.

Starnes also pleaded with pilots to *trust* their parachutes. "A parachute that is airworthy," he promised, "will not fail to open."

Even though Starnes had gone a long way toward eliminating many of the common misconceptions about freefall, the one thing he had never been able to eliminate was uncertainty about how a human body was likely to behave once it left an airplane. As he wrote in his treatise to the airmen of World War II: "After leaving the plane I may somersault, roll, fall head first or face downward." And though he had made some real progress in learning to counteract certain types of undesirable movement, such as his discovery that by suddenly throwing one's arms and legs outward it was possible to arrest a moderate flat spin, his remedies were all reactions to random circumstance. Starnes never guessed that there might be a proactive approach to the problem, that with proper technique, jumpers might take mastery of their own fate as they fell.

Ten years before Starnes's great jump from the Lodestar, a young man named Spud Manning had fallen 15,000 feet with his body in a "cross" position: arms outstretched, feet together, and generally parallel to the ground. Manning didn't spin or tumble, but remained in the same attitude for the duration of his jump, becoming the first to employ a technique that would, years later, come to be known as "skydiving." As Manning experimented with his freefall position, he discovered that he could maneuver himself as he fell, increasing and decreasing his rate of fall at will. By 1932, he was demonstrating aerobatic moves during freefall. Floyd Smith at McCook Field was aware of Manning's technique and published an article in 1934 that discussed the concept of controlled freefall.

But, unfortunately, most of the parachuting world ignored the notion that, with some practice, it was indeed possible to control a fall. Jumpers went right on rolling and tumbling and spinning. Even experienced jumpers like Art Starnes were apparently unaware of skydiving techniques throughout the '30s and '40s. So it fell to an eccentric Frenchman to discover skydiving all over again, to perfect it, and to popularize the technique. His name was Leo Valentin.

Valentin made his first parachute jump in 1938 at the age of 19 during an assignment with the French Armée de l'Air in North Africa. Like Starnes and most of the rest of the parachuting world, Valentin was unaware that it was possible to regulate and control the body during freefall. But after watching one French jumper after another tumble to his death, he understood the dangers of uncontrolled freefall. "One never knows," Valentin wrote. "When a man leaves the plane he falls anyhow; he tumbles about the sky; he twirls like a sack of potatoes; it is enough for a foot or an arm to get caught in the rigging lines to prevent the normal opening. . . . All of us, and I was no exception, jumped like sacks of flour."

After the war, Valentin began to study the properties of falling bodies in search of an answer to the problem of instability, and particularly to the dreaded flat spin, which he referred to as "making a mayonnaise." He looked for inspiration in the movements of acrobats and dancers and divers. Then one day he observed a funnel falling from a second-story windowsill: it tumbled for a split second, but then righted itself in a spout-down configuration and fell cleanly to the ground. Valentin theorized that if the human body could present a concave shape to the airstream, it might be capable of cleaving through the air like a funnel. He reasoned that the only practical way for a human being to be concave during a fall would be in a spread-eagle, chest-forward position. And this, he realized, was precisely the configuration that a bird or an airplane used to push itself through the air.

He was sure he had hit on something, and in May 1947, he attempted to prove it. He jumped from 9,000 feet and tried to assume a spread-eagle shape with his arms out, his head up, his feet together, and his back arched. But the experiment was disappointingly inconclusive. He found it awkward to maintain the position he wanted, and he found it equally difficult to fall without his hand in the customary and reassuring position adopted by most jumpers: securely on top of the D-ring.

But when he tried it again the following day, it worked. He assumed the arched, spread-eagle position and—as he gained confidence—found that indeed he could remain perfectly stable for as long as he wanted. In succeeding jumps, he learned that freefall could be a serene, reflective experience when the body was stabilized. He felt that he was gliding through the air. He also learned, through experimentation, that by careful movements of his arms and legs he could maneuver and control his attitude. It was like swimming, he thought. Freefall was no longer something to be endured: it was fun, and the longer one fell, the more fun it was.

Valentin became a prophet of skydiving in French aeronautical circles, demonstrating his technique and training other jumpers. "I knew now that I could leap from any height and control my fall. From now on, I no longer fell at between 180 and 190 feet per second but at 170 or even 160; to a certain extent I was therefore beginning to glide."

But Valentin was a restless man. Beginning to glide was not enough. He wanted to fly. Like a bird. He wanted not only to control himself in the air and to be able to adjust his rate of descent, he wanted the power to ascend and to remain aloft indefinitely on the currents of air, to ride for hours on a thermal column like a hawk. After spending many months enjoying his newfound control over freefall, he set a French freefall record, and then a world record for freefall without a respirator (20,000 feet). But he remained unsatisfied.

Man no longer figures in the game. An aeroplane does not mean man in the sky: it is the machine in the sky. A few of us want to open up the air to man on his own. When machinery reaches its limit, man feels the need to return to simplicity. There comes a time when he wants to get out of his car and walk and so, getting out of a supersonic aircraft, he wants to fly with his own wings.

Valentin studied the work of Otto Lilienthal, who constructed something resembling today's hang-gliders in the latter years of the nineteenth century. Lilienthal had been able, with a running start, to glide from hilltops for distances of up to 300 yards, to rise above his takeoff point, and to execute controlled turns. But even more interesting to Valentin was an American named Clem Sohn who had used canvas wings attached to his arms to glide during freefall after jumping from airplanes. In the thirties, Sohn had toured France and become known as the Bird Man. But it was a dangerous business and Sohn died during an exhibition in Vincennes in the spring of 1937 when his parachute rigging fouled around his feet.

Valentin, undeterred, built his own set of canvas wings and began to experiment. He gave his first public demonstration at Villacoublay in April 1950 for a crowd of 300,000 spectators. And while the flight did not go particularly well—Valentin had trouble finding stability with the unwieldy wings attached to his shoulders—he survived and the crowd was ecstatic. The papers referred to Valentin as "The New Clem Sohn," or simply as "L'homme-Oiseau"—the Bird Man.

Four days later, Valentin made a repeat attempt and succeeded in gliding, turning, and controlling his airspeed. It was another public triumph, but Valentin was still not content. He had been unable to achieve lift with the wings, and blamed it on the canvas. By spring of 1951, he had built new wooden wings and had tested them in a wind tunnel. Satisfied, finally, with their aerodynamics, he began a series of test jumps—some of them from a special platform that hung off the side of a helicopter. In May of 1954 he jumped from 9,000 feet with his balsawood wings (they measured 13 feet from tip to tip and weighed, along with their harness, 28 pounds) and for the first time actually achieved moments of lift during a controlled freefall. He was hailed as the first human being ever to fly.

Valentin's last jump came in May of 1956 before a crowd of 100,000 in Liverpool, England. He jumped with his latest wooden-wing design from an altitude of 8,500 feet. As he attempted to leave the plane, one of his wings was snatched by the slipstream and hurled against the fuselage. Valentin tumbled, his wings splintered and misshapen. When he opened his main parachute, it immediately fouled around the wings. Moments later he frantically pulled open his chest-pack reserve chute, but it too wrapped itself around the wooden pieces dangling from his harness. He died on impact.

Roy "Red" Grant, an American who billed himself as "The Last of the Birdmen" continued jumping with attached wings—"batwings" as they were often called—into the 1960s. He jumped for the final time in a demonstration for the CBS television show "Sunday Sports Spectacular" on February 19, 1961. Not only was this Grant's last jump, but it may have been the last winged jump ever. Grant estimates that no more than seventy-five "bird men" ever attempted to fly. By his count, of those seventy-five, four retired—including himself. The rest met the hard fate of Leo Valentin.

By the end of World War II, the armed forces of the world had accepted the parachute not only as a survival device for pilots, but also as a strategic weapon. And when the Allied paratroopers returned home after the armistice, the sport of skydiving began to emerge in the West. (Sport jumping had already become a phenomenon in the Soviet Union.) Clubs popped up from coast to coast across the United States. But the real center of postwar sport parachuting in the West was France, where Valentin and his followers had popularized skydiving techniques. The first world championship skydiving event, held in Yugoslavia in 1951, was completely dominated by French jumpers.

A Frenchman who had become a U.S. citizen, Jacques Istel, traveled to France in the early 1950s and studied advanced skydiving maneuvers. He returned to the United States in 1956 and founded the first American competition parachuting team, which competed in the World Championship in Moscow that year, placing sixth in a field of ten.

Freefall parachuting and the very concept of sport jumping was officially anathema to the U.S. Armed Forces up until the mid-fifties. In fact, delayed openings could land a paratrooper in court-martial proceedings. In 1958, however, the Army did an abrupt about-face and fielded a team of competition jumpers. Other branches of the service shortly followed suit. By 1962, while emphasizing the sport aspect of parachuting, a twenty-man Army parachute team announced that it was going to make an all-out assault on world parachute records—most of which were in the hands of Soviet-bloc countries. The Americans made some inroads, but parachuting competitions continued to be dominated by the Soviet Union and Czechoslovakia into the 1980s.

Meanwhile, the military—particularly the Air Force and the Army—continued to experiment with new parachute technology. Aircraft design and performance were racing ahead at breakneck speed, and if parachutes were to continue to be a viable option at the new heights and speeds made possible by the latest generation of jets, chute designers and jumpmasters would have to sprint to keep pace.

In the early 1950s, John Paul Stapp proved with his rocket-sled experiments that it was physically possible to survive tremendous deceleration. Simultaneously, pioneer USAF test jumpers (Henderson, Post, Sperry, and Neilsen, among others) were testing new chute designs and new aircraft-ejection systems under increasingly punishing conditions. Then, in 1955, Air Force test pilot George Smith became the first human being to survive an emergency bailout at supersonic speed. Smith was exposed to wind-blast of 1,280 pounds of pressure per square inch and deceleration forces of 25 Gs, yet he endured the ejection and landed safely beneath his parachute.

The next challenge was to find a way to bring pilots back from the upper reaches of the stratosphere. First Project High Dive, and then Project Excelsior groped for the answer.

eight

"The Mission Is Canceled"

At Colonel Stapp's insistence, Project Excelsior had operated in relative secrecy from the beginning. And so even after Joe Kittinger's harrowing experience on his fall from the stratosphere, the Air Force was able to feed the press its own version of *Excelsior I*. Briefings back in Alamogordo made no mention of helmet problems or flat spin or fouled parachutes.

Kittinger was asked whether he had been afraid as he leapt from the gondola. "Oh no," he told the reporters with typical Kittinger deprecation, "it was the quickest way down." During the freefall, he continued, he had been much too busy to be scared. He neglected to cite unconsciousness due to centrifugal motion as one of the activities that had kept him occupied. The young captain had felt no ill effects, the Associated Press assured readers, and had survived the fall in "good shape."

But as medical personnel rushed to Kittinger's landing site in the sand on November 16, 1959, they found a man who had suffered terribly during his descent. His reserve chute had saved him, but as events were pieced together over the following days, it was clear that—once again—Joe Kittinger had been a very lucky man.

Thanks in large part to the extensive collection of cameras onboard the gondola and attached to Kittinger himself, it was possible to review the exit and freefall in excruciating, slow-motion detail. The films revealed the following: As Kittinger stood poised in the door of the gondola and jerked on the lanyard that was designed to pull two knobs on his parachute harness, knobs that would activate the staged openings of the multistage parachute, the lanyard failed to pull free. It had worked perfectly scores of times in tests on the ground, but at altitude, for some unknown reason, the lanyard remained attached. Kittinger jerked again, with added force, but still the lanyard was attached to the harness. He paused, then tried one final time—and the lanyard came free. The problem was that Kittinger had been unable to see the knobs due to their position on the harness, and had been unaware that his first tug on the lanyard had in fact pulled one, but not both, of the knobs out. And that seemingly insignificant mechanical glitch had nearly doomed both Kittinger and Excelsior.

One of the knobs on the harness activated an aneroid device that would trigger the opening of the main parachute canopy at an altitude of approximately 18,000 feet. (It was necessary to arm the aneroid at altitude to avoid the chute opening as the balloon passed through 18,000 feet on the way up.) This was the knob that did *not* come free until Kittinger's final jerk on the lanyard. The other knob activated a timer that was designed to release the pilot chute that would in turn deploy the stabilization chute after the jumper had reached approximately 75 percent of his terminal velocity: a delay of roughly 16 seconds. And this was the knob that had popped out with the first pull on the lanyard. So, as Kittinger stood in the doorway of *Excelsior I* fighting to pull the lanyard free, the timer on the stabilization chute was already running. It ran for 11 seconds before Kittinger left the gondola, and then released the first stage of the parachute exactly 2.5 seconds later.

Two and one-half seconds of freefall provided nowhere near the airspeed needed for the pilot chute to bite into the thin atmosphere. The tiny chute popped from the backpack and drifted around Kittinger like a damp dishtowel. It twirled between his legs, drifted up near his shoulders, and finally encircled his neck. Kittinger, seemingly hanging in space, groped for the chute, feeling for it around his thighs and knees.

The falling man's airspeed increased. He went into a moderate flat spin, recovered, and then—suddenly—began twirling like a propeller. Blood surged into his brain and he blacked out. At 18,000 feet, the main canopy of the Beaupre chute opened and immediately snarled around the spinning body. Next, at 11,000 feet, with Joe Kittinger still unconscious and still spinning, a second aneroid device opened the reserve chute in his chest pack. The reserve snarled with the other chute and Kittinger spun on toward the desert floor.

Then, due to a fortuitous safety feature designed into the system by Francis Beaupre, Kittinger was spared. Beaupre had deliberately used shroud lines of a weaker strength on the main canopy of the BMSP for just such an emergency. In the event of a high rate of spin that would render the jumper unconscious and therefore incapable of manually separating a fouled main canopy prior to activating his reserve, Beaupre reasoned that the lines of the main canopy ought to break free on their own. And this is precisely what happened. At a mere 6,000 feet from the ground, the weaker lines snapped away and the main chute was freed, allowing the reserve to blossom out and fill with air—and deposit Kittinger in the sand.

After reviewing the entire episode on the films, Kittinger was angry with himself, furious that his own failure to properly arm the aneroid and the timer at altitude had nearly destroyed all that the Excelsior team had worked for. He felt that he had personally let the project down, and specifically that he had let Francis Beaupre down. The BMSP was a sound design, he was sure. It would work.

Shortly after the flight and jump, Kittinger and the Excelsior crew returned to Dayton and began not only to study the parachute itself, but to attack some of the other problems that had cropped up during the flight.

Before the project could consider launching a second balloon, five main areas would have to be addressed:

1. The difficulties related to the arming of the opening devices;
2. The condensation on the helmet faceplate;
3. The intermittent glare and resultant sun-blindness at altitude;
4. The potentially deadly tendency of the helmet to creep upward from the pilot's neck due to internal pressure; and
5. The awkwardness of the overall exit procedure—the jumper needed to be able to stand, do a few simple chores, and then leave the gondola without further ado.

Once back in Dayton, Kittinger immediately requested authorization for a second flight. The Air Force brass was still breathing down Stapp's neck, reminding him how lucky he was that Kittinger hadn't been killed. Again, Stapp had traveled to Washington to plead with missionary passion before the mahogany desks. And again he won his case. He gave Kittinger the green light, and Kittinger, confident that the mechanical problems of the maiden flight could be solved in short order, scheduled the launch of *Excelsior II* for December 11. That gave Robert Daniels and the rest of the team less than three weeks to complete preparations.

Working night and day, Francis Beaupre and his assistants rethought and redesigned both the BMSP and the procedure for arming the aneroid and timer. To simplify matters, it was decided that Kittinger should arm the aneroid for the main canopy during the ascent—at about 30,000 feet. This would eliminate the need to do it later. Beaupre also repositioned the knob for the stabilization chute's timer. The angle of the lanyard's pull on the knob was now more positive. Kittinger was dressed in full flight gear in order to test the procedure. He pulled the lanyard fifty times—from every conceivable body position and with a variety of arm and hand movements—and each time it popped the knob out and set the timer. They were convinced that there was no way the device could fail to perform as intended.

The condensation on the helmet faceplate had been a surprise. The Excelsior team had tested the faceplate extensively prior to the flight and had never had problems with moisture. Unfortunately, the coldest temperatures the decompression chamber at Wright could achieve were in the range of –70° Fahrenheit. As it turned out, the effects at true stratospheric temperatures—as much as 30 degrees colder—were very different. Daniels made a trip back down to Holloman where the huge new altitude chamber allowed for truer temperature testing and personally made simulated flights to 110,000 feet at temperatures of 110° below zero. Inside this steel chamber, 18 feet high and entered through an airlock anteroom, he was able to readjust the automatic defogging system built into the faceplate so that no moisture appeared.

Back in Ohio, a searchlight was directed into the open door of the gondola to simulate the glare of the sun in the stratosphere. The crew studied the angle of the light and considered a number of possible solutions to the problem of the sun-blindness Kittinger had experienced. Finally, they hit upon an effective remedy: a cardboard sunshade to surround the instrument panel. Once again, in the spirit of Auguste Piccard, a well-trained crew of highly technical aviation personnel had eschewed the complex for the fundamental and had arrived at a classic bootleg solution any child could have envisioned.

The helmet rising up on Kittinger's head at altitude represented the most serious of the problems. The potential for catastrophe was obvious should the helmet pop free at jump altitude. If it hadn't been for the safety cords attached to the helmet, the postflight press conference in Alamogordo might have been very different. The helmet had been secured to the nylon webbing around Kittinger's chest by straps that were held together by metal clamps. The straps had slipped during the flight because, as the nylon became extremely cold, the teeth of the clamps were no longer able to grip the fabric. The tremendous internal pressure of the helmet simply pulled the clamps free. It was decided that the only trustworthy solution would be to pull the straps tight and then sew them together with heavy nylon thread.

The final piece of the puzzle was to make sure Kittinger could stand without obstruction and exit easily. The styrofoam seat was reworked and the water bottles were repositioned so that they could not snag the instrument pack and impede movement up and away from the seat.

Everything was set. The team was confident and Kittinger was anxious to return to the heights where he could prove that the BMSP worked, that it was possible to freefall from the stratosphere with confidence.

The launch of *Excelsior II* occurred on schedule in the predawn hours of December 11, 1959. The gondola pulled away from the desert floor and rose with the sun. As he passed through 30,000 feet, Kittinger armed the aneroid on the main canopy's opener. He passed through the tropopause without problem, and continued steadily into the stratosphere. This time, no condensation crept inward from the edges of the faceplate. His vision was clear as he looked out across the broad surface of the earth below. And although the bright needles of sunlight stabbed at him as before, the cardboard around the instrument panel cut off the glare and made it possible for him to note his altitude, his rate of climb, the air temperature, the amount of oxygen remaining, and—to his immense relief—his helmet pressure gauge. Best of all, the helmet itself stayed firmly in position this time.

It took one hour for the balloon to reach the altitude from which Kittinger would jump: 74,700. He stood and positioned himself in the open doorway. He started the cameras. He pulled the lanyard to arm the timer. It pulled free easily this time. Then he jumped.

Fourteen seconds later, the pilot chute popped free, caught air, and deployed the stabilization chute. Kittinger fell through the stratosphere at hundreds of miles per hour, but this time there was no flat spin. With the three-foot chute taut above him, he dropped—feet first—cleanly and predictably toward the earth. At 18,000 feet, the aneroid sensed the air pressure and fired the pins on the 28-foot main canopy. The chute unfurled and snapped open.

Kittinger dropped again into the white sands, exultant this time. The flight and the jump had gone off like clockwork. It had taken him a grand total of 12 minutes and 32 seconds to return from a height of more than 14 miles. Again, Kittinger downplayed his role to the press. It was "simple," he told them, "like riding a motorcycle."

But for the Excelsior crew and their project officer, the job was far from over. Now that preliminary flights had proven the workability of the system and the procedures, and that it was in fact possible to retrieve a human being from the deep stratosphere, a final flight was needed to fulfill their charter: a jump from 100,000 feet, a full five miles higher. And as everyone connected with the project was acutely aware, they were five extremely difficult and cruel miles.

If some people are driven to accomplish great deeds through a desire to conquer private demons or compensate for inadequacies of character or personal history, such was not the case with Joe Kittinger Jr. His father was an office equipment salesman in Orlando, Florida, who liked to fly airplanes. One morning in 1930, Joe Sr. took his two-year-old son up in a Ford trimotor Tin Goose. The boy wouldn't remember the flight, which only lasted 10 minutes, but he would refer back to it years later as the first significant event in a life that would be defined by extraordinary events in the air.

Joe Jr. does have very early memories of airports and airshows, balloons and parachutes. Before he could read he was building model airplanes, and as soon as he could understand them he was collecting books and magazines about airplanes and air adventures. He would stand transfixed on the roof of the family home, gazing at the clouds or launching rubber band–powered aircraft into the summer breezes.

The Kittingers owned a ramshackle, 10-horsepower, flat-bottomed houseboat called the *John Henry* in which they cruised the St. Johns River. They cooked their meals onboard over a gasoline stove and fished for black bass and the big catfish that lurked under the cut banks. The St. Johns wound through a rich bird sanctuary and through exotic swampland that held a wide variety of wildlife. Joe and his younger brother Jack became expert not only at hunting and fishing, but also at gigging frogs and trapping alligators. By the age of 11, Joe was allowed to take off on the boat by himself or with his brother. At 16, he began to race speedboats and before long was winning consistently. After graduation from high school, he turned pro and enjoyed a short, successful career as a hydroplane racer. But as expert as he would become at guiding powerful machines across the surface of the water, his first love was always in the air above. "From the time I was a kid," he would say, "I never wanted to do anything but fly airplanes and have adventures."

During World War II, Orlando became a major flight training center and the skies over the Kittinger home regularly buzzed with all kinds of aircraft. By the time he was 17, Joe was soloing in a Piper Cub and living out his fantasies of only a few years before. He graduated from the Bolles School, a military prep school, in 1946.

After an unsatisfying year and a half at the University of Florida, Kittinger was accepted into USAF aviation school and was assigned to Goodfellow Air Force Base in San Angelo, Texas, for basic training. He found the strict military discipline stifling, but he loved flying airplanes enough to endure it. He graduated in 1950 and was promoted to second lieutenant. The Air Force immediately shipped him off to Neubiberg Air Base in Germany, where he was assigned to the 526th Fighter Bomber Squadron, 86th Fighter Bomber Group. In Germany, Kittinger found himself flying not the new Air Force jets he had expected, but a classic prop airplane with a special place in aviation history: the tough-as-nails Republic F-47 Thunderbolt. It was serendipitous duty for the young man who only a few years before had lain awake at night and fantasized about flying the Thunderbolt fighter against the great German aces.

Nine months after arriving in Germany, red-headed Joe Kittinger met a beautiful red-headed fraulein named Pauline Bauer. After a year-long courtship, they married—just as Kittinger was assigned new duty as a test pilot. Shortly afterward, the newlyweds moved to Copenhagen, where Joe flew experimental aircraft for the North Atlantic Treaty Organization (NATO). It was a plum assignment he landed by cutting cards with the two other volunteers for the job back in Neubiberg.

When his assignment to NATO was completed, Kittinger asked the Air Force for more test-pilot duty. It was a job he felt he was born to do and, reviewing his 200-plus mishap-free test flights, his superiors agreed. The Kittingers moved to New Mexico in July 1953, where Joe began a five-year stint with the Fighter Test Section at Holloman. After accumulating a great many hours in a variety of experimental jet fighters and working extensively with a number of guided-missile systems, Kittinger volunteered for the Air Force's zero-gravity program and was assigned to fly parabolic patterns for Dr. David Simons's medical research flights, which led eventually to Project Manhigh and a manned-balloon altitude record.

As jet flying safety officer at Holloman, Kittinger became an instructor in survival and bailout techniques. He made his first parachute jump in El Centro, California, in January of 1956, and then jumped nine more times that summer while preparing for his role in Manhigh. But the real jump test came later, in 1957, barely a month after Simons's *Manhigh II* flight. It happened during takeoff on what was supposed to have been a routine test flight in an F-100C Super Sabre fighter jet. Just as Kittinger cleared the runway and attempted to retract the landing gear, the Super Sabre lost all hydraulic pressure. Kittinger fought the plane into a level attitude and attempted to re-enter the traffic pattern for an emergency landing, but in spite of all the force he could apply on the stick, the nose kept tipping up—then finally pitched vertical. The 14-ton jet stalled and dropped toward the ground.

Kittinger pulled the canopy release and the wind blast ripped the helmet off his head. He groped for the ejection-seat trigger and squeezed it. He was only 800 feet from the ground when he was blown out of the cockpit of the wobbling fighter. He tumbled through the air, rolled, and then heard the snap of his parachute canopy somewhere above his head. Pilot and jet touched down simultaneously a quarter of a mile apart, the Super Sabre exploding into a mammoth orange fireball.

Joe Kittinger's luck had held once again. Within an hour after the accident, he was back in the officer's club telling the story. But to keep his accounts with fate squared up, he made a point of tracking down the man who had packed his chute that day and presenting him with a bottle of whiskey.

Kittinger was not Buck Rogers. Nor was he a daredevil or thrill-seeker. He was a modern-day test pilot: intense, focused, usually quiet and always polite, with firm religious convictions and a powerful sense of loyalty. If he was often stubborn, uncompromising, and demanding, he also dealt fairly and respectfully with those who came into contact with him. He was a straight arrow and a straight shooter. But Dr. Marvin Feldstein, who was appointed chief medical officer for *Excelsior III* and who came to know his project officer as a friend, says flatly, "The man is not the hero stereotype."

The luck that seems to have been Joe Kittinger's companion for life was not blind. He stalked his luck like the alligators he hunted in his Florida childhood. His parents gave him the responsibility that led to a supreme self-confidence, if not arrogance, but Kittinger never allowed his faith in himself to degenerate into complacency. Years afterward, remembering a violent speedboat accident he experienced as a young man—an accident that nearly killed him—Kittinger listed the lessons gleaned from the disaster: "First: know your abilities and don't overestimate yourself. Second: know the capability of the equipment you are using and don't demand more than it can give you in service and performance. Third: don't become complacent."

It was the same prescription for success he would take into the final difficult phase of Project Excelsior. Alan Shepard, who would later become the first American to ride a rocket into space, recalled his Air Force days with Kittinger: "He'll outwork you and out-think you. He just stays with it and stays with it."

The launch date for the third flight was targeted for summer. The second test flight from 75,000 feet had gone without a hitch, but 100,000 feet was something else again. The Manhigh flights had been there, but not without the considerable protection of a pressurized capsule. To send someone to that height with nothing between him and the vacuum but his suit required altogether another level of performance and confidence, and presented altogether another level of danger. Complacency would truly be the enemy now. The additional five miles of altitude would be psychologically challenging. Kittinger knew that if his pressure suit or oxygen system failed at 75,000 feet, he had at least a fighting chance of survival. With a quick exit, he would be able to fall into more hospitable air space within a couple of minutes. Above 100,000 feet, there was no margin for error. It was a strange situation, even for an experienced test pilot. Normally, even the most dangerous of assignments have backups and contingencies. But at 100,000 feet, nothing could help if any part of the survival system failed. If the poison fingers got to you up there, there would be nothing anyone could do. First your saliva begins to bubble, then your skin starts to puff up in spots; your stomach bloats and your eyes swell and pop outward; then the pressure ruptures the veins and arteries as boiling blood seeks an escape. In Kittinger's own estimation, "You're gonna be a dead son of a bitch."

On the afternoon of August 15, 1960, Kittinger was sedated and put to bed while the Excelsior launch crew prepared the site. They would launch the following morning from an old dirt airstrip that cut across the jackrabbit-infested yucca and squawbush north of the town of Tularosa, 18 miles from Holloman and due east of Trinity Site. That is, they would launch as long as the weather held. Duke Gildenberg had his wary eye on a Texas storm front.

At 7:00 P.M., Kittinger's rest was interrupted for a meal of lean beefsteak. After eating, he phoned his wife back in Dayton. She had been through such waits before, and as the wife of a veteran test pilot she had learned to live with uncertainty. But this time she was worried. He could hear it in her voice. And he could only pretend that it did not bother him. He went back to sleep until awakened by Francis Beaupre one hour before midnight.

While Kittinger ate breakfast, a convoy of vehicles pulled out of the main Holloman gate without him and headed toward Alamogordo. The string of pickup trucks, helium tankers, communications vans, press cars and TV vans, flatbeds hauling the balloon and gondola and other equipment required for launch—stretching a full three city blocks in length—turned north on Highway 54 and rumbled through the darkness toward Tularosa. A yellow crescent moon floated on the horizon and the headlights of the trucks swarmed with tiny insects.

At the launch site east of town, bright white searchlights lit up the night and the busy crew of electrical technicians with their checklists scurrying back and forth across the dirt runway, the gondola crew, the balloon crew, the life-support and pressure-suit personnel, and the photographic systems people. This team had been together now for a year and a half, and each member moved with a sense of purpose. The occasional tiny flares of matches lighting cigarettes and illuminating faces bent to cupped hands appeared in the shadows on the periphery, and the wisps of steam from thermoses of coffee drifted across the beams of the searchlights.

The assistant project officer and operations officer for *Excelsior III* was Capt. Billy Mills. He had served as jumpmaster for the original jump tests of the BMSP, but now—with Kittinger being suited up for a wild ride to the edge of space—he was in charge. Mills chomped nervously on a cigar and squinted at his own checklist. It contained more than 1,000 items.

One of those items concerned a piece of equipment supplied by Kittinger's five-year-old son, Mark, who had reasoned that no vehicle ought to undertake a major journey without some sort of official identification. Mark had carefully cut a cardboard license plate from the side of a cereal box and had his mother send it to New Mexico. So, in the early hours of August 16, members of the gondola crew carefully taped a replica of a tiny Oregon license plate to the side of *Excelsior III*. The gondola was now stratosphere-legal.

At 2:00 A.M., Joe Kittinger arrived by helicopter, escorted by Francis Beaupre and photographic systems engineer Ken Arnold. One reporter likened it to the entrance of a movie star onto a Hollywood set. As always, Kittinger wore an old red hunting cap—it was his trademark good luck charm. Members of the Holloman Balloon Branch crew, as well as those from Kittinger's Excelsior team from Wright, momentarily stopped their chores to catch a glimpse of the leading man. Photographers clicked away and motion-picture cameras whirred. Kittinger smiled and waved to his faithful supporting cast.

But within minutes, Kittinger was whisked inside the crowded air-conditioned van in which he would be prepared for his ordeal. Inside, the "dressing" crew waited: Robert Daniels, George Post, Medical Officer Richard Chubb, and T.Sgt. Eugene Fritz. Also present were Rowe Findley and Kurt Wentzel from *National Geographic,* who would provide "pool" pictures for the rest of the news organizations present. The first step was to denitrogenize the blood; Daniels strapped an oxygen mask to Kittinger's face and had him recline for another half-hour of rest. The air-conditioned environment was necessary to ensure that Kittinger did not perspire. August in New Mexico is hot—even at 3:30 in the morning.

Then, with the door of the van sealed tight and the temperature at an acceptable 50° Fahrenheit, just as Kittinger had pulled on the first set of longjohns, the crew inside heard the staccato backfire and stammer of the generator that sat outside on the desert floor. The gush of cool air died and an eerie silence filled the van.

At that precise moment outside the van, a member of the launch crew, M.Sgt. Gene Fowler, happened to hear the backfire of the generator's motor. He saw the implications right away: without an air conditioner, the launch would likely be scrubbed. He reasoned, correctly, that parts to repair the motor were not available at the launch site. It would take a couple of hours—minimum—to locate and retrieve parts. And that would be too late to save the launch or the partially inflated balloon.

Fowler quickly removed a plate that covered the generator and saw that a ground wire had come off the magneto. The motor continued to cough and sputter. The ground wire was at the back of the engine, a full arm's length inside the generator. Without consulting anyone, Fowler reached inside the motor that was still running spasmodically, found the wire with his fingers, and held it against the post of the magneto. It was a delicate operation: not only was the engine hot and full of moving parts, but if the ground wire were to slip and make contact with a plug, Fowler risked a powerful jolt of electricity.

But he held it steady against the magneto post and the engine roared back. There was no way with one hand—and that was absolutely all that would fit into the motor—to attach the wire. Fowler had to kneel there and hold it. So he held it. Inside the van, the launch crew heard the sound of the motor smooth out, followed by the welcome hiss of cool air. Without knowing who or what had saved them, they were able to resume the dressing procedure.

Outside, Fowler continued to hold the wire. For two long hours he held it. It was an almost superhuman effort, one that had completely exhausted him by the time Kittinger, Daniels, and the rest emerged from the van. No reporters would interview him and no record books would record his contribution, but without Master Sergeant Fowler's quiet dedication, *Excelsior III* would not have launched that morning.

Duke Gildenberg and meteorologists from the missile range were still concerned about the Texas storm. The skies over New Mexico were clear and full of bone-white stars, but that could change in a matter of hours. Rain had already been reported on the northern perimeter of the range. Billy Mills was furious when word came down that a 30-minute hold had been ordered on the launch, moving Kittinger's departure time back to 5:30. But the hold provided a more comfortable margin of safety. If the front was going to move north and east, it should begin to show signs by then. Small pilot balloons were released from the launch site hourly to provide up-to-the-minute data on wind direction and velocity.

The gondola sat waiting on a flatbed truck. Kittinger, fully laden, weighed over 300 pounds and had to be helped up onto the bed of the truck and then into the cramped gondola itself. The gondola was equipped with a new feature for this flight, courtesy of *National Geographic:* a twelfth camera, this one loaded with color film and positioned at the apex of the frame's tepee. It was 5:00 in the morning as the crew maneuvered Kittinger into a sitting position. The air conditioner was transferred from the van to the truck and cold air was continually hosed over Kittinger's flight suit to keep his body temperature down during the wait.

Last-minute checks and double-checks kept Melvin Johnson's launch crew darting and hovering around the truck, swarming around the gondola like wasps on a fallen apple. Daniels personally lowered the helmet carefully into position and verified the integrity of the seal. It was a sober moment for Kittinger: "The helmet is lowered over my head, and suddenly I feel a man apart."

A flare was set off to mark 10 minutes to launch. The truck bearing the gondola was driven slowly under the balloon launch arm and the gondola's harness was attached to the glossy balloon that rose a full 360 feet into the dawn sky. Kittinger could feel the power of the gas surging against the restraining lines. Then, almost before he was ready, he could hear the muffled pop as a squib fired and the first of the lines was blown free.

Duke Gildenberg, back in the weather van with his maps and meteorological reports, had struggled with his decision up until the final instant. The worrisome storm showed no signs of abating. As the final minutes before launch ticked down, he agonized. Then, finally, he did the only thing he could do under the circumstances. The main problem with this particular storm, he felt, was likely to be the interruption of optical tracking, but a storm was a storm and a plastic balloon was the wrong aircraft with which to tempt fate. The life of Joe Kittinger and the success of an entire program were at stake. After consulting with authorities from the White Sands Missile Range, Gildenberg issued the order to cancel the mission. The launch was off.

A messenger sprinted from the van toward the truck shouting Gildenberg's order: "The mission is canceled!" But his words were punctuated by the small explosion that released the second restraining line. *Excelsior III* was airborne one minute early, at 5:29 A.M.

As the messenger reached the truck, breathless, he watched helplessly as the gondola lifted quickly away, a diminishing silhouette against a blood-red sunrise.

nine

▼

One Man Alone

The *Excelsior III* gondola and pilot together weighed 1,250 pounds and the inflated balloon weighed another thousand, yet the entire package jumped off the earth as if it had been spring-loaded. The ascent rate held steady at 1,200 feet per minute as Kittinger rose through the warm morning air.

Almost immediately, the flight encountered its first difficulty: the UHF radio was not working. This wasn't a total disaster; voice messages could still be sent through the high-frequency system that would also be used to transmit pulse and respiratory rate. But it was a definite irritation. In order to monitor ground communication, Kittinger would be forced to listen to the drum of his own heartbeat and the slow, rhythmic rasp of his own breathing for the entire ascent.

As he rose, Kittinger could see the sky taking on color above him, but instead of the deep blue he was expecting, he saw a white swath of thin stratus awaiting him at about 15,000 feet. The sight was more than vaguely troubling. Unless the clouds moved, his view of the earth from altitude would be obstructed. If the clouds thickened, he might be able to see nothing at all of the ground. And if the cover dropped a few thousand feet lower and his flight path took him over one of the mountain ranges that bordered the Tularosa Basin and he was forced to fall through the clouds into the peaks. . . . Kittinger sat back and consoled himself with the knowledge that Duke Gildenberg would never have approved the launch if there was any danger of that.

The next sign of trouble did not manifest itself until the gondola had passed through the thin lace of clouds and then risen nearly to the tropopause. Everything seemed to be going normally—with the exception of the malfunctioning radio—when Kittinger noticed something odd. At this altitude, the air bladders in the partial-pressure suit were filled with pressurized oxygen and were squeezing his body firmly to compensate for the near-vacuum conditions. A gauge revealed the pressure inside his helmet, but only his body told him whether or not the suit itself was working properly. Every so often, he would flex his fingers and toes in order to feel the welcome resistance that told him the suit was pressurized even in its extremities.

At 50,000 feet, he flexed his fingers out of habit. His right hand felt wrong. He repeated the exercise. There was no resistance. The tube that fed the oxygen into the pressure glove had cracked; no gas was flowing into the right glove. Kittinger was well schooled in high-altitude physiology. He knew exactly what would happen to his hand if he continued to ascend. The air trapped beneath the skin would expand as the pressure decreased; the blood in the hand would become thick and heavy; the hand would swell grotesquely and, due to lack of circulation, would grow painfully cold.

Kittinger did not immediately radio his discovery to his crew on the ground. He was worried about his hand; he was afraid of what would happen as pressure continued to decrease. But he was also worried and afraid for Project Excelsior. There was no question that if he shared the facts about the unpressurized glove with the ground, Capt. Marvin Feldstein, Chief Medical Officer for the flight, together with Billy Mills, would order him to valve gas and descend without delay and without discussion. And he would have no choice but to comply.

Joe Kittinger faced a moment of decision. If he descended, there was a reasonable chance that Excelsior might never get this far again. There were funding problems, battles with the Air Force bureaucracy, technical issues to resolve—all of which might conspire to keep the project from achieving its goal. If he continued toward his destination at 100,000 feet, his hand might be damaged beyond repair. At the very least, the pain would be excruciating. And yet it did not take him long to reach a conclusion. In fact, the decision had been made before the balloon had ever left the ground. Kittinger had long since resolved that nothing short of the threat of death would cause him to abort this mission voluntarily. Too much work by too many people had brought them to this point. If he was not prepared to suffer hardship and some pain, he reasoned, he had no business setting foot in the gondola in the first place. Others had risked the same punishments and others had suffered. It was a price he decided he was willing to pay.

The problem with the glove would not affect his ability to perform the tasks necessary to complete the mission. He would still be capable of performing his measurement and monitoring chores during the ascent. He would still be able to communicate with the crew. And once at altitude, he would still be able to activate the timer and get out of the open door. Nowhere was his competency threatened by the situation.

It was really no decision at all. Kittinger simply refrained from mentioning the glove. "My reactions had absolutely nothing to do with fearlessness," he would write later. He had been acutely aware of his own fear. "My reactions were *pre*determined; I continued the ascent."

At this point, the ground crew monitoring voice communications became aware that the pilot was upset, but they did not yet appreciate the cause. Kittinger's brief observations of the stratosphere were peppered with the word "hostile." His communications were short and brusque. He refused attempts to draw him into further conversation.

The great balloon rose. At 60,000 feet the rate of ascent had increased to 1,300 feet per minute and Kittinger was instructed to valve some gas in order to slow himself down. If he rushed upward too quickly, the tenuous polyethylene could become stressed. The temperature was 94° below zero and a crack in the brittle plastic skin was always a very real possibility.

But while he monitored his ascent and tried to keep his mind off the nagging, stiffening ache in his right hand, conditions many miles below were changing. At 80,000 feet, Kittinger looked down and noticed that the thin layer of stratus he had observed earlier had become a substantial blanket of thick clouds. Gildenberg confirmed that the cloud layer was now more than a mile deep, stretching from approximately 15,000 feet to their tops at 21,000 feet. There was no cause for great alarm—communication was still possible and radar could still track the balloon's position—but Kittinger was tremendously disappointed to have his visual observation of the ground cut off. He could not see the white sands of the desert basin from which he had come and to which he hoped to return, and his crew who had worked so hard to put him where he was could no longer see his progress.

As he rose, the sensation of separation engulfed him. He was acutely aware that it was an overreaction, but the knowledge was no solace. He needed his crew and it was as if they had been blotted out. He became angry and bitter that the clouds had robbed him of this essential camaraderie. He warned himself that his emotions were threatening to deprive him of the concentration he would need to complete the mission and bring success back to his team on the ground, but these moments of lucid self-evaluation were fleeting. Helplessly, he felt his anger begin to boil.

Then, as the balloon rose through 85,000 feet, Dr. Feldstein, who had been monitoring the HF radio searching for clues as to his patient's psychological state, noticed a dramatic change. Suddenly, instead of the curt statements and irritated responses Joe Kittinger had been transmitting for the previous six miles of altitude, he began to gush words. It was uncharacteristic. Launching into lengthy, meticulous descriptions of the sights before him, Kittinger's monologues became increasingly sober and clinical.

This was not good news to Marvin Feldstein. The Joe Kittinger he knew and understood was the man who was forever reassuring his crew with glib asides ("No sweat") and jokes in the face of mortal danger ("Come and get me"). Now he was approaching the literal pinnacle of his career, the moment his entire life had prepared him for, the event he had gambled his career on—and he had turned coldly descriptive, impersonal, and humorless. Feldstein tried to cajole him into some lighthearted exchanges, but it did not work. "I was responsible for his safety," Feldstein wrote later, "but felt powerless, frustrated by my inability to help him."

Up in the *Excelsior* gondola, Joe Kittinger had indeed undergone a psychological sea change. After the initial fear and anger at his visual separation from the ground, he forced himself to evaluate his situation. Everything had been done for him that could possibly be done, he realized. His team had prepared the gondola, the balloon, and all the associated equipment as well as it could possibly have been prepared. He himself had been trained for this role as thoroughly as anyone could possibly have been trained. He had already accepted the risks associated with the mission and had come to terms with them. There was nothing more to do. His anger made no sense. He must accept his fate and trust in the competence of his equipment, his crew, and himself. In a fatalistic way, it was a comforting realization.

As the balloon rose through 90,000 feet, Kittinger radioed back long, vivid descriptions of the gradations of sky color from the pale horizon on up to the deep, dark blues and violets of the vertical.

On the ground, Marvin Feldstein finally thought he was getting a handle on what was happening to the mind of Joe Kittinger, why he had switched so suddenly from short, unrevealing responses to catalogic monologues.

He wanted to be certain that we knew everything he saw, that the dangerous beauty he had fought against would not be lost. The solemnity of his words, the earnest care with which he chose them, humbled me. And suddenly I realized why his remarks produced such a profound response in me; these were the words of a departing man. Joe thought he was going to die. He had accepted this possibility as fact and had now turned to view his surroundings with calm realism.

The balloon passed through 100,000 feet and continued to rise. Feldstein decided that the best thing he could do at this point was to provide whatever emotional support he could for his patient.

"Everybody's with you, Joe," he radioed.

Minutes later, *Excelsior III* was floating at 102,800 feet. Duke Gildenberg, who had never brought a balloon down more than a quarter mile from its target, asked that the balloon float at that altitude for 11 minutes while it drifted over the preferred drop site 20 miles below. As the balloon had risen through the troposphere, westerly winds had blown it 15 miles to the east of the launch site. Easterlies in the stratosphere had then sent it back nearly to the western edge of the Tularosa Basin. Kittinger had several minutes to observe and to send his report earthward.

We're at 103,000 feet. Looking out over a very beautiful, beautiful world . . . a hostile sky. As you look up the sky looks beautiful but hostile. As you sit here you realize that Man will never conquer space. He will learn to live with it, but he will never conquer it. Can see for over 400 miles. Beneath me I can see the clouds. . . . They are beautiful . . . Looking through my mirror the sky is absolutely black. Void of anything. . . . I can see the beautiful blue of the sky and above that it goes into a deep, deep, dark, indescribable blue which no artist can ever duplicate. It's fantastic.

Kittinger made a discovery as he surveyed the sights out the gondola door.

There are clouds at my altitude. They are so thin that I see them only when my vision comes within 30 degrees of the sun, but then they reflect the light with a dazzling whiteness. I remember reports of clouds this high, but the actual sight of them is fantastic.

Only an hour and a half earlier, Joe Kittinger had been on the surface of the earth. Now he hung suspended in the no-man's land between the familiar world and the black void of outer space. And suddenly, in a rushing surge of emotion and realization, he understood how special this moment really was. His right hand had swollen to twice its normal size, blood pooling beneath the skin and the circulation all but gone. The pain was ferocious. His eyes burned from the intensity of the sun's glare. Yet these distractions were somehow distant and inconsequential as he gazed with raw wonder across the wide expanse of clouds and stratospheric sky.

For the first time during the flight, he was able to appreciate the accomplishment. Over 99 percent of the earth's atmosphere was beneath him, and nothing stood between his eyes and the poison fingers of the stratosphere but the thin face shield of his helmet. It was an awesome moment, and Joe Kittinger savored it in silent jubilation.

Marvin Feldstein had started a countdown over the HF radio and Kittinger began to prepare himself to leave the gondola. When the count reached 90 seconds, Kittinger finally passed on the information he had been withholding.

"For your information, Marv," he announced casually, "my right hand is not pressurized."

Feldstein, appropriately alarmed, immediately began grilling Kittinger on the performance of the rest of the pressure suit and on the pressurized oxygen delivery system. He was worried that his subject might be keeping more, and possibly more alarming, news to himself.

It was Kittinger's turn to try and reassure the ground crew. "Okay," he said. "No sweat. No sweat."

Seconds later, as directed by the pre-exit checklist, Kittinger jettisoned the radio antenna that hung beneath the gondola. There would be no more news from *Excelsior III*. From here on out, Joe Kittinger would be very much on his own.

Feldstein, Mills, and Gildenberg in the command post on the desert floor were likewise on their own. They could no longer transmit messages to the gondola or listen to the pilot's voice. They couldn't even monitor his pulse or respiration for clues. They had only radar data that tracked the location of *Excelsior III* and would track Kittinger as he fell. Only later, with tape recordings recovered from the gondola, would they be able to examine the medical data.

Before Kittinger even raised himself off the styrofoam seat to begin the final preparations, his pulse rate jumped from 106 beats per minute to 136. He staggered to the door of the gondola—due to the decrease of gravity with altitude, he actually weighed three pounds less than he had on the ground—and positioned himself with the toes of his boots protruding slightly beyond the edge of the floor piece, then took a deep breath of pure oxygen and held it. A printed sign at the base of the door, inches below his toes, read: "HIGHEST STEP IN THE WORLD." He stood motionless as the gondola twirled beneath the bulging balloon and provided a slow pan of the scene out the open door. Haze obscured portions of the panorama, but he could clearly see a thunderhead building above Flagstaff, Arizona, 350 miles in the distance.

He looked up at the dark cosmos above him, then down at the rumpled carpet of clouds. He turned and pushed the button that activated all twelve cameras simultaneously; even inside his helmet he could plainly hear the clicking whir of all the tiny motors. Then he tried to grasp the familiar lanyard with his swollen, ice-cold right hand, and realized immediately that there was no way he could grip the lanyard, much less pull it. He let it drop. He would have to trust his weight to pull it and arm the timing knob on the harness as he fell.

Joe Kittinger steadied himself and shifted his weight slightly forward. He placed his hands on the sides of the gondola door and looked up one last time. His final words aboard *Excelsior III* were not addressed to the crew. They were audible only to himself and to the flight tape recorder.

"Lord, take care of me now."

Kittinger fell forward as he had done on the two previous flights, but it was different this time. This time he was convinced he was going to die.

At 7:10 A.M., he was out. He was floating. It was like before: no rush of wind, no sensation of falling, no perception of movement at all. The universe was calm. He hung suspended, nearly 103,000 feet above the earth, in complete silence. His pulse raced at 156 beats per minute, twice the normal rate. He had not taken a breath since leaving the gondola and so not even the sound of his own respiration intruded on the astonishing emptiness. It was all impossibly beautiful.

He forced himself to kick and twist his torso. Then he was on his back, looking up. A white ball of light—the 200-foot-wide balloon—shot away as if snapped from a huge rubber band, retreating into the inky-black backdrop of outer space. He knew that in reality it was he who was moving away from the balloon, falling at tremendous speed, accelerating, gaining 22 MPH of speed each second, but it was nearly

"The highest step in the world." Kittinger falls from the *Excelsior* gondola on the final flight: "Lord, take care of me now." *(Source: Volkmar Wentzel, © National Geographic Society)*

impossible to believe it as he watched the ball of light shrink. He still imagined that he was floating.

He searched the blackness for stars. For years he had wondered what it would be like to view the stars from above the atmosphere. But now that he was here, he couldn't find them. And then he understood with a shock of intense disappointment that he had been light-blinded by the brightness of the sun's reflection on the huge plastic balloon. He would not see the stars after all.

Then, precisely 16 seconds after leaving the familiar confines of the gondola, he felt a gentle shudder on his back. And then a slight jolt as the stabilization chute opened and filled above him. He realized that somehow—without his being aware of it—his position had changed and that now he was falling feet earthward in a perfectly stable attitude. The first stage of the Beaupre chute had worked flawlessly.

The instrument kit that was strapped to Kittinger's rear end contained a tape recorder. The device had proven problematic during the earlier Excelsior jumps, but technicians from the Air Force's Aerospace Medical Laboratory's Bioelectronics Section had worked to improve the mechanism and on this attempt the recorder functioned without a hitch. As Kittinger fell through the stratosphere, not only were his heartbeat and respiration recorded, but his voice was captured as well.

"Chute opened," he said after realizing that the stabilization chute had deployed. Kittinger gasped and sucked in a deep breath, his first since leaving the gondola. He began to monitor the stopwatch and altimeter on his wrist and record the readings.

"Thirty seconds." He had been hurtling through the stratosphere for half a minute now. As he fell through the 90,000-foot mark he was traveling at an almost unbelievable airspeed of 614 MPH, on the verge of the speed of sound.*

"Multistage is working perfectly," he reported. At this point, he began to be aware of the tug of the stabilization chute on his harness. Very gradually, the air thickened and the chute began to exert a slight drag.

Then, as he fell, Kittinger felt a familiar choking sensation. He had experienced the same thing for a brief moment on *Excelsior II*. But this was worse. He could not breathe. He was strangling. Fear gripped him as he felt consciousness ebbing.

---

*The speed of sound varies with temperature. On a summer day at sea level near the equator, it is approximately 740 MPH. In the cold of the tropopause, it is only about 660 MPH.

"Can't get my breath . . ."

He gasped, trying to find air. He fought against the strangling, determined to keep his senses and work past the choking.

"Can't get my . . . breath . . ." He felt himself going light-headed and bore down, refusing to fade.

And then, suddenly, the sensation disappeared as mysteriously as it had come. He could breathe again. The terrible pressure in his throat had vanished and he relaxed.

His position remained unchanged. He sped toward the earth feet first, in complete control of his fall.

"Seventy thousand."

With the choking gone, a feeling of joy and accomplishment enveloped Kittinger. The BMSP was vindicated.

"Perfect stability. . . . Beautiful!"

He had now been falling for over a minute and a half.

"Multistage. . . . Beautiful stability. . . . Multistage perfect." He could not get over what was happening. He was hurtling through the stratosphere and he was in complete control of himself and his equipment. It was the most incredible ride ever taken and he was cruising in comfort. He fell through 60,000 feet. Then 50,000.

"Perfect stability," he repeated. His airspeed had now been reduced to about 250 MPH and he was fast approaching the troposphere. If his pressure suit were to fail now, he knew, he would probably have a chance at survival. Another 30 seconds and he would be safe. He felt the elation course through him again. It seemed almost impossible to believe that he was going to survive this jump. He was feeling secure enough now to experiment with his body position. Just how well could he control movement?

"I'm going to turn to the right." He dropped his right shoulder and kicked his leg.

"Beautiful. . . . Perfect!"

As he approached the 40,000-foot region, he entered the coldest part of the atmosphere. The temperature measured 98° below zero.

"Face plate getting fogged up." The familiar condensation began to creep in from the edges of his face shield.

"Forty thousand. . . . Two minutes thirty seconds." He could feel now that the constriction of the partial-pressure suit had relaxed.

"Out of positive pressure. . . . The face plate fogged up a little bit. . . . Thirty-five thousand."

The familiar world was coming up to receive him. From this point on, the air would grow progressively warmer. The pressure of the air would continue to increase. The molecules that make up the atmospheric gases would become denser and his rate of fall would decrease. He began to check his stopwatch and his altimeter every few seconds. They were his confirmation that he was going to survive this 20-mile jump.

"Little cold in my legs. Thirty thousand. No . . . correction: thirty-four. Coming up on three minutes. Perfect stability!"

He continued to struggle with the condensation on his face shield. The parachute system was working so well—it was annoying to have his vision impaired. He lifted the sun visor on the shield to see if that would help.

"Awful bright." He fell through the 30,000-foot mark. Three and a half minutes had elapsed since he first stepped out of the gondola.

At this point, Kittinger noticed the layer of clouds that had worried him so much on the ascent. He had managed to put them out of his mind, but now here they were, rushing up. He had never fallen through thick cloud cover before and didn't find the prospect appealing. In spite of the fact that his brain told him the white formations were nothing more than water vapor and that he would burst through them as if they were puffs of smoke, his gut told him it was bad to fall through anything other than clear space. His pulse raced again and his voice became anxious.

"Undercast beneath me." He also thought of his main parachute canopy. It was set to open at 18,000 feet, but he felt for the manual override ring just in case. "Override in my hand for the pack opening. Coming up on twenty thousand! Multistage is beautiful. . . . Perfect stability. Four minutes! The undercast beneath me. The multistage is going perfect. . . . Beautiful! Four minutes ten seconds. I can turn around perfect. Can do everything."

The anticipation of the main chute opening mixed with the elation of the entire experience. Kittinger checked the instruments on his wrist.

"Twenty thousand. Four minutes twenty-five seconds." He could see the clouds coming up like mountains of cotton. He pulled his legs up as if to prepare for impact.

"Four minutes thirty seconds. We're going into the overcast. . . . Into the overcast!" His heart pounded. "The main chute just opened. . . . Right on the button!"

It was too much to believe.

"Four minutes and thirty-seven seconds free fall. Eighteen thousand feet. Ahhhhhh boy!"

With the main red-and-white canopy open above him and his rate of descent slowed to 18 feet per second, Kittinger was finally able to relax. The almost unimaginable stress that had gripped him for the better part of the ascent and during the long freefall seeped gradually away as he approached the ground. No longer was his goal simply the earth. It was more than the earth now. It was New Mexico. The White Sands. Holloman. His crew and friends were waiting for him. As he came out of the clouds, he looked down to see a desert very different from the one he had left that morning. The Texas storm front had brought rain and the sands were pockmarked with hundreds of small lakes. His respiration slowed, his heartbeat slowed.

"Thank you, God, thank you," he murmured. "Thank you for protecting me during that long descent. Thank you, God. Thank you."

For the last minute and forty-five seconds of his jump from the stratosphere, Joe Kittinger repeated those words. "Thank you, God. . . . Thank you."

But in spite of this emotional release, Kittinger did not have the luxury of simply drifting down to the desert floor. There was still work to do.

First he disconnected his electric gloves. The pain in his swollen right hand had not abated. Next he removed a special hook-bladed knife from a compartment on one forearm of his flight suit and slashed through the nylon tie lines that secured the left side of the bright red instrument kit to his back side. The kit weighed 80 pounds and needed to be released before landing. The kit had its own parachute that would drop it safely to the ground. He disconnected several hoses that were attached to the kit. His altimeter read 1,000 feet. Then he disarmed the reserve chest parachute. The pain in his right hand made him wince.

He noticed two helicopters hovering nearby, ready to drop down to his landing spot. He struggled to cut the tie lines to the right side of the instrument kit, slashing at them, but his right hand was useless. He could barely grip the knife. He got through everything but one hose. The last hose was impossible. He couldn't cut it. Finally, he gave up. He resigned himself to landing with the heavy kit attached.

"I can't get the kit off," he said. Instead, he raised the face shield on his helmet and drank in the fresh air. The temperature was in the neighborhood of 100°, but the air felt like a cool breeze.

"Oh, gee, it feels good. That cold air." He looked down. The ground was coming up fast. "Now, let's see . . ."

Kittinger smashed into the ground 27 miles west of Tularosa weighing, with his gear and the instrument kit, 320 pounds. It was the hardest landing he would ever experience. The instrument kit slammed into his leg. He rolled out on the sandy, sage-covered ground like a stuffed doll tossed in the dirt. He glanced at the stopwatch on his wrist and noted that a total of 13 minutes and 45 seconds had elapsed since he had plunged from the open door of the *Excelsior* gondola and embarked on the journey of a lifetime. But now it was over and he was alive. It still seemed almost impossible.

As medical personnel, press, and friends poured out of the helicopters and surrounded Kittinger, he glanced up and managed a relieved smile through the open faceplate of his helmet.

"I'm very glad to be back with you all," he said.

At 10:00 that same morning, before having anything to eat or even phoning his wife, Kittinger—dressed now in a crisp, blue USAF uniform—met the press in a briefing room back at Holloman. "I was the lucky one," he told them. "I made the jump. But without all these ground people we couldn't have done it at all. We tested everything we could first, and then this human test was necessary. It showed us among other things that man's only limit is his imagination." If the cynical press had been charmed by McClure before and after the *Manhigh III* flight, it fell in love with Joe Kittinger. They listened like children to the telling of a fairy tale. And when Kittinger had finished, the room erupted in applause.

"Could you see the Grand Canyon?" one reporter shouted.

"Not with the overcast," he said, "but I could have seen it."

"What could you see from float altitude?"

"I could see El Paso," Kittinger answered. "And Guadalupe in the distance."

Three hours after landing, the swelling in Kittinger's right hand was gone and circulation was back to normal. He sat with his feet up on a desk in a Holloman office, surrounded by members of the crew and others, and—in the best test-pilot tradition—relived the story of the longest jump ever attempted.

The following morning, the entire Excelsior brain trust assembled at Holloman for a postmortem. It was a revelation for Kittinger to sit and listen to the voice tape made on his way down through the stratosphere. He could hear the gamut of emotion in his comments and inflections: from terror to exultation. Yet when he heard his voice during the final two minutes of the fall, after the main canopy had opened and he had finally been able to find release from the steely tension that had gripped him, he was dumbfounded. He heard his voice repeating "Thank you, God. . . . thank you," but he had trouble believing what he was hearing. He was completely unable to remember saying those things. He listened to the tape again. It was his voice but he still couldn't believe it.

He became angry. "That is the voice of a coward!" he snapped. Somehow, whether it was the words themselves or something in the sound of his voice, he was not able to accept that he had ended the greatest event of his career with a litany of prayer. Dr. Feldstein tried to explain:

The remark is obviously not true. Joe was afraid; he was not a coward. Perhaps this reaction of his explains the reason why this event remained submerged beneath the other mass of information that he had related to us. Rather than a literal interpretation of his statement, it would be more accurate to say that an emotional release of this nature was not included in Joe Kittinger's personality profile of himself and, as such, was subconsciously repressed. This incident dramatically emphasizes the inherent inadequacies of the human observer.

In spite of the radio problems and the malfunction in the right pressure glove, *Excelsior III* was judged an almost total success. This was good news to George Post who was scheduled to repeat Kittinger's performance and jump from 103,000 feet himself in *Excelsior IV*.

One additional problem, though, would have to be worked out. For at least 30 seconds during the jump, Kittinger had been subjected to the mysterious choking sensation. Anything that hinders one's breathing is by definition serious. They would have to pinpoint the cause and eliminate it before Post's flight could proceed.

Kittinger and crew wasted no time. They immediately set up full-dress "hanging" tests in which both Kittinger and Post were suspended in their parachute harnesses to simulate actual jump conditions. One possible culprit was a steel cable that bound the helmet to the pressure suit: the cable tended to slip up and tip the back of the helmet forward, causing the front of the helmet and neck ring forward against the subject's windpipe. This might have caused Kittinger's choking incident, but it was impossible to be certain that they had solved the problem.

Unfortunately, the postmortem and hanging tests pointed to other potential trouble spots in the pressure suit. It was agreed that the suit and pressurization system would need to be rethought and perhaps overhauled. The loss of pressurization in a glove was one thing. If a larger failure should occur, the jumper's life would be at serious risk.

Back at the Aeromedical Laboratory in Ohio, Colonel Stapp weighed the evidence. Excelsior had already achieved a great deal. He had to determine whether the possible gains of another flight offset the hazards to the life of the pilot/jumper. Stapp at first postponed the flight until more information about the pressure suit problems could be gathered. Then, reluctantly, he made the decision to cancel the program.

The cancellation was a crushing blow to George Post, the man whom Joe Kittinger has called the greatest parachutist in the history of the Air Force. Post had already received the Distinguished Flying Cross for his work on the ejection seat tests in the mid-fifties, but he wanted his own chance to make a jump from the upper stratosphere. He saw it as the crowning achievement for his career as a jumper. Kittinger and Stapp and the entire Excelsior team hated to see the project canceled before Post got a chance at his big jump, but the decision had been made. It was over.

And though it had ended prematurely, Excelsior had achieved a great deal. Stated simply, the project had established that fliers could leave their craft at extraordinary—previously unthinkable—altitudes and freefall back into the earth's atmosphere. Kittinger had done it three times in a row and was none the worse for wear. And he had not worn loads of exotic survival equipment unavailable to the average jet pilot. True, he had worn electrically heated socks and gloves. But those had been necessary because of exposure during the slow balloon ascent that would not be an issue for someone in an enclosed cockpit. Otherwise, he had worn standard-issue high-altitude pilot gear, which included the partial-pressure suit and helmet. His jumps had been realistic tests.

A friend and colleague of Kittinger's, and the man who would fly the final Mercury mission for NASA two and one-half years later, Gordon Cooper, attests to the significance of Project Excelsior:

It was absolutely vital. We had to know if we could build the right kind of equipment to sustain life, and certainly Joe's job was the ideal test of hardware and equipment. . . . We didn't have any idea about the body's stability at high altitudes or what kind of dynamics the human body would go through or how to build a drogue chute that would stabilize it. It was totally unknown. Everybody who came along conjectured a different theory. You never knew whether any of them had any merit or were totally wrong until it was done. You had to send a guy up to do it.

Another of the original Mercury astronauts who remained an active member of the NASA team through Apollo, Deke Slayton, offers his own assessment of Kittinger and Excelsior:

We knew damned little at that point in time. That was an ambitious thing he did, and it was a valuable thing for the space program because when we got into *Gemini,* we had ejection seats for the first time, and a lot of the information Joe gathered went right into the design. He also tested prototypes of the pressure suits we wore.

Kittinger's rare blend of drive, guts, brains, and prudence impressed another former colleague who went on to play a key role in NASA, Alan Shepard. "Would I have jumped out of that balloon?" Shepard asks incredulously. "That's easy. Hell no. Absolutely not." Cooper seconds the motion: "I don't know if I'd have made that jump or not. It was way, way out for those times. It still is. It's never even come close to being equalled."

The technical breakthrough that had brought success to Excelsior was Francis Beaupre's radical multistage parachute. It had effectively eliminated the insidious flat spin that had tormented high-altitude jumpers for decades. It made descent from extreme heights not only feasible, but—as Kittinger could attest—comfortable and potentially exhilarating: "It was a blast!"

The balloon itself had also been a success, thanks in large part to the Holloman Balloon Branch headed by Maj. Irving Levin. In spite of the fact that it had been little more than a vehicle for ferrying Kittinger up to jump altitude, it was worth noting that a new unofficial balloon altitude record had been set in the process. *Excelsior III* had risen several hundred feet higher than had David Simons in *Manhigh II.* Clearly, there were other useful applications for a vehicle capable of floating for some period of time at that height. There was a wealth of scientific and medical knowledge still to be gained from the balloon-borne experiments and observers. Training for space travelers was an obvious application. There was also the possibility that a balloon platform might someday prove valuable for launching satellites into orbit.

A valuable physics lesson reinforced by Excelsior concerned the effects of direct solar radiation on a human being above earth atmosphere. The effects of the sun at 100,000 feet are nearly twice as intense as at sea level and a great deal of care must be taken to adequately protect the exposed person from extremes of heat and cold. When the atmosphere is thin or nonexistent, our conception of temperature becomes irrelevant. At 100,000 feet, the ambient temperature might be measured at 35° below zero—but this is extremely misleading. For although the temperature of the surrounding "air" is extremely cold, a human exposed to the direct rays of the sun at that altitude will feel extreme heat. In fact, a body suspended in air at 100,000 feet without thermal protection would boil on the surface exposed to the sun and freeze on the surface away from the sun. Kittinger, protected by his survival clothing, found that he would sweat beneath areas of his flight suit that received the direct rays of the sun, and that a steamy vapor would begin to rise from those same areas the moment they were covered with shadow. So even though the stratosphere is very cold, protection from the intense heat of the sun is critical.

Both Kittinger and Stapp were extremely pleased with Project Excelsior. They had done what they set out to do and shared the satisfaction of success with an extraordinary team of individuals: Beaupre, Daniels, Gildenberg, Post, Mills, and many others. As Kittinger put it: "One man alone is nothing; one man supported by people like these . . . can do anything."

Yet the long-term legacy of Project Excelsior is not without its disappointments. For one, the Air Force never adopted the Beaupre multistage chute for high-altitude pilots and never developed an adequate high-altitude pilot ejection system. Instead, the prevailing dictum was that pilots should remain with their aircraft until they were back down into the lower atmosphere before ejecting. Parachutes were eventually added to both high-altitude aircraft and spacecraft, but no real provision was made for escape from a burning jet at higher stratospheric altitudes. Air Force statistics on survival rates of pilots who eject above 40,000 feet with a standard parachute are grim indeed.

Nor was NASA very interested in the Excelsior-style survival system. Kittinger and Stapp were convinced that it was mostly politics. Why should a huge organization like NASA, already operating in what Tom Wolfe would call the "billion-volt, limitless-budget future" even take notice of a two-bit bootleg balloon program run by renegade doctors and test pilots? All three Excelsior jumps had been accomplished for a total cash outlay of about $30,000, a trivial amount that was within the margin of error on NASA ledgers.

"There was a lot of bickering because we stepped on a lot of people's toes by what we'd done," Kittinger explained. "NASA was in a world all their own. If they didn't invent it, they didn't want anything to do with it."* And like David Simons's bitterness over NASA's refusal to adopt a Manhigh-like multigas capsule atmosphere, Kittinger believes that the space program's failure to adopt a stratospheric escape system for some of its later vehicles led to equally tragic results. "If they would have used our system, when the *Challenger* blew up, those people would have had a chance. Those people were alive when they hit the water." The space shuttle *Challenger* exploded at about the same altitude from which Kittinger jumped from *Excelsior III.* "The space shuttle is the only experimental aircraft ever used by man that does not have a means of escape for the most critical point of the flight: takeoff. They still don't have it." He reiterates in a tone that resonates with missionary hatred: "Those people were alive!"

Kittinger's feet rested squarely on the shoulders of other equally brave and dedicated individuals who had pioneered the use of parachutes for high-altitude survival. Not only George Post, but many others before him. Yet it was Joe Kittinger who drove the Excelsior program to the success that had eluded Project High Dive. It was Kittinger whose relentless insistence on perfection and dogged refusal to be denied had catalyzed a team and focused it on a single objective. And it was fitting that Kittinger should get the accolades.

He had already received the Distinguished Flying Cross for his flight in *Manhigh I,* but the honors really started to pile up now. (He would eventually receive five Oak Leaf Clusters for his Cross.) In September, President Eisenhower presented Kittinger with the Harmon International Trophy in a White House ceremony. He also received the Leo Stevens Parachute Medal and the John Jeffries Award for "outstanding contributions to the advancement of aeronautics through medical research."

Life magazine ran an article, based on an exclusive postflight interview, chronicling Kittinger's triumphal jump and glorifying the young

---

*After learning of Kittinger's work on Excelsior, Alan Shepard tried to convince NASA to include a personal parachute system for astronauts on Project Mercury so that escape from a malfunctioning spacecraft within the earth's gravity might be survivable. After the spectacular success of the final Excelsior flight, NASA was compelled to consider such an escape system. In the end, though, the notion of putting a personal parachute on board was abandoned.

captain as a "new space hero." Like David Simons before him, Kittinger strove to clarify the project's objectives and tried to draw attention to the real significance of what had been accomplished: "This project was no stunt, you see. And never meant to be. Sometimes the news gets it wrong, or builds it wrong, but I want you to understand, this was done for scientific knowledge and nothing else. . . . We've got to know all about those hazards up there, out in space." Dramatic full-page, black-and-white photographs taken from one of the gondola-mounted cameras showed Kittinger in mid-jump as a tiny, doll-like form against a background of billowing clouds. Another picture showed a bare-chested Kittinger sitting up amid the sage and salt grass, the waffle-weave pattern of the long underwear embedded in his skin, lighting a cigarette and wearing a genuine hero's grin. *Time* called him "steel-nerved" and made the inevitable comparison with Buck Rogers. *National Geographic* hired him to supply text to accompany a stunning collection of photographs. E. P. Dutton in New York gave him a book contract for a first-person account of his adventure.

As the weeks following the jump passed, Kittinger began to take advantage of the press attention that came his way to talk about other projects he envisioned. There was some discussion of putting him in the nose cone of a Redstone rocket and ejecting him 100 miles up into space, to be followed by a freefall back to earth. Kittinger believed it was possible and he wanted to try it. But he never lost interest in balloon-borne vehicles. Balloons, he believed, could provide the perfect platforms with which to prepare for manned space missions. They could provide testing for equipment and for space travelers. He also harbored a special love for and fascination with astronomy, he explained. The problem was, the earth's atmosphere distorts our view of the heavens. He remained disappointed by his inability to see stars as he fell from the *Excelsior III* gondola. What he wanted to do now, he announced, was to ascend in a balloon to a satisfactory height and train a telescope on the stars.

At the very least, high-altitude astronomy represented a potential return ticket to the stratosphere. Kittinger had gone four times into that barren frontier already, and three of them had flirted with disaster.

Now he wanted more.

ten

▼

Analog for Space Flight

In the face of such highly successful Air Force programs as Manhigh
and Excelsior, it is easy to overlook the fact that the first super-high-
altitude manned balloon trip since the thirties had been made not by
one of the USAF balloon groups but by the U.S. Navy. In November
of 1956, well over a year after the founding of Project Manhigh, but still
several months before Kittinger's test flight, lieutenant commanders
Malcolm Ross and Lee Lewis set a new balloon altitude record—76,000
feet—with a plastic, helium-filled balloon called *Strato-Lab,* one of the
descendants of the Office of Naval Research's influential but ultimately
failed Project Helios.

After the cancellation of Helios in 1947, while the Air Force's
Cambridge Research Labs were in the early phases of the Moby Dick
balloon program and James Henry and David Simons were sending animals up in the nose cones of V-2 rockets, the ONR founded Project
Skyhook. The ONR contracted first with General Mills to build a series
of single-cell, unmanned plastic balloons for testing. The 200,000-cubic-
foot balloons, constructed of one-mil polyethylene, were designed to
carry a 70-pound payload to 100,000 feet. When Otto Winzen left
General Mills to form Winzen Research in 1948, the Skyhook contract
went with him. The ONR and Winzen, using the University of
Minnesota as a research facility, developed a number of high-altitude
experiments for the project.* Skyhook ultimately proved to be a valuable

---

*The University of Minnesota physics department began its association with the
ONR during Project Skyhook in 1948. Using newly discovered nuclear emulsions,
the group conducted unmanned high-altitude balloon experiments that resulted in
major discoveries of cosmic radiation components, establishing the presence of
helium nuclei and other heavy nuclei like iron in the primary flux of cosmic rays.

scientific program, collecting data on a number of atmospheric and meteorological subjects, but especially on cosmic radiation.

By 1949, Charles B. Moore (originally of the balloon team at New York University), who had replaced Winzen at General Mills, had reestablished contact with the ONR and secured a contract for the company to build plastic balloons for the Navy once again. Moore spent a great deal of his energy arguing the case for manned balloon flights, and on November 3 he became the first human being to fly a plastic balloon. Moore, as fearless as he was curious, would make several flights using Skyhook balloons connected to nothing more than a parachute harness. On one such flight, much to his wife's horror, he used cushions borrowed from the family sofa to pad the harness straps. (The balloon/parachute-harness concept was later considered as a means of getting U.S. agents across the Iron Curtain.)

Then, in 1954, thanks largely to Moore's insistence, but also to Lewis and Ross who had been assigned by the ONR to the General Mills balloon team, Project Strato-Lab was born. The idea was to create a manned, balloon-borne laboratory that would serve as a stratospheric platform for a wide range of atmospheric and biomedical endeavors. The stated objectives were threefold:

1. To provide a high-altitude research platform;
2. To provide an opportunity to study human reaction to a high-altitude environment; and
3. To provide an opportunity to conduct specific scientific experiments.

The early days of the program saw Jean Piccard's old aluminum Helios gondola retrieved from storage and given to Winzen Research for refurbishing. Balloon technologies, pressure suits, and instrumentation were evaluated by a large group of expert consultants from all branches of the service, from the universities, from private industry, and from scientific organizations. Winzen Research tested the closed-gondola system extensively, sometimes employing unique methods. In a report to the ONR, one such technique was noted: "During one 8-hour [climatic] test, Mr. Winzen took his loyal dog, Brandy, in the gondola with him, together with another co-worker. Brandy, true to his usual Boxer form, obliged by providing the necessary odors, thus giving a clue to the absorption capacity of the system."

Meanwhile, in August of 1956, Ross and Lewis rode in an open gon-

Otto Winzen (*right*) poses with Dr. Vern Suomi, a Winzen Research consultant, and the *Strato-Lab* gondola. (*Source: Vera Simons*)

dola to a height of 40,000 feet to test pressure suits and balloon control. (A B. F. Goodrich engineer named Carroll Krupp had worked with the Navy to develop a sophisticated pressure suit. The design was unique and testing had been classified as top secret.) Even though this flight went largely unnoticed, it was the first penetration of the stratosphere by

Americans since *Explorer II* in 1935; it was also the first manned strato-spheric flight to employ a polyethylene balloon.

Three months later, at 6:19 in the morning on a frozen November 8, *Strato-Lab I* was launched from the historic Stratobowl in the Black Hills of South Dakota. As Lewis pulled the second of the gondola's two hatches shut, he saw for the first time a drawing someone on the crew had pasted there. It was a caricature of a smiling Indian chief with arrows piercing his head and chest. A note read: "Keep Smiling—Have Faith. Good Luck!"

The 2-million-cubic-foot balloon lifted off from the same spot as had *Explorer II* almost exactly 21 years before. The ascent went smoothly and the two balloonists sipped coffee and chatted with their ground crew as they rose. Jean Piccard's gondola was a far cry from the cramped quarters of the Manhigh capsule. Ross and Lewis had enough room to stand up and exchange seats. They marveled at the view and struggled to describe the strange coloring of the sky. To underscore the difficulty all the high-altitude balloonists had with the colors, Ross and Lewis, sitting only inches apart, could not agree on what they saw. According to postflight reports:

> To Lee the sweep of sky adjacent to earth seemed an intense white, but this intensity vanished almost immediately above the horizon. It became part of a band of white, several degrees in width, that shaded to a very delicate blue-white at its upper extreme. Here, with definite demarcation, the sky changed to blue, light at first but soon deepening to the shade we knew as earth dwellers. Above that narrow band of familiar blue—and again abruptly—the color gradually darkened into a hue seemingly alien to the sky, a magnificent shade indescribable in its richness.
>
> Thus Lee saw two narrow bands, one of white and one of light-to-medium blue, and the second was terminated by a well-defined deeper color. Mal, on the other hand, saw the distinct white band, but the blue above it shaded very gradually into the darker tones.

They remained at peak altitude for only a few moments, but at 76,000 feet, they had established a new unofficial manned balloon record.

Then, unexpectedly, they began to drop. The two men assumed that the balloon had ripped, although the cause would later be identified as a faulty helium release valve that began spilling gas prematurely.

Lewis radioed the ground: "We are in an emergency situation. We

A *Strato-Lab* flight is launched from the iron pit mine near Crosby, Minnesota.
(Source: U.S. Navy)

hit 76,000 feet, and now we are descending rapidly. We are standing by to pass 70,000. We are buckled in with our seat belts. No shoulder harness. We have our faceplates on but not down. We are rotating and have a decided elevator feeling."

They dropped some steel-shot ballast, but it had no effect. They sank through the tropopause at 4,000 feet per minute. They discussed cutting the balloon free and taking their chances under the big emergency drogue chute, but worried about their location over the sharp crags of the Badlands. At the urging of their ground crew, they elected to stay with the balloon. Lewis updated their condition: "We are cool, calm, and collected. We think we will stay with the balloon as long as we can."

Once the balloon fell back into the survivable region of the atmosphere, Lewis and Ross opened the portholes on the gondola and began jettisoning whatever they could get their hands on in order to slow their descent—all together, some 200 pounds worth of hardware. Out went oxygen tanks and converters, the air regenerator, the instrument panel, the radio. "We will be out of communication for some time," the last transmission from the gondola informed the ground crew.

The pair managed to land unharmed on a desolate stretch of sandy soil on a ranch near Brownlee, Nebraska. "I can't say we were scared," the 37-year-old Lewis told the press later, "but of course we were a little concerned." Ross, six years his senior, also downplayed the largely out-of-control descent: "It was a smooth, uneventful landing on a relatively level stretch of land." They labeled the scientific achievements of *Strato-Lab I* "65 percent successful." In spite of its problems, the flight was a clarion call announcing that the United States was now officially back in the business of exploring the stratosphere by means of balloon. President Eisenhower bestowed Harmon International Aviation Awards on both men the following August, even though by then their altitude record had been eclipsed by *Manhigh I*.

By the time Ross and Lewis went up in *Strato-Lab II* on October 18, 1957, much had changed in the world of aviation and aeronautics since their first ascent. Not only had Kittinger shattered the balloon altitude record and Simons broken the 100,000-foot barrier and spent the night in the stratosphere, but *Sputnik* had gone into orbit. That explains the scant attention paid to the second Strato-Lab ascent, which lasted only 10 hours and reached a maximum altitude of 86,000 feet. Among other scientific goals, *Strato-Lab II* carried instruments to measure the physiological responses of the pilots and to evaluate both mental and physi-

The Navy's pioneers of the stratosphere inspect the interior of *Strato-Lab*. Lee Lewis (with cap): "Everybody's favorite man in the world . . ." Malcolm Ross: "Manager, planner, the seeker of funds, operational organizer, project engineer, then finally and anti-climactically, pilot, medical subject, and sometimes semi-scientist." *(Source: Vera Simons)*

cal fatigue. The third Strato-Lab flight (launched on July 26, 1958) kept Ross and Lewis aloft for 34½ hours, surpassing Simons's marathon, but with a peak altitude of only 82,000 feet the world was not impressed.

It was not long after *Strato-Lab III* when Lee Lewis—as operations chief at Winzen Labs—went to work on the Air Force's Project Manhigh. Lewis was a popular figure in American military balloon circles who had been a project officer for the Navy's Bureau of Aeronautics. In the estimation of Vera Winzen: "Everybody's favorite man in the world was Lee Lewis. He was the kindest, quietest, most reasonable man. Everybody loved him." In the 1940s, he had suggested the use of stratospheric balloon-borne platforms as launching pads for rockets—later known as "rockoons."* Shortly after the third Manhigh flight, Lewis was killed in a freak accident while testing a gondola-suspension rig in a gymnasium at the University of Minnesota. A 75-pound wooden pulley block snapped loose and fell from about 75 feet, catching him full force on the back of the neck and most likely breaking his neck and back simultaneously. His death was a blow to the Air Force and the Navy, as well as to Winzen Research. Otto Winzen had been very close to Lewis and became severely depressed by his sudden death.

The ONR made a number of substratospheric balloon flights during this period. In October of 1958, for example, Ross and Charlie Moore ascended in a nylon and plywood gondola into a storm cloud that was developing over Mount Withington in central New Mexico in order to observe firsthand the formation of rain and the generation of electricity. Despite some rough treatment by the violent downdrafts on the edge of the storm ("a giant, frothy waterfall with ice crystals and moisture drops cascading down the side"), and a wild landing, Ross and Moore returned with some dramatic photos and a series of electricity readings taken inside the turret of a cumulus cloud.

The ONR made some overtures to the scientific community and attempted to make its stratospheric laboratory available to scientific organizations and companies that could pay their way. The October 31, 1958, issue of *Science* included this appeal: "Would a manned balloon-borne stratospheric laboratory assist or further your research and development activities? How? What functional requirements, that is, stability, weight, etc., would these activities impose on the Strato-Lab?" Malcolm Ross was more than willing to take the program's case to the physicists, physiologists, and astronomers himself: "The visionaries dream of satellites and space ships for this application," he told them. "Some day their dreams will materialize. But why wait?"

And although the next stratospheric flight would not go up for another full year, when it did, the agenda was a purely scientific one. *Strato-Lab*

---

*The first successful rockoon was launched from the deck of a ship off the Greenland coast in August of 1952. A research team from the University of Iowa, working with the Navy and supervised by physicist James Van Allen, raised a rocket into the stratosphere by means of a balloon and fired it from a height of 70,000 feet. The rocket went on to hit a peak altitude of 40 miles.

IV would raise a 16-inch Schmidt infrared telescope mounted on top of the gondola into the relatively distortion-free region of the stratosphere for the purpose of attempting to detect the presence of water vapor in the atmosphere of Venus and for making observations of the canals of Mars. Balloon-borne astronomy was an idea whose time had come. In New Mexico in 1950, the Navy had first considered the idea of viewing the planets from a perspective above the earth's atmosphere. It was suggested that balloons be used to raise a telescope, a concept that became Project FATSO—First Astronomical Telescopic and Spectrographic Observatory. In the spring of 1959, French astronomer Audoin Dollfus, son of the great French balloonist and aeronautical historian Charles Dollfus, ascended to 42,000 feet beneath a string of weather balloons to make observations of Venus. And four months later, Ross himself made an open-gondola flight to 38,000 feet in order to carry out some solar coronal studies.

Commander Ross would serve as pilot for *Strato-Lab IV,* accompanied by a scientific observer in charge of astronomy-related tasks. Dr. John Strong of Johns Hopkins University, who had been involved with Project FATSO and who proposed the experiments that defined the flight's scientific agenda, was originally slated to be the first astrophysicist to take sophisticated instruments high into the stratosphere,* but he was later replaced by Charlie Moore. The flight was launched from the Stratobowl on the afternoon of November 28, 1959, and ascended to a peak altitude of 81,000 feet. The night was spent in observation of Mars, and the two men landed safely the following afternoon near the town of Manhattan, Kansas. In terms of astronomy, the results were negligible, but as a first step toward an ultimate goal of satellite-borne astrolabs, the flight offered promise.

The final and most celebrated of the Strato-Lab flights would occur a year and a half later. By that point, the Office of Naval Research's balloon program had been in existence for a full seven years and earth-orbiting satellites were no longer the latest rage. In April of 1961, Maj. Yuri Gagarin, a Soviet, had become the first man in space, orbiting the

---

*Harry Mikesell of the Naval Observatory became the first astronomer to make observations from the stratosphere during a 12-hour, open-gondola ONR flight with Malcolm Ross to 40,000 feet in May of 1958, nearly two months before the launch of *Strato-Lab III*. After the flight, Mikesell raved about the opportunity—even though he admitted to being uncomfortable with heights. "The stars were startling. Jupiter looked as big as a weather balloon."

globe at a speed of 18,000 MPH in a spherical, 10,000-pound space capsule called *Vostok I*. In spite of this remarkable feat and the building anticipation over how the U.S. space program would acquit itself,* the *Strato-Lab V* balloon flight managed to command its own share of attention partly because of its own record-setting achievements, but also because of its tragic ending.

Strato-Lab V did have some scientific goals. Nuclear emulsions would be carried aloft in an attempt to capture heavy cosmic ray particles; meteorological devices would measure air pressure, temperature, winds, and water vapor; cameras would provide time-lapse records of cloud formations and infrared photographs of the earth. But the major objective of this fifth ONR balloon lab flight was to test pressure suits for NASA's Project Mercury. These were not the partial-pressure suits worn by Simons and Kittinger; these were true spacesuits, designed for orbital astronauts by the B. F. Goodrich Company and fully pressurized to five pounds per square inch. The pilots of *Strato-Lab V* hoped to put these suits to the test in an open gondola that would expose them to conditions no human being had ever experienced. They intended to surpass even Joe Kittinger's extreme altitude mark of 102,800 feet.

The pressure suits were only a part of the survival clothing that would protect Malcolm Ross and Dr. Victor Prather. Lieutenant Commander Prather, a medical officer with the Naval Medical Research Institute in Bethesda, Maryland, would make his third balloon flight on *Strato-Lab V*. As flight surgeon, he would have a chance to study firsthand the biomedical effects of a super-high-altitude environment. Beneath the suit, the men would wear underwear made of a new porous, nonabsorbent fabric (a by-product of peanut shells) that was designed to wick perspiration away from the skin and provide increased warmth, as well as electrically heated mittens and socks. A four-ply "breakaway" garment was worn over the pressure suit. This outer layer was made of rubberized nylon that was coated with silicone. A plastic helmet with plastic face shield contained a tube that led to a water bottle housed within the pressure suit. This allowed the wearer to sip on a liquid mixture of water, sugar, salt, and flavoring at any time by simply turning the head and sucking on the

---

*Less than a month after Gagarin's flight, and one day after the launch of *Strato-Lab V*, a Redstone missile launched Alan Shepard from Cape Canaveral into a 15-minute suborbital flight, marking the first manned flight of Project Mercury and the United States' first attempt at true manned space travel.

tube. The total weight of the clothing was about 25 pounds, but once the pressure suit was inflated (this would occur automatically at about 26,000 feet), it was impossible to rise from a sitting position. In fact, only limited head, arm, and leg movements would be possible. It was a system intended for the demands of orbital flight, an activity that was now more than speculation.

The biomedical monitoring was also more sophisticated than on previous balloon flights. Not only were pulse, respiration, and temperature checked, but electrocardiograms and electroencephalograms were now part of the telemetering system. Sensors were glued to the pilots' chests and heads with rubber cement.

The balloon built for *Strato-Lab V* by Winzen Research was also state of the art. In fact, it was the largest balloon ever to be used for manned flight (a record that still stands today), with a capacity of 10 million cubic feet. It took seven acres of polyethylene (weight: one ton) to construct it. Its diameter at full inflation at peak altitude would be 300 feet—the length of a football field. The balloon's height was 411 feet—equivalent to a forty-story building. In ascent, with the 70-foot orange and white cargo parachute that stretched between the gondola and the balloon, and with the antenna that trailed beneath the gondola, the entire package spanned the height of an eighty-story building.

The gondola, also built by Winzen, was like nothing seen before. It was not an enclosed—or even partially enclosed—ball or cylinder. Instead, it was the frame of a cube. One and one-half–inch aluminum tubes served as the framework and cross pieces of the cube, the floor was a solid sheet of aluminum, and the front was wide open. It was not a perfect cube: 6 feet wide by 5 feet deep by 5 feet high. The walls and top were nothing more than standard Venetian blinds in nine independent, separately controllable racks with slats that were covered with aluminized mylar on one side and painted black on the other. This arrangement allowed the pilots to turn the exterior of their aircraft black for heat absorption as they passed through the frigid tropopause, and then to switch to silver for solar reflection in the upper reaches of the stratosphere. They could also raise the blinds completely if they wanted an unobstructed view. The batteries were stored on a shelf beneath the cube's floor and the two pilot seats were arranged side by side within the gondola. Several strategically placed mirrors allowed both men to see every nook and cranny of their vehicle in spite of the severe restrictions imposed by the pressure suits.

* * *

Unlike Joe Kittinger, Malcolm Ross did not grow up with a single-minded obsession that would govern the pattern of his life. Born and raised in the Midwest, he tried a career in radio after graduating from Purdue with a physics degree in 1941. After a stint as a commercial announcer in Chicago, Ross became a news and sports reporter in Indianapolis. He joined the Navy in 1943 and served as a meteorologist at Pearl Harbor and aboard the aircraft carrier *Saratoga*. After the war, he ran an advertising agency with his wife in Pasadena, California. He was recalled for duty in Korea in 1950. By the time that war was over, his work with the Office of Naval Research had captivated him to the point that he remained with that organization as a civilian physicist. His meteorology work had acquainted him with balloons, and his fascination with them had led him deeper and deeper into lighter-than-air experimentation.

By 1961, Ross had become the world's most experienced stratospheric balloonist. A successful flight in *Strato-Lab V* would give him over 100 balloon hours in the stratosphere. Yet in his own mind, he was never the intrepid explorer or space hero. He described his role, instead, as "manager, planner, the seeker of funds, operational organizer, project engineer, then finally and anti-climactically, pilot, medical subject, and sometimes semi-scientist." Yet early in the morning of May 4, 1961, he was helped into his chair inside the strange box-frame gondola in preparation for one of the most monumental journeys ever undertaken. And it would begin not from the bottom of an iron mine or an arid high-desert basin, but from the deck of a ship in the middle of the Gulf of Mexico.

At 7:00 A.M. the aircraft carrier *Antietam* was cruising 138 miles southeast of New Orleans, attempting—with the aid of a small weather balloon—to exactly match the wind's direction and speed in order to provide calm conditions for the launch.* On the massive deck of the carrier, inflation of the largest balloon ever constructed was being personally supervised by its creator, Otto Winzen (now rehabilitated from his balloon accident in Wisconsin prior to *Manhigh III*). As the endless acres of clear polyethylene were laid out, they were fed through rollers as helium

---

*At General Mills in the forties, Jean Piccard had proposed launching a balloon from the bed of a truck moving in the direction of and at the speed of the wind, and the Navy used "no wind" ocean-going launches for their rockoon flights in the Arctic in the early fifties.

screamed through an inflation tube and lifted the filmy material—yard by yard—into the air. As the billowing bubble of plastic levitated above the ship and the sailors, it caught the salmon-pink glow of the tropical sunrise, undulating like a grotesque and elongated flower waving on the bottom of a coral sea.

The launch was delayed for several moments when a parachute shroud line caught on one of the carrier's deck cleats. Once the snag was freed, the tie-downs were cut and the great balloon lifted the gondola from the deck at 7:08.

Rising quickly, Ross and Prather were at 26,000 feet exactly 26 minutes later. The temperature was –27°. Moments later, the two men heard the welcome moaning and hissing of the valves on their pressure suits as the bladders inflated. In spite of their layers of clothing and electrically heated gloves and socks, the cold was bitter as the temperature dropped to –40°. Kittinger had been partially surrounded by the metal walls of his gondola, but aboard *Strato-Lab V* there was nothing to break the fast-approaching jet-stream winds but insignificant racks of Venetian blinds. As they rose toward the tropopause, the blinds were turned black side out to absorb whatever heat might be available. At 43,000 feet, the temperature had plunged to –73°.

Then, things began to happen. First, both pilots' face shields began to fog up. The helmets were rigged with heating elements designed to eliminate the condensation, but which were also capable of melting the plastic shields. Warning lights would alert a pilot when the temperature of his shield reached 135°, but Ross and Prather nevertheless turned up their helmet heaters with some trepidation.

Next, Ross became aware of a hissing sound. He first thought that his pressure suit had ruptured and was leaking. At that same instant, a small vapor cloud poured out from beneath him and drifted away through the opening on the front of the gondola. He wanted to bend over and inspect his suit, but the constriction of the bladders made such a maneuver impossible. He radioed his concerns to the ground. Seconds later, *Strato-Lab V* lost radio contact with the *Antietam*. Attempts to establish contact with a monitoring airplane proved fruitless. Beginning to panic, Ross tried the international emergency channel. But there was no response.

To make matters worse, Ross also noticed that the balloon's rate of ascent had slowed. The gauge showed that they were only climbing at 600 feet per minute. Without voicing his fear to Prather, Ross concluded that the envelope had developed a leak. Instead, he announced that they had likely hit a temperature inversion—without really believing it. Luckily, that in fact turned out to be the explanation. A small pocket of warmer air had slowed them down. As they moved on up to 53,000 feet, they picked up speed again as the air cooled to –94°.

As the rate-of-climb indicator read 750, the mysterious hissing sound stopped. Whatever had caused it had not been a leak in a pressure suit. And then, at 71,000 feet, the radio came alive and the voice of Comdr. John Sparkman, the flight's technical director, crackled in the pilots' helmets. Sparkman was in the process of informing Ross and Prather that their face shields were overheating. The timing was good, since the warning light on the helmet heaters had failed. A few more minutes and the plastic shields would have blistered and cracked open.

By 90,000 feet, with the sudden succession of emergencies behind them, Ross decided to raise the blinds on the front of the gondola. Temperatures were on the rise again as they climbed into the upper region of the stratosphere and –40° struck them as relatively balmy. The front of the gondola's cube was constructed without aluminum cross bracing and provided an unobstructed "picture window" effect as the blinds were hoisted up.

Ross described the sensation: "I caught my breath as I looked out. The scene as we topped 100,000 feet was utterly magnificent. For long moments we drank in the beauty of earth, sky, and sea." As the gondola rotated slowly beneath the swollen balloon, which had assumed the shape of a gigantic onion, the two men looked out across a vast tableau. Their gaze took in half a million square miles of the southern United States. They could see from Texas to Florida and they could clearly identify New Orleans; Mobile, Alabama; Vicksburg, Mississippi. Ross even thought he could pinpoint Cape Canaveral on the edge of the Atlantic Ocean. They could also track the *Antietam* by her wake as she moved about in the blue Gulf.

They sat in silence and simply stared out at the world and the strange, ineffable colors of the sky: "In silent awe, we contemplated the supernal loveliness of the atmosphere."

Their reverie was interrupted at 9:47 by the distinctive German accent of Otto Winzen.

"Mal, this is Otto. Do you realize you have already broken the record?"

The burgeoning *Strato-Lab V* was now floating at its peak altitude: 113,740 feet—nearly 11,000 feet beyond Kittinger's mark. At $21^{1}/_{2}$ miles above the earth, it was higher than a balloon had ever been, higher than anyone had ever been without a pressurized compartment for protection. Yet as he surveyed the scene out the picture window, Ross remarked to Prather that he had forgotten all about the record, and that it no longer seemed to have any significance.*

Not long after reaching the top, Ross began to valve gas for the descent. As usual, with the rising sun warming the helium, the descent started slowly. After nearly an hour of repeated valving, the rate of fall was only 70 feet per minute. Because their oxygen supplies were limited, Ross decided to leave the valve open for a solid 15 minutes, and that brought them down to 90,000 at a rate of 750 feet per minute. As they descended through 75,000 feet, they lowered the blinds and turned the black sides out again. It was getting cold and the pilots' feet, especially, were feeling the effects.

As they passed through the tropopause, they began to fall faster. Too fast. At 28,000 feet they were coming down at a rate of 1,140 feet per second. It was time to ballast. After dropping the batteries beneath the aluminum floor, they released all 125 pounds of steel shot. Next went the power supply unit and the oxygen converter and the radio—out the picture window. For the last few thousand feet, they continued to toss items overboard—but with a lessened sense of urgency. In fact, just below 7,000 feet, both pilots lit cigarettes and allowed themselves to enjoy the final moments. The Venetian blinds were cut down and tossed over. Then their boots and items of cold-weather clothing.

The *Antietam*, meanwhile, had tracked the falling gondola and had attempted to maneuver itself into position to make a "running catch." It would save a helicopter rescue if *Strato-Lab V* could manage to land on the wide deck of the carrier. But as the gondola came down, the *Antietam* was a good two miles away. As it turned out, it didn't matter anyway, since Prather had jettisoned the drag line that would have been necessary to make a safe carrier landing.

As the aluminum-frame cube splashed into the waters of the Gulf at 4:00 P.M.—nearly nine hours after launching—Ross hit the button that released the big balloon and pulled a knob designed to release half of the shroud lines attached to the huge emergency parachute. Prather pulled a similar knob to release the rest of the shroud lines. Only

---

*The manned-balloon altitude mark of Ross and Prather in *Strato-Lab V* remains on the books today.

Prather's lines came free, however, and the parachute—still partially attached—fouled, allowing the canopy to partially inflate. There was potential for disaster if the chute caught enough air to drag the gondola across the surface, but luckily the striped silk flared once or twice and then settled harmlessly in the water. As the two men looked about them, they saw the objects that they had tossed out surrounding them now, bobbing on the swells like debris from a shipwreck. "Landing in our own 'mess' was poetic justice," Ross would admit.

The first helicopter to reach the landing site lowered a cable with a rescue hook and sling toward the gondola. Ross secured the cable and told Prather to get on. Prather deferred.

"You go ahead. I'll come later."

Ross stepped onto the hook. "See you later," he said. The carrier was about a mile and a half away at this point, bearing toward the gondola. As the helicopter pulled up, Ross's feet slipped off the hook, half submerging him. He held on to the cable with his hands and pulled himself back up. The copter lifted away.

A few minutes later, a second helicopter lowered itself down toward the small aluminum raft and dropped a hook to Vic Prather. He stepped on and the helicopter lurched upward. And then, like Ross before him, he slipped off. Unfortunately, unlike Ross, he was not able to hang on to the cable and pull himself back on. Prather splashed into the sea. A flood of water immediately rushed through the open face shield and flooded the helmet. The heavy pressure suit also took on water.

In spite of quick action on the part of Navy rescue divers who were out of the helicopter and immediately into the water, Prather, after having completed one of the most remarkable flights in the history of aeronautics, drowned.

At first, Prather's death overwhelmed Malcolm Ross. Reporters at the postflight press conference avoided the subject in the face of Ross's obvious grief. Instead, he was asked to evaluate the mission in light of its objectives.

"It was a wonderful flight," Ross told them. "The basic objectives we had in mind—testing capabilities of the suit and further acquisition of physiological data—were met."

But Prather's death was a blow from which the program never recovered. In spite of Ross's insistence that the flight had been a success and that his copilot had not died in vain, and in spite of the White House ceremony in which President Kennedy awarded the Distinguished

Flying Cross to Prather's widow, Strato-Lab had flown for the last time.

A year later, addressing the Second National Conference on the Peaceful Uses of Space in Seattle, Ross reflected on the contributions of Project Strato-Lab. He focused on three areas. First of all, there were the technological advances (such as balloons, gondolas, subsystems, human factors). Next were the specific scientific achievements (atmospheric measurements, telescopic and spectrographic observations, photographs, biomedical data). But most important of all, according to Ross, Strato-Lab served as an analog for manned scientific space research. He told the conference that the ONR balloon work served as "a catalyst to crystallize manned space science efforts. It helped focus early thinking by some of the best scientific minds in America on a fundamental question before our nation actually had a formal space program." That fundamental question was whether or not scientists themselves should be aboard the vehicles that travel into space. Ross pleaded his case: "Scientific man *must* go into space," he declared. Astronauts and aviators alone would not do.

A debate was already raging within NASA between the scientists and the engineers. The organization's Office of Space Sciences, like Robert Millikan and other researchers of the 1930s, originally argued for unmanned missions. Human cargo, they maintained, became an obstruction to scientific objectives by placing an unnecessary burden—economic and technological—on the vehicle and its subsystems. The astronaut would only get in the way. In fact, when Eisenhower signed the bill establishing NASA in July of 1958, he openly expressed skepticism about the value of manned missions, and his chief scientific advisor, James Killian (the respected former president of MIT), urged the United States not to compete with the Soviets stunt for stunt, but to develop, calmly and rationally, its own scientific objectives and agenda. Killian asked policymakers to focus on unmanned space flight. A likely contributing factor to the administration's reluctance to support manned flight was the national recession; manned space missions would be more expensive and Eisenhower had gone public with his intention to balance the federal budget.

Meanwhile, NASA's Office of Manned Space Flight lobbied hard on behalf of the astronaut. During the early months of NASA's existence, as Congress sought a national consensus on what the objectives of the space program ought to be, Ernst Stuhlinger, an associate of Wernher von Braun, stated the case: "The main objective in outer space, of course, should be man in space; and not only man as a survivor in space, but man as an active scientist, a man who can explore out in space all those things which we cannot explore from Earth." The cause was bolstered first by *Sputnik* and later by Kennedy's extraordinary address to Congress on space policy. In his "Special Message to Congress on Urgent National Needs" on May 25, 1961, the young president committed the nation to putting a man on the moon and bringing him home safely—all before the end of the decade. Kennedy's vision had nothing to do with science. The space race would be principally about national prestige, and an unmanned mission—regardless of its outcome and any scientific achievements—could never counter the spectacle of Russians strutting about on the surface of the moon. According to NASA's own history of Project Apollo, the moon shot "would be an end in itself, needing no justification in terms of its contribution to some larger goal, and it would demonstrate the nation's superiority in space technology to all the world."

Outside of NASA, a third camp refused to align itself either with the ivory-towerism of the academics (too often narrowly focused on their own scientific specialties and pet projects) who supported only unmanned space missions or with the gung-ho rocket men who burned to "put America back on top" by whipping the Russians in the race to the moon. This third camp was represented in the public policy debate by the National Academy of Sciences, and in the field by such men as Malcolm Ross, David Simons, and John Paul Stapp. They were men of science, but they also believed that humanity itself was the key to the entire endeavor. You couldn't leave people behind when the rockets took off. The human race had no choice but to go into space: to learn, to grow, to survive. For these men, the issue was never *whether* humans should go into space, but what *kind* of individual should be selected. And on this they were in agreement: trained scientists must join the ranks of the astronaut.

In his Seattle speech, Ross proposed a specific plan to encourage formal training for prospective space scientists. "I have a sincere fear," he told the conference, "that when our technology of manned space flight is sufficiently advanced to permit a 'seat open,' we may have plenty of astronauts, but not enough 'astroscientists.'" Ross outlined his plan:

It is recommended that professorships in astroscience (merely areas of extra-terrestrial physical scientific investigations utilizing man as a scientist) be established at three of our leading universities. These might be geographically located with one on each coast and one in the central portion of the United States. It would be hoped that the "chairs" would attract three of our nation's most scholarly, eminent, and mature scientists. Each professor would head up a staff with a graduate program of learning, aimed generally at providing an opportunity for the students to conduct their own creative and imaginative research as scientists in future manned scientific space missions. The plan would be implemented on a trial basis, but should be established with an initial five-year longevity so it will have a reasonable opportunity to demonstrate its value.

It is anticipated that liberal funding would be provided each of the three universities for unique laboratory facilities which might be required. It is also presumed that the government, as part of its long-range national space program, would be most generous in providing support for special research activities of the young space scientists. This would allow them to develop specific instrumentation for semi-space research platforms, such as very high-altitude aircraft and balloon systems. These kinds of special tools also would be made available so that their graduate school investigations would produce creative efforts with useful results. This type of effort would allow them to become deeply involved in the field of space exploration. The studies, experiments, and associated activities would be controlled only by the university and the professor in charge of the program at each institution.

Complete scientific freedom, thus, would be available for the type of scientific expression and accomplishment which can be developed best in the university atmosphere.

Once the space race had been won, Malcolm Ross's contention that aviators alone would not suffice would eventually be acknowledged. But while scientists were gradually phased into the Apollo program as astronauts, the nation's space policymakers ignored Ross's plan for graduating trained astroscientists. The status of the scientist would never equal that of the engineer within the halls of the great house of NASA.

Meanwhile, Joe Kittinger—aviator—had held onto his goal of returning to the stratosphere, and had continued to pursue astronomy as the ticket that would get him there. True, Strato-Lab had already taken a telescope high into the stratosphere, but the Navy had not put an astronomer up there with it—and despite the rhetoric of Malcolm Ross and others at the ONR, no truly definitive astronomy had ever really been done at extreme altitudes. So when Project Excelsior ended, Kittinger did not have to look far to find the opportunity he needed.

Nothing about Project Stargazer had ever been easy. The program was a joint venture that involved, at one time or another, the Air Force, the Navy, the Smithsonian Institution, several universities, a smattering of private industry, and a number of other organizations both public and private. The goal was never modest: to raise an astronomer, a high-powered telescope, and a stable observation platform far enough above the distorting influence of the earth's atmosphere to allow the first unencumbered look at our universe. Nor were the claims humble. Dr. J. Allen Hynek, chairman of Northwestern University's astronomy department and scientific test director for Stargazer, stated flatly that if the project were to achieve its principal objectives it would represent "the greatest breakthrough in astronomy since Galileo."

The idea for the project originated at a conference on balloon capabilities and requirements at the Air Force Cambridge Research Laboratory (AFCRL) in January 1958. Project High Dive had already ended and Excelsior was yet to be born. The AFCRL's Balloon Research Group was discussing possible uses of High Dive flight equipment for astronomical research. Followup discussions involved Dr. Fred Whipple of the Smithsonian, astronomers at the University of Maryland, and an advisory committee to the National Academy of Sciences. Finally, a written proposal called for a series of four high-altitude manned balloon flights in a pressurized gondola to be equipped with a sophisticated telescope. All four flights were to occur between the spring and fall of 1961.

Astronomical observation from high-altitude balloon platforms was not a radical idea. James Glaisher made ten balloon ascents with a telescope in the nineteenth century. Russian balloonists had tried to make telescopic observations of the sun from a balloon in the 1930s. British astronomers from Cambridge had launched an unmanned astro-observatory in 1956 and a French astronomer at the Meudon Observatory had done the same. These efforts proved of very little scientific value, however, since the balloons never rose high enough to escape significant atmospheric distortion. In the United States, Martin Schwarzschild of Princeton did much better. His first balloon, the unmanned *Stratoscope* (which was originally sponsored by the Office of Naval Research), launched from New Brighton, Minnesota, in 1957, ascended well into the stratosphere (80,000 feet), and returned with spectacular photographs of the surface of the sun despite stabilization problems with the 12-inch reflecting telescope on board. *Stratoscope II* carried a 36-inch infrared telescope, $9^{1}/_{2}$ feet long, designed specifically by the Perkin-Elmer Corporation for the observation of Mars.

The AFCRL Balloon Branch and its test director, Maj. Thomas Spaulding, had reason for optimism. Sophisticated new gyro-electronic gear supplied by the Instrumentation Lab at MIT, technology first developed for inertial guidance systems in ballistic missiles, promised a higher degree of stabilization than had been possible before. A new launch vehicle, a modified Le Tourneau log loader, would allow the project to launch in winds up to 10 MPH. And new balloon construction techniques and materials promised stronger, more controllable balloons capable of lifting heavier and heavier payloads and capable of maintaining precise altitudes. Astronomers would be forced into fewer compromises in their selection of instruments for the new floating astrolabs and balloon pilots had a more maneuverable aircraft to work with.

A number of experiments were suggested for Stargazer, several of them by Dr. Hynek. Among the ideas he proposed were to view regions in deep space that had previously been beyond the reach of our telescopes, to view previously invisible infrared star "companions," to map the Milky Way and the canals of Mars, and to scout landing sites on the moon. He also waxed lyrical about the possibility of satellite-borne astrolabs and a permanent national balloon observatory on the edge of outer space—an idea the Air Force considered. Hynek was a man of great imagination. He would later serve as a consultant to the Air Force on issues relating to unidentified flying objects and write several books on the subject to go on the shelf alongside his technical astrophysics texts. He also worked as a scientific consultant on a Hollywood story of extraterrestrial visitors, *Close Encounters of the Third Kind.** In the end, Stargazer settled on three very specific—if unromantic—astronomical objectives:

---

*In 1972, drawing on more than two decades of research into UFO reports, Hynek wrote about what he called "close encounters." He divided such experiences into three classifications, the third of which involves physical contact with extraterrestrial "humanoids." His conclusion? "Although I know of no hypothesis that adequately covers the mountainous evidence, this should not and must not deter us from following the advice of Schroedinger: to be curious, capable of being astonished, and eager to find out."

1. To measure atmospheric turbulence;

2. To measure star brightness variations caused by high-altitude turbulence; and

3. To reveal how water vapor in the air affects light emanating from planets and stars.

In fact, Hynek finally admitted, if the project did nothing more than determine the height at which the effects of scintillation (the atmospheric turbulence responsible for the illusion that stars twinkle) were no longer apparent, then Stargazer could be counted a rousing success. (Never mind that such an objective was a questionable argument for a *manned* ascent.)

The goal of four manned flights by the fall of 1961 turned out to be a pipe dream, even though Joe Kittinger, fresh from his triumphs with Excelsior, was brought in as test director at John Paul Stapp's insistence. Stapp had lobbied for Stargazer in the halls of the Air Force's Aeromed Lab and had encountered the usual resistance. The Air Force wasn't sure what the project would contribute. Stapp argued that while Stargazer would not contribute to the physiological protection of pilots (the charter of the Aeromed Lab), astronomical observation was still of great importance to science and should be pursued. They had the opportunity to do important work and they ought to do it. The project was eventually approved, but with a bootleg-size budget and warnings that additional funding would be out of the question.

Five test flights of unmanned balloon platforms were carried out at various locations in the desert Southwest during the winter and spring months of 1961, and all five failed. The first three balloons were simply not strong enough to lift the required 4,500-pound payload—the heaviest ever attempted. The fourth had problems with its ballast hopper and with its gas valve, but was grounded for good when the inflation tube snagged on the launch arm and ripped the balloon. The fifth test resulted in an overinflated balloon that burst during ascent. This last failure was particularly galling to Kittinger, who found the civilian-military launch crew inadequate to the task. The predawn layout of the balloon, for example, had been accomplished with only a flashlight for illumination because no one had arranged for proper lighting. The crew went about its business without rigorous checklists and with poorly developed procedures, which resulted in the overinflation. Kittinger's report on the incident blasted the crew as "unprofessional." His analysis of the botched flight concluded, "The cause was poor operational control and procedures."

By the following spring, with a new crew, a refurbished gondola to be used only for the manned flight, improved launch procedures, and a general reorientation of the entire program, Kittinger and company were ready to try again. On March 4, 1962, the first test flight of the new Stargazer balloon astrolab was launched from the AFCRL's field at Chico, California. If everything went right with this test, Kittinger and an astronomical observer would attempt a manned flight a few weeks later. The 400-foot-tall balloon, filled with 3 million cubic feet of helium, left the earth at dawn and rose for one hour and twelve minutes before rupturing at 41,900 feet. The gondola, laden with instrumentation and cameras, fell into the deep snowpack of the Sierra Nevada mountains.

After a week's delay due to bad weather, a helicopter retrieved the gondola, relatively undamaged, from the mountains. The manned flight, which would occur in the new gondola, was postponed and additional tests of the unmanned system were carried out that March. The balloon collapsed at 200 feet on the next test flight due to valve failure, but rose to 88,000 feet and remained aloft for 26 hours on the subsequent one—a welcome and unqualified success.

In August of 1962, General Mills—the balloon contractor—delivered a new dacron-reinforced mylar balloon (one-half of one-thousandth of an inch thick) to Holloman and two more tests of the unmanned lab took place. Both were successful flights, reaching heights above 83,000 feet. One additional test occurred during this period, an unmanned launch of the gondola that would be used for the manned flight. This one went to 81,500 feet without encountering significant problems. It was time to try the real thing.

As the scientific observer for the flight, Dr. Hynek selected a civilian astronomer, 40-year-old William White from the China Lake naval weapons center. Kittinger, of course, announced that he himself would serve as balloon pilot. His return trip to the stratosphere had finally materialized.

The two-man gondola, an aluminum cylinder 14 feet high (with telescope on top) and 7 feet wide, had originally been built by Grumman for Project Mercury to use in high-altitude escape procedure tests. When Mercury decided against using balloons for astronaut drills, the hardware was made available to the Air Force. The gondola, more impressive visually than either the Manhigh or Excelsior vehicles, had a styrofoam base and had received a silver-foil coating in the effort to improve passive temperature control. The cabin would be pressurized with a 50% oxygen/50% nitrogen mixture from liquid oxygen and nitrogen converters, and both prospective passengers would undergo altitude chamber tests in the gondola. Flight procedures called for both men to wear partial-pressure suits and full survival gear but, as on the Manhigh flights, they would wear their helmet faceplates up (in the open position).

The 12.5-inch telescope was mounted on top of the gondola on a lazy-Susan turntable. In theory, once the telescope was "locked" on its target—for instance, a star—it would track the target precisely despite any pitching or turning of the gondola itself.

The rugged new mylar balloon was not as tall as the earlier Stargazer balloons (only 200 feet at full inflation), but its capacity was greater by 200,000 cubic feet. The launch crew prepared it for ascent in the early morning hours of December 13, 1962, at Holloman. After a two-hour hold due to a problem with some carbon dioxide cylinders, Stargazer was launched.

Kittinger and White rose above Alamogordo at 500 feet per minute (much slower than either Manhigh or Excelsior due to the weight of the astronomy lab) and climbed into the bright winter sky. Two hours later, they hovered at float altitude: 81,500 feet. For the next 13 hours, William White—with Kittinger's help—worked his way methodically through the flight's astronomical agenda in spite of the bulky suit and gloves. Dr. Pierre St. Amand, a geophysicist colleague of White's at China Lake, was White's communication link on the ground at Holloman.

After a cold, busy night aloft, Kittinger—with the able assistance of Duke Gildenberg's valving instructions on the radio—brought Stargazer down for a landing early the following morning. Gildenberg always attempted to bring balloons down as near to a road as possible to ease the retrieval operation. With Stargazer, he practically put it down on the road. In fact, there was some last-minute discussion about whether or not they should try to land the gondola directly onto the bed of the waiting truck. For safety's sake, it was decided that Kittinger should touch down a few yards from the truck.

White immediately labeled the flight a "huge success" and a followup flight was announced. In the meantime, the project conducted chamber tests in order to diagnose unspecified "problems that occurred during the manned flight." These problems were related to "telescope stabilization and excessive noise in radiation detectors."

Kittinger and White were sealed into the pressurized gondola once again in the early morning hours of April 20, 1963. At dawn, only moments before the scheduled launch of *Stargazer II,* a static-electric charge tripped a release prematurely and freed the helium-filled balloon. The huge mylar envelope, estimated to be worth $53,000, sped up into the sky and, within a few short minutes, disappeared from sight, leaving two very frustrated men sitting ingloriously in the stratosphere-ready but very earthbound capsule.

Stapp had been reassigned by this point, and two days later, without an advocate to argue at the mahogany desks, Dr. Hynek announced that Project Stargazer had been discontinued. In spite of the fact that $100,000 and six additional weeks might have rescued the program, Hynek said, there would be no more funds. The total bill for Stargazer to that point was estimated at $750,000, much of which had been spent for balloon testing.

It was a disappointing coda to the stratospheric adventures of Joe Kittinger. He would never punch through the tropopause in a balloon again. Nor would anyone else in the armed forces of the United States. By mid-1963, Project Mercury was well under way and astronauts were orbiting the earth and chatting jovially with awed newscasters on live TV while they did it. President Kennedy would die that fall in Dallas, but the nation was solidly and irrevocably committed to the achievement of the objective laid out in his "moon challenge" two years earlier: a manned lunar landing before the end of the decade.

Three days after Stargazer was officially mothballed, a voluble Joe Kittinger waxed optimistic to the *Albuquerque Journal* about the future of manned high-altitude balloon work. He no longer had any desire to become an astronaut, he said. When NASA had first announced its plans for Project Mercury, Kittinger had told Stapp that he wanted to volunteer. He had already completed most of the selection process that the eventual astronaut candidates would go through during his training for Manhigh. And although Stapp, along with General Flickinger, would serve on the panel that would examine and select the thirty-seven finalists for the Mercury flights, he talked Kittinger out of applying. Project Excelsior was in full swing and Stapp had wanted Kittinger to continue with high-altitude escape work.[*]

---

[*]In a similar move, Don Flickinger reportedly talked X-15 pilot Scott Crossfield out of applying for Mercury.

Kittinger estimated that it would take at least three years before orbital flight could produce the kind of scientific knowledge that balloons were already capable of delivering. Stargazer had been cheap and simple, but it had never received the benefit of the public relations machinery or the influence of the big corporate contractors available to NASA. To Kittinger, the whole thing was a golden opportunity wasted. "When you're above 100,000 feet," he explained, "you're above 99% of the earth's atmosphere. There's no need to go any higher to do astronomy. We could still be doing astronomical research for a thousandth of the cost of the NASA programs."

Hynek went even further: "By no means should the use of balloons be considered an interim technique, to be abandoned when observatories in orbit become commonplace, for even then a satellite should not be sent to do a job a balloon can do better. . . . Only when, some day, permanent observatories on the moon have become routinely established can we dispense with balloons (as well as local earth satellites)."

But no one was willing to support the balloon programs Kittinger and Hynek envisioned. High-altitude gas ballooning simply had not produced the spectacular scientific results that would guarantee continued funding. Project Stargazer had been a bust, William White's claims to the contrary notwithstanding. The project had failed to solve the problems of platform stabilization and, in the end, contributed little of scientific value. In return, the entire enterprise was ignored by the mass media and historians alike. In fact, a definitive study of manned scientific ballooning in America by David DeVorkin of the National Air and Space Museum manages to conclude on page 364 without a single mention of Project Stargazer. Likewise the excellent general history of American ballooning by DeVorkin's colleague at Air and Space, Tom Crouch, gets through its 667 pages without Stargazer.

NASA's aggressive schedule had rendered balloons all but irrelevant as practice platforms for space flight—as least as far as the national space agency was concerned—and the final stratospheric flight of Kittinger and the Air Force represented the muffled last gasp of the science-oriented manned balloon flights. As late as 1965, Otto Winzen was still arguing tirelessly for the manned balloon as a cost-effective space research vehicle and trainer. At the Sixth International Symposium on Space Technology and Science in Tokyo, he gamely pleaded his case:

The plastic balloon vehicle, native to the United States, is a valuable, proven test platform which could serve to fill the gap between earth-bound simulators and final space flight. . . . In the search to reduce the exorbitant cost of test programs leading to manned and unmanned space flight, we would be remiss not to explore its unique capabilities. . . . The most significant contributions the balloon vehicle can make may still lie ahead.

But in reality, it was already over. Balloons would continue to ply the stratosphere, but without human beings aboard. "In the space age," DeVorkin's study concludes, "manned stratospheric ballooning lost visible purpose." With regard to astronomy, which had been the balloonists' last hope for justification, he elaborates:

The few astronomers who did participate in manned ventures were no longer enthusiastic after the first flights. . . . Without exception, when sufficiently stable automatic platforms became available along with sufficient funding, all turned to unmanned sondes, satellite berths, or completely different modes of observation after they tasted manned ballooning.

And although Joe Kittinger was denied further trips into the stratosphere, he never lost his taste for the romance of ballooning or the elixir of the frontier. "If life is not an adventure," he insisted, "then it's nothing at all."

eleven

Track Meet in the Sky

As *Sputnik* and Gagarin had so clearly demonstrated, much to the horror of the American press (and—consequently—of the American public), the Soviet Union of the early 1960s had every intention of claiming and defending the title of undisputed master of outer space. The Soviets had a long history of high-altitude aeronautical achievement upon which to build and had always been ready to compete—and compete fiercely—with the Americans for the various prizes that had presented themselves over the years. The competition began in earnest in the 1930s.

While Tex Settle and crew prepared for the *Century of Progress* flight in the summer of 1933, everyone connected with the Chicago venture was acutely aware that a group of Soviets was also preparing for an ambitious stratospheric flight of their own. Two months after Settle's abortive ascent from Soldier Field, a combined military-civilian crew on the other side of the globe took the larger Red Army balloon *Stratostat* to 53,153 feet and established a new manned-balloon altitude record. When Auguste Piccard (who had publicly eschewed the significance of altitude records) learned that his own record had been broken, he immediately charged that the Soviet flight had been nothing more than a stunt, since no science had even been attempted—the purpose, he claimed, had been simply to set a record. The Soviets claimed otherwise. But regardless of whether or not the *Stratostat* gondola had contained a few scientific instruments, the Soviets had made their point. And the Americans, ignoring Piccard's charges, acknowledged it: the Soviet record was now the one to beat.

The next Soviet balloonists to enter the stratosphere were the three ill-equipped civilian pilots of the *Osoaviakhim*. They set what would have been a new record, but died on impact when their balloon ripped loose from the gondola during descent. The great Russian balloonist Prokofiev, who flew the *Stratostat* and who would reach an even higher mark in 1935, conducted an exhaustive analysis of the tragedy. Prokofiev charged, among other things, that the preparations for the flight of *Osoaviakhim* had sacrificed too much in weight and emergency safety equipment in order to attain a record altitude. His words are reminiscent of Leo Stevens's analysis of Hawthorne Gray's final flight—the message was the same: altitude is gained at a cost, and the aeronaut must never pay a price higher than his system and experience can afford.

As the Americans suffered the near disaster of *Explorer I*, and went aggressively forward with plans for a followup flight, the race continued. In June of 1935, a Soviet scientific flight, the *USSR1-Bis*, reached the stratosphere just as the balloon began to rip apart. A physicist named Verigo and an engineer named Prilutsky both parachuted to safety while the balloon's pilot, Zille, managed to bring the damaged craft down to a safe landing. This string of tragedies and near-tragedies took its toll on the morale of the future crew of *Explorer II*, who recounted suffering tremendous stress in the days leading up to their record-breaking flight—the flight that ended the "space race" of the thirties. The bad luck and equipment failures also had an effect on the project's benefactor and figurehead, National Geographic's Gilbert Grosvenor, who wavered in his support for Explorer while insisting that in the event that Stevens and Anderson *did* fly, it was imperative that they make every effort to set a record in the process. The scientific agenda was important, but Grosvenor and others connected with Explorer proved more than willing to barter science for altitude by cutting instrumentation in order to shave pounds off the total weight.

In many respects, the high-altitude balloon competition of the 1930s precisely prefigures the Cold War rocket race of the 1960s: Russians and Americans vying for the latest, most spectacular, prizes in the sky. The winners weren't merely those who went highest, farthest, and fastest—but those who had most adroitly captured the public imagination or who had fulfilled some transient political purpose. The Soviet Union in the early Stalin era was often accused of using high-altitude balloon stunts to deflect attention from the obscenities of the purges and to create a new venue for national glory. But it is naive to suggest that the United States went into the stratosphere with nothing but bright eyes, pure hearts, and a noble desire to advance the holy cause of science. In fact, science was regularly and often dishonestly used as a justification for America's journeys into the stratosphere which, in truth, had as much to do with bolstering the national morale in the face of the Great Depression as it did with discovering the origin of the cosmic ray. It had been important for both the Soviets and the Americans to be first and go highest—but not always for the reasons stated.

Three years before the outbreak of the first World War, a Russian inventor named Kotelnikov offered his parachute designs to his country's air force. Unfortunately, Kotelnikov's vision was afforded a treatment similar to that of his counterparts in Europe and the United States at the time. The commander of the czar's air corps reportedly rejected the concept of emergency bailout on the theory that the very presence of a parachute in the cockpit might tempt faint-hearted pilots to abandon perfectly good—and perfectly expensive—airplanes at the first sign of trouble. The official attitude toward parachutes and pilots changed little with the overhaul of the political system. For nearly a decade following the Revolution, emergency escape technology was practically nonexistent. In 1927, the first Russian pilot saved his life with a parachute, and thus began a love affair between the Soviet Union and the parachute.

The Russian public first became acquainted with parachutes during a Moscow sports festival in 1930. The young factory workers who made the demonstration drops were members of one of the earliest Soviet parachute clubs, and they held accuracy competitions that were promoted and staged as sporting events. Parachute clubs popped up across the Soviet Union, primarily organized by factories and schools, but rarely without some military connection. Soon, the clubs began to hold formal competitions with each other. At a time when parachuting was largely an escape procedure for military pilots in most of the rest of the world, the Soviet populace embraced it as a form of both recreation and entertainment.

By 1933, the clubs were so numerous that they were incorporated into a central umbrella organization known as "Osoaviakhim," or the Society for the Promotion of Aviation and Chemical Defense. This organization seems to have been something like a cross between an athletic club and a civil defense corps. Members were trained to defend the Soviet populace against chemical and gas attacks, and to provide a variety of emergency rescue services. In the course of their training, the groups specialized in parachuting from gliders, airplanes, and balloons.

The clubs were popular throughout the 1930s. Chapters were formed in crowded cities and in remote villages. It was not unusual for high-school-age students to be proficient parachutists. Jump towers—some of them modernistic steel derricks with spiral ramps and staircases, others no more than wooden frames—sprang up in parks and playgrounds. Smaller platforms with cable-assisted harnesses allowed young children to experience the sensation.

Soon young Soviets were competing to set records: altitude records, freefall records, accuracy records, records for water landings and night jumps. In August of 1940, a Russian parachute celebrity named Kharokhonov—while making his 599th jump—set an unofficial world freefall record of 38,700 feet. At about that same time, a record for mass-jumping was set when twenty-nine men jumped together out of a plane at an altitude of 23,000 feet.

It is hard to appreciate how popular the sport became in the pre–World War II Soviet Union. Sport jumping was officially sanctioned and encouraged by the government for the first time in 1933. During 1934, 4,500 jumps from airplanes were recorded, while 300,000 jumps were made from various training towers. In 1935, 11,000 jumps were made from planes and 800,000 from towers. The numbers continued to soar. In 1936: 30,000 jumps from planes; 1,600,000 jumps from towers. And these are only civilian numbers. It is estimated that over a million young Soviets were taught the art of parachuting in 1940.

With all this activity, it is not surprising that the Soviets were pioneers in both parachute design and jumping techniques. In 1938, the Doronin brothers tested and built one of the first automatic-opening parachutes. A timing mechanism would pop the canopy after a preset interval had elapsed. The Soviets also became experienced in the art of skydiving, although it is unclear at what point Soviet jumpers first became aware of freefall stabilization techniques. Soviet paratrooper squadrons were the first to realize Benjamin Franklin's 150-year-old notion of using strategically placed airborne soldiers. These units, outfitted with skis and capable of jumping from planes into remote, snow-covered mountain terrain, predated similar American units. The Soviets also led the way in the use of parachutes for dropping medical supplies into inaccessible regions and for dropping brigades of trained firefighters onto the perimeters of wilderness blazes.

And parachute training schools eventually became proving grounds for cosmonauts. In 1963, Valentina Tereshkova, a former sport parachutist, became the first woman in space.

* * *

In November of 1962, a little more than twelve months after the resolution of the Cuban Missile Crisis and nine months after John Glenn's flight in *Friendship 7,* the Soviet Union announced what it claimed was a new world record: Maj. Yevgeny Andreyev had taken a balloon to a height of 83,500 feet and, like Joe Kittinger before him, had jumped out. Andreyev had fallen 79,560 feet before opening his parachute. The Soviets made immediate public claim to the freefall record. Not only had Kittinger's longer jump never been officially sanctioned by the FAI, but Kittinger had used a stabilization device, which—according to both the Soviets and the FAI—would have disqualified him anyway. According to the FAI, the record Andreyev broke was one held by another Soviet, Nikolai Nikitin, who had made a free fall of 46,965 feet a year earlier. These Soviet jumps made no pretense to being scientific or research activities. The goal was straightforward: they were after world records.

Andreyev had launched from Saratov in a balloon called the *Volga* with another aeronaut and parachutist aboard, Col. Peter Dolgov. Both men were veterans in the art of parachute jumping, each with an impressive string of national and world records to his credit. Dolgov, in addition, was a developer and tester of ejection systems—both for jets and for spacecraft.

Andreyev left the balloon at 10:13 A.M. after an ascent of two hours and twenty minutes. He fell the first 20,000 feet with his back turned to the earth in order to keep the faceplate on his helmet from icing up. His maximum speed was later given as 550 MPH. As he fell, Andreyev reported, he witnessed a "dark purple sky with an orange fringe along the horizon." He also reported seeing bright stars—a sight Kittinger had longed for. According to reports, Andreyev controlled his body position during the fall solely through the use of skydiving techniques—no multistage parachute was involved. In fact, Andreyev said that he was able to control his fall to such a degree that he successfully altered his descent path in order to avoid landing in the Volga River by joining his legs together and turning one palm or the other outward to initiate turns.

After Andreyev's exit, Dolgov remained in the balloon and continued to ascend. At 93,970 feet, he jumped. For some unreported reason, Dolgov's parachute deployed immediately after he left the balloon and he died sometime during the long descent. (One of the world records Dolgov had held was the highest parachute opening at 48,671 feet in June of 1960.) The Soviet military newspaper *Red Star* originally announced only that Dolgov had died "while fulfilling his duties." A cause of death was never given, but it is reasonable to assume that Colonel Dolgov either froze to death or ran out of oxygen to breathe. Some have speculated that the opening shock delivered by a parachute at that altitude could itself have caused death.

The newspaper of the Soviet defense ministry, *Krasnaya Zvezda,* claimed that Andreyev's jump—made without the aid of any kind of stabilization device—disproved the theory advanced by Project Excelsior that a body falling from such tremendous heights would succumb inevitably to flat spin. Proper skydiving techniques could be employed to provide stable and controllable freefall at any altitude, the Soviets argued. And they were right. Major Andreyev had made over 1,500 parachute jumps before attempting his jump from the upper stratosphere. He was well versed in skydiving techniques and had experimented with variations of those techniques in the thin air of the upper atmosphere many times. In contrast, Joe Kittinger had made only a relative handful of jumps before his long leap from *Excelsior III.* It is quite probable that the spin problems Kittinger experienced on the first Excelsior jump could have been avoided by a more experienced jumper. But that had never been the point for the Americans.

Unlike the two men in the *Volga,* the Excelsior team had not been interested in altitude records per se. The goal for Kittinger—and certainly for John Paul Stapp—had been to pioneer the technology and the processes necessary to protect pilots (or astronauts) forced to bail out at extreme altitudes. It was not realistic to pretend that those pilots would be experienced skydivers on the order of Major Andreyev. Flat spin would remain the biggest problem for the dazed aviator unfamiliar with freefall at near-supersonic speed, and something like the Beaupre chute would be required for any chance of survival.

Meanwhile, on both sides of the Atlantic, the race to the moon pressed on—with the Americans usually about a month, sometimes only days, behind the Russians. Gordon Cooper's twenty-two-orbit flight in 1963 was the final chapter of the Mercury project. The next step was to orbit larger, more sophisticated capsules capable of carrying more than a single astronaut. The first Soviet *Vokshod* ("Sunrise") flight carried three cosmonauts—including a civilian scientist—into space, and in March of 1965 *Vokshod 2* featured the first space walk. Lt. Col. Aleksei Leonov crawled through an airlock and left the spacecraft, spending 10 minutes hanging in oblivion before wriggling back inside.

Only five days after Leonov's historic "coffee break" in space, the United States' Gemini program put Gus Grissom and John Young into orbit in a capsule that provided them the ability to maneuver the position of the spacecraft and manually alter the configuration of orbit. The next Gemini flight, in June of that same year, gave Americans a look at one of their own walking in space as Edward White spent 21 minutes outside the capsule and used a hand-held gas gun to jet himself around.

The United States then scored a first with *Gemini 5* in August by keeping Cooper and Conrad in space for almost eight days, for a total of 120 orbits around the earth—a new space endurance record. In December, two separate manned spacecraft were launched by NASA one week apart and maneuvered to within 12 inches of each other nearly 185 miles above the earth and flew in formation for eight hours.

But while both Soviet and American rocket programs continued their stunning string of achievements in space, a competition that had become the track meet in the sky that John Paul Stapp had warned against, preparations for an obscure alternate event, a grudge match, were reaching a head in St. Paul, Minnesota. There were few spectators and almost no press. The lone competitor was a 33-year-old former pet-store owner from New Jersey who was neither an astronaut nor a military pilot. He had no connection whatsoever with NASA or the armed forces.

Nicholas Piantanida was a dark-eyed loner. As a skinny, awkward kid growing up in Union City, New Jersey, he fought a stubborn and painful bout with a potentially crippling bone disease called osteomyelitis that distanced him from childhood society, in particular from sports and outdoor games. In his late teens, the disease behind him, Nick took up flying and found a sense of peace and accomplishment in the skies above his hometown. He joined the Army and—as a testament to his regained health—fought eleven times as a heavyweight boxer. When his two-year tour of duty was up, he retired from the ring undefeated and resigned from the service.

Free of his obligation to his country, and still looking for his place in life, his mission, Piantanida traveled to Venezuela to prospect for diamonds. He did not get rich, but he did find a challenge in the dense mountain terrain of the Guiana Highlands: Angel Falls, the highest waterfall in the world. Piantanida developed a sudden interest in rock climbing and became one of the first climbers in the world to scale all 3,212 feet of the vertical rock wall alongside the tumbling waters of the Rio Churun.

Piantanida returned to the States resolved to pursue an academic career. He ended up in Kansas at St. Mary College where he majored in biology and went out for the basketball team. He made Catholic College Basketball All-American and led the nation's Catholic colleges in scoring in 1959–60. The next year he transferred to the University of Wichita where he began to collect animals—lots of animals. By the end of his second year on campus he had incurred the wrath of school officials with his personal menagerie of ground squirrels (some 200 of them), and a growing collection of alligators, snakes, and tropical birds. He left school and hauled his personal zoo back to New Jersey where he went into business as a pet dealer. That was in 1961; Nick was 28.

Two mostly uneventful years later, he married a beautiful 18-year-old named Janice McDowell who lived next door in Union City. They settled down together into what looked like it might be a stable and relatively normal life. Then, one day, Nick was driving by the parachute center in Lakewood. He pulled off to watch the jumpers floating out of the sky and circling down toward the drop zone. After giving it some thought, he returned the next day and paid $35 for some preliminary instruction and a static-line parachute jump. In the quick moment before his chute caught air, as he fell away from the airplane's drone and plunged into the wind, Nick found an exhilaration beyond anything he had ever known.

He started jumping regularly, passionately, driving out to the parachute center every chance he got. Soon he was off the static line and pulling his own ripcord, then making longer and longer freefalls. He learned the techniques of stable freefall—techniques that had been modified only slightly since the days of Valentin—and learned to maneuver himself in the air, turning, rolling, and tumbling end over end, but always in complete control. He had made hundreds of jumps and had worked his way up to a class D expert license when he heard about a Russian named Andreyev who had jumped from a helium balloon at 83,000 feet and set a new world freefall record. He decided almost immediately to recapture the record for the United States. He knew that he, personally, was capable of doing it. It was just a matter of proper training, of getting up there with survival gear adequate to the environment.

With his wife's blessing, Piantanida took a job driving trucks so that he could keep his weekends free. His long hours on the highway gave him time to work through the necessary preparations in his mind. He dove into research: meteorology, balloon technology, survival systems, high-altitude aerodynamics. He began writing and calling everyone he could think of who might be able to help. Lee Guilfoyle at the Lakewood Parachuting Center agreed to provide facilities for jump testing.

A key contact turned out to be Jacques Istel, the father of American sport parachuting and president of Parachutes Incorporated, an organization that developed freefall training programs. Istel took a personal interest in the project. He helped gather the equipment that would be needed to make a stratospheric jump and, in 1965, helped Piantanida form a corporation called Survival Programs Above a Common Environment: SPACE, Inc. The principals in the corporation were the Pioneer Parachute Company, Parachutes, Inc., and Nick Piantanida himself.

Nick spent much of his time on the phone or writing letters, asking—begging—for information, gear, training facilities. He ran into brick walls at NASA, in spite of offers to share his data and offers to modify his procedures in any way that would suit NASA's research purposes. He eventually received some assistance from the Air Force, which provided facilities at Tyndall Air Force Base in Panama City, Florida, for physiological training and from the Federal Aviation Administration who agreed to let the project use the Civil Aeromedical Research Center in Oklahoma City. Piantanida put himself into cold chambers and decompression chambers and made test jumps up to 36,000 feet. Much of the equipment was either donated or provided at, or below, cost. As the project picked up steam, driven by the focused determination of a single man, the gear began to roll in. The parachute harness and containers came from Pioneer Parachute Company. The survival suit was a full-pressure Air Force suit that had been modified by the David Clark Company who built suits for the Gemini astronauts. General Electric's Re-Entry Systems Division agreed to provide personnel and equipment capable of capturing precise velocity measurements.

By mid-1965, Piantanida's dream had acquired a name: Project Strato Jump. And four very specific objectives had been established:

1. To set an official world freefall record;
2. To set an unofficial manned balloon altitude record (since Piantanida planned to jump from his balloon at peak altitude, he would not be able to fulfill one of the FAI's requirements for an altitude record: that the pilot land with his craft);
3. To investigate the effects of supersonic speeds on a human body; and

4. To prove that it was possible to make a high-altitude (100,000+ feet) jump without the aid of a stabilization device.

In fact, Andreyev had already established that a stabilization device was unnecessary for a properly trained jumper, but given the climate of the lingering Cold War, some in the West stubbornly refused to believe it. Falling bodies in the upper atmosphere tumble, the common wisdom insisted, and eventually enter an unrecoverable flat spin. Piantanida, Istel, and Guilfoyle were all sure that skydiving techniques could provide stability, even at 100,000 feet where there is no air and where aerodynamics are essentially nonexistent. But interestingly enough, the braintrust of Project Strato Jump was never so certain of point number 4 that they were willing to bet Piantanida's life on it. The main parachute canopy would be the highly maneuverable Para Commander, which provided a slower rate of descent, set to open automatically at 6,500 feet, backed up by a reserve set to open at 4,000. But in addition, the system included an emergency six-foot drogue chute, much like the one that had been incorporated into Francis Beaupre's design for Project Excelsior . . . just in case point 4 turned out to be trickier than expected.

The months of research, training, and fundraising finally came together in the fall of 1965. The launch was set for October 22 at a small airport in New Brighton, Minnesota, north of Minneapolis. Early that morning, the balloon—a 5-million-cubic-foot polyethylene monster constructed by the Applied Science Division of Litton Industries—was elevated between two trucks and readied for the helium inflation. The gondola, a 4-foot by 4-foot by $5^{1}/_{2}$-foot polystyrene box with a frame of welded aluminum tubes, was rolled into place a few hours prior to launch. Once the laborious process of being sealed into the pressure suit and denitrogenization of his blood was complete, Piantanida was led to the open gondola and helped into his seat. Like Kittinger, he wore electrically heated socks and gloves and, like Malcolm Ross, a heated helmet face shield. The gondola was outfitted with four separate oxygen systems and three radios. As his wife, now the mother of two with a third on the way, watched the prelaunch scramble of the Strato Jump crew, observers noted her nervousness, but also her faith in her husband: "I trust Nicky's judgement," she told them.

Less than half an hour after launch, Strato Jump hit 22,700 feet and a six-knot wind sheared the top right off the balloon. Nick jumped from the gondola and, seeing that he was on course for downtown St. Paul, pulled his D-ring at 10,000 feet—much higher than he would normally pull—so that he could maneuver himself toward a safer landing spot. The failed balloon drifted off and landed in a school playground, but Nick touched down just off U.S. Highway 12 . . . in the St. Paul city dump.

There was never any question that they would try again. Piantanida's obsession, like Hawthorne Gray's before him, had taken on a life of its own. A fellow jumper who knew Nick during his preparations for Strato Jump confirms that there was absolutely no scientific drive involved: "He was just a real ballsy guy. Kind of a loose cannon sometimes. A little showy, maybe arrogant. But he was well equipped and prepared." And he wasn't going to give up without a fight. The Air Force and Navy balloon programs had suffered similar setbacks. He had worked too hard to quit. He knew he had to regroup, analyze the problems, retool or change procedures as necessary—and then go again. All he needed was money. And a new balloon.

Raven Industries in Sioux Falls had already supplied the gondola and the personnel responsible for launch operations and the entire tracking and recovery operation. Ed Yost, who had invented the modern hot-air sport balloon and who founded Raven in 1956,* had agreed to serve as balloon program director. And for the second Strato Jump flight, Raven would manufacture the balloon as well. And so it only made sense to move the entire project—including the launch site—to Sioux Falls. The unofficial headquarters for Strato Jump became the Town House Motel and Smoky Jim Lee's barbecue joint. Piantanida, Istel, Yost, Raven's meteorologist, Dr. Frisby, and the others would gather for ribs and beers and talk the flight through over and over again. As winter wore on, optimism soared.

The launch was set for the first day of February 1966, but Frisby scrubbed the flight because of weather. They set up to try again the following morning. As dawn spread across the Minnesota prairies and fell on Joe Foss Field on the outskirts of Sioux Falls, a heavy ground fog clung to the flat earth. It was −13° with a three-knot wind. Frisby put a hold on the launch, but revoked it once the fog had begun to dissipate.

The balloon was rolled out and the hoses from the helium trucks

---

*Yost was himself an accomplished balloonist. In addition to his transatlantic attempt, he made a 1963 hot-air crossing of the English Channel with Don Piccard, son of Jean and Jeanette.

were attached. The gondola, with a new nameplate bearing the words "Second Chance," was trucked from the hangar and rolled into position. At 11:40, Piantanida, wearing the orange pressure suit, was driven out to the gondola where his wife and launch crew awaited him. As they waited together, Piantanida sat down on the tailgate of a station wagon and wrote out a letter to his first daughter who was three years old. He sealed the letter in an envelope and gave it to his wife. If he should die, he said, his daughter was not to open the letter until 1981, when she would be 18.

In spite of the cold, it was a perfect day for a balloon launch. The winds had not picked up since dawn and visibility was unlimited. Once Nick was installed in the gondola and the trucks pumped 28,000 cubic feet of helium into the 324-foot-long plastic bag—a volume of gas that would expand to 5 million cubic feet at altitude—it was time. At 12:11, *Strato Jump II* left the ground. The crew, spectators, and the small huddle of reporters and photographers, along with the state police who were on hand to provide security for the launch operation, all stamped their feet and rubbed their hands to keep warm, while craning their necks to watch as the gondola "Second Chance" gradually diminished into the clear blue sky. The skies over South Dakota were so clear that day that the crowd was able to watch the balloon's journey all the way to the top. You could still see the sun shining on the huge ball of plastic even as it hung 23 miles above the surface of the earth.

This time the ascent went without a hitch. Piantanida kept the gondola's double doors open for the view until he reached 30,000 feet. Then he closed them for the trip through the tropopause to lessen the effect of the bone-chilling temperatures and fierce jet-stream winds. At 60,000 feet, he was able to open the doors again. As he continued to rise, he noted the distortions in the rural-checkerboard panorama below him and realized he was seeing the curvature of the earth. The sky above him was now a dark purple. A few moments later and it appeared black.

At 1:53, Piantanida reported an altimeter reading of 120,500 feet and announced that he was beginning a five-minute countdown to what would be the world's longest jump. He snapped the sun visor down over his face shield, released his seat belt, and activated his bailout unit—the portable oxygen system that he would use during the jump. The next task was to disconnect his on-board oxygen unit, which would effectively sever him from any physical connection to the gondola. But when he tried to turn the valve that would release the oxygen hose, he found that it wouldn't turn. He jiggled it and applied all the pressure he could to try and move it, but it was frozen. And with the pressure gloves on his hands, he did not have the dexterity to do anything very fancy. He kept cranking on the disconnect valve, but it would not budge.

As he worked, he kept up a chatter with his ground crew. "Disconnect, having problem with oxygen . . . disconnect. . . . Going overtime. Ground control, do you read me? We've got problems."

Piantanida's breath came heavy and rasping through the receivers on the ground. "Isn't this a bitch. . . . Can't disconnect the oxygen. . . . I don't believe it, I can't separate the hose."

Tense minutes went by. The ground crew struggled for answers as Piantanida kept up a running commentary.

"Oh God, let me get this hose." The crew could hear the labored breathing. "Don't make me talk. I don't believe it. I just don't believe it."

Meanwhile, the balloon continued to rise until it was hanging at an altitude that would later be officially recorded as 123,500 feet. It was two miles higher than any balloonist had ever gone. And if he could simply disconnect himself from the gondola, he could leap out and shatter the world freefall record. It was right there for him. Only he couldn't get the oxygen hose loose. And he couldn't just tear it or cut it loose. It was too risky. If he pulled a fitting out or otherwise damaged the pressure suit, he'd die in an instant. But he had to get the hose disconnected somehow.

At 2:03, Piantanida's voice came across the radio again. "How in hell can this thing be stuck?" He was reaching the limits of his tolerance. "God damn crescent wrench."

After a moment: "It's getting so damn hot. . . . God, I just don't believe it." As the minutes went by, he continued to struggle with the valve. It seemed inconceivable that he would not be able to get it loose somehow. He knew what would happen if he couldn't disconnect. They would have to separate him from the balloon. And that wasn't a very comforting thought, since there was nowhere near enough air at this height to open the big drogue parachute canopy. If they cut him loose, the gondola would freefall for 30,000 feet before the chute would open. And not only would he have to worry about being thrown around the interior, but no one really knew what the opening shock would be like at the speeds he would be traveling. Many people were positive it could not be survived. And even if Piantanida got past the opening shock, the rest of the trip down remained an unknown quantity.*

"I'll try one more time. . . . What a stinking . . . Please make it come loose."

Then Ed Yost's sober voice on the radio told Piantanida to reconnect his seat belt. Obviously, a decision had been made. Now Piantanida struggled with the restraint system.

"I can't hook up the belt. . . . There is no way of making it. . . . Nobody will believe it."

"Try, Nick," Yost pleaded. "Try."

"I've got no control with the gloves. . . . Can't do it."

After a few moments, the dejected voice from the stratosphere came through again.

"I just can't release this gadget. Let me know if you're going to cut me down."

The voice of the ground controller broke in. "Nick, I'll give you a countdown from 10. Brace yourself against the seat, put your feet on each side of the door and hold on tight."

Without the insurance of the seat belt, it would be a battle between Nick Piantanida and the invisible forces that he knew could buck him out of the gondola at any point during the upcoming ride. It would take all of his considerable strength to hang on. The track meet in space had become a rodeo.

It was Ed Yost's voice again. "Nick, do you read me?"

"Who's going to cut me down?"

"I will, Nick," Yost assured him. "Make sure you have a good hold."

Yost's voice began to crackle and cut out.

"Can't hear you, Ed," Piantanida said. "Let Sioux Falls take it."

The voice of Ground Control in Sioux Falls came on immediately. "Nick, we're cutting you down on Yost's signal."

Piantanida's heavy breathing continued as he listened to an explanation of the separation procedure that he already knew by heart.

"O.K., Roger," he responded. "When it comes, I'm braced."

---

*Albert Stevens, following the flight of *Explorer II* in 1935, had marveled innocently at the idea: "The fall of such a gondola on a parachute in the extremely thin upper air of the stratosphere would be for tens of thousands of feet before the parachute would really retard it. That *would* be a ride!"

Ground Control began the countdown. Piantanida steeled himself, pushing with his legs and his arms against the aluminum frame of the gondola.

" . . . 5, 4, 3, 2, 1!"

The "Second Chance" was falling like a rock. As he braced himself, Piantanida thought of his daughter, and tried to imagine her at age 18 as she opened the letter. The gondola was in freefall for a full 35 seconds, but to Piantanida's tremendous relief, there was no tumbling or spinning at all. The box just dropped straight down in the exact attitude it had assumed beneath the balloon. But his worries were far from over. The chute would be released at 97,000 feet and he was prepared for a violent opening shock. He was falling at about 600 MPH.

Then it came. The chute was open and Piantanida was still in the gondola. He hadn't fallen out and he hadn't been blown through the floor. In fact, as it turned out, the shock wasn't really that much worse than the normal opening shock of a parachute in the lower atmosphere. But in spite of the fact that he was still on board and still alive, Piantanida wasn't celebrating.

"I'm going to keep quiet for a while," he told the crew.

At 65,000 feet, Ed Yost broke the silence and asked how Piantanida felt.

"I'm getting sick," was the answer. "These oscillations." As the gondola descended beneath the parachute, it swung wildly from side to side. In preparation for such a situation, Piantanida had eaten nothing the night before the launch so that there would be no danger of him vomiting inside the helmet and suffocating himself.

There was some discussion about whether Piantanida ought to try to jump from the gondola once it had reached a safe altitude, but it was a moot point since he was still unable to disconnect the oxygen hose.

At 46,000 feet, Piantanida was still feeling sick.

"How could one tiny bit of stinking equipment screw up like that?" he asked no one in particular.

At 30,000 feet, Ground Control suggested that he begin to open his face shield for short intervals to see whether fresh air alleviated the nausea. A couple of minutes later, Piantanida began to think about the aneroid that was set to open his main canopy automatically.

"Ground control, do you read me? My main parachute is going to activate at 6,500 feet."

"The only thing you can do," the voice said, "is sit back when it does and hold it in the gondola." If the canopy were allowed to escape out into the wind, it would jerk Piantanida right out with it—and it probably wouldn't be a very clean exit.

Jacques Istel's voice came on. "Nick, deactivate your reserve."

"I already did," he said.

Istel continued. "Nick, put your main parachute under you to absorb the landing shock."

The voice of Ground Control added, "Nick, stand up just before landing. It will help absorb the shock."

The gondola hit the ground at 2:45 P.M., some 32 minutes after being separated from the balloon at 123,500 feet. The first thing Piantanida did after landing was fish out a pocket knife and go to work on the oxygen disconnect valve, eventually prying it loose.

A recovery helicopter sped to the landing site in an Iowa cornfield. As Nick climbed out of his curious-looking spacecraft, he saw a middle-aged farmer approaching on foot. But unlike the cool characters who had encountered David Simons after his trip to the edge of space, this guy was awestruck. As it turned out, the sight of Piantanida in his orange pressure suit emerging from the strange white box was just too much. The farmer dropped in his tracks, stricken by a heart attack.

As the helicopter landed, Piantanida directed the doctor who was assigned to administer his postflight examination to the farmer and boarded the chopper for a ride back to Sioux Falls. There was an upbeat but awkward press conference ("If only I had a damned $1.25 wrench, gravity would have done the rest," a haggard Piantanida explained), and a private steak and champagne dinner with Janice in their room back at the Town House Motel, but there was little peace for Nick Piantanida. His balloon altitude mark would forever be unofficial, and the world freefall record still belonged to the Russians.

The total expenses for the second attempt stood at about $120,000. Could the project afford a third try? At a time when the nation's armed forces were mired in a shooting war and NASA was pumping furiously to stay on the track in its race for the moon, could the freefall record continue to interest anyone? Somehow, Piantanida's insistence convinced crew and sponsors to go for one last shot.

And so, for the third time in seven months, Project Strato Jump was readied for yet another launch date: May Day—not only the international distress signal, but also the biggest holiday on the Soviet calendar. There were those who wondered whether or not this coincidence would prove auspicious, but Nick Piantanida probably wasn't one of them.

It was a cold, clear morning when the new balloon was rolled out at Joe Foss Field and the gondola was once again trucked out from the hangar. A small crowd had gathered on the tarmac to watch the launch and ascent. The balloon was attached to the gondola, and minutes later the big mechanical arm that secured the balloon sprang back with a sharp crack and *Strato Jump III* was airborne. Janice Piantanida waved goodbye. She turned to Jacques Istel and whispered, "Oh God, he has to make it this time."

At a steady ascent rate of 1,000 feet per minute, it took a little under one hour for the balloon to reach 57,600 feet. Then it happened. Ground Control heard a sudden gush of air in their monitors and headphones and then Piantanida's voice, gasping and screaming.

"Emergency!"

It took the ground crew 17 seconds to determine what had happened, that the helmet or the suit had, for some unknown reason, developed a leak—the consequences being that Piantanida's entire pressurization system had failed and exposed him to the vacuum. The point at which oxygen and nitrogen will literally boil in a man's veins is pegged at 63,000 feet, only about a mile above the gondola. There was no doubt that they were in real trouble. The poison-fingered hand had finally gotten a grip.

The gondola was immediately separated from the balloon, but unfortunately the gondola's drogue parachute deployed—as designed—and slowed the descent. Four critical minutes later, the gondola had still only fallen to 43,000 feet. A total of 25 minutes elapsed before Piantanida was back on the ground. The landing spot was just outside the town of Lakefield, Minnesota. An Air Force rescue team was on the spot and dragged Piantanida, moaning and sucking for breath, from his seat. They stuck a tube down his throat to facilitate breathing and rushed him to the Worthington Municipal Hospital where doctors performed an emergency tracheotomy followed by an hour-long surgery. The doctors emerged from the operation to console a sobbing Janice Piantanida. Nick's prognosis was said to be fairly good. The following day they transferred him to Hennepin County General in Minneapolis and put him in a high-pressure oxygen chamber. In spite of the fact that he remained unconscious, Piantanida's breathing improved and by week's end the doctors were beginning to sound encouraging, while admitting that brain damage was probably a foregone conclusion.

What had gone wrong? Those monitoring the radio transmission heard a rush of air. Did the helmet's face shield develop a hairline crack? Was the heating element to blame? Was there a problem with the seal of either the helmet or the suit? Did Piantanida crack open the face shield for just the briefest instant to clear condensation as some later charged and others vehemently denied? After years of litigation and rumors circulating among parachuting circles, we still don't know the truth.

What we do know is that Nick Piantanida suffered the most severe explosive decompression ever endured by a human being. He never woke up from his coma. He was moved to Veterans' Hospital in Philadelphia during the summer and he died there on August 29.

twelve

▼

Stair Steps

The era of manned ballooning in the upper stratosphere ended with the Stargazer astronomy flight; Piantanida was little more than a curious postscript. Neither the armed forces nor private industry had the will to continue. The main event of the celestial track meet, the race to the moon, was about to enter the breathtaking bell lap: the development of the Saturn rocket-launch vehicles and the Apollo payloads they would ferry into deep space was well under way. The entire scenario for the lunar-landing flight had already been scripted in full technical and procedural detail: a trio of astronauts would take a three-module spaceship into lunar orbit, at which point one of the modules—carrying two of the men—would detach itself and swoop down to land on the moon's surface. It had never been easy for the public to believe that all the calculations and training and unfathomably complex technology would actually succeed in depositing a mortal human being on the surface of the moon and, more unbelievably still, retrieving him from the void and delivering him to his home planet no worse for the wear. It was mind-boggling, almost beyond comprehension. Only a few years earlier, an ONR spokesman familiar with the problems of high-altitude exploration assessed a manned assault on outer space: "The moon seems sure to be man's first destination in space. A landing there might be achieved within 50 years." To believe that the goal could in fact be accomplished before the end of the present *decade* required a certain faith in the laws of science, and in human genius and character. But as the Apollo program worked through its crowded agenda, and in spite of the occasional setbacks, the ultimate goal as originally outlined by Kennedy began to take on the heady aura of inevitability. Meanwhile, the Soviets fell quietly out of the race after a coup displaced Nikita Khrushchev and installed Leonid Brezhnev. Brezhnev listened to his military leaders, who wanted practical weapons hardware rather than spaceships, and to his top scientists, who convinced him that unmanned space missions would be more cost-effective. The 1966 death of Sergei Korolev, the man most responsible for the Soviets' earlier triumphs, signaled the eventual collapse of the Soviet lunar mission program.

Michael Collins, a former test pilot who went into earth orbit with *Gemini 10* in 1966 and who would later pilot the command module on *Apollo 11* while Armstrong and Aldrin took mankind's giant leap into the lunar dust, has written that testing vehicles and procedures for space flight was like no other type of flight testing: "It was not possible to stair-step into orbit, to test the craft by making a long series of flights, each with a small incremental increase in performance. It tended to be all or nothing, zooming out to the four corners of the envelope on the first try."

Yet in the beginning, NASA had no choice but to use the substantial high-altitude balloon research done by the Air Force and the Navy as its stair steps into space. It was the best available information on how to pick the right man for the mission, on how he might be expected to function in a space environment, and on what sorts of hardware and processes would be needed to keep him comfortable and alert. With the exception of the rocket itself, few major systems aboard the Mercury, Gemini, and Apollo spacecraft had not been influenced in some way—and often profoundly—by Manhigh, Strato-Lab, and Excelsior. And as surely as the advances in rocketry that carried men to the moon were rooted in the German experiments of the forties (just as the Germans themselves had based their work on Robert Goddard's breakthroughs in the twenties and thirties), the roots of the space program are forever entangled with the high-altitude balloon flights of the fifties and early sixties. J. Gordon Vaeth, a Navy engineer and contributor to Project Helios, predicted this relationship and our incremental progress toward space back in 1956:

There will be no sudden "all-out" climb into interplanetary space. Altitude will be gradually and carefully increased. There will be many flights and series of flights. The crews who make them will be the true pioneers. Theirs will be the responsibility of proving—by going up and coming back alive—that man can safely explore the emptiness and loneliness of space.

The stratospheric balloonists were genuine pioneers, and they suffered the attendant hardships and disadvantages. Too often they were forced to cope with inadequate budgets and bargain-basement equipment, without computers or well-trained technical staffs, improvising and bootlegging and generally making due. "Compared to the first men who ventured into the thin, cruel air of the upper atmosphere," Martin Caidin wrote in 1963 of the high-altitude balloonists, "our astronauts are almost pampered." The bureaucrats who controlled funding and authorization were too often impediments to progress, motivated by the knee-jerk conservatism of the bureaucracy and by the petty jealousies of organizational politics. But if the balloonists suffered their share of difficulties, they also enjoyed immense personal satisfactions. As the first human being to witness sunset and sunrise from above the atmosphere, looking down at the warped horizon and surveying the blackness that was so black it was more felt than seen, David Simons experienced a unique moment of exaltation, seeing the virgin extraterrestrial panorama years before NASA astronauts would have a chance to see these things with their own eyes. John Glenn's celebrated descriptions of the colors of sunset as seen from space were slightly less poetic versions of the same descriptions radioed back to earth by the more articulate Simons on *Manhigh II;** Glenn's observations of the glowing cloud forms of an electrical storm were also repeats. And Joe Kittinger took his own free walk in space years before the orbital astronauts—tethered, at first, securely to their capsules—would do the same.

There is some comfort in the knowledge that monumental achievements do not—as they sometimes first appear—spring magically from nothing; that they come in gritty, painstaking stages, one following from another, each major success contingent upon the numberless smaller ones that preceded it. And if the foremost technoscientific moment of mankind in the twentieth century is the lunar landing, then a measure of tribute is due those frontiersmen who first punched their way into the upper stratosphere and smuggled back its secrets. They are the forgotten heroes of our greatest collective triumph.

---

*The balloonists were, if not always more articulate, certainly more colorful communicators than the NASA astronauts of the 1960s, who relied mostly on a technospeak code through which they could talk to the engineers in Houston without the nuisance of being understood by the TV-watching public. Some of the Apollo pilots didn't like to talk much at all. Norman Mailer wrote that Neil Armstrong "surrendered words about as happily as a hound allowed meat to be pulled out of his teeth."

The pre-astronauts were a unique strain of driven, brilliant men for whom the years of the manned balloon programs contained the defining moments of their lives. And for them all, the glory days were over too soon. In their minds, their work was unfinished, and their contributions were too soon forgotten.

But for those few years, they *were* the space program.

During the time of *Manhigh III,* the marriage of Otto and Vera Winzen was disintegrating. Subject to volatile mood swings and severe guilt following the balloon crash that had badly injured Grover Schock, Otto Winzen was slow to recover from his own injuries. After his release from the hospital, he and Vera divorced. She sold her interest in Winzen Research and enrolled in art school in Washington, D.C. Two years later, she married another recently divorced balloonatic, David Simons.

By the early seventies, having made a name for herself in international art circles, Vera Simons conceived of ways to incorporate aspects of ballooning and balloon technology into her art. In 1972, following an exhibition of her work in Amsterdam, she began plans for what she called Project Da Vinci: a series of gas balloon flights involving both scientific research and original kinetic art. She renewed her contacts in the balloon world, including those with Otto Winzen, and eventually partnered with Dr. Rudolf Engelmann, chief scientist of the National Oceanic and Atmospheric Administration. Engelmann, a former Air Force meteorologist, was an authority on the migration of lower-level atmospheric pollutants and assembled a research package composed of experiments from some twenty-five universities. After convincing the National Geographic Society and the Atomic Energy Commission to provide funding for Da Vinci, Vera spent two years designing and supervising the construction of a double-decker, fiberglass gondola and a polyethylene balloon, receiving assistance from a handful of private companies as well as from NASA.

The genesis of the project was rooted in a desire to meld science and art. To Vera, it was anything but a contradiction. "I found, all those years of working with scientists, that their creative processes were similar to mine. Their minds fascinated me. And I thought: Why can't artists work with scientists?"

Da Vinci began with a 12-hour night-time flight from Las Cruces to Wagon Mound, New Mexico, in November 1974, in which detailed temperature and air-flow data were collected. Vera's old friend Duke

Gildenberg served as launch advisor. The project's second flight, from St. Louis to Griffin, Indiana, in the summer of 1976, gathered data on the mix and movement of urban air pollutants while Vera photographed landscape and cloud images. After another flight from St. Louis, Vera Simons and Engelmann began preparations for their final flight, a *pièce de résistance* that would be known as *Da Vinci Transamerica*. Sponsored primarily by the Seven-Up Company (with additional support provided by Louisiana-Pacific, NBC, and the Washington Post), the 216,000-cubic-foot helium balloon lifted off from Tillamook, Oregon—a few miles from the shore of the Pacific Ocean—on the morning of September 26, 1979. The crew, which consisted of Simons (pilot), Engelmann (chief scientist), Fred Hyde (flight surgeon, communications director, and copilot), and NBC cameraman Randy Birch (photographer), hoped to make the first nonstop manned balloon expedition to cross the continental United States. The desire to set the overland distance record became, finally, the focus of the flight and the focus of an aggressive public relations campaign by Seven-Up. *Da Vinci* was shooting for Norfolk, Virginia.

As the eleven-story balloon and its split-level gondola rose above the mountains of the Oregon Coast range, Vera dropped tiny tetrahedron balloons carrying Douglas fir seedlings into clearcuts. Then, as *Da Vinci* drifted eastward, she took time-lapse photographs, made sound recordings, and used mirrors to create special lighting effects for spectators on the ground. Throughout the $5^{1}/_{2}$ -day journey, the balloon never rose above 23,000 feet, and spent most of its time relatively close to the ground. This was by design. Simons had never had any particular desire to make a high-altitude flight on the order of Manhigh or Strato-Lab, nor to spend any time at all in a space capsule. She explained,

> I want to do something more romantic, more people-oriented. I like the connection with people on the ground vs. the balloon, establishing this dialogue cross-country. . . . Having a bird fly and land on your gondola. It is so romantic, so exciting, and so elevating—emotionally and physically.

The balloon drifted east-southeast, crossing the Cascades and then the Rockies. Bad weather struck first in eastern Kansas, forcing *Da Vinci* to drop down near the surface and tether for the night, a kind of airborne parking. Then, over western Ohio, a storm subjected the crew to high winds and driving rains and coated the gondola with snow and ice. After the jettisoning of all available ballast, including several cases of 7 Up,

Inflation of *Da Vinci Transamerica* in Tillamook, Oregon. Vera Simons (pilot) and Dr. Fred Hyde (copilot) look on. *(Source: Vera Simons, photographer unknown)*

the balloon was forced down in a soybean field near Spencerville. On impact, one of the heavy NBC cameras (which had been used to capture images for the "Today Show") tore loose and broke Vera Simons's left leg. She was taken to a hospital in nearby Lima and treated for multiple compound fractures.

Da Vinci landed 500 miles short of its goal, although a new overland distance record had been established: 2,003 miles. Simons and Engelmann expressed disappointment; the flight was publicly referred to as a failure. Yet the series of *Da Vinci* flights, spanning six years, constitute a unique chapter in the saga of ballooning. Vera Simons established something more significant than any records she may have set or failed to set (in fact, she holds most of the significant women's balloon records on the books): she added another element, an alternate sensibility, to the business of exploring the atmosphere. She found something beyond height or distance or cosmic rays. She found ways to bring ballooning to people on the ground, and ways to open our minds and our eyes to the atmosphere. "I feel pretty good," she says, "about the fact that I have been able to use the technology that I learned, and the various facets of it, and put it into what I really care about. . . . I thought all those years running a balloon factory would be lost as far as my art career was concerned. But they weren't."

Since *Da Vinci,* Vera Simons has continued to produce art that incorporates lighter-than-air technology. In 1984, she staged Project Aeolus, in which three plastic balloons, lit from within and connected by gracefully looping strings of lights, were launched simultaneously into the night-time New Mexico sky. Joe Kittinger piloted one of the balloons. Legendary aeronaut Larry Newman flew another. And in the third balloon with Vera Simons was Ben Abruzzo who, along with Newman, had been part of the *Double Eagle* transatlantic crossing six years earlier. But she is reluctant to embark on another manned balloon project. For one thing, it takes many months and often a great deal of money to plan and execute a manned flight. For another, she is afraid that ballooning is too much of a distraction in her chosen sphere, the art world: "The artists consider me a balloonist and the balloonists consider me an artist." But she will never lose the desire to fly gas balloons. "You never get it out of your blood," she admits, gazing out across the green Texas hill country west of Austin where she lives and works. "I'd go in a minute."

In spite of some unpleasant memories, she remembers the days of the great high-altitude balloon programs with obvious fondness. To her, the period of Manhigh and Strato-Lab was a romantic era full of great purpose. And she assesses her role with a firm pride. "My contribution was in building really damn good balloons." In fact, no woman—with the debatable exception of Jeanette Piccard—played a more important role in the development of modern balloon technology and atmospheric exploration. And though she received a gold medal for her contributions to balloon research while representing the United States at the 30th International Gas Balloon Races in Holland, she has been largely forgotten outside of the art world.

Winzen Research's bid to build the Mercury space capsule was unsuccessful, but the company did very well for itself in the 1960s. Contracts were plentiful. Otto Winzen built a personal collection of some fifty automobiles that he kept in a hangar at Fleming Field. Then, after moving the manufacturing plant to Texas and selling off chunks of Winzen Research to his employees, Otto gradually began to lose control. The engineering staff no longer looked to him for input, and his frequent traveling was curtailed. Depression set in, exacerbated by an unhappy second marriage.

In 1976, at age 58, Otto Winzen killed himself. "It's a macabre thing," Vera Simons recalls. "Otto picked my birthday to commit suicide."

The Navy's most influential proponent of high-altitude balloon research in the 1940s, George Hoover, must be recognized as one of the pioneers who paved the way for the glory flights of the 1950s and '60s—and, ultimately, as one of the founders of the U.S. space program. Hoover attributes his own success to the fact that he always understood the value of setting clear goals and objectives, and claims that this discipline afforded him the ability to visualize the solution to a problem long before others even understood the nature of it.

Hoover is now at work on his autobiography at his home in Pacific Palisades, California. His book, he says, will tell the whole story behind the events at the ONR in the 1940s. According to Hoover, other organizations within the Navy, civilian contractors, and—later—the Air Force all attempted to gain control of and take credit for the ideas and technology involved in Project Helios. "I had to work on these things secretly, give them code names, and bury them inside all the other projects I had going on. Let me tell you, it was a real cut-throat operation."

To Hoover and other ONR researchers who had been involved with high-altitude studies and who had been thinking about manned balloon ascents to heights of 100,000 feet since the forties, David Simons's Manhigh seemed to have come from out of the woodwork. As one of Hoover's colleagues put it: "Who is this guy? Where did he come from? We were the show, and all of a sudden the Air Force starts coming in." To hear Navy veterans of the ONR talk about the Air Force balloon programs is to hear Air Force veterans of Manhigh and Excelsior talk about NASA.

The concept of a manned balloon research flight to near-space altitudes actually originated with the Navy. And much of the early theoretical groundwork necessary to make such a flight a reality was carried out at naval research facilities like the Air Development Center in Pennsylvania and the School of Aviation Medicine in Pensacola, Florida. Nevertheless, because the Air Force had the resources and the charter to make super-high-altitude ascents a reality, the Air Force dominated the decade leading up to Project Mercury and the full flowering of the space age. And, fair or not, it is the Air Force that receives the lion's share of the credit for opening the door to outer space.

Malcolm Ross made more balloon trips into the stratosphere than anyone else. His Strato-Lab flight in the winter of 1956, the flight that touched off the era of the pre-astronauts, marked the first time a human had taken a polyethylene balloon through the tropopause. But after the deaths of the two men with whom he had shared his greatest accomplishments, Lee Lewis and Vic Prather—both, ironically, due to accidents on the ground—Ross retired from the Navy and from ballooning. He had never set out to be a balloonist, much less a space hero. He didn't care much about records, being first or going highest. His interests were too varied. He had worked in radio and advertising and enjoyed civilian life too much. He went to work for the Space Defense Corporation, and then for General Motors, where he headed the environmental sciences section. He died at age 65 at his home in Birmingham, Michigan, not far from the Indiana countryside where he grew up. A recipient of several prestigious awards, including the Distinguished Flying Cross and the Harmon International Trophy, Ross was buried in Arlington National Cemetery.

J. Gordon Vaeth, who knew (and in most cases worked with) all of the Navy's principal players in the high-altitude drama, points out that scientific and technological milestones are always achieved by individual contributors who catalyze organizations and will them into action:

All major technical advances are achieved because of people who are banging the drums and blowing the whistles. This was true of Von Braun and the space program. And in the case of manned stratospheric ballooning, it was because there were people like Mal Ross who was operating at the seat of power—so to speak—in the Office of Naval Research right there in Washington. And there was Lee Lewis, who was the Navy's representative on the scene, in the field. And last, but not least, was Charlie Moore. Along with George Hoover, these men made much of this possible.

After Excelsior, Francis Beaupre spent most of the 1960s working on a variety of escape systems and survival gear in the Aeromed Lab at Wright-Patterson. Having grown up a hundred miles away in Indianapolis, he found Dayton a comfortable and convenient place to settle in for the long haul. He interviewed with NASA after Excelsior ended, but decided to turn down the job that was offered. "I didn't want to subject my family to that kind of a life in a place like Washington or Houston," he says. "And I didn't want to subject myself to all the political mumbo-jumbo." The Air Force did investigate Beaupre's stabilization chute and at least considered adopting the design for high-altitude jet pilots. An explanation for why the chute was scrapped was never offered. The Air Force's study was classified and, according to Beaupre, everyone connected with Project Excelsior was shut out. NASA also looked into the multistage chute, but Beaupre was never given the results of their analysis. There is the suspicion that NASA remained infected with the NIH avoidance syndrome: Not Invented Here.

In 1979, Francis Beaupre retired, although he has worked on the investigations of a number of aircraft accidents since then. He recalls his Excelsior days with pleasure. "Joe Kittinger was one of the fairest people I've ever worked for, and Stapp was the hammer with the big stick. We were do-ers, action people. Those were the kinds of people Kittinger and Stapp surrounded themselves with."

Beaupre, incidentally, agrees with Kittinger that the victims of the *Challenger* disaster might have survived if they had had some kind of personal escape system. But he holds little hope for the bureaucratic snarl of NASA. "The *Challenger* tragedy," he says sadly, "was the result of a lot of selfish political people who just didn't give a shit."

It had appeared obvious to some that the high-altitude balloonists would naturally inherit the controls of the rocket vehicles that would sling us into orbit and, eventually, on into deep space. The pre-astronauts ought, logically, to have become the first astronauts. Having endured their trials by fire, surely they had earned the assignment. Lynn Poole, writing in 1958, before the final Manhigh flight, before the later Strato-Lab flights, before Project Excelsior, saw clearly the value of the balloon as a trainer for would-be spacemen: "Undoubtedly the first person to man a space rocket . . . will undergo space testing in a stratosphere balloon ascension."

If anyone can ever be said to have been born for a purpose, Clifton McClure was born to be an astronaut. He burned to go into space. He had dreamed about it, prepared for it, was willing to do anything for the opportunity. *Manhigh III* should have been his ticket, but events conspired against him. The death of Pope Pius XII on the morning after McClure's flight knocked the would-be space traveler off the front pages of the nation's newspapers, and off the cover of the following week's *Life* magazine as well. The burst of publicity that would normally have attended a spectacular ordeal like *Manhigh III* was diluted; McClure never got the attention that Simons and Kittinger had enjoyed. And when time came to draw up a list of potential NASA astronauts, few remembered the name of Clifton McClure—if, in fact, they had ever heard it at all.

NASA just wanted all these old guys. John Glenn was 15 years older than I was, old enough to have been Gagarin's father.[*] I could've done it. If you look strictly at qualifications, I was more qualified than any of those guys. But nobody knew who I was. A lot of the information on *Manhigh III* didn't come out until two years later and by then it was too late.

Originally, Manhigh was to have been followed by another high-altitude program (to be called Skylab); McClure had hoped to get involved in that, but the project never materialized. After Manhigh, McClure played a minor role in Project Excelsior.

They asked for a backup pilot. They called me over there. See, [Kittinger] had two options: he had a sealed gondola and an open gondola. And if

---

[*]The Soviets had always emphasized youth in the astronaut selection process. Given the time and expense of training astronauts, they wanted those men and women available for service for as long as possible. The Soviet space program built a roster of professional space travelers. In contrast, early U.S. space policy designated astronaut service as a temporary duty for selected military personnel.

he'd gone with the sealed gondola, he would've had to have had a pilot in there to bring it back down. But if he had a pilot in there, he'd have had to supply him with another chute just like the one he had. . . . The way Kittinger figured, if he jumped out, I'd go up 3,000 feet and jump out and then before he got to the ground, I'd set the world altitude record right behind him. *[McClure laughs deeply.]*

If he couldn't go into space, what he really wanted to do was just to keep flying. Like Kittinger, he preferred combat duty to an office. But with his engineering degrees, the Air Force would assign him to fly nothing more exhilarating than a desk. McClure resigned and joined the Air National Guard where he could once again slide into the cockpit of the latest and greatest wonders of aviation science.

McClure believes he narrowly missed a second shot at fame and glory during his tenure with the Guard. He was stationed in South Carolina in 1962 and followed the Soviet arms buildup in Cuba through newspaper stories like everyone else. But when secret high-altitude Soviet reconnaissance flights were detected over the base that fall, McClure requested permission to go after them. He had earned a reputation as one of the sharpest high-altitude pilots in the service, and he was eager to avenge Americans who had been shot down over the Soviet Union. But permission was not forthcoming. Later, official spokesmen would deny that the Russian overflights had occurred. Air Force Chief of Staff Curtis LeMay, Assistant Secretary of Defense for Public Affairs Arthur Sylvester, and White House Press Secretary Pierre Salinger kept up a litany of denials even as key members of the Senate Foreign Relations and House Armed Services Committees clamored for an official investigation. Walker Stone, editor-in-chief of the Scripps-Howard newspaper chain in which the Russian overflight stories broke, continued to insist on the unassailability of his reporters' sources, which came, according to Stone, from high in the Kennedy administration's military establishment. No definitive account of the incident ever surfaced, however, and Clifton McClure never had a chance to win the Cold War trophy he wanted.

Today, McClure owns a company in Huntsville, Alabama, that has produced special hydrogen pumps for the Air Force and breathing-air systems designed for workers subjected to toxic environments. McClure watched the investigation into the explosion of the *Challenger* with great personal and professional interest. He studied the reports and he is convinced that NASA misunderstood—and continues to misunderstand—the hardware problems that led to the space-shuttle disaster. He does not believe that any external heat source (such as the flame from the solid rocket booster with the faulty O-ring seal) could have damaged the huge external fuel tank enough to have caused the explosion. He is sure that the external heating caused the hydrogen in the big tank to boil and that the liquid hydrogen vent/relief valve (designed for use on the ground) allowed hydrogen to escape where it was ignited, causing a flashback into the tank.

> And the reason I know this is from a practical thing. That's where a lot of these guys go wrong. There is a very simple way to test this. Go tell a welder that you want him to take a hot torch and burn through a one-inch aluminum piece, that you're going to have a tank and you're going to have water in the tank. And he's gonna fall over laughing at your ass. He'll say, "You gotta take the water out first. Any fool knows that." Now water is nowhere near what hydrogen is. Water'll go to 212 degrees before it vaporizes. But hydrogen is gonna keep it colder.

McClure thinks the vent/relief valve opened, and that the volatile hydrogen did what physics says it must do: it ignited and flashed back to its source. He believes that liquid hydrogen, and not just vapor, escaped through the valve. "This is so basic. I just can't believe that I can't find anybody who'll listen." McClure has written numerous letters to individuals at NASA, and even had intermediaries more influential than himself hand-deliver his data, along with recommended solutions, to NASA officials. He has never received any acknowledgment from anyone connected with the agency, much less an indication that his findings were considered.

"I know I'm right about this," he says angrily, but with a touch of regret in his voice. He agrees with Kittinger's assessment that the *Challenger* crew was likely still alive when the wreckage hit the ocean. "The problem still exists, and it could happen again." He pauses. "It could happen again."

Duke Gildenberg, who was a major player in all the Air Force high-altitude manned balloon programs, continued through the sixties, seventies, and eighties to contribute to high-altitude research both for the Air Force and for NASA. Gildenberg participated in the Air Force's re-entry and reconnaissance testing for a number of NASA projects, including Apollo. Most of this work was considered highly sensitive and was conducted in secret. The first successful atmospheric re-entry of an American satellite was made possible by Air Force balloon tests at White Sands; the testing and calibration of NASA cameras (including a classified recon camera that went to the moon) was conducted at Holloman.

Today, the soft-spoken, affable Gildenberg is a cattle rancher in Tularosa on the eastern edge of the White Sands Range. His knowledge of upper air patterns and the technical problems of balloon tracking remains unparalleled, and his curiosity about the universe and our place in it remains unabated. A conversation with Gildenberg skips with seamless ease from the latest techniques in animal husbandry to the colonization of space to the interpretation of ancient religious texts. He recalls the pioneer days of the balloon programs with great fondness. A wide smile creases his leathery face and his eyes sparkle as he remembers the early animal flights.

Winzen had a competition between his air crew and his ground crew: whoever got to the capsule first would get a beer. They put beer in the instrumentation package. So whoever got there first would get the beer. And so they had competitions. And the guys would try to hide the landing locations from each other so they could get there first.

So one day they were flying a monkey, and the ground crew had all the equipment and the doctors. The air crew had just one pilot, all by himself in a two-seat trainer. The pilot found the landing site and figured, "Boy, I'm gonna get that beer!" So he lands on the road near where the capsule had come down before anybody else gets there, and he figures, "Jeez, I better get the monkey out or he's gonna die with the heat on the ground." So he just tips the capsule up and loads the monkey in the aircraft and slams the top shut. He got in with it and takes off and this monkey's still free inside the plane. So the monkey gets on top of his head and starts pulling his hair out. And he's trying to fly the aircraft and the monkey's crapping all over the damn plane. He comes down with the aircraft full of monkey crap and his hair all pulled out.

But he got the beer. Ha!

After leaving the Air Force, David Simons continued to work on the leading edges of medical research. His most recent contributions to medical science have been focused on pain research. As a clinical professor at the

University of California–Irvine, Simons has broken new ground in the diagnosis and treatment of myofascial pain. *The Trigger Point Manual,* which Dr. Simons has written in conjunction with Dr. Janet Travell of the George Washington University School of Medicine, is referred to as "the bible" by physicians who treat patients with chronic pain. Like his father so many years before, David Simons continues to hurl his scientific arsenal against the realities of ignorance and suffering, fired by his own personal spark of missionary hatred.

Simons lives in a small house in Huntington Beach, California, a few blocks from the ocean. A framed remnant of the *Manhigh II* balloon, autographed by John Paul Stapp, hangs in his stairwell. In the early evening, he can walk down the beach and watch the colors of the sunset spread across the Pacific, and remember the sunset he once witnessed from the brink of outer space: "I have a ringside view of the heavens—it is indescribable."

Life is still an adventure for Joe Kittinger. His résumé of aeronautical achievements spans several pages—of small type. He gets regular letters and phone calls from people who want to break his freefall record. He believes that someone will do it, someday, but he never responds to those asking for his advice and counsel. They don't understand what they're getting into, he says, or how difficult the task will be. "Getting the balloon and launch services is the easy part. The tough part is getting up and back down alive." They don't understand that long months of testing and retesting must precede an actual stratospheric jump. And Kittinger does not want to be associated with a tragedy like Nick Piantanida's. He still ranks his jump from 102,800 feet as his greatest achievement.

After Stargazer, Kittinger volunteered for the Aero Commandos. He had been too young for World War II and had been involved with flight testing and other research during Korea. After Vietnam turned serious, Kittinger—against the wishes of his superiors who valued his skills as a test pilot and project director—decided to jump into a new phase of his career: aerial combat. It was a tough decision to leave high-altitude research just as the space age was coming into its own, but Kittinger made it without regret. "Even though I didn't go into space, I helped people get there. . . . I could have stayed in research and development and gotten deeply involved in Apollo and other exotic space ventures, but I was a fighter pilot, and I felt I owed it to my Air Force and my country to go to Vietnam. I guess it was a simplistic view, but that's how I felt."

He logged over 1,000 hours of combat flight in Southeast Asia in the sixties and early seventies. During his three tours of duty, he flew a total of 483 missions, including one in March of 1972 in which he shot down a Soviet MiG-21. Two months later, he was himself shot down over North Vietnam and taken prisoner. He spent 11 months in solitary confinement in the infamous "Hanoi Hilton." When his captors read in *Stars and Stripes* that their redheaded guest was a plum American hero who had flown hundreds of missions against them, they tortured him severely. Among numerous military decorations, he would receive—in addition to the Distinguished Flying Cross awarded him after Project Excelsior—the Silver Star, Bronze Star, Legion of Merit, Purple Heart, and Republic of Vietnam Cross of Gallantry.

Like most prisoners of war and hostages, especially those in solitary confinement, Kittinger found that he needed some sort of mental gymnastics in order to keep himself sane. Men have built imaginary houses, cataloging each nail and board and length of pipe. Others have scored symphonies, performed mathematical calculations, and written epic-length poetry in their minds. Joe Kittinger, instead, thought about balloon adventures—perhaps the ultimate metaphor for freedom. When he had first arrived at Wright Field in 1958, he asked a meteorologist there whether it would be possible to fly a balloon across the Atlantic Ocean. After some calculations, the man had replied that it was theoretically possible. It would be tricky, but it could be done. So, in his Hanoi cell, Kittinger painstakingly developed the detailed systems and procedures that would be required in order to cross the Atlantic in a gas balloon. He covered everything: logistics, designs, materials, processes, routes, economics.

After his release in the spring of 1973, Kittinger returned to the States and a desk job with the Air Force. Dissatisfied, he retired and went to work for Martin-Marietta, a defense contractor in his hometown of Orlando. It was there that he took up balloon racing and began talking to other balloon experts about the idea of an Atlantic crossing. The only thing he needed, he insisted, was a sponsor. He knew what would be required and how to do it. Kittinger rushed to New York to talk with officials of a tobacco company who had indicated a willingness to underwrite the attempt. Unfortunately, he learned that a condition of sponsorship would require him to take along a "Lark Cigarette Girl" for publicity. Kittinger refused.

In 1976, Kittinger served as flight operations director for another balloonist's (friend Ed Yost) attempt to cross the Atlantic in a balloon. Yost took off from the United States' Eastern Seaboard and landed in the Azores, short of the goal. Then, in 1978, Kittinger found a sponsor and was preparing for his own Atlantic crossing when Maxie Anderson, Ben Abruzzo, and Larry Newman beat him to the punch by about a month. When Kittinger first learned of his competition and of their head-start, he challenged them to a transatlantic race. The three weren't interested. In their balloon *Double Eagle,* they completed the first manned balloon crossing of the Atlantic.

Meanwhile, Kittinger continued to pursue "impossible" balloon adventures. His achievements during the mid-1980s are legendary: after breaking a shoulder and nearly freezing to death in Wyoming after a crash-landing in one Gordon Bennett competition, Kittinger was allowed to retire the coveted Gordon Bennett Trophy after three consecutive victories. He captured the world distance record in a 1,000-cubic-meter gas balloon flying from Las Vegas to Franklinville, New York (2,001 miles). He then set a new world distance record in a 3,000-cubic-meter balloon as he became the first balloonist to make a *solo* crossing of the Atlantic Ocean in 1984, traveling 3,543 miles from Maine to Italy (a logistical nightmare of a journey). As he neared the French coast, Kittinger was contacted by an air traffic controller in Biarritz who asked where the balloonist intended to land.

"There's no sense in landing if you've got a nice pattern to fly in and good weather," Kittinger replied. After his balloon, the *Rosie O'Grady,* crashed in a grove of trees in the mountains near Savona, Italy, breaking his ankle, he was helicoptered to a hospital in Nice where he met reporters. "You just have to go for it, go for it," he told them. "That's the American way." He added that he had secretly wanted to make it all the way to Moscow.

Today Joe Kittinger has his sights set on what he calls "the last great balloon adventure." It would be the ultimate distance quest: around the world, *solo.* "It's the only big one left," Kittinger says quietly, anticipating the adventure, "and I want to be the one to do it." There is no question in his mind that it can be done, and there isn't anybody who knows Joe who doubts it.

While locked in his cell at the Hanoi Hilton, Kittinger worked not only on plans for an Atlantic crossing, but also on a circumnavigation of the planet. And while he originally thought that a gas balloon was the proper vehicle, he is now convinced that the greater altitude control and reduced thermal complications of a hot-air system are preferable. He has engineers and meteorologists committed and ready to go. All he needs now is a sponsor with about a million dollars. It will take eight days. He'll use a pressurized gondola, rise up into the jet stream, and "just go like a bat out of hell."

He grins when he says it. He can't wait: "From the time I was a kid, I never wanted to do anything but fly airplanes and have adventures. When I grow up, I want to be exactly what I am right now."

The real genius behind all of it [says Kittinger] was John Paul Stapp. He was the visionary. He was the one who knew what had to be done, and when, and how, and the importance of it. He had people like Dave Simons and myself around, but he was the one who gave us the tools to do the job. Everything I did in the research business was because of Stapp. Every project I was associated with happened because of his genius. I had the desire, but he gave me the tools and the opportunity.

To Duke Gildenberg's way of thinking, Stapp's most valuable role was the work he did behind the scenes—politicking with the Air Force brass, pleading for authorization and funding—simply keeping the programs alive. He ran interference between the mahogany desks and the men in the field doing the nuts-and-bolts work. "There are people that want to do, and people that want to be," Clifton McClure explains. "Stapp was a 'do' person, and he surrounded himself with 'do' people. . . . [He] started it all. He was the guy that had the brains. He was the guy who took all the heat. . . . I mean, I can't say enough about that dude."

"The true worth of a scientist," Stapp himself is wont to say, "can be measured by the degree to which he's willing to do battle with the savages and cannibals of management." On the basis of such criteria and his own collection of battle scars, Stapp ought long ago to have made his trip to Stockholm and shaken hands with the king.

"When it came time to go to space," Kittinger explains, "much of the knowledge we had was because of Stapp. He never made general because he wasn't a politician. But he's not bitter: he just laughs about it."

Stapp's indirect contributions to America's space program are legion. If the Air Force—rather than NASA—had been selected to oversee the nation's space agenda, Stapp might well have been an integral figure throughout the push to reach the moon. In April 1958, the Air Force published its own development plan: two exploratory projects that would send man into space, followed by a lunar reconnaissance mission, followed by a manned lunar landing and return to earth—all to be accomplished in seven years at a cost of $1.5 billion. In June of that year, the Air Force contracted with Rocketdyne to build a single-chamber rocket that would burn kerosene and liquid oxygen. In the end, the Air Force may have priced itself out of the space program by demanding millions of dollars for an extensive network of worldwide surveillance installations; Congress balked and gave the program to NASA.

As it was, Stapp was forced into a bootleg role. And while NASA may never acknowledge the degree to which the rocket-sled research and the balloon research programs set the stage for manned space travel, that organization did use Stapp's direct services a number of times in the late fifties and early sixties. Stapp was on the panel that winnowed the original thirty-seven Mercury astronaut candidates down to twelve (and finally seven), and in 1963 he managed the Apollo landing-impact tests using a rocket sled and a tubular-rail track of his own invention called the Daisy Track, so named because of the rails' resemblance to the barrel of the Daisy air rifle. Interestingly, Stapp never applied for a single patent for any of the devices he invented. Nor has he ever asked for or received a dime in medical compensation for any of his rocket-sled injuries either during or after his tenure with the Air Force.

Today, Stapp lives in Alamogordo and serves on the board of the Space Center, a museum founded in 1975 and dedicated to preserving the history of rocketry and space exploration. The museum houses the International Space Hall of Fame; Stapp recently nominated Galileo—who was subsequently inducted. Always a man of ideas and radical schemes, his huge, penetrating intelligence still acute in his ninth decade, Stapp will ramble off through the desert in his 1965 Cadillac, with John Coltrane on the radio, and wax lyrical about the future of our exploration of the universe. But his thoughts are not all extraterrestrial. He has plans for Planet Earth, too. We feed the poor and hungry along the country's Eastern Seaboard with produce grown in giant agricultural caverns beneath Washington, D.C.; these caverns are accessed by the Metro (the District's subway system) which is closed to riders between the hours of 2:00 and 4:00 A.M. to allow for the transportation of food to the markets. We rescue failing commuter airlines with a battery-operated fly-by-wire air trolley system that is pollution-free and ultra-convenient: converted DC-10s are flown into landing bays on the twelfth floors of urban office buildings and disgorge passengers in the center of town. We revise the Pledge of Allegiance to honor not the flag but the

Constitution. "I'm not a genius," Stapp insists. "I'm simply an unconventional thinker."

But Stapp's greatest contribution of all might be his work with vehicle safety. While he was in charge of the Aeromed Lab at Wright-Patterson, Stapp looked at base casualty reports and noticed an astonishing fact: more Air Force men were killed and injured each year in ground vehicle accidents than in aircraft mishaps. This led him to require the use of lap belts for anyone riding in cars and trucks on the base. When it became clear that the new order was saving lives and reducing the number and severity of injuries, Stapp was off on another missionary crusade that has really never ended. The rocket-sled research had provided insight into what a human was capable of surviving if properly restrained. Representatives from the Society of Automotive Engineers first visited Stapp at Holloman in 1955 after hearing about the deceleration research. And to Stapp's great satisfaction, General Motors subsequently adopted some of his ideas and test methodologies. If a human could survive a sudden stop in a vehicle going 600 MPH, why couldn't he routinely walk away from car crashes? Even airplane crashes?

Stapp conducted the first car-crash tests to use anthropomorphic dummies. He didn't invent the three-point seat belt, but he improved it and perfected its application. He didn't invent the air bag, but his research led directly to it. What he did was raise the world's consciousness about the issue of vehicle safety and crash survival. Put padded dashboards in cars, he said. And turn airplane seats around so that the passengers face backwards. The rocket sleds had shown that a great deal more punishment could be survived if the passenger was slammed into the back of his seat during deceleration. Stapp's discoveries were responsible for the rear-facing seats in some military transport aircraft, although no commercial airlines ever seriously considered turning their seats around. But for the most part, the world listened to Stapp when he told it how to make cars and trucks safer. He has received countless awards and honors from automobile manufacturers and professional organizations. He was presented with the National Medal of Technology by President Bush. He has testified before congressional committees and written scores of articles and technical papers. And the Society of Automotive Engineers' 35th Annual Stapp Car Crash Conference (in which Dr. Stapp presented his exhaustive sourcebook on human biomechanics) was recently held in San Diego where hundreds of industry experts met to discuss vehicle safety and restraint systems.

Stapp remains a missionary, and the fires of missionary hatred still smolder within him. He rails against the reactionary forces that oppose new ideas. He has little sympathy for the unimaginative. "The definition of a bureaucrat," he'll tell you, "is one who sticks to his guns even after shooting himself in the foot."

Of his many accomplishments, John Paul Stapp remains proudest of the fact that in all his years running some of the most dangerous research projects in the history of the Air Force, "the really hairy stuff," not a single person under his command ever lost his life or sustained a disabling injury. We can do things to prevent death and injury, we can fight back—that is the crux of Stapp's teaching, of the missionary rage: "There is no requirement that we submit supinely to an act of God beyond our control. . . . And there is no call to yield integrity because the heads of state can brandish thunderbolts that go around the earth."

Although scientific balloon activity has waned, Holloman Air Force Base and its desert environs are still a center of aviation and space research. The desolate White Sands Missile Range to the north, administered by the Army, remains the most sophisticated overland tracking complex in the world, with hundreds of instrumentation sites and survey points amid the thorns of ocotillo and prickly pear and devil's finger. Long-range cameras, telescopes, theodolites, radar and microwave installations make it the most thoroughly instrumented piece of desert in existence. Thousands of missile firings are still conducted each year. Range personnel also carry out scores of other tests on the missiles: shake and shock tests, extreme cold and heat tests. The hardware is subjected to nuclear radiation and saltwater. The propulsion materials are tested and evaluated in order to determine their impact on the flora and fauna of the region.

By the mid-sixties, the Air Force balloon experts of the Research and Development Test Branch at Holloman had become the most experienced balloon crew in the world, launching aerostats with capacities up to 13 million cubic feet. And long after the manned balloon programs were gone, Holloman-launched balloons continued to probe the fringes of space and were responsible for gathering most of the important scientific data about the atmospheric regions up to 25 miles.

The city of Alamogordo (literally: "fat cottonwood"), originally just another whistlestop in the desert, a mill town built on the harvest of lumber from the Sacramento Mountains, boomed with the expansion of the bombing range and the establishment of the Army—and later, Air Force—base. The population of the area was only a few thousand in the summer of 1945 when the Trinity bomb blew, but had reached 25,000 by the mid-sixties. Today, more than 30,000 people live there, and, like the inhabitants of any other military town, their fortunes still rise and fall with the ebb and flow of defense politics and world events.

The Alamogordo Chamber of Commerce markets the town as the Missile Capital of the World. And although the White Sands Range is off-limits to the public, on two days every year, once in April and again in October, the Chamber of Commerce, in cooperation with the U.S. Army, organizes civilian car caravans out to Trinity Site, complete with full military escort and souvenir trucks selling T-shirts and coffee mugs. Pregnant women and very young children are discouraged from approaching ground-zero, and visitors are asked not to remove the chips of trinitite, the dull green glass made of the sand melted in the blast in 1945.

Both the armed forces and the scientific community are out of the stratospheric manned balloon business—at least for now, and perhaps forever—but they still use unmanned balloons to probe the skies and to capture data on the ozone layer, on temperature and wind patterns, on sky brightness. Low-altitude balloons are used to capture other kinds of data. In 1990, Kuwait first detected the Iraqi invasion with a balloon-borne radar system floating at 10,000 feet; the U.S. Customs Service drug interdiction operations use the same Westinghouse-built system at certain high-traffic border points.

Probably the most exciting use of balloon technology, though, is in planetary exploration, where state-of-the-art aerostats may give us intimate contact with the rest of the solar system. In 1986, a joint Soviet-French space mission, in the culmination of a 20-year-old project, successfully dropped two superpressure balloons into the atmosphere of Venus. (Superpressure systems use very strong polyester films that will not burst with helium expansion, allowing for long, unballasted flights.) Instruments carried by the balloons, which stabilized at an altitude of 34 miles above the surface, sent back wind measurements and other data. And an international team is already planning to drop more sophisticated balloons, made of a special film that is a mere nine microns thick, into the skies of Mars where their payloads would be able to float slowly across a thousand of miles of Martian landscape over a period of 10 days, dropping down to an altitude of 300 feet above the surface.

A Mortal Mercury

Immediately following the cancellation of Project Excelsior, Joe Kittinger found himself looking around for a suitable followup program, something to rival the long, lonely leap from 103,000 feet. What could you do after taking the "highest step in the world"? What was the step after that? One idea being kicked around by the Air Force intrigued him: he would be strapped into the nose cone of a Redstone rocket, much like one of the dogs or chimpanzees that had already been into space, and fired at the heavens. Then, at approximately the altitude from which he had jumped from *Excelsior III,* he would be explosively ejected and launched on a climbing trajectory that would send him hurtling like a fleck of cosmic debris toward the perimeter of the stratosphere. It was pure stunt: Joe Kittinger, Human Cannonball! But it was, at the very least, an irresistible scenario: In an instant he leaves behind the thrust and bone-humming thunder of the rocket, and finds himself sailing off into oblivion. Perhaps it is like the eerie moment when he first stepped out of the balloon and found himself suspended in quasi-space. Only now the earth is rushing away from him, and without the massive globe of plastic to reflect the sun's glare the stars are clearly visible before him, spread like a dense cape of white lights.

As he plunges on, he ascends through the stratosphere. And as he races away from the earth, a strange thing happens: the frigid temperatures of the lower stratosphere are warming. At 30 miles above the planet, in the ozone-rich layer of the atmosphere, it is balmy: about 65°.

He continues to ascend, rushing toward the distant lights, but rushing without the sensation of movement, through the portals of the stratosphere and into the mesosphere, where the temperature begins to drop again. This is where meteors are incinerated by their impact with the atmosphere. At a height of 50 miles, it is as cold as anywhere in the universe. He hurtles through icy noctilucent clouds and on toward the stars.

Now he crosses into yet another atmospheric layer: the thermosphere, the "airglow" region, where energized atoms of the ionosphere create a soft background light. These same atoms occasionally agitate the ionosphere and erupt into one of the full-blown auroras that are visible in the polar regions of Earth below.

He is slowing now; the boost from the Redstone is nearly dissipated. The invisible grip of gravity is wrestling for the upper hand. He nears the 100-mile mark: 500,000 feet above the surface of the earth. The V-2s didn't get much higher than this. The invisible poison fingers of the vacuum are scratching all around his space suit now, probing for a weakness. Not only is there no air, but what few oxygen molecules do exist here are beginning to dissociate into individual atoms. At this height, even the very concept of emptiness is challenged.

As he nears the apex of his trajectory, he can feel it warming up once again. If he were to keep going, the heat would melt his suit before long. Eighty miles higher and he would encounter temperatures of 3,600°. And beyond that the radioactive cosmic plasma of the exosphere and interplanetary space await.

Still he feels no motion. It is the sensation of floating, of liquid prebirth. But now his momentum has stopped and for an instant he is literally floating, as at the top of one of the zero-gravity flights he and David Simons flew so often at Holloman in the days before Manhigh. He begins to fall and pick up all the speed he lost on the way up. And soon he is freefalling well beyond Mach 1. Even so, the earth below, its giant ball shape clearly discernible, appears to come no closer. There seems to be no connection between him and it.

Again he is a man alone, a single point of matter speeding through the void: a human spacecraft with a trusty parachute on its back.

He is Alan Shepard without the Mercury capsule.

The 100-mile freefall through space never got beyond the discussion stage. Joe Kittinger gave up and spent the decade of the space race in, and often just above, the suffocating jungles of Southeast Asia. But he was ready to try it. He believed it was possible.

"Hell," he says, at age 66, "I'd do it today if they'd offer it to me."

▼

Notes

Prologue

The material on Hawthorne Gray is based primarily on the following sources: Crouch, *The Eagle Aloft;* Stehling and Beller, *Skyhooks;* Maurer, *Aviation in the U.S. Army;* Payne, *Lighter than Air;* Friedlander and Gurney, *Higher, Faster, and Farther; New York Times,* November 6, 1927, 1; November 8, 1927, 30; November 12, 1927, 18; November 13, 1927, 3, and sec. 20, p. 9.

5   "Okay, let her go": Crouch, *The Eagle Aloft,* 596.
7   "Symptoms of Ricketts": *New York Times,* November 6, 1927, 1.
7   "Sky deep blue": Friedlander and Gurney, *Higher, Faster, and Farther,* 76.
8   "It is perfectly possible": *New York Times,* November 8, 1927, 30.
8   "A larger balloon": Ibid.

one The Ghost of Muroc

The material on the pre-Muroc career of John Paul Stapp is based primarily on the following sources: interviews by the author; Stapp's own "Biographical Sketch"; Thomas, *Men of Space;* Friedlander and Gurney, *Higher, Faster, and Farther;* Haggerty, "Fastest Man on Earth," 29; "The Fastest Man on Earth," 82–85; Stanton, "John Paul Stapp," 34–37; and *Alamogordo Daily News,* "Fastest Man Alive: A Legend for His Pioneer Work," c. 1988, and December 7, 1987, 12.

11   "In spite of calculations": Szasz, *The Day the Sun Rose Twice,* 79.
13   "at altitudes between 12 and 50 miles": Von Braun et al., *Space Travel: A History,* 198.
13   "That Professor Goddard": Friedlander and Gurney, *Higher, Faster, and Farther,* 243.
14   "If it breathed": Stanton, "John Paul Stapp," 35.
14   "I was taught the value": Interview with John Paul Stapp.
14   "You might shake off": "Fastest Man Alive: A Legend for His Pioneer Work."

15   "dumped": Interview with John Paul Stapp.
15   "pure scientists": "The Fastest Man on Earth," 85.
15   "a nightmare": Thomas, *Men of Space,* 72.

The material on Stapp's rocket-sled experiments at Muroc and at Holloman is based primarily on the following sources: interviews by the author; Stapp's own "Biographical Sketch"; Thomas, *Men of Space;* Kittinger with Caidin, *The Long, Lonely Leap;* Burrows, *Exploring Space;* Meeter, *The Holloman Story;* Haggerty, "Fastest Man on Earth," 25–29; "The Fastest Man on Earth," 80–88; Armagnac, "How Near Is Space Travel?" 130, 131, 296; Stanton, "John Paul Stapp," 34–37; *Alamogordo Daily News,* December 7, 1987, 1, 12, and "Fastest Man Alive: A Legend for His Pioneer Work."

The material on the early days of Project Manhigh is based primarily on the following sources: interviews by the author; Simons with Schanche, *Man High;* Kittinger with Caidin, *The Long, Lonely Leap;* von Braun et al., *Space Travel: A History;* Meeter, *The Holloman Story;* Swenson et al., *This New Ocean: A History of Project Mercury;* Kennedy, *Project Manhigh.*

16   "men at the mahogany desks": "The Fastest Man on Earth," 86.
21   "We were naive as hell": Interview with Duke Gildenberg.
21   "The drive for myself and my colleagues": Burrows, *Exploring Space,* 42.
22   "What these blockbusters": Armagnac, "How Near Is Space Travel?" 130, 131.
24   "Dave, would *you* be interested": Interview with David Simons.
24   "The animals did nothing": Kittinger with Caidin, *The Long, Lonely Leap,* 73.
25   "track meets in the sky": Interview with John Paul Stapp.
25   "What we call upper atmosphere": Swenson et al., *This New Ocean,* 35.
28   "Subject had considerable apprehension": Thomas, *Men of Space,* 83.
29   "shimmering salmon-colored field": "The Fastest Man on Earth," 81.
29   "somewhat like the extraction": Kittinger with Caidin, *The Long, Lonely Leap,* 59.
29   "I've never been unconscious": Interview with John Paul Stapp
30   "The first thing I felt": Meeter, *The Holloman Story,* 108.
30   "Why are we always": Thomas, *Men of Space,* 84.
31   "He was not addressing himself": Simons with Schanche, *Man High,* 12.
31   "lost in space": Ibid., 37.
32   "We've lost number two engine": Ibid., 32.
32   "I'm coming straight in": Ibid., 33.
32   "Thanks for the information": Ibid.
33   "Joe, here's your approval": Interview with Joe Kittinger.
34   "for the hell of it": Ibid.
35   "Without wind whistling": Simons with Schanche, *Man High,* 60, 61.

The material on the history of ballooning from 1783 to 1906 is based primarily on the following sources: Crouch, *The Eagle Aloft;* Stehling and Beller, *Skyhooks;* Dwiggins, *Riders of the Winds; The Romance of Ballooning.*

two **The Sport of the Scientist**

The material on the stratospheric flights and subsequent American visit of Auguste Piccard is based primarily on the following sources: Piccard, *Earth, Sky, and Sea* and *Between Earth and Sky;* DeVorkin, *Race to the Stratosphere;* Stehling and Beller, *Skyhooks;* Stehling, *Bags Up!;* Friedlander and Gurney, *Higher, Faster, and Farther; New York Times,* May 31, 1931, 3; October 16, 1932, 4E; January 18, 1933, 10; December 30, 1934, sec. 4, p. 7.

40   "The modern scientific seeker": Piccard, *Earth, Sky, and Sea,* xii.
41   "We must have a hermetically sealed cabin": Ibid., 6.
42   "Physicists cannot explain": Piccard, *Between Earth and Sky,* 79.
42   "There we were": Piccard, *Earth, Sky, and Sea,* 11.
43   "I made this flight": *New York Times,* May 31, 1931, 3.
43   "All is going well": Friedlander and Gurney, *Higher, Faster, and Farther,* 77.
44   "It will be a fine day": Piccard, *Earth, Sky, and Sea,* 16.

The material on the U.S. and Soviet flights of the 1930s, and on the Office of Naval Research projects of the 1940s, is based primarily on the following sources: interviews by the author; Crouch, *The Eagle Aloft;* DeVorkin, *Race to the Stratosphere;* Stehling and Beller, *Skyhooks;* Friedlander and Gurney, *Higher, Faster, and Farther;* Vaeth, "When the Race for Space Began"; "Your Society Sponsors an Expedition to Explore the Stratosphere"; Stevens, "Exploring the Stratosphere"; Stevens, "Man's Farthest Aloft"; *New York Times,* August 5, 1933, 1, 8; August 6, 1933, 2:1, 2; November 21, 1933, 1, 3; November 22, 1933, 3; January 17, 1934, 21; July 29, 1934, 1, 20, 21; January 17, 1935, 13; November 12, 1935, 1–5, 18; November 13, 1935, 2; May 28, 1939, 18; June 11, 1939, 2; July 12, 1939, 15; July 22, 1939, 25; September 14, 1939, 7.

47   "I am sorry": *New York Times,* August 6, 1933, sec. 2, p. 2.
48   "very marvelous performance": *New York Times,* October 1, 1933, 39.
48   "Yesterday's events did more": *New York Times,* October 2, 1933, 11.
50   "Hearty congratulations": *New York Times,* November 22, 1933, 3.
50   "greatest of all unexplored regions": Ibid.
50   "There probably is plenty of poetry": Ibid.
52   "Mere attainment of altitude": "Your Society Sponsors an Expedition to Explore the Stratosphere," 528.
54   "The bottom of this balloon": *New York Times,* July 29, 1934, 1.
54   "No one made a move": Stevens, "Exploring the Stratosphere," 397.
55   "crushed like an eggshell": Ibid., 418.
55   "wonder gas": DeVorkin, *Race to the Stratosphere,* 186.
56   "Oh! Just give me a chance": Crouch, *The Eagle Aloft,* 631.
57   "Going with open eyes": DeVorkin, *Race to the Stratosphere,* 265.
59   "The earth could be seen": Stevens, "Man's Farthest Aloft," 80.
60   "soft as a feather": *New York Times,* November 12, 1935, 4.
60   "Boy, I sure got a kick": Ibid.

60 "Thus it happens": Ibid., 18.
61 "sham," "fad": DeVorkin, *Race to the Stratosphere,* 189.
62 "compelling symbols": Ibid., 4.
62 "the whole thing started": Interview with George Hoover.
63 "OK, you've got a job": Ibid.
63 "Jean Piccard knew what he was talking about": Ibid.

The material on the preparation for *Manhigh I* that appears toward the end of this chapter is based on the same Manhigh sources listed for chapter 1, as well as on "Prelude to Space," 52. The material on Winzen Research and early plastic balloon technology also relies on DeVorkin, *Race to the Stratosphere;* Winzen, "10 Years of Plastic Balloons"; Winzen Research, "The Story of Winzen Research"; and on various USAF sources.

65 "I think they eventually funded": Interview with John Paul Stapp.
66 "I want Kittinger": Simons with Schanche, *Man High,* 66.
66 "I didn't want much": "Prelude to Space," 52.
66 "He didn't want anybody to steal the thunder": Interview with Joe Kittinger.
67 "They had better quality control": Interview with David Simons.
70 "What I liked about flying": Interview with Vera Simons.
71 "To see what you've made": Ibid.
71 "Balloons are the most complicated": USAF publicity release, "The Rebirth of the Balloon," n.d., 6.
72 "It almost appears that there is no limit": Winzen, "10 Years of Plastic Balloons," 8.

three **"Come and Get Me"**

This chapter relies on the same Manhigh sources listed for chapters 1 and 2, as well as on the following sources: Winzen Research, "Manhigh I Flown by J. W. Kittinger" and "Progress Report, Air Regeneration Development"; Clark and Graybiel, "The Break-Off Phenomenon," 2; "Getting the High Notes," 72.

76 "Although Kittinger was far more alert": Simons with Schanche, *Man High,* 36.
77 "He relished the delightful experience": Ibid., 70, 71.
77 "Difficult as it is": Ibid., 72, 73.
78 "They were both emotional guys": Interview with Vera Simons.
79 "If Duke Gildenberg looked up": Simons with Schanche, *Man High,* 68.
80 "like being loved by an octopus": "Prelude to Space," 52.
81 "No sweat": Simons with Schanche, *Man High,* 79.
82 "absolutely frightened the hell out of me": Kittinger with Caidin, *The Long, Lonely Leap,* 82.
82 "R-E-P-O-R-T F-O-L-L-O-W-S": "Getting the High Notes," 72.
83 "How does it feel": Ibid.
83 "C-O-M-E A-N-D G-E-T M-E": Simons with Schanche, *Man High,* 87.

84 "V-A-L-V-I-N-G G-A-S": Ibid., 88.
84 "Well, God, they said": Interview with Joe Kittinger.
86 "Not a red hair of his head": "Prelude to Space," 52.
86 "I suspect": Interview with David Simons.
87 "It was kind of a stupid thing": Ibid.
87 "I was just trying to be funny": Interview with Joe Kittinger.
87 "You don't neglect testing": Ibid.
87 "One of the reasons": Interview with David Simons.
87 "[Simons] was looking for an excuse": Interview with Joe Kittinger.

four **Floating at the Ceiling**

This chapter relies on the same Manhigh sources listed for chapters 1–3, as well as on the following additional sources: Vaeth, *200 Miles Up;* Dwiggins, *Riders of the Winds;* Crouch, *The Eagle Aloft;* Houston, *Going Higher;* Hart, *The Prehistory of Flight;* Simons, "Air Force Missile Development Center Technical Report: Manhigh II"; "Space Pioneer," *Time* 70 (September 2, 1957): 44, 46; *Life,* September 2, 1957, 19–26; "Ringside in Heaven," *Newsweek,* September 2, 1957, 49, 50.

88   "a text of the physical sciences": Vaeth, *200 Miles Up,* 3.
89   "We had difficulty": Dwiggins, *Riders of the Winds,* 39.
90   "I dimly saw Mr. Coxwell": Ibid., 137.
92   "The body and mind weaken": Houston, *Going Higher,* 60.
93   "the stratosphere was far more": Crouch, *The Eagle Aloft,* 595.
94   "One monkey on this flight is enough.": Interview with Vera Simons.
95   "I didn't care": Interview with David Simons.
98   "He knew as well as I did": Simons with Schanche, *Man High,* 118.
99   "so we could be under the stars": *Time,* September 2, 1957, 46.
99   "Major, you are about to reach": *Life,* September 2, 1957, 20.
99   "My body tingled": Simons with Schanche, *Man High,* 122.
101 "like a lady holding onto her skirt": Simons, "Technical Report: Manhigh II," 111.
101 "It's like no earthly quiet": *Time,* September 2, 1957, 46.
102 "floating at the ceiling": Simons, "Technical Report: Manhigh II," 111; Simons with Schanche, *Man High,* 135.
102 "Looking down": Simons, "Technical Report: Manhigh II," 112.
102 "You wouldn't see it": Interview with David Simons.
103 "I tried to compare the color": Simons, "Technical Report: Manhigh II," 113.
103 "Where the atmosphere merged": Simons with Schanche, *Man High,* 136.
103 "As one ascends toward heaven": Hart, *The Prehistory of Flight,* 6.
104 "We've got a problem, Dave": Simons with Schanche, *Man High,* 144.
104 "It's up to you": Ibid., 145.
105 "With your permission": Ibid., 147.
106 "Paradoxically, I was still suspended": Ibid., 150, 151.
106 "The stars glow": "Ringside in Heaven," 49.
106 "Interestingly enough": Simons, "Technical Report: Manhigh II," 120.

107 "Close behind the setting sun": Simons with Schanche, *Man High,* 152, 153.
108 "The clouds were becoming sirens": Simons, "Technical Report: Manhigh II," 142.
109 "Are you certain": Simons with Schanche, *Man High,* 169.
110 "I'm right on top of them": Ibid.
110 "reddish blue-purple . . .": Simons, "Technical Report: Manhigh II," 124.
111 "I felt as if I no longer belonged": Simons with Schanche, *Man High,* 174.
111 "This cloud layer": Ibid., 175.
112 "Gentlemen": *Time,* September 2, 1957, 46.
115 "Hello"; "Howdy": *Life,* September 2, 1957, 26.
115 "Look! There's a helicopter": Ibid.

five **"This Is God"**

This chapter relies on the same Manhigh sources listed for chapters 1–4, as well as on the following additional sources: Meeter, *The Holloman Story;* Brooks et al., *Chariots for Apollo;* Swenson et al., *This New Ocean;* Compton, *Where No Man Has Gone Before;* Gray, *Angle of Attack;* Caidin, *Overture to Space;* Hallion, *Test Pilots;* Kennan and Harvey, *Mission to the Moon;* Riabchikov, *Russians in Space;* Hoyt, *The Space Dealers;* von Braun and Ordway, *History of Rocketry and Space Travel;* von Braun et al., *Space Travel: A History;* Bilstein, *Orders of Magnitude;* USAF, "Air Force Missile Development Center Technical Report: Manhigh III"; *The Holloman Rocketeer,* October 10, 1958; "Picking the Men," 42–48; Heppenheimer, "Lost in Space," 60–72; *New York Times,* August 20, 1957, 29; August 22, 1957, 26; August 25, 1957, 56; November 8, 1957, 10.

116 "a valor above and beyond": *New York Times,* August 25, 1957, 56.
116 "daring young Air Force officer": *New York Times,* August 20, 1957, 29.
116 "the gallant major": *New York Times,* August 22, 1957, 26.
116 "made the trip for all of us": Ibid.
116 "He was sort of a one-man band": "Ringside in Heaven," 49.
117 "Was it a spiritual experience?" (and subsequent quotes from the press conference): Simons with Schanche, *Man High,* 195.
117 "I had a profound resentment": Interview with David Simons.
117 "After I saw Kittinger and Stapp": Ibid.
118 "The time will come": Riabchikov, *Russians in Space,* 150, 151.
119 "If you mentioned the word": Caidin, *Overture to Space,* 67.
119 "Almost 12 years ago": Ibid., 77.
119 "In a sense": Ibid., 79.
120 "a hunk of iron": Ibid., xii.
120 "captured all the German scientists": Ibid., xiii.
120 "We could fall behind": *New York Times,* November 8, 1957, 10.
121 "spoke our language": Interview with David Simons.
122 "The people who had opposed me earlier": Ibid.
122 "The real challenge we face": Heppenheimer, "Lost in Space," 62.
122 "the psychological problems": Swenson et al., *This New Ocean,* 48.

123   "At this time no decent": Interview with Clifton McClure.

124   "There was a personality conflict": Interview with Duke Gildenberg.

124   "What we're looking for": "Picking the Men," 42.

126   "Somebody panicked": Interview with Vera Simons.

128   "It . . . wasn't a matter of whether you had to grit your teeth": USAF, "Technical Report: Manhigh III," 79.

128   "thoroughly enjoyed the experience": Ibid., 83.

128   "I've never to this day met anybody any smarter": Interview with David Simons.

129   "He was an absolute monster": Interview with Duke Gildenberg.

129   "McClure was a nice man": Interview with Vera Simons.

129   "I think Joe Kittinger": Ibid.

130   "It was supposed to be a detriment": Interview with Clifton McClure.

130   "I started getting myself evaluated": Ibid.

130   "I'm a better shot myself": "The Holloman Rocketeer," October 10, 1958.

132   "to supervise and direct the scientific study": Hallion, *Test Pilots,* 72.

132   "for the benefit of all mankind": Brooks et al., *Chariots for Apollo,* 2.

134   "Hessberg was a parachutist": Interview with Clifton McClure.

135   "I was the only person": USAF, "Technical Report: Manhigh III," 139. 140.

138   "I see a blanket like a halo": Meeter, *The Holloman Story,* 33.

138   "I see the most fantastic thing": Simons with Schanche, *Man High,* 228.

139   "It was like a Hollywood movie": Interview with Duke Gildenberg.

140   "I don't want to come down": Simons with Schanche, *Man High,* 233.

144   "I don't know what all the fuss is about": Meeter, *The Holloman Story,* 35.

144   "He's the only one who could've survived": Interview with Joe Kittinger.

145   "It was ridiculous to send him off": Ibid.

145   "Something went wrong with our calculating": Crouch, *The Eagle Aloft,* 656.

145   "The various chapters of this report": USAF, "Technical Report: Manhigh III," 1.

145   "Apparently because Lt McClure": Ibid., 126.

145   "Essentially, he blew the experiment": Interview with Vera Simons.

146   "Here's what happened": Interview with Clifton McClure.

146   "I really don't think he deserves": Ibid.

147   "I leaned over with my head": Simons with Schanche, *Man High,* 250.

147   "About two hours after 95,000": USAF, "Technical Report: Manhigh III," 133.

147   "Under stress": Ibid., 134.

147   "Oh, no, it was nothing like that": Ibid.

148   "An essential quality necessary to an astronaut": Simons with Schanche, *Man High,* 249, 250.

149   "Neither branch could decide": Interview with David Simons.

149   "What I was offering was so far ahead": Ibid.

149   "There were even articles in the newspaper": Interview with Duke Gildenberg.

150   "every system for survival": Interview with John Paul Stapp.

150   "It is now generally recognized": Crouch, *The Eagle Aloft,* 653.

151   "extensive distribution of combustible materials": Brooks, et al., *Chariots for Apollo,* 221.

▼

Notes

151   "unaware of the intensity": Compton, *Where No Man Has Gone Before,* 93.

151   "It's the wrong thing to do": Gray, *Angle of Attack,* 138.

152   "at the time of initial Apollo development": Kennan and Harvey, *Mission to the Moon,* 138.

152   "many deficiencies in design": Gray, *Angle of Attack,* 244.

153   "Things are set in motion" (and subsequent McClure quotes in this chapter): Interview with Clifton McClure.

six Truth or Consequences

The material in this chapter is based primarily on interviews by the author and on Kittinger with Caidin, *The Long, Lonely Leap.*

156   "They were a bunch of real sharp guys": Interview with Joe Kittinger.

158   "one brilliant son of a bitch": Ibid.

160   "Our entire program soon began to revolve": Kittinger with Caidin, *The Long, Lonely Leap,* 141.

161   "hordes of engineers and scientists": Ibid., 138.

161   "mathematical tables were of little use": Ibid., 142.

161   "The average person at Wright Field": Interview with Joe Kittinger.

162   "The gun was loaded against Stapp": Ibid.

162   "for peanuts": Interview with Duke Gildenberg.

168   "Gentlemen, enclosed is your passport": Kittinger with Caidin, *The Long, Lonely Leap,* 154.

171   "I felt the first quiver of motion": Ibid., 165.

seven Aerial Maniacs and Birdmen

The material on Joe Kittinger's jump from the *Excelsior I* gondola relies on the same Excelsior sources listed for chapter 6. The material on the history of parachuting is based primarily on the following sources: Sellick, *Skydiving* and *The Wild, Wonderful World of Parachutes and Parachuting;* Zim, *Parachutes;* Caidin, *The Silken Angels* and introduction to Kittinger's *The Long, Lonely Leap;* Horan, *Parachuting Folklore;* Starnes, *Aerial Maniac* and *Delayed Opening Parachute Jumps and Their Life-Saving Value;* Valentin, *Bird Man.*

179   "Me for staying with the old bus": Caidin, *The Silken Angels,* 42.

184   "The chute that I was using": Starnes, *Aerial Maniac,* 17.

185   "This little volume is dedicated": Starnes, *Delayed Opening Parachute Jumps,* 5.

186   "I had only two moments of fear": Horan, *Parachuting Folklore,* 142.

187   "by swallowing . . .": Starnes, *Delayed Opening Parachute Jumps,* 46.

187   "Don't stick your foot out": Ibid., 54, 55.

187   "I find rapid somersaulting": Ibid., 30.

187   "practical or necessary": Ibid., 36.

187   "A parachute that is airworthy": Ibid., 48.

187   "After leaving the plane": Ibid., 28.
188   "One never knows": Valentin, *Bird Man,* 15.
188   "making a mayonnaise": Ibid., 52.
189   "I knew now that I could leap": Ibid., 61, 62.
189   "Man no longer figures in the game": Ibid., 81.

eight **"The Mission Is Canceled"**

This chapter relies on the same sources listed for chapter 6, as well as on the following additional sources: Kittinger, "The Long Lonely Leap," 854–73; *New York Times,* November 21, 1959, 1, 9; December 12, 1959, 2; Clark, "Roll Chuck Yeager and Evel Knievel into One," 17–28.

193   "Oh no, it was the quickest way down": *New York Times,* November 21, 1959, 9.
198   "simple . . . like riding a motorcycle": *New York Times,* December 12, 1959, 2.
198   "From the time I was a kid": Clark, "Roll Chuck Yeager and Evel Knievel into One," 18.
200   "The man is not the hero stereotype": Kittinger with Caidin, *The Long, Lonely Leap,* 234.
201   "First: know your abilities": Ibid., 49.
201   "He'll outwork you and out-think you": Clark, "Roll Chuck Yeager and Evel Knievel into One," 23.
201   "You're gonna be a dead son of a bitch": Interview with Joe Kittinger.
204   "The helmet is lowered over my head": Kittinger, "The Long Lonely Leap," 862.
205   "The mission is canceled!": Kittinger with Caidin, *The Long, Lonely Leap,* 194.

nine **One Man Alone**

This chapter relies on the sources listed for chapters 6 and 8, as well as on the following additional sources: Meeter, *The Holloman Story;* Wolfe, *The Right Stuff;* "The 20-Mile Fall," 16; "Fantastic Catch in the Sky," 20.

208   "My reactions had absolutely . . .": Kittinger with Caidin, *The Long, Lonely Leap,* 199.
209   "I was responsible for his safety": Ibid., 237.
210   "He wanted to be certain": Ibid., 237, 238.
210   "Everybody's with you, Joe": Ibid., 208.
210   "We're at 103,000 feet": Ibid.
210   "There are clouds at my altitude": Kittinger, "The Long Lonely Leap," 866.
211   "For your information, Marv": Kittinger with Caidin, *The Long, Lonely Leap,* 211.
211   "Okay. No sweat": Ibid.
212   "Lord, take care of me now": Ibid., 213.
214   "Chute opened" (and all subsequent Kittinger quotes during his fall to earth): Ibid., 216–22.

218   "I'm very glad to be back": Ibid., 224.

218   "I was the lucky one" (and all subsequent quotes from the postflight press conference): Meeter, *The Holloman Story,* 49–51.

219   "That is the voice of a coward!": Kittinger with Caidin, *The Long, Lonely Leap,* 241.

219   "The remark is obviously not true": Ibid.

220   "It was absolutely vital": Clark, "Roll Chuck Yeager and Evel Knievel into One," 18.

221   "We knew damned little at that point": Ibid., 19.

221   "Would I have jumped out of that balloon?": Ibid., 18.

221   "I don't know if I'd have made that jump": Ibid.

221   "It was a blast!": Ibid.

222   "One man alone is nothing": Kittinger with Caidin, *The Long, Lonely Leap,* 245.

222   "billion-volt, limitless-budget future": Wolfe, *The Right Stuff,* 231.

223   "There was a lot of bickering": Interview with Joe Kittinger.

223   "If they would have used our system": Ibid.

223   "The space shuttle is the only experimental aircraft": Ibid.

223   "Those people were alive!": Ibid.

223   "outstanding contributions": "Fantastic Catch in the Sky," 20.

224   "new space hero": Ibid.

224   "This project was no stunt": Ibid.

224   "steel-nerved": "The 20-Mile Fall," 16.

ten **Analog for Space Flight**

The material on Project Strato-Lab (and other associated Navy projects) is based primarily on the following sources: interviews by the author; Compton, *Where No Man Has Gone Before;* Brooks et al., *Chariots for Apollo;* DeVorkin, *Race to the Stratosphere;* Crouch, *The Eagle Aloft;* Ross, "A Consideration of the U.S. Navy Strato-Lab Balloon Program and Its Contributions to Manned Space Flight"; Winzen, "10 Years of Plastic Balloons"; Winzen Research, "The Strato-Lab Gondola—A Space Laboratory" and "Final Report, Stratolab High No. 5"; Ross and Lewis, "To 76,000 Feet by *Strato-Lab* Balloon"; Ross, "We Saw the World from the Edge of Space"; *Saturday Review,* October 4, 1958, 50; "Balloon-Borne Laboratory"; *New York Times,* November 9, 1956, 1, 58; November 10, 1956, 2; May 6, 1961, 12.

226   "During one 8-hour [climatic] test": Winzen Research, "The Strato-Lab Gondola—A Space Laboratory," 15.

228   "To Lee the sweep of sky": Ross and Lewis, "To 76,000 Feet by *Strato-Lab* Balloon," 278.

228   "We are in an emergency situation": Ibid., 279.

230   "We are cool, calm, and collected": *New York Times,* November 9, 1956, 1.

230   "We will be out of communication": Ibid., 58.

230   "I can't say we were scared": *New York Times,* November 10, 1956, 2.

230   "It was a smooth, uneventful landing": Ibid.

230   "65 percent successful": Ibid.

231   "Everybody's favorite man": Interview with Vera Simons.

232   "a giant, frothy waterfall": *Saturday Review,* October 4, 1958, 50.

232   "Would a manned balloon-borne stratospheric laboratory": "Balloon-Borne
       Laboratory," 1074.

232   "The visionaries dream of satellites": DeVorkin, *Race to the Stratosphere,* 307.

233   "The stars were startling": *Newsweek,* May 19, 1958, 63.

236   "manager, planner, the seeker of funds": Ross, "A Consideration of the U.S.
       Navy Strato-Lab Balloon Program," 7.

238   "I caught my breath as I looked out": Ross, "We Saw the World from the
       Edge of Space," 679.

238   "In silent awe, we contemplated": Ibid., 681.

238   "Mal, this is Otto": Ibid.

240   "Landing in our own 'mess'": Ibid., 683.

240   "You go ahead," "See you later": Ibid.

240   "It was a wonderful flight": *New York Times,* May 6, 1961, 12.

241   "a catalyst to crystallize manned space science efforts": Ross, "A
       Consideration of the U.S. Navy Strato-Lab Balloon Program," 4, 5.

241   "Scientific man *must* go into space": Ibid., 7.

241   "The main objective in outer space": Brooks et al., *Chariots for Apollo,* 6.

242   "would be an end in itself": Compton, *Where No Man Has Gone Before,* 4.

242   "I have a sincere fear": Ross, "A Consideration of the U.S. Navy Strato-Lab
       Balloon Program," 8.

242   "It is recommended": Ibid., 9.

The material on Project Stargazer and the fate of high-altitude manned balloon
flight is based primarily on the following sources: DeVorkin, *Race to the Stratosphere;*
J. Allen Hynek in Sagan and Page, eds., *UFOs—A Scientific Debate;* Winzen, "The
Balloon as a Stepping Stone to Space Flight"; USAF, "Aeronautical Systems
Division History," 2:14, 3:15–22; USAF, "Star Gazer Unmanned Test Flight Nr.
5," c. April 15, 1961; "MDSGL-2, Environmental Test Section, Guidance and
Control Division, AFMDC," January 29, 1963; *Newsweek,* May 19, 1958, 65;
"Project Star Gazer," 14; Clark, "Roll Chuck Yeager and Evel Knievel into One,"
17–26; *Albuquerque Journal,* April 25, 1963; *New York Times,* December 15, 1962, 4;
September 18, 1984, B8; September 19, 1984, 1, 17.

244   "the greatest breakthrough in astronomy": USAF, "Aeronautical Systems
       Division History," 2:14.

245   "Although I know of no hypothesis": Hynek in Sagan and Page, eds., *UFOs—
       A Scientific Debate,* 51.

246   "unprofessional": USAF, "Star Gazer Unmanned Test Flight Nr. 5," 4.

248   "huge success": *New York Times,* December 15, 1962, 4.

248   "problems that occurred during the manned flight": USAF, "MDSGL-2,
       Environmental Test Section, Guidance and Control Division, AFMDC," 1.

250   "When you're above 100,000 feet": Interview with Joe Kittinger.

250   "By no means should the use of balloons": "Project Star Gazer," 14.

251   "The plastic balloon vehicle": Winzen, "The Balloon as a Stepping Stone to Space Flight," 665.

251   "In the space age": DeVorkin, *Race to the Stratosphere,* 311.

251   "The few astronomers who did participate": Ibid.

251   "If life is not an adventure": Clark, "Roll Chuck Yeager and Evel Knievel into One," 18.

eleven **Track Meet in the Sky**

The material on the general history of Soviet parachuting is based primarily on Zim, *Parachutes,* and Moshkovsky, *Parachute-Jumping and Gliding.* The material on the jumps of Andreyev and Dolgov is based on the following sources: *Aviation Week and Space Technology,* November 12, 1962; "Russia Claims Mark for Freefall," 37; "Russian Officer Set Altitude Parachute Record," 11–16; *New York Times,* November 15, 1962, 1, 13.

The material on Nick Piantanida is based primarily on the following sources: interview by the author; Horan, *Parachuting Folklore;* Sellick, *The Wild, Wonderful World of Parachutes and Parachuting;* Payne, *Lighter than Air; Life,* May 13, 1966, 3, 33–38; Evans, "Project Strato-Jump," 11–16; "Emergency 11 Miles High," 67; *Aviation Week and Space Technology,* November 12, 1962; "Russia Claims Mark for Freefall," 37; *Washington Post,* August 30, 1966, C-3; *Evening Times* (Trenton, N.J.), August 31, 1966; *New York Times,* October 23, 1965, 19; February 3, 1966, 33; May 2, 1966, 40; August 30, 1966, 41.

256   "dark purple sky": "Russia Claims Mark for Freefall," 37.

257   "while fulfilling his duties": *Aviation Week and Space Technology,* November 12, 1962.

261   "I trust Nicky's judgement": Evans, "Project Strato-Jump," 13.

262   "He was just a real ballsy guy": Interview with Jim Bates.

264   "Disconnect, having problem with oxygen" (and all subsequent quotes from Piantanida and his ground crew during the flight of *Strato Jump II*): Evans, "Project Strato-Jump," 11–16.

268   "Oh God, he has to make it this time": *Life,* May 13, 1966, 38.

268   "Emergency!": Ibid.

twelve **Stair Steps**

The material in this chapter is based primarily on the following sources: interviews by the author; Vaeth, *200 Miles Up;* Hallion, *Test Pilots;* Poole, *Ballooning in the Space Age;* Caidin, *Overture to Space;* Thomas, *Men of Space;* von Braun et al., *Space Travel: A History;* Mailer, *Of a Fire on the Moon;* O'Toole, "The Man Who Didn't Walk on the Moon"; "Ballooning Up!"; Brown, "The Midnight Ride of Balloon DaVinci," 36–40; "Sky Light," 36; *Newsweek,* September 2, 1957, 49, 50; Vaeth, "Landings in Space," 29, 64, 65; "Completed Careers," 8.

270   "The moon seems sure to be": Vaeth, "Landings in Space," 65.

271   "It was not possible to stair-step": Hallion, *Test Pilots*, x.

271   "There will be no sudden": Vaeth, *200 Miles Up*, 241.

272   "Compared to the first men": Caidin, *Overture to Space*, 10.

272   "surrendered words about": Mailer, *Of a Fire on the Moon*, 27.

273   "I found, all those years" (and all subsequent quotes from Vera Simons in this chapter): Interview with Vera Simons.

277   "I had to work on these things secretly": Interview with George Hoover.

277   "Who is this guy?": Interview with J. Gordon Vaeth.

278   "All major technical advances": Ibid.

279   "I didn't want to subject my family" (and all subsequent quotes from Francis Beaupre in this chapter): Interview with Francis Beaupre.

280   "Undoubtedly the first person": Poole, *Ballooning in the Space Age*, 10.

280   "NASA just wanted all these old guys" (and all subsequent quotes from Clifton McClure in this chapter): Interview with Clifton McClure.

283   "Winzen had a competition": Interview with Duke Gildenberg.

284   "I have a ringside view of the heavens": "Ringside in Heaven," 49.

284   "Getting the balloon and launch services" (and all subsequent quotes from Joe Kittinger in this chapter): Interview with Joe Kittinger.

287   "There are people that want to do": Interview with Clifton McClure.

287   "The true worth of a scientist" (and all subsequent quotes from John Paul Stapp): Interview with John Paul Stapp.

290   "There is no requirement": Thomas, *Men of Space*, 88.

Epilogue

294   "Hell, I'd do it today": Interview with Joe Kittinger.

▼

Bibliography

Books, Technical Reports, and Papers

Allen, Oliver E. *Planet Earth: Atmosphere*. Alexandria, Va.: Time-Life, 1983.

Andree, S. A., Nils Strindberg, and K. Fraenkel. *Andree's Story*. New York: Viking, 1971.

"Ballooning Up!" Press kit for Project Da Vinci, 1979.

Berghaust, Erik. *Murder on Pad 34*. New York: G. P. Putnam's, 1968.

Bilstein, Roger E. *Orders of Magnitude: A History of the NACA and NASA, 1915–1990*. Washington, D.C.: National Aeronautics and Space Administration, 1989.

Brooks, Courtney G., James M. Grimwood, and Loyd Swenson. *Chariots for Apollo: A History of Manned Lunar Spacecraft*. Washington, D.C.: National Aeronautics and Space Administration, 1979.

Burrows, William E. *Exploring Space*. New York: Random House, 1990.

Caidin, Martin. *Barnstorming*. New York: Duell, Sloan, and Pearce, 1965.

———. *Overture to Space*. New York: Duell, Sloan, and Pearce, 1963.

———. *The Silken Angels*. New York: Lippincott, 1964.

Clark, Carl, and Ashton Graybiel. *The Break-Off Phenomonon: A Feeling of Separation from the Earth Experienced by Pilots at High Altitude*. Authors' abstract, San Jose State College and Naval School of Aviation Medicine, Pensacola, Fla. Research project no. NM 001 110 100, Report No. 43. August 1956.

Compton, William D. *Where No Man Has Gone Before: A History of Apollo Lunar Exploration Missions*. Washington, D.C.: National Aeronautics and Space Administration, 1989.

Coombs, C. *Survival in the Sky*. New York: William Morrow, 1956.

Cottrell, Leonard. *Up in a Balloon*. New York: Phillips, 1970.

Crouch, Tom D. *The Eagle Aloft*. Washington, D.C.: Smithsonian Institution Press, 1983.

Darby, R. *Space Age Sport: Skydiving*. New York: Julian Messner, 1964.

DeVorkin, David H. *Race to the Stratosphere: Manned Scientific Ballooning in America*. New York: Springer-Verlag, 1989.

Dobson, G.M.B. *Exploring the Atmosphere*. Oxford: Oxford University Press, 1968.

Dwiggins, Don. *Riders of the Winds*. New York: Hawthorn Books, 1973.

Fillingham, Paul. *The Balloon Book.* New York: David McKay, 1977.

Friedlander, Mark P., Jr., and Gene Gurney. *Higher, Faster, and Farther.* New York: William Morrow, 1973.

Gedzelman, Stanley. *The Science and Wonders of the Atmosphere.* New York: John Wiley and Sons, 1980.

Glines, C. V. *The Compact History of the United States Air Force.* New York: Hawthorn Books, 1963.

——, ed. *Lighter-than-Air Flight.* New York: Franklin Watts, 1965.

Gray, Mike. *Angle of Attack.* New York: W. W. Norton, 1992.

Greenwood, James R. *The Parachute from Balloons to Skydiving.* New York: E. P. Dutton, 1964.

Gregory, Howard. *Parachuting's Unforgettable Jumps.* N.p.: Howard Gregory Associates, 1974.

Gurney, Gene, and Clare Gurney. *Cosmonauts in Orbit.* New York: Franklin Watts, 1972.

Hallion, Richard P. *Test Pilots.* Washington, D.C.: Smithsonian Institution Press, 1981.

Hart, Clive. *The Prehistory of Flight.* Berkeley: University of California Press, 1985.

Horan, Michael. *Index to Parachuting, 1900–1975.* Richmond, Ind.: Parachuting Resources, 1979.

——. *Index to Parachuting, 1976–1980.* Richmond, Ind.: Parachuting Resources, 1981.

——. *Parachuting Folklore: The Evolution of Freefall.* Parachuting Resources, 1980.

Houston, C. S. *Going Higher: The Story of Man and Altitude.* Boston: Little, Brown, 1987.

Howard, Joseph L. *Our Modern Navy.* New York: D. Van Nostrand, 1961.

Hoyt, E. P. *The Space Dealers.* New York: John Day, 1971.

Kennan, E., and D. Harvey. *Mission to the Moon.* New York: William Morrow, 1969.

Kennedy, Gregory P. "Project Manhigh: A Balloon Borne Predecessor for Project Mercury." Author's collection.

Kirschner, Edwin J. *Aerospace Balloons.* Blue Ridge Summit, Pa.: Aero, 1985.

Kittinger, Capt. Joseph W., Jr. "Biographical Summary." Author's collection.

Kittinger, Capt. Joseph W., Jr., with Martin Caidin. *The Long, Lonely Leap.* New York: E. P. Dutton, 1961.

Lucas, John. *The Big Umbrella.* New York: Drake, 1973.

McCarry, Charles. *Double Eagle.* Boston: Little, Brown, 1979.

Mailer, Norman. *Of a Fire on the Moon.* Boston: Little, Brown, 1969.

Maurer, Maurer. *Aviation in the U.S. Army, 1919–1939.* Washington, D.C.: Office of Air Force History, 1987.

Meeter, George F. *The Holloman Story.* Albuquerque: University of New Mexico Press, 1967.

Moran, Peter. *A Speck in the Sky.* Poole, Dorset, England: Blandford Press, 1987.

Moshkovsky, Y. *Parachute Jumping and Gliding.* Moscow: Foreign Languages Publishing House, 1939.

Oberg, James E. *Red Star in Orbit.* New York: Random House, 1981.

[Office Of Naval Research: Technical Information Office]. *Stratolab High #5 Background Information.* Washington, D.C., 1961.

Payne, Lee. *Lighter than Air.* New York: Orion Books, 1991.

Piccard, Auguste. *Between Earth and Sky.* London: Falcon Press, 1950.

———. *Earth, Sky, and Sea.* New York: Oxford University Press, 1956.

Poole, Lynn. *Ballooning in the Space Age.* New York: McGraw-Hill, 1958.

Rhodes, Richard. *The Making of the Atomic Bomb.* New York: Simon and Schuster, 1986.

Riabchikov, Evgeny. *Russians in Space.* New York: Doubleday, 1971.

Robinson, Douglas H., and Charles L. Keller. *"Up Ship!" U.S. Navy Rigid Airships, 1919–1935.* Annapolis, Md.: Naval Institute Press, 1982.

The Romance of Ballooning: The Story of the Early Aeronauts. New York: Viking, 1971.

Ross, Malcolm D. "A Consideration of the U.S. Navy Strato-Lab Balloon Program and Its Contribution to Manned Space Flight." Prepared for presentation during the panel, "Report on Manned Space Flight," Second National Conference on the Peaceful Uses of Space, May 8–10, 1962.

Sagan, Carl, and Thornton Page, eds. *UFOs—A Scientific Debate.* New York: W. W. Norton, 1974.

Sellick, Bud. *Skydiving.* Englewood Cliffs, N.J.: Prentice-Hall, 1961.

———. *The Wild, Wonderful World of Parachutes and Parachuting.* Englewood Cliffs, N.J.: Prentice-Hall, 1971.

Simons, Lt. Col. David G. "Air Force Missile Development Center Technical Report: Manhigh II." June 1959.

Simons, Lt. Col. David G., with Don A. Schanche. *Man High.* New York: Doubleday, 1960.

Stapp, John Paul. "Biographical Sketch." Author's collection.

Starnes, Arthur H. *Aerial Maniac.* Hammond, Ind.: Delaney Printing, 1938.

———. *Delayed Opening Parachute Jumps and Their Life-Saving Value.* Chicago: Parachute Science Service, 1942.

Stehling, Kurt. *Bags Up!* Chicago: Playboy, 1975.

Stehling, Kurt, and William Beller. *Skyhooks.* New York: Doubleday, 1962.

Swanborough, Gordon and Peter M. Bowers. *United States Navy Aircraft since 1911.* Annapolis, Md.: Naval Institute Press, 1968.

Swenson, Loyd S., James M. Grimwood, and Charles C. Alexander. *This New Ocean: A History of Project Mercury.* Washington, D.C.: National Aeronautics and Space Administration, 1966.

Szasz, Ferenc M. *The Day the Sun Rose Twice.* Albuquerque: University of New Mexico Press, 1984.

Tascione, Thomas F. *Introduction to the Space Environment.* Malabar, Fla.: Orbit Book Co., 1988.

Thomas, Shirley. *Men of Space,* vol. 1. Philadelphia: Chilton, 1960.

U.S. Air Force. "Aeronautical Systems Division History," vols. 2 and 3. January–June, 1962.

———. "Air Force Missile Development Center Technical Report: Manhigh III, USAF Manned Balloon Flight into the Stratosphere, as reported by Pilot and Task Scientists (Holloman Air Force Base, New Mexico)." April 1961.

———. "Contributions of Balloon Operations to Research and Development at the Air Force Missile Development Center (Holloman Air Force Base, New Mexico)." 1947–1958.

——. "Geophysics Research Directorate: Annual Report 1960 (AFCRL)."

——. "History of Research in Space Biology and Biodynamics at the Air Force Missile Development Center (Holloman Air Force Base, New Mexico, 1946–1958."

——. "History of Air Force Missile Development Center" (ARDC), vol. 1. July–December 1960.

——. "History of Air Force Missile Development Center (Air Force Systems Command), vol. 1, July–December 1961."

——. "History of Air Force Missile Development Center (Air Force Systems Command), vol. 1, January–June 1962."

——. "History of the Air Force Missile Development Center (Air Research and Development Command), July 1, 1959–June 30, 1960."

——. "Major Achievements in Biodynamics: Escape Physiology of the Air Force Missile Development Center (Holloman Air Force Base, New Mexico), 1953–1958."

——. "MDSGL-2, Environmental Test Section, Guidance and Control Division, AFMDC." January 29, 1963.

——. "Star Gazer Unmanned Test Flight Nr. 5." Technical report, c. April 15, 1961.

——. *Your Body in Flight AFP 160-10-3*. Washington, D.C.: USGPO, 1960.

Vaeth, J. Gordon. *200 Miles Up*. New York: Ronald Press, 1951.

Valentin, Leo. *Bird Man*. London: Hutchison, 1955.

Vladimirov, Leonid. *The Russian Space Bluff*. New York: Dial Press, 1973.

Von Braun, Wernher, and Frederick I. Ordway. *History of Rocketry and Space Travel*. New York: Thomas Y. Crowell, 1975.

Von Braun, Wernher, Frederick I. Ordway III, and Dave Dooling. *Space Travel: A History*. New York: Harper and Row, 1985.

Walker, Lois, and Shelby Wickam. *From Huffman Prairie to the Moon*. Washington, D.C.: USGPO, mid-1980s.

Winzen, Otto C. "The Balloon as a Stepping Stone to Space Flight." Proceedings of the Sixth International Symposium on Space Technology and Science, Tokyo, 1965. University of Minnesota "Winzen collection."

——. "10 Years of Plastic Balloons." Based on a paper given by Otto Winzen, presented under the auspices of the American Rocket Society at the Eighth International Astronautical Congress, Barcelona, Spain, October 6–12, 1957. University of Minnesota "Winzen collection."

——. "The 3 Manned Stratosphere Balloon Ascents of 1957." Based on a paper presented by Otto Winzen before the joint meeting of the IAS and AMS in New York, January 27–30, 1959. University of Minnesota "Winzen collection."

[Winzen, Otto C.] "Final Report, Stratolab High No. 5 (Winzen Research, Inc. Portion)." Prepared for the Office of Naval Research, August 1961. University of Minnesota "Winzen collection."

——. "Manhigh I Flown by J. W. Kittinger." Prepared for the Air Force Missile Development Center, June 1959. University of Minnesota "Winzen collection."

——. "Progress Report, Air Regeneration Development." Prepared for the Aero-Medical Field Laboratory, Air Force Missile Development Center, April 1958. University of Minnesota "Winzen collection."

——. "Project Stratolab Instruction Book." Prepared for Office of Naval Research, November 1955. University of Minnesota "Winzen collection."

——. "The Story of Winzen Research." (n.d.) University of Minnesota "Winzen collection."

——. "The Strato-Lab Gondola—A Space Laboratory." Prepared for the Office of Naval Research, November 1956. University of Minnesota "Winzen collection."

Wirth, Dick, and Jerry Young. *Ballooning*. London: Marshall Editions, Ltd., 1980.

Wise, John. *Through the Air*. Salem, N.H.: Arno Press, 1972.

Wolfe, Tom. *The Right Stuff*. New York: Farrar, Straus, and Giroux, 1979.

Young, Louise B. *Earth's Aura*. New York: Knopf, 1977.

Zim, Herbert S. *Parachutes*. New York: Harcourt, Brace, 1942.

Periodicals

Abbreviations

AIAA	*American Institute of Aeronautics and Astronautics*
AWST	*Aviation Week and Space Technology*
NG	*National Geographic*
NTIS	National Technical Information Service
PS	*Popular Science*

Alexander, M., et al. "Fear of Death in Parachute Jumpers." *Perceptual and Motor Skills* 34 (February 1972): 338.

Alicotti, L. "Hypoxia." *Skydiver* 5 (December 1963): 28.

Armagnac, Alden. "How Near Is Space Travel?" *PS* 167 (September 1955): 130.

"Balloon-Borne Laboratory." *Science* 128 (October 31, 1958): 1074.

Barmine, A. "They Learned about Parachuting from Us." *Aviation* 41 (March 1942): 142.

Belikov, V. "Working Day of a Space Pioneer." NTIS, N64-33669, August 9, 1963.

Booda, L. "Jumps Prove USAF Survival Concepts." *AWST* 73 (October 17, 1960): 105.

Brown, Dick. "The Midnight Ride of Balloon DaVinci." *Ballooning* 8 (Winter 1974–75): 36–40.

Burton, W. E. "Twenty-One Mile Parachute Leap." *PS* 133 (August 1938): 42.

Cameron, L. C. "Birdman." *Skydiver* 5 (July 1963): 14.

——. "NASA and Skydiving." *Skydiver* 6 (December 1964): 8.

Carlson, A. J. "Life at High Altitudes." *Nature* 148 (December 27, 1941): 774.

Charette, W. J. "Jumping in the Troposphere." *Parachutist* 5 (February 1964): 12.

Clark, Carl, and Ashton Graybiel. "The Break-Off Phenomenon." *Journal of Aviation Medicine* 28 (April 1957): 2.

Clark, K. "Roll Chuck Yeager and Evel Knievel into One, and You Get an Idea of Joe Kittinger's Thirst for Danger." *Chicago Tribune Magazine,* June 26, 1988, 17–28.

Colin, J., et al. "Thermal Protection from Jumping at High Altitudes." *AIAA* (May 1964): A65-80119.

"Completed Careers" (Malcolm Ross obituary). *Buoyant Flight* 33 (January–February 1986): 8.

Cotterell, A. "Sergeant's High Jump." *Scholastic* 44 (May 22, 1944): 25.

Courts, D. E., et al. "Sport Parachuting and Hypoxia." *AIAA* (April 1965): A65-80951.

Demarest, D. "Barnstorming Days." *Parachutist* 15: pt. 1 (May 1974): 15; pt. 2 (June 1974): 12; pt. 3 (July 1974): 12; pt. 4 (August 1974): 18; pt. 5 (September 1974): 28.

Dunlap, L. "Jump Your Walk around Bottle." *Parachutist* 10 (April 1969): 12.

Elliott, C. D. "Hypoxia." *Parachutist* 7: pt. 1 (October 1966): 13; pt. 2 (November 1966): 16.

"Emergency 11 Miles High." *Newsweek* 67 (May 16, 1966): 67.

"End of a Winged Man." *Life* 40 (June 4, 1956): 53.

Engelmann, R., and Vera Simons. "Laboratory in a Dirty Sky." *NG* 150 (November 1976): 616–21.

Evans, H. "Project Strato-Jump." *Parachutist* 7 (April 1966): 11–16.

——. "Project Strato-Jump." *Skydiver* 8 (April 1966): 8.

"Falling Ten Miles without Moving." *Science Digest* 31 (February 1952): 14.

"Fantastic Catch in the Sky." *Life* 49 (August 29, 1960): 20.

"The Fastest Man on Earth." *Time* 66 (September 12, 1955): 80–88.

Fenz, W. D., et al. "Stress: In the Air." *Parachutist* 11 (January 1970): 14.

Fisher, G. "Nightmare in the Stratosphere." *Coronet* 45 (December 1958): 29.

"Freefall: Starnes Dropped 29,300 Feet." *Time* 38 (December 1941): 34.

Garr, D. "Balloon + Chute = Ballute." *PS* 200 (April 1972): 71.

Gately, M. J. "Soviet Airborne Operations in World War II." *Military Review* 47 (January 1967): 14.

Gauthier, P., et al. "Initial Results of a Psychophysiological Study of Certified Parachutists." *AIAA* (September 1972): A73-36917.

"Getting the High Notes." *Newsweek* 49 (June 17, 1957): 72.

Girnth, H. "Dangers Inherent in Oxygen Deficiency for Parachute Sport Jumpers." *AIAA* (April 1965): A65-22759.

Grabow, R. "Aerodynamics of Skydiving." *Skydiver* 4 (March 1962): 12.

Gross, F. "Studies on the Simultaneous Effects of Cold and Oxygen Deficiency on Man." *Rivista di Medicina Aeronautica* (in Italian with an English summary) 15 (1952): 13.

Gustafson, P. "They Bail Out 8 Miles Up." *Saturday Evening Post* 227 (November 20, 1954): 34.

Haggerty, J., Jr. "Fastest Man on Earth." *Collier's* (June 25, 1954): 25–29.

Hamilton, J. S. "Into the Tropopause." *Parachutist* 8 (May 1967): 5.

Hammerton, M., et al. "Investigation into the Effects of Stress upon Skilled Performance." *Ergonomics* 12 (November 1969): 851.

Hawkins, A. R. "I Had to Bail Out at Supersonic Speed." *Saturday Evening Post* 222 (March 13, 1954): 32.

Heppenheimer, T. A. "Lost in Space: What Went Wrong with NASA." *American Heritage* 43 (November 1992): 60.

"High Altitude, Low Opening." *Ebony* 22 (May 1967): 40.

Holloman Rocketeer (October 10, 1958).

Horan, M. "Peak Experience at 6:45 A.M." *Parachutist* 16 (May 1975): 20.

Hunt, G. "The Cameras Worked, the Balloon Failed." *Life* 60 (May 16, 1966): 2.

Hunter, G. S. "Hot-Air Balloons Studied for Pilot Rescue." *AWST* 89 (August 12, 1968): 56.

Istel, J. A. "Skydive to Moscow." *Flying* 58 (April 1956): 32.

"Jumper Drops 17,500 Feet Breaking Record." *Newsweek* 1 (June 3, 1933): 17.

"Jumping Russians." *Time* 64 (August 16, 1954): 37.

Kahn, R. "Crucial Part Fear Plays in Sport." *Parachutist* 4 (January 1963): 7.

Katser, J. "Rivals in the Sky, Friends on Earth." *Soviet Life* (March 1975): 11.

Kennedy, J. V. "Partial Pressure Suit in High Altitude Escape." *AIAA* (September 29, 1952): AD 14 350.

Khlebnikov, G. F., et al. "Dynamics of Emotional-Volitional Processes of Cosmonauts during Parachute Jumps." *AIAA* (September 1964): A65-80045.

Kittinger, J. "Descent to the Future." *Time* 74 (November 1959): 17.

———. "The Long Lonely Leap." *NG* 118 (December 1960): 854–73.

"Leaping for a World's Record with a Parachute." *Literary Digest* 99 (November 10, 1928): 70.

"The Long, Lonely Leap" (book review). *Parachute Magazine* 2 (March 1964): 17.

McClimans, R. A. "High Altitude Jumps." *Skydiver* 3 (May 1961): 6.

McFarland, R. A. "Human Problems Associated with High Speed and High Altitude Flight." *AIAA* (July 1955): 4585.

"Magic Alloy Makes Stratospheric Jumping Safer." *Business Week* (December 17, 1955): 96.

Martin, J. "Bailing Out at High Flying Speeds." *AIAA* (January 1957): 8042.

Maury, C. "Jumping with H.A.L.O." *Skydiver* 10 (January 1968): 6.

Mazza, V. "Eight Mile High Jump." *Science Digest* 30 (September 1951): 6.

Miller, P. C. "Physics of the Atmosphere." *Skydiver* 3: pt. 1 (September 1961): 13; pt. 2 (October 1961): 13; pt. 3 (November 1961): 13.

Miller, R. "Emotional Feelings as Considered in Parachuting." *Parachutist* 6 (February 1965): 5.

Morton, K. "32,000 in an Apache." *Parachutist* 10 (October 1969): 6.

"Nightmare Fall." *Time* 74 (August 17, 1959): 21.

O'Toole, Thomas. "The Man Who Didn't Walk on the Moon." *New York Times Magazine* (July 17, 1994): 26–29.

"Parachute Jumper Wears Aerial Diving Suit." *PS* 134 (March 1939): 99.

"Parachute Peril: Jumps from a Jet Plane." *Newsweek* 34 (November 21, 1949): 54.

"Parachuting behind the Iron Curtain." *AWST* 65 (September 3, 1956): 71.

"Parachuting Youth of Peking." *Life* 42 (March 25, 1957): 63.

"Parachutist Dives Record 29,300 Feet in Freefall." *Life* 11 (November 10, 1941): 44.

"Partial Pressure Suit Training." *AIAA* (November 1955): 4753.

Phillip, S. "1969 Soviet Nationals." *Skydiver* 12 (January 1970): 10.

———. "Soviet Views on the Need for Change." *Skydiver* 13 (May 1971): 16.

"Picking the Men." *Collier's* (February 28, 1953): 42–48.

Pletcher, K. E., et al. "USAF Emergency Escape Experience 1950–59." *Aerospace Medicine* 32 (June 1961): 524.

"Prelude to Space." *Time* 69 (June 17, 1957): 52.

"Project Star Gazer." *Science Digest* 52 (October 1962): 14.

"Radio Reports Chutists Pulse in Six Mile Fall." *Popular Mechanics* 77 (January 1942): 6.

"Record-Breaking Fall from Six Miles Up." *Illustrated London News* 240 (February 10, 1962): 225.

Renemann, H., et al. "Heart Frequency during Parachute Jumps." *AIAA* (1968): A70-23010.

"Research Notes: Stratolab High V Flight Sets Record." *Naval Research Reviews* (June 1961): 20, 21.

Ride, Sally. "Single Room, Earth View." *Air and Space* 1 (April–May 1986): 14.

"Ringside in Heaven." *Newsweek* (September 2, 1957), 49, 50.

"Rocket to Survival." *Skydiver* 4 (December 1962): 8.

Ross, E. W. "General Theory of Parachute Opening." *Journal of Aircraft* 9 (April 1972): 257.

Ross, M. "We Saw the World from the Edge of Space." *NG* 120 (November 1961): 671–84.

Ross, M., and Lee Lewis. "To 76,000 Feet by *Strato-Lab* Balloon." *NG* 111 (February 1957): 269–82.

Ross, Malcolm D. "The Role of Manned Balloons in the Exploration of Space." *Aerospace Engineering* (August 1958): 52.

Rudakow, M. G. "Thirty Years of Soviet Airborne Forces." *Military Review* 41 (June 1961): 42.

"Russia Claims Mark for Freefall." *AWST* 27 (November 26, 1962): 37.

"Russian Officer Set Altitude Parachute Record." *Parachutist* 4 (February 1963): 11–16.

"Russians Build Better Chute." *Life* 41 (November 19, 1956): 117.

Sagan, Carl. "Skies of Other Worlds." *Parade* (May 1988): 10.

Schane, W. P., et al. "Continuous ECG Recording During Free-Fall Parachuting." *Aerospace Medicine* 39 (June 1968): 597.

Seliverstov, A. "Parachute Oxygen Apparatus." NTIS, N73-24141, June 1972.

Shepard, J. "15,000 Ft. in 30 Minutes." *Skydiver* 8 (May 1966): 14.

Simons, Maj. David G. "A Journey No Man Had Taken." *Life* 43 (September 2, 1957): 19–26.

Simpson, T. E. "They'll Jump 17 Miles from the Sky." *Popular Mechanics* 105 (March 1956): 97.

"Six Mile Drop." *Scholastic* 39 (November 10, 1941): 6.

"Sky Light." *Monogram* 62 (Fall 1984): 36.

Snyder, S. "No. 1000 from a Balloon." *Skydiver* 9 (December 1967): 12.

"Space Pioneer." *Time* 70 (September 2, 1957): 44, 46.

Stafford, J. "Seven Mile Jump." *Science News* 39 (January 18, 1941): 4.

Stanton, E. "John Paul Stapp." *Del Sol New Mexico* (December 1982): 34–37.

Starnes, A. H. "Dropping Two or Three Miles Makes Jumper Think Better." *Science News* 40 (October 4, 1941): 213.

Starr, S. "Accurate Freefall Tables." *Skydiver* 3 (January 1961): 8.

Stevens, A. "Exploring the Stratosphere." *NG* 66 (October 1934): 397–434.

———. "Man's Farthest Aloft." *NG* 69 (January 1936): 59–94.

——. "Scientific Results of the Stratosphere Flight." *NG* 69 (May 1936): 693–714.

Stiller, Jay. "High Gs, High Risk." *Air and Space* (October–November 1987): 66.

"Story of USSR Cosmonaut Training Center Related." NTIS, N70-30513, June 8, 1970.

Strong, H. L. "Air Force Box Score." NTIS, AD 14 342, September 30, 1952.

Swain, M. "Want to Make a High One?" *Parachutist* 10 (March 1969): 27.

Swift, J. E. "4500th Physiological Training Flight." *Parachutist* 9 (January 1968): 15.

"Touching the Stars." *Newsweek* 71 (May 19, 1958): 65.

Towner, D. "Pressure Suit." *Parachutist* 12 (July 1971): 10.

Turbiville, G. H. "Soviet Airborne Troops." *Military Review* 53 (April 1973): 60.

"The 20-Mile Fall." *Time* 76 (August 29, 1960): 16.

Vaeth, J. Gordon. "Landings in Space." *Flying* 58 (January 1956): 29, 64, 65.

——. "When the Race for Space Began." *U.S. Naval Institute Proceedings* (August 1963): 68–78.

Vaughan, R. "Heroic Sky-Dive Venture." *Life* 60 (May 16, 1966): 32–39.

Volotskov, I. "Air Descent." *Literary Digest* 124 (November 6, 1937): 29.

Walcher, O. "Parachutist's Spin Problem." *AIAA* (December 1960): 12355.

"Way to Fall at High Altitudes." *Newsweek* 37 (February 19, 1951): 90.

Webster, A. P. "High Altitude-High Velocity Flying with Reference to the Human Factors." NTIS 2230, 1953.

Wick, R. L. "To Pull or Not to Pull." *Parachute* 1 (December 1962): 23.

Wilson, Jack. "The World in Space." *Look* 21 (January 8, 1957): 36.

Winzen, Otto C. "Plastic Balloons in the Rocket Age." *Missiles and Rockets* (March 1957).

Wise, W. A. "Pressure Suit for High Altitude." *Parachutist* 7 (February 1966): 7.

Wollenberg, E. "Red Parachute Corps." *Spectator* 161 (December 2, 1938): 939.

"World's Largest Free Balloon to Explore Stratosphere." *NG* 61 (July 1934): 107–10.

Yaffee, M. L. "Ballute." *Parachutist* 5 (September 1964): 8.

Young, D. H. "High Altitude Breathing Equipment." *AIAA* (November 1956): 6495.

"Your Society Sponsors an Expedition to Explore the Stratosphere." *NG* 60 (April 1934): 528–30.

Zeller, A. F. "Psychologic Factors in Escape." *Journal of Aviation Medicine* 28, no. 1 (February 1957): 90.

Interviews

Francis Beaupre, Dayton, Ohio, March 8, 1992.

Duke Gildenberg, Alamogordo, N.M., October 3, 1991.

George Hoover, Pacific Palisades, Calif., January 5, 1994.

Joseph Kittinger, Las Vegas, September 17, 1991.

Clifton McClure, Huntsville, Ala., March 2 and August 10, 1992.

Dr. David Simons, Huntington Beach, Calif., September 11, 1989.

Vera Simons, Austin, Tex., June 15 and 22, 1992, and June 5, 1994.

Dr. John Paul Stapp, Alamogordo, N.M., October 3–5, 1991.

J. Gordon Vaeth, Olympia, Wash., December 2, 1993.

Index

Index

▼

About the Author

Craig Ryan grew up in Oklahoma and Tennessee. He graduated from Reed College in 1977 with a B.A. in English literature. He spent two years in the Brown University Writer's Workshop, where he was awarded the Feldman Prize for Short Fiction; he received an M.A. in English literature and writing from Brown in 1982 and won the Transatlantic Review Award for New Fiction the following year. He is the author of two travel books, *Beautiful New Mexico* and *Beautiful New York*.

Ryan has spent thirteen years in the computer industry as a technical writer and editor, and has published several articles in the computer and electronics trade press. His *Technical Writer's Guide* earned the Award of Excellence from the International Society for Technical Communication in 1986. He currently manages software engineering projects for Sequent Computer Systems in Portland, Oregon, where he lives with his wife and two daughters. He is working on a novel.

The **Naval Institute Press** is the book-publishing arm of the U.S. Naval Institute, a private, nonprofit society for sea service professionals and others who share an interest in naval and maritime affairs. Established in 1873 at the U.S. Naval Academy in Annapolis, Maryland, where its offices remain, today the Naval Institute has more than 100,000 members worldwide.

Members of the Naval Institute receive the influential monthly magazine *Proceedings* and discounts on fine nautical prints and on ship and aircraft photos. They also have access to the transcripts of the Institute's Oral History Program and get discounted admission to any of the Institute-sponsored seminars offered around the country.

The Naval Institute also publishes *Naval History* magazine. This colorful bimonthly is filled with entertaining and thought-provoking articles, first-person reminiscences, and dramatic art and photography. Members receive a discount on *Naval History* subscriptions.

The Naval Institute's book-publishing program, begun in 1898 with basic guides to naval practices, has broadened its scope in recent years to include books of more general interest. Now the Naval Institute Press publishes more than seventy titles each year, ranging from how-to books on boating and navigation to battle histories, biographies, ship and aircraft guides, and novels. Institute members receive discounts on the Press's nearly 400 books in print.

For a free catalog describing Naval Institute Press books currently available, and for further information about subscribing to *Naval History* magazine or about joining the U.S. Naval Institute, please write to:

Membership & Communications Department
U.S. Naval Institute
118 Maryland Avenue
Annapolis, Maryland 21402-5035

Or call, toll-free, (800) 233-USNI.

DATE DUE

GAYLORD			PRINTED IN U.S.A.

A17901929750